MATHEMATICS
FOR THE
INFORMED CONSUMER

Mary Wallace
Larry Pitz

gage EDUCATIONAL PUBLISHING COMPANY
A DIVISION OF CANADA PUBLISHING CORPORATION
TORONTO ONTARIO CANADA

Canadian Cataloguing in Publication Data

Wallace, Mary.
  Mathematics for the informed consumer

Includes index.
ISBN 0-7715-0462-4 (v.1)

1. Mathematics — 1961–   2. Finance, Personal.
3. Consumer education. I. Pitz, Larry. II. Title.

QA39.2.W34 1985   513′.9   C85-099424-1

Project Editor/Mary Agnes Challoner
Design/Michael van Elsen Design Inc.
Photographer/Gail Kenny

ISBN: 0-7715-**0462-4**
1 2 3 4 5 6 7 8 9 0 JD 2 1 0 9 8 7 6 5
Written, Printed, and Bound in Canada

PREFACE

This revised edition has been written to provide an up-to-date course for students of consumer mathematics. In particular, interest rates, tax rates, wage scales, and prices have been raised to reflect current levels. Sections on problem solving and estimating have been added. An effort has been made to clarify and simplify terms and procedures where possible.

The text is completely metric and can be used with or without business machines. The material is valuable for personal use, as preparation for further studies in the business field, or for job preparation. It applies knowledge of business world practices and basic arithmetic processes to the solution of personal financial problems. The mathematical calculator is used as a tool to remove the drudgery of lengthy arithmetic computations. The text can be used successfully with various makes of calculators or without any machines. Since many students have access to computers, a section has been added on their use. All problems in the text may be solved with the aid of a personal computer.

The material has been tested in several classrooms and found valuable for personal use and preparation for a vocation. Comments of students and teachers have been responsible for several changes and additions.

This is a book for students. Much care has been taken to make it interesting and easy to read. Where possible, examples and problem situations relevant to students's personal experiences have been used.

The book is intended to develop speed, accuracy, and facility in fundamental mathematical processes, and in the arithmetic processes associated with personal financial problems. It will also develop current techniques and operational skills on business machines. Included are units on the cost of credit, basic statistics, buying and pricing for resale, earnings and deductions, compound interest, ordinary annuities, costs of owning an automobile, and mensuration.

The comma, used traditionally to separate groups of three digits, has been replaced by a space with the exception of the reprints of machine tapes. At this time machines still print the comma or do not separate groups of digits regardless of the number of digits in a number.

A workbook is available. This workbook is not absolutely essential as sufficient problems are provided in the text for many students. However, it does provide much additional material to enable students to acquire mastery of the concepts presented in the text. All the problems in the workbook are different from the problems in the text.

We are grateful to the teachers and students who piloted the materials in this text and to other business educators who offered suggestions to aid us in our selection of topics and determination of the aims of the course. We would also like to thank the following firms and organizations for providing material for illustrations: Bank of Nova Scotia, Toronto Stock Exchange, Revenue Canada, Olivetti Canada, National Trust, Canadian Imperial Bank of Commerce, Central Mortgage and Housing Corporation, Silva Limited, and Mutual Life Assurance Company of Canada.

M. WALLACE
L. PITZ

CONTENTS

UNIT 1

Using Your Calculator

Centuries ago our ancestors counted on their fingers or used pebbles and sticks. Today we use highly sophisticated electronic equipment to perform both routine and complicated mathematical calculations.

1.1   THE ELECTRONIC CALCULATOR

Electronic calculators are widely used. There are several types and sizes, but they all display the calculation or answer to a problem in a small screen near the top of the calculator. The most common electronic calculators are:

1. The small hand or pocket calculator.

2. The desk-top calculator which is similar to the hand or pocket calculator but larger and designed to sit on a desk.

3. The printing calculator which both displays the answer on a screen and prints it on a paper tape.

All electronic calculators have the same 10 numeral keys and are operated by touch. All perform operations instantaneously and almost noiselessly. Many models have two registers and special keys for calculating percents and square roots. Some models have special keys that help the operator perform complicated mathematical and scientific computations.

A   The Keyboard

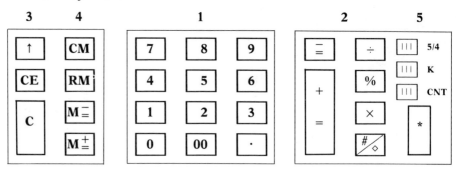

Section 1 shows numeral keys.
Section 2 shows operation keys.
Section 3 shows clear and correction keys.
Sections 4 and *5* show special purpose keys.

Section 1   The numeral part of the keyboard is operated by the first 3 fingers of the right hand. The *home row* of 4, 5, and 6 is operated by the index finger on the 4, the middle finger on the 5, and the third finger on the 6. The index finger moves up to operate the 7 and down to operate the 1. Similarly, the middle finger operates the 8 and 2, and the third finger operates the 9 and 3. Since efficiency depends on speed and accuracy, it is *extremely important* to master this simple touch system.

Section 2   The operation keys are depressed by the little finger. You may find your little finger weak. Keep using it. After some practice it will become stronger and its use *is* necessary to build up your efficiency. The arrangement of these keys will vary from one make of machine to another.

| ‗ | Minus and negative multiplication equal key |

| + ‗ | Plus and equal key |

| ÷ | Division key |

| % | Percent key (not on all machines) |

| × | Multiplication key |

| #⁄◊ | Subtotal and non-add key |

This key enables the operator to number problems without the number affecting the calculations.

| * | Total key |

Section 3   The keys in this section may be arranged in a different order on the machine you are using. They include a *clear key* to remove all calculations, except those in memory register, a *correction key* to remove the last entry when an incorrect numeral key has been depressed, and the *paper advance key* to move the tape forward.

| C | CLEAR |

| CE | CORRECTION |

Section 4   Some machines have special purpose keys. Numbers to be used later in a problem may be placed in a memory bank by depressing the correct *memory key*, memory minus and equal or memory plus and equal. These numbers can be recalled for use later by depressing the *recall key*. The *memory clear key* clears the memory register.

| M ‗ | MEMORY MINUS |

| M + ‗ | MEMORY PLUS | | ||| | 5/4 ROUND-OFF |

| RM | MEMORY RECALL | | ||| | K   CONSTANT |

| CM | MEMORY CLEAR | | ||| | CNT COUNTER |

Section 5   The *round-off key* is used to round-off decimal answers to the desired number of decimal places. The *constant key* allows the operator to multiply or divide a series of numbers by a constant number. Depression of the *counter key* counts and prints the number of items entered into the machine.

The special purpose keys help the operator perform complex operations faster. Where necessary, the use of special purpose keys will be explained in greater detail later in this text.

All machine tapes reproduced in this text were made by an electronic printing calculator and margin instructions apply specifically to the same machine. However, since many students will be using other machines, the basic instructions are broad enough to adapt to all electronic calculators.

B   Machine Instructions in Text

CLEAR   Clear machine of all previous entries and answers.

SET DEC 2 Set decimal to 2 places. This will give the answer correct to 2 decimal places on machines with an automatic round off. If there is no round-off feature on your machine, set the decimal to 3 and round off manually.

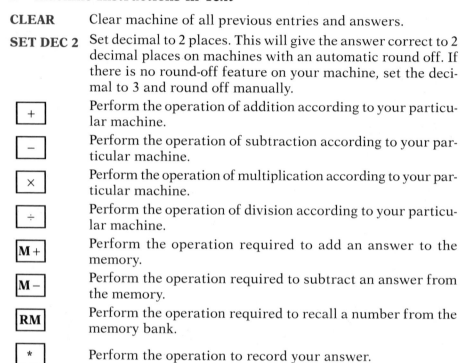

Perform the operation of addition according to your particular machine.

Perform the operation of subtraction according to your particular machine.

Perform the operation of multiplication according to your particular machine.

Perform the operation of division according to your particular machine.

Perform the operation required to add an answer to the memory.

Perform the operation required to subtract an answer from the memory.

Perform the operation required to recall a number from the memory bank.

Perform the operation to record your answer.

C   Before You Start

1. Make sure the power is on and the machine is plugged into the electrical outlet.

2. Move on-off switch to on position.

3. Clear the machine.

4. Place fingers on home row: index finger on 4, middle finger on 5, and third finger on 6.

5. Practice briefly moving your fingers vertically up and down–the index finger to 7 and 1, the middle finger to 8 and 2, the third finger to 9 and 3.

6. Place thumb on zero.

Now you are ready to learn to add, subtract, multiply, and divide on your machine. Remember that the machine is only a tool and performs only as well as its operator. Be careful and accurate. Your speed and efficiency will improve.

D   Basic Machine Operations: Addition

Example

Add.   26
          35
          82
          97

Solution
Machine
Instruction

CLEAR

SET DEC 2

Enter 26

Press    +

Enter 35

Press   +

Enter 82

Press   +

Enter 97

Press   +

Press   *

Use the correct
fingers to depress
each key. ————→

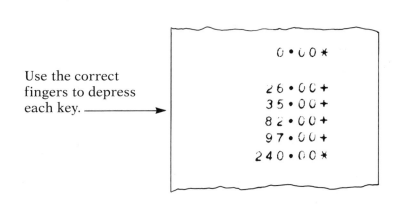

```
        0 • 00 *

      26 • 00 +
      35 • 00 +
      82 • 00 +
      97 • 00 +
     240 • 00 *
```

EXERCISE 1.1
Add the following.

1. (a) 45   (b) 78   (c) 12
        64   97   32
        56   87   23
        46   79   21

2. (a) 456
        564
        645
        654

    (b) 789
        897
        798
        978

    (c) 123
        132
        312
        231

3. (a) 483
        491
        673
        592

    (b) 285
        347
        172
        395

    (c) 732
        389
        491
        562

4. (a) 862
        743
        129
        136
        812
        643
        678
        910
        702
        336
        491

    (b) 951
        675
        482
        349
        907
        620
        426
        783
        709
        562
        783

    (c) 129
        587
        671
        372
        195
        473
        508
        904
        672
        530
        407

5. (a) 672
        95
        408
        17
        6
        207

    (b) 19
        423
        60
        120
        8
        104

    (c) 6

        190
        74
        862
        18

6. (a) 15 496 782
        43 572 867
        672 486
        721 009 602
        3 784 692
        209 467 306

    (b) 103 739 921
        1 046 284
        29 460 032
        893 459 187
        794 001 005
        30 031 672

7. (a) 380 + 49 + 83 + 91 + 118 + 55 + 209 + 16 + 923
    (b) 560 + 24 + 317 + 288 + 190 + 67 + 59 + 110 + 227 + 38
    (c) 274 + 117 + 289 + 53 + 29 + 62 + 795 + 112 + 333

8. (a) 683 472 001 + 574 774 229 + 5 473 882 + 36 340 382
    (b) 33 536 278 + 4 397 + 415 667 + 94 356 222
    (c) 739 496 974 + 551 639 231 + 503 471 332 + 3 401

1.2   THE MICROCOMPUTER

Miniaturization of the parts inside the processor has made it possible for manufacturers to produce small, lightweight models that are becoming increasingly less expensive. More and more, average consumers have their own personal computers. They are the calculators of the future. Many now come equipped with a number pad having the same arrangement of the nine numeral keys as the electronic calculator. Home computers may be used as a calculator without being programmed.

A   The Keyboard

Keyboard of a computer

The keyboard of a computer is very similar to that of a typewriter. If you type by touch, you will have no difficulty using the computer keyboard. The "hunt and peck" method is less efficient and not recommended but is used by people who are unable to touch type. There are a few command keys not seen on a typewriter and the printing may be all in capital letters.

As previously mentioned, some computers have an additional number pad on the right side of the keyboard. The numerals on this pad are arranged in the same manner as those on the calculator. You may perform all arithmetical operations on a computer without this number pad by using the numerals in the top row of keys.

7	8	9
4	5	6
1	2	3

B   Machine Instructions in Text

Since each model varies in the precise instructions required to set the computer in a mathematical mode, instructions given in this text will apply after you have set your computer in the BASIC language according to the manual for your particular machine.

Examples of signals used to indicate that the computer is ready to help you calculate solutions to problems are:

(a)] □

(b) READY

The blinking square is called a *cursor*. It will be used in this text to indicate that the machine is ready.

$\boxed{+}$	Perform the operation of addition.
$\boxed{-}$	Perform the operation of subtraction.
$\boxed{*}$	Perform the operation of multiplication.
$\boxed{/}$	Perform the operation of division.
$\boxed{\textbf{RETURN}}$	Perform the operation to record your answer.
PRINT	Perform the operation to enter information or to recall stored values.

C Before You Start

(1) Set your machine in the mathematical mode.

(2) The computer does not know the difference between 0 for zero and 0 for capital letter "oh" unless you tell it. Always use the number $\boxed{0}$ key for zero. The screen may show it as Ø and the letter "oh" as 0.

D Basic Machine Operations: Addition

Remember that the computer will do *exactly* as you tell it to do. Be careful and accurate.

Example
Add.   26
        35
        82
        <u>97</u>

Solution
Machine Ready

          ] ▢

Type   PRINT 26 + 35 + 82 + 97

          ]PRINT 26 + 35 + 82 + 97

Note: 0 for zero Press $\boxed{\textbf{RETURN}}$

          ]PRINT 26 + 35 + 82 + 97
          240
          ] ▢

Note: It is not necessary to leave spaces between commands and numbers when you type. The computer gives the same answer if you type PRINT26 + 35 + 82 + 97. However, spaces make your readout more attractive and we are accustomed to seeing spaces between numbers and words and operational signs.

Exercise 1.2

1. (a) 48
       75
       68
       57
       ‾‾

   (b) 41
       53
       36
       25
       ‾‾

   (c) 71
       83
       29
       19
       ‾‾

2. (a) 987
       978
       789
       897
       ‾‾‾

   (b) 312
       321
       132
       231
       ‾‾‾

   (c) 564
       645
       546
       465
       ‾‾‾

3. (a) 832
       562
       382
       892
       ‾‾‾

   (b) 576
       472
       194
       926
       ‾‾‾

   (c) 419
       736
       172
       359
       ‾‾‾

4. (a) 982
       429
       498
       650
       105
       910
       294
       305
       593
       772
       129
       ‾‾‾

   (b) 764
       387
       637
       428
       386
       538
       375
       784
       862
       292
       936
       ‾‾‾

   (c) 491
       562
       672
       910
       426
       347
       812
       439
       671
       743
       951
       ‾‾‾

5. (a) 35
       172
       89
       89
       334
       9
       ‾‾

   (b)   4
        38
       728
       356
        19
       110
       ‾‾‾

   (c) 129
       428
       7
       39
       586
       72
       ‾‾

6. (a) 526 732
       2 388 709
       8 382 352
       552 783
       5 126 700
       7 336 782
       ‾‾‾‾‾‾‾

   (b) 29 460 032
       712 938 284
       5 714 639
       47 602 337
       392 718 456
       259 814
       ‾‾‾‾‾‾‾

7. (a) 892 + 734 + 29 + 48 + 402 + 340 + 91 + 336 + 4 + 15
   (b) 139 + 375 + 34 + 94 + 67 + 138 + 879 + 192 + 17 + 3
   (c) 702 + 256 + 63 + 84 + 7 + 395 + 15 + 839 + 5 + 556

8. (a) 437 652 + 53 336 728 + 6542 + 867 925 431
   (b) 94 553 + 530 449 510 + 149 376 + 148 885 601
   (c) 241 573 101 + 183 562 440 + 186 335 + 97 397 302

1.3   DECIMALS

Many students get the right figures to an answer but put the decimal point in the wrong place, thus making the answer incorrect. Machines are only a useful tool. The operator must instruct the machine. For example, a machine cannot calculate $12\frac{1}{2}\%$ of \$4.26. The operator must change the $12\frac{1}{2}\%$ to its decimal form, must set the machine for the correct number of decimal places, and must express the answer 0.53 as \$0.53.

All the numbers we use make up the decimal number system. Each place value is 10 times the value of the place on its right. For example, in the number 666 each 6 has a different value. The 6 on the extreme left means 6 hundreds, the middle 6 means 6 tens, and the last 6 means 6 units.

The following table shows the place value of digits in our decimal system. The use of zero as a *placeholder* is vitally important.

1 000 000 000	thousand million	
100 000 000	hundred million	millions
10 000 000	ten million	
1 000 000	million	
100 000	hundred thousand	
10 000	ten thousand	thousands
1 000	thousand	
100	hundred	
10	ten	
1	unit	
0.1	tenth	
0.01	hundredth	
0.001	thousandth	
0.000 1	ten-thousandth	
0.000 01	hundred-thousandth	
0.000 001	millionth	
0.000 000 1	ten-millionth	
0.000 000 01	hundred-millionth	
0.000 000 001	thousand-millionth	

Chart of Place Values for Numbers in the Decimal System

A   Reading Decimals

(1) Numbers are separated into groups of three by a *space*, starting from the decimal point and moving right and left.

(2) Starting at the left, read the first group and state its group name.

(3) Do not read "and" after hundred, such as one hundred and twenty-five.

(4) Do not use a group name for tens and units.

(5) Read "and" for the decimal point.

(6) Read the number after the decimal point as if it were a whole number and state its group name.

Examples
- 3 425 678 921.782 345 reads three thousand four hundred twenty-five million six hundred seventy-eight thousand nine hundred twenty-one and seven hundred eighty-two thousand three hundred forty-five millionths
- 692.421 reads six hundred ninety-two and four hundred twenty-one thousandths
- 0.423 1 reads four thousand two hundred thirty-one ten-thousandths
- 0.056 reads fifty-six thousandths
- 0.456 78 reads forty-five thound six hundred seventy-eight hundred-thousandths
- 0.000 028 62 reads two thousand eight hundred sixty-two hundred-millionths
- 4.12 reads four and twelve hundredths
- 4.125 reads four and one hundred twenty-five thousandths

In actual practice, whole numbers are often read in groups of three with a pause between groups and no mention of the group names. "Point" is often read to indicate the decimal, and the number to the right of the decimal point is read as a single series of digits.

Example
462 675.725 436 is sometimes read as four sixty-two (pause) six seventy-five point seven two five (pause) four three six.

B   Writing Numbers

Practice writing numbers clearly so that other people will not make errors when they read them. Avoid all loops. Close the 0, 6, 8, and 9.

1. Read aloud the following numbers.
   (a) 53 489 012.003 52   (d) 0.345 786 222
   (b) 132 483.597 01   (e) 0.37
   (c) 34.139 009 12   (f) 0.000 020 9

2. Write the following numbers in words.
   (a) 546 398.467
   (b) 939 876.953 67
   (c) 1.001 3
   (d) 0.000 5
   (e) 0.865 32
   (f) 672.03

3. Write the following numbers in numerals.
   (a) Ten thousand four hundred million six hundred eighty-five thousand one hundred forty-four and ten thousandths
   (b) Four hundred sixty-two thousandths
   (c) Eight hundredths
   (d) Ninety-eight thousand three hundred forty-eight and fifty-two hundredths
   (e) Two tenths

C   Adding Decimal Numbers on a Machine

Example
Add 426.38 and 32.5

Solution

	Machine Instruction	Computer
	CLEAR	Use the ⎡ · ⎤ for the decimal point. The computer will automatically position the decimal point in the answer.
	SET DEC 2	
	Enter 426.38	
	Press ⎡ + ⎤	
	Enter 32.5	
	Press ⎡ + ⎤	
	Press ⎡ * ⎤	

```
  0 • 00 *

4 26 • 38 +
  32 • 50 +
4 58 • 88 *
```

EXERCISE 1.3
Add the following.

1.
(a)	(b)	(c)	(d)	(e)	(f)
62.34	78.34	82.34	96.34	10.25	30.84
78.38	39.54	73.59	94.56	38.48	21.75
10.11	20.45	48.53	33.45	64.78	10.31
12.91	31.45	79.54	68.35	72.48	30.32
83.54	79.32	83.46	49.58	13.84	49.28
59.35	29.10	78.35	39.56	22.48	39.58
10.43	36.50	10.41	78.95	18.34	27.65

2. (a) 13 467.45 + 93.4 + 1 437.85 + 11 938.29 + 6 784.03
   (b) 6.45 + 345.73 + 83.41 + 23 683.5 + 8 927.19 + 12.01
   (c) 98.98 + 378.65 + 345 392.6 + 936.4 + 14 673.09

3. (a) 792.56   (b)   0.1   (c)   395.44   (d)   92.63   (e)   138.9
       0.26   23.45   137.62   537.10   2 658.47
       426.7   91.6   3 289.54   34.50   356.72
       38.09   194.73   147.35   4.1   19.2
       67.45   395.82   8 356.39   0.83   86.42
       119.06   46.73   9.3   525.63   4 882.61
       0.18   9.61   10.05   673.91   8 364.2
       45.67   106.45   2 364.68   928.37   15.24

1.4   SUBTOTALS

Subtotals provide useful data when dealing with many numbers. In adding monthly sales figures, for example, businesspeople would be interested in knowing the first quarter total, the half-yearly total, and the yearly total.

Example

Add.   539
        6 392
        8 123
          592
        ▄▄▄▄ S
          540
          600
        1 120
        ▄▄▄▄ S
        5 673
        4 297
          183
          462
        9 893
        ▄▄▄▄ T

Solution
Machine
Instruction

CLEAR

SET DEC 2

Enter 1st group of numbers, following each by | + |

Press | ◇ |

```
        0 • 0 0 *

      5 3 9 • 0 0 +
    6,3 9 2 • 0 0 +
    8,1 2 3 • 0 0 +
      5 9 2 • 0 0 +
  1 5,6 4 6 • 0 0 ◇
      5 4 0 • 0 0 +
      6 0 0 • 0 0 +
    1,1 2 0 • 0 0 +
  1 7,9 0 6 • 0 0 ◇
    5,6 7 3 • 0 0 +
    4,2 9 7 • 0 0 +
      1 8 3 • 0 0 +
      4 6 2 • 0 0 +
    9,8 9 3 • 0 0 +
  3 8,4 1 4 • 0 0 *
```

Enter next group with [+]

Press [◇]

Enter last group with [+]

Press [*]

EXERCISE 1.4
Add the following.

1.		3.		5.	
	34		246.98		$998.37
	92		538.20		48.33
	48		453.75		63.27
	75		834.49		5.45
	12		149.83		638.90
	▪S		485.66		145.54
	38		887.39		▬S
	87		▬S		792.46
	42		257.56		374.90
	27		557.42		156.72
	▪S		892.39		66.67
	56		662.84		▬S
	92		▬S		435.67
	44		139.24		389.64
	62		995.33		196.37
	79		489.99		35.92
	▪T		▬T		▬T

2.		4.		6.	
	243		$149.58		34 592.35
	948		385.13		19 375.39
	126		6.37		5 416.23
	743		152.19		13 980.46
	509		▬S		▬S
	▪S		463.87		12 859.39
	112		46.57		7 463.92
	945		33.11		6 387.65
	378		9.34		▬S
	▪S		▬S		13 692.40
	288		37.70		27 839.26
	137		481.82		1 888.93
	275		199.98		▬S
	439		65.72		5 539.75
	837		803.25		45 693.67
	111		1.97		8 276.49
	▪T		▬T		▬T

1.5 ADDING NUMBERS WITH A VARIETY OF DECIMAL PLACES

Set the decimal for the largest number of decimal places in any of the numbers to be added. Press the decimal key whenever a decimal occurs and the machine automatically positions the decimal correctly.

Example
Add 13.45 + 1.268 + 0.1 + 32 + 8.369 2.

Solution
The largest number of decimal places is four.

CLEAR

SET DEC 4

Enter each number followed by | + |

Press | * |

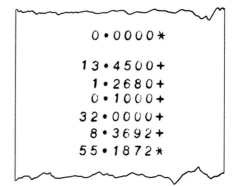

```
0•0000*

13•4500+
 1•2680+
 0•1000+
32•0000+
 8•3692+
55•1872*
```

The computer has only nine digits to work with. If an answer or an input number has more than nine digits, the computer rounds off or uses scientific notation.

EXERCISE 1.5
Add.

1.
(a)	(b)	(c)	(d)	(e)
0.39	1.34	0.56	145	6
135.234 99	15.44	10.6	1.2	8.267
14	0.42	11.789	11.865 3	12
18.693	6.792 11	8.2	196.1	35.693 82
385.88	139.3	149.34	16.23	7.573

2.
(a)	(b)	(c)	(d)	(e)
0.101	36.558	41.58	1 436.012 6	0.234
1.34	584.55	164.39	369.312	10.2
0.000 1	325.333 6	18.342	34.01	357.45
8.67	894.437 7	386.489 1	6 539.1	892
45	0.3	45.3	7 528.996 5	2.9
6.2	763.742 8	34.972	728.335 6	56
125	88.56	486.38	3 493.5	92.9
8.1	34.901	367.84	368.2	847.35
16	638.45	74.5	4 389.565 2	17.67
4.3	25.7	6	43.5	4

1.6   CROSS BALANCING

This is a useful device used to check arithmetical accuracy.

Example
Add columns horizontally and vertically.

$$
\begin{array}{rrrr}
38 + & 78 + & 92 = & 208 \\
65 + & 14 + & 78 = & 157 \\
36 + & 23 + & 56 = & 115 \\
97 + & 39 + & 42 = & 178 \\
85 + & 62 + & 76 = & 223 \\
\hline
321 + & 216 + & 344 = & \blacksquare
\end{array}
$$

Solution
881 is the total of the total column and also the total of the totals of each of the columns.

EXERCISE 1.6
From the following chart, find
(a) the total sales for each salesperson,
(b) the total sales for each month,
(c) the total sales for the second quarter of the year.

Month	Ranu	Camil	Callas	Grey	Total
April	$13 601	$ 8 724	$10 000	$12 460	■■■
May	15 750	10 900	6 637	9 350	■■■
June	14 500	10 350	11 980	10 500	■■■
Total	■■■	■■■	■■■	■■■	■■■

1.7   SUBTRACTION

Subtraction is the inverse or opposite of the addition operation. If you add 5 and 8, you have $5 + 8 = 13$. Inversely, 8 taken away or subtracted from 13 gives 5, as in $13 - 8 = 5$.

Where decimals are involved, the decimal point must be vertically aligned as in addition.

Example 1   On Your Calculator
Subtract 35.4 from 426.829.

Solution
Machine
Instruction

CLEAR

SET DEC 3

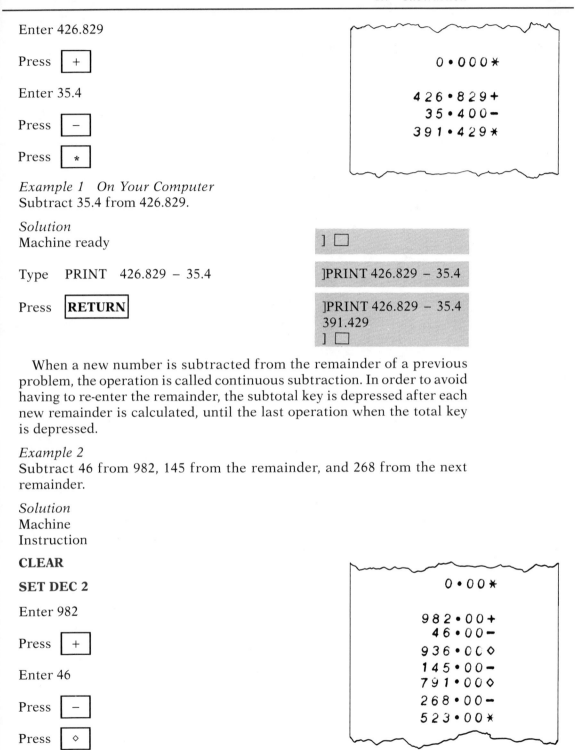

Enter 426.829

Press ☐ +

Enter 35.4

Press ☐ −

Press ☐ *

```
      0•000*

   426•829+
    35•400−
   391•429*
```

Example 1   On Your Computer
Subtract 35.4 from 426.829.

Solution
Machine ready

] ☐

Type   PRINT   426.829 − 35.4

]PRINT 426.829 − 35.4

Press   **RETURN**

]PRINT 426.829 − 35.4
391.429
] ☐

When a new number is subtracted from the remainder of a previous problem, the operation is called continuous subtraction. In order to avoid having to re-enter the remainder, the subtotal key is depressed after each new remainder is calculated, until the last operation when the total key is depressed.

Example 2
Subtract 46 from 982, 145 from the remainder, and 268 from the next remainder.

Solution
Machine
Instruction

CLEAR

SET DEC 2

Enter 982

Press ☐ +

Enter 46

Press ☐ −

Press ☐ ◇

```
      0•00*

   982•00+
    46•00−
   936•00◊
   145•00−
   791•00◊
   268•00−
   523•00*
```

Enter 145

Press [−]

Press [◇]

Enter 268

Press [−]

Press [*]

If the number being subtracted is larger than the number it is being subtracted from, the answer will be a negative or credit balance.

Example 3
Subtract 896 from 742.

Solution

$$
\begin{array}{r}
742 \\
-896 \\
\hline
-154
\end{array}
$$

EXERCISE 1.7
Find the following.

1. (a) 6 789   (b) 9 342   (c)   546   (d) 8 731   (e) 9 382
        −   782   −1 691   − 99   −   403   −1 869

2. (a) 467.82   (b) 986.93 (c) 938.62   (d) 811.02 (e) 364.98
        − 32.94   − 4.2   − 46.19   − 3   −240

3. (a) 436.813 4   (b) 33.458 (c) 8.2   (d) 5.118   (e) 0.075
        − 6.802   −13.58   −0.468   −2.34   −0.07

4. Subtract.

   (a) $ 325.46   (b) $ 889.68   (c) $ 1 045.62   (d) $ 935.67
        − 62.70   −120.37   −   438.56   − 38.70
        ▮▮▮▮▮▮   ▮▮▮▮▮▮   ▮▮▮▮▮▮   ▮▮▮▮▮▮

        −109.24   −   3.45   −   100.00   − 19.35
        ▮▮▮▮▮▮   ▮▮▮▮▮▮   ▮▮▮▮▮▮   ▮▮▮▮▮▮

        −   3.60   − 62.78   −   19.72   −345.00
        ▮▮▮▮▮▮   ▮▮▮▮▮▮   ▮▮▮▮▮▮   ▮▮▮▮▮▮

        − 92.42   −278.46   −   290.50   − 29.42
        ▮▮▮▮▮▮   ▮▮▮▮▮▮   ▮▮▮▮▮▮   ▮▮▮▮▮▮

(e) $ 792.63
   − 0.58
▆▆▆
− 345.67
▆▆▆
− 17.23
▆▆▆
− 89.02
▆▆▆

(f)   497
  − 38
▆▆
− 122
▆▆
− 256
▆▆
− 14
▆▆

(g)   492
  − 122
▆▆
− 34
▆▆
− 19
▆▆
− 113
▆▆

(h)   794
  − 350
▆▆
− 108
▆▆
− 62
▆▆
− 201
▆▆

5. Total the following columns and indicate credit balances where appropriate.

(a)	(b)	(c)	(d)	(e)
392	− 467.4	49.579	135.462	875.94
− 867	− 76.3	− 1.62	− 92.4	− 2.61
62	8.7	24.001	1.972	24.003
− 41	− 19.25	− 38.267	− 89.73	− 672.38
678	6.38	1.34	3.445	275.406

6. Complete the balance column by subtracting the debits and adding the credits.

Blinwood Shopping Centre P.O. Box 7114, STN B Nanaimo, BC V9R 5M6	CENTRAL BANK	Ms. Gisla Diachuk 714 Jostad Ave. Cranbrook, BC V1C 2A3
ACCOUNT NO. 01-58823	TRANSIT NO. 4452 760512	BALANCE FORWARD 2 085.01

CHEQUES	DEPOSITS	DATE	BALANCE
10.85		04 14	
	95.48	04 15	
	7.71	04 19	
101.92	6.86		
	450.00		
870.98		04 20	
319.10			
62.43			
1.75			
13.67		04 21	
	10.00	04 22	
145.76	38.76	04 23	
35.76		04 27	
17.15		04 29	
23.56		05 02	
124.00			
2.18SC		05 11	

Use the subtotal key.

7. In each of the following inventory cards, calculate the balance on hand on each date by using your subtotal key. At the end of the month, total the columns to prove your arithmetic.

(a)

Inventory Card

No. 249 B

ITEM Steam Iron

DATE	REC'D	SOLD	BALANCE
05 01			182
03	82		
04		112	
05	108	67	
10	110	32	
11	314	225	
19		145	
21	162	19	
22	12	35	
23	124	137	
25	167	79	
28	63	102	
29	83	17	
31	102	74	

(b)

Inventory Card

NO. 259 C

ITEM Toaster

DATE	REC'D	SOLD	BALANCE
05 01			96
03	92		
04	105	97	
09	138	85	
10		130	
12	215	113	
18		95	
20		84	
21	193	138	
22	96	15	
23	30	162	
27	215	82	
29		93	
31	112	16	

1.8 MULTIPLICATION

We say that the product of 12 and 6 is 72. The product is the same for 12×6 and for 6×12. For practical purposes it is usually faster to multiply by the smaller number. For example,

$$\begin{array}{r} 62\ 534 \\ \times\ \ \ \ 65 \\ \hline \end{array} \quad \text{rather than} \quad \begin{array}{r} 65 \\ \times 62\ 534 \\ \hline \end{array}$$

A Shortcuts for Mental Multiplication

(1) Multiply by multiples of 10

Examples
- $78 \times 10 \quad = 780$
- $78 \times 100 \quad = 7\ 800$
- $78 \times 1\ 000 = 78\ 000$

To multiply by 10, 100, 1 000, and so on, add the number of zeros in the multiplier to the number you are multiplying.

Examples
- $78 \times 40 = (78 \times 4) \times 10 = 312 \times 10 = 3\ 210$
- $78 \times 600 = (78 \times 6) \times 100 = 468 \times 100 = 46\ 800$

To multiply by a multiple of 10, 100, 1 000, and so on, multiply by the number multiplying the ten, then multiply by the 10.

(2) Multiply 697 by 25.

$$25 \times \frac{100}{4}$$

$$\therefore \ 697 \times 25 = 697 \times \frac{100}{4} = \frac{69\ 700}{4} = 17\ 425$$

To multiply by 25, multiply by 100 and divide by 4.

(3) Multiply 843×125.

$$125 = \frac{1\ 000}{8}$$

$$\therefore \ 843 \times 125 = 843 \times \frac{1\ 000}{8} = \frac{843\ 000}{8} = 105\ 375$$

To multiply by 125, multiply by 1 000 and divide by 8.

(4) Multiply 784×99.

$$99 = 100 - 1$$
$$\therefore \ 784 \times 99 = (784 \times 100) - (784 \times 1)$$
$$= 78\ 400 - 784$$
$$= 77\ 616$$

To multiply a number by 99, multiply by 100 and subtract the number.

(5) Multiply 425×98.

$$98 = 100 - 2$$
$$\therefore \ 425 \times 98 = (425 \times 100) - (425 \times 2)$$
$$= 42\ 500 - 850$$
$$= 41\ 650$$

To multiply a number by 98, multiply by 100 and subtract twice the given number.

(6) Multiply 682×102.

$$102 = 100 + 2$$
$$\therefore \ 682 \times 102 = (682 \times 100) + (682 \times 2)$$
$$= 68\ 200 + 1\ 364$$
$$= 69\ 564$$

To multiply a number by 102, multiply by 100 and add twice the given number.

B Multiplying on Your Electronic Printing Calculator

This machine uses the "times equals" equation.

Example 1
Multiply 382 × 796.

Solution
Machine
Instruction

CLEAR

SET DEC 2

Enter 382

Press | × |

Enter 796

Press | = |

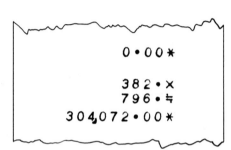

```
       0 • 00 *

     382 • ×
     796 • ≒
304,072 • 00 *
```

When the calculator is used as a tool to remove the drudgery of arithmetic, it is only as accurate as the operator. To ensure accuracy, you should estimate your answer whenever you can.

To estimate an answer, round off each number to simpler numbers that you can multiply mentally.

Example 2
Multiply 38 × 72.

Solution
Estimate 40 × 70 = 2 800.

Using your calculator 38 × 72 = 2 736. Since 2 736 is close to 2 800, it is a reasonable answer.

Multiplying on Your Computer

Example 3
Multiply 382 × 796.

Solution
Machine ready

Type   PRINT   382 * 796

Press **RETURN**

```
] □
```

```
]PRINT 382 * 796
```

```
]PRINT 382 * 796
304 072
] □
```

C Multiplying with Decimals

To determine the number of decimal places in the product, add the number of decimal places in the numbers being multiplied.

Example 1

$$4.56 \times 2.2 = 10.032$$
$$2 + 1 = 3$$

After determining where the decimal point belongs, you may need to round off the answer to a specified number of decimal places.

(1) If the digit after the required number of decimal places is 5 or higher, add 1 to the previous digit and omit the rest.

(2) If the digit after the required number of decimal places is less than 5, omit all remaining digits.

Round Off Rules

Examples
- $4.85 = 4.9$ correct to 1 decimal place
- $0.43 = 0.4$ correct to 1 decimal place
- $62.354\,8 = 62.35$ correct to 2 decimal places
  - $= 62.355$ correct to 3 decimal places
  - $= 62.354\,8$ correct to 4 decimal places

Example 5
Find the product of 367.42 and 9.372 1 correct to 1 decimal place.

Solution
Machine
Instruction

CLEAR

SET DEC 2

Enter 367.42

Press $\boxed{\times}$

Enter 9.372 1

Press $\boxed{=}$

Write answer as 3 443.5.

If your machine does not round off automatically, set the decimal for 3 places and round off manually.

D   Addition of Products

Example

Find the sum of the following products.

$$23 \times 44 = \text{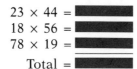}$$
$$18 \times 56 = $$
$$78 \times 19 = $$
$$\text{Total} = $$

Solution

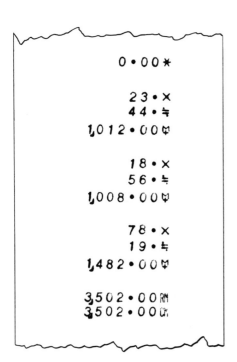

```
        0 • 0 0 *

        2 3 • ×
        4 4 • ⹌
  1,0 1 2 • 0 0 ⹌

        1 8 • ×
        5 6 • ⹌
  1,0 0 8 • 0 0 ⹌

        7 8 • ×
        1 9 • ⹌
  1,4 8 2 • 0 0 ⹌

  3,5 0 2 • 0 0 RM
  3,5 0 2 • 0 0 CM
```

		Machine Instruction
		CLEAR
		SET DEC 2
Enter 23		
Press	×	
Enter 44		
Press	M+	Product is printed and stored in memory.
Enter 18		
Press	×	
Enter 56		
Press	M+	Product is printed and stored in memory.
Enter 78		
Press	×	
Enter 19		
Press	M+	Product is printed and stored in memory.
Press	RM	The accumulated total is recalled from memory.
Press	CM	Memory is cleared.

On Your Computer

Machine Ready

] ☐

Type   PRINT A = 23 * 44

Press   **RETURN**

]PRINT A = 23 * 44

Type   PRINT B = 18 * 56

Press   **RETURN**

]PRINT B = 18 * 56

Type   PRINT C = 78 * 19

Press   **RETURN**

]PRINT C = 78 * 19

Type   PRINT A + B + C

Press   **RETURN**

]PRINT A + B + C
3502
] ☐

E   Multiplying Products

Products can be multiplied on electronic calculators without having to reinsert the first product to be multiplied by the third factor.

Example
Multiply 35 × 64 × 72.

Solution
Machine
Instruction

CLEAR

SET DEC 0

Enter 35

Press   ☒ ×

Enter 64

Press   ☒ ×

Enter 72

Press   ☐ =

```
                         35 • X
                         64 • X
                         72 • ⅍
              1 6 1,2 8 0 • 0 0 *
```

On Your Computer

Machine ready

] ☐

Type   PRINT 35 * 64 * 72

Press   **RETURN**

]PRINT 35 * 64 * 72
161280
] ☐

EXERCISE 1.8
1. Multiply mentally.

(a) 672 × 99	(f) 847 × 100	(k) 425 × 98
(b) 436 × 25	(g) 531 × 125	(l) 32 × 101
(c) 521 × 125	(h) 922 × 99	(m) 724 × 50
(d) 862 × 98	(i) 726 × 25	(n) 321 × 102
(e) 684 × 102	(j) 392 × 30	(o) 867 × 100

Multiply the following, estimating your answer each time.

2. (a) 45 × 67	(e) 33 × 74	(i) 91 × 64
(b) 83 × 56	(f) 46 × 72	(j) 38 × 72
(c) 72 × 43	(g) 79 × 38	(k) 42 × 37
(d) 34 × 85	(h) 65 × 58	(l) 63 × 54

3. (a) 847 × 870	(e) 768 × 347	(i) 483 × 752
(b) 824 × 553	(f) 113 × 322	(j) 516 × 909
(c) 649 × 123	(g) 501 × 857	(k) 587 × 742
(d) 572 × 438	(h) 384 × 165	(l) 451 × 119

4. (a) 34 853 × 639	(d) 3 469 × 842	(g) 18 546 × 82 503
(b) 17 385 × 145	(e) 2 995 × 52	(h) 9 461 × 2 596
(c) 86 435 × 666	(f) 6 752 × 964	(i) 7 328 × 8 476

5. Correct to 2 decimal places.

(a) 34.5 × 63.62	(c) 74.64 × 83.5	(e) 65.4 × 13.45
(b) 119.46 × 38.33	(d) 84.59 × 32.1	(f) 37.62 × 21.49

6. Correct to 3 decimal places.

(a) 37.549 × 0.101	(c) 1.75 × 8.25	(e) 1.382 9 × 0.9
(b) 0.253 × 35.1	(d) 79.24 × 1.369	(f) 24.35 × 8.462

7. Correct to 3 decimal places.

(a) 38.469 × 0.000 1	(c) 8.2 × 4.63	(e) 25 × 0.736 2
(b) 823.56 × 4.57	(d) 0.127 × 0.004	(f) 25.378 × 8.35

8. Find the total of the products. Make each product correct to 2 decimal places.

(a) 38.56 × 3.7 = ▉	(e) 103.45 × 36.2 = ▉
72.39 × 18 = ▉	97.362 × 1.13 = ▉
6.392 × 1.1 = ▉	284.3 × 0.003 = ▉
Total = ▉	Total = ▉

(b) 82.22 × 954   =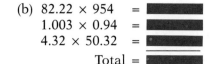
     1.003 × 0.94   =
     4.32 × 50.32   =
           Total =

(f) 83.41 × 0.64   =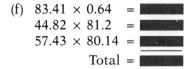
     44.82 × 81.2   =
     57.43 × 80.14 =
           Total =

(c) 53.21 × 9.43   =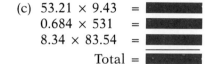
     0.684 × 531   =
     8.34 × 83.54   =
           Total =

(g) 44.3 × 41.01   =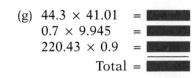
     0.7 × 9.945   =
     220.43 × 0.9   =
           Total =

(d) 83.11 × 8.953 =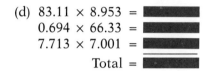
     0.694 × 66.33 =
     7.713 × 7.001 =
           Total =

(h) 43 × 2.3   =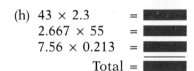
     2.667 × 55   =
     7.56 × 0.213   =
           Total =

9. Extend and total the following bills correct to the nearest cent.

(a)

Bay Groceteria 19 Huron Drive Leduc, AB T9E 1W7 Sold to: 19__ 10 04 K. Broome, 11 River Rd.		
4 kg	tomatoes @ 1.65/kg	
1 doz	cucumbers @ 0.29 each	
3 heads	lettuce @ 0.59 each	
14 tins	Campbell's soup @ 2/0.95	
250 g	cookies @ 3.75/kg	
$7\frac{1}{2}$ kg	potatoes @ 0.59/kg	

(b)

Bay Groceteria 19 Huron Drive Leduc, AB T9E 1W7 Sold to: 19__ 10 08 J. Swartz, 12 Lake Ave.		
14 pkgs	macaroni dinner @ 0.49	
200 g	blue cheese @ 0.85/100 g	
250 g	cheddar @ 0.63/100 g	
2 ctns	cereal @ 1.32	
$3\frac{1}{2}$ kg	sirloin roast @ 8.98/kg	
1 kg	wieners @ 4.89/kg	
$4\frac{1}{2}$ doz	eggs @ 1.12/doz	
400 g	tea @ 0.88/100 g	

10. Find the following products without re-entering the first product
     (record final answer correct to 2 decimal places).
     (a) 374 × 46 × 82
     (b) 18 × 72 × 91
     (c) 23 × 48 × 84
     (d) 2.7 × 67.2 × 8.1
     (e) 350.01 × 34.67 × 0.94
     (f) 17.8 × 25.3 × 66.7
     (g) 35.6 × 86.38 × 6.22
     (h) 3.4 × 46.2 × 95.7
     (i) 5.1 × 6.23 × 8.43
     (j) 38.1 × 2.5 × 0.12

1.9   DIVISION

Division is the inverse of multiplication. For example, if $8 \times 6 = 48$, then $48 \div 8 = 6$ and $48 \div 6 = 8$. There are 3 parts to any division problem, the dividend, the divisor, and the quotient. In the equation $48 \div 6 = 8$,

the dividend is 48,
the divisor is 6,
the quotient is 8.

A   Shortcuts for Mental Division

(1) Division by One-Digit Divisors
These problems should be done mentally.

Example
• $198\ 644 \div 4 = 49\ 661$

(2) Division by 10, 100, 1 000, . . .
These problems should also be done mentally. Simply move the decimal point one place to the left for each zero in the divisor.

Examples
• $4\ 926.83 \div 10 = 492.683$
• $4\ 926.83 \div 100 = 49.268\ 3$
• $4\ 926.83 \div 1\ 000 = 4.926\ 83$

(3) Divide 8962 by 25.

$$25 = \frac{100}{4}$$

$$\therefore 8962 \div 25 = 8962 \div \frac{100}{4}$$

$$= 8962 \times \frac{4}{100}$$

$$= 89.62 \times 4$$

$$= 358.48$$

To divide by 25, divide by 100 and multiply the result by 4.

(4) Divide 43 678 by 125.

$$125 = \frac{1\ 000}{8}$$

$$\therefore 43\ 678 \div 125 = 43\ 678 \div \frac{1\ 000}{8}$$

$$= 43\ 678 \times \frac{8}{1\ 000}$$

$$= 43.678 \times 8$$

$$= 349.424$$

To divide by 125, divide by 1 000 and multiply by 8.

(5) Divide 892 by 50.

$$892 \div 50 = 892 \div \frac{100}{2}$$

$$= 892 \times \frac{2}{100}$$

$$= 8.92 \times 2$$

$$= 17.84$$

To divide by 50, divide by 100 and multiply by 2.

B   Division with Whole Numbers

Example
Divide 1 008 by 18.
Estimate = 1 000 ÷ 20
        = 50

Solution
Machine
Instruction

CLEAR

SET DEC 0

Enter 1008

Press   ÷

Enter 18

Press   =

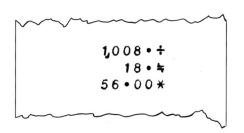

On Your Computer

Machine ready

Type   PRINT 1008/18

] ☐

Press   **RETURN**

] PRINT 1008 / 18
56
] ☐

C   Division with Decimals on Machines with a Decimal Set Key

Set your decimal for the desired number of decimal places, then enter the numbers as they appear, including the decimal point where it occurs. If the number is less than one, enter a zero before the decimal point. The machine will show the decimal in the correct place.

Example
Divide 79.367 8 by 0.24, correct to two decimal places.

Solution
Machine
Instruction

CLEAR

SET DEC 2

Enter 79.367 8

Press

Enter 0.24

Press

```
79•3678÷
   0•24≒
330•70*
```

EXERCISE 1.9
1. Divide mentally (correct to 2 decimal places).
    (a) 463 ÷ 4   (f) 625 ÷ 25
    (b) 89 648 ÷ 6   (g) 387 500 ÷ 125
    (c) 876 872.45 ÷ 7   (h) 7 800 ÷ 2.5
    (d) 15 500 ÷ 25   (i) 100 000 ÷ 1.25
    (e) 364 662.87 ÷ 100   (j) 87.5 ÷ 25

2. Find the following quotients.
    (a) 481 ÷ 37   (f) 4 420 ÷ 34
    (b) 5 568 ÷ 116   (g) 1 092 ÷ 78
    (c) 1 440 ÷ 45   (h) 5 194 ÷ 53
    (d) 19 888 ÷ 904   (i) 2 592 ÷ 72
    (e) 2 268 ÷ 12   (j) 29 032 ÷ 382

3. Divide correct to 2 decimal places.
    (a) 972 ÷ 37   (g) 6 452 ÷ 10.8   (m) 12 593 ÷ 389
    (b) 1 126 ÷ 409   (h) 342 ÷ 0.002   (n) 79 ÷ 83
    (c) 81.9 ÷ 4.5   (i) 1 605 ÷ 903   (o) 34.6 ÷ 48.2
    (d) 634 ÷ 1.12   (j) 331 ÷ 59   (p) 99.3 ÷ 45
    (e) 157 ÷ 42   (k) 794.35 ÷ 0.9   (q) 545.1 ÷ 80.22
    (f) 793 ÷ 59   (l) 60.34 ÷ 0.23   (r) 9 056 ÷ 38

**Remember
to
estimate.**

REVIEW EXERCISE 1.10

1. 492.4 + 593.44 + 1.398 + 0.01 + 3.356 + 6.75 + 4.567

2. 35.8 + 66.378 − 44.2 + 65.43 − 23.95 + 267.1 + 48.356

3. Add, indicating subtotals and total.

(a)	(b)	(c)
988.73	941.95	642.89
835.02	583.31	33.84
354.57	7.63	72.56
438.94	251.91	5.45
941.38	▬▬ S	908.36
584.68	364.21	455.41
▬▬ S	157.19	368.13
18.72	485.82	▬▬ S
9.35	0.04	364.96
839.66	▬▬ S	843.11
▬▬ S	355.49	387.07
17.91	971.16	▬▬ S
382.11	546.72	195.83
593.35	867.24	335.44
947.56	33.96	752.68
▬▬ T	▬▬ T	▬▬ T

4. Find the total cost of the following long distance telephone calls. Use your memory key and then recall the accumulated total.

Mo.	Day	Location	Regular Charge	Discount	Amount
10	14	Freelton	53	23	
10	17	Oakville	98		
10	18	Stoney Creek	98	33	
10	19	Stoney Creek			M* 30
10	23	Burlington	3.03	1.51	
10	24	Dundas			M 30
11	03	Ottawa	6.48	4.32	
11	05	Ottawa	3.52	1.76	
11	10	Oakville	2.07	1.38	
*minimum charge					

5.

(a)	(b)	(c)
456.72	973.66	12 556.49
− 65.78	− 443.72	− 3 682.46
▬▬	▬▬	▬▬
− 79.35	− 8.72	− 956.26
▬▬	▬▬	▬▬
− 126.17	− 331.95	− 5 725.18
▬▬	▬▬	▬▬
− 92.48	− 85.46	− 852.39
▬▬	▬▬	▬▬

6. Total the following columns and indicate credit balances where appropriate.

(a)   –   46.79
        1.86
      58.578
   4 637.2
   –   0.925 8
      72.1
  – 3 938.0

(b)   357.224 89
  – 395.39
   – 48.1
     9.074
   77.2
  117.35
  – 292.1

(c)   30 552.78
  10 662.58
   –   0.456
  – 19 507
  – 22 995.56
   864.2
     0.905

7. Complete the balance column.

(a)

Add	Subtract	Balance
		368
35	16	
52		
163	39	
	42	
	114	
356	72	
89	41	
	56	
237	136	
42	418	
190	308	
	19	

(b)

Add	Subtract	Balance
		984
112	88	
	92	
403	972	
151		
382	543	
	16	
	92	
78	54	
	38	
	129	
220		
48	43	

8. Multiple or divide mentally.

(a) 368 × 25   (b) 1 784 × 125   (c) 389 ÷ 50   (d) 1 850 ÷ 125

9. Multiple or divide correct to 2 decimal places.

(a) 14 572 × 0.104   (d) 486 ÷ 18   (g) 52.3 × 68 × 0.4
(b) 3.45 × 87.63   (e) 45 835 ÷ 1.245   (h) 1.56 × 85.2 × 63
(c) 501.24 × 682.12   (f) 1.356 ÷ 14   (i) 38.42 × 17.2 × 81.3

10. Find the sum of the following products using the memory key.

(a) 38 × 46 =   (c) 115 × 79 =
    24 × 78 =   318 × 42 =
    63 × 85 =   296 × 56 =
   Total =   Total =

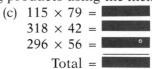

(b) 72 × 95 =
    59 × 64 =
    23 × 72 =
   Total =

UNIT 2

Basic Operations

In the business world and in the world of personal finance answers seldom work out evenly and fractions are used frequently. In order to use a calculator or a computer, you must have all such fractions in the form of decimal fractions. Also, the metric system is based on decimal fractions. A familiarity with common fractions, their functions and uses, is most helpful in your work with decimal fractions.

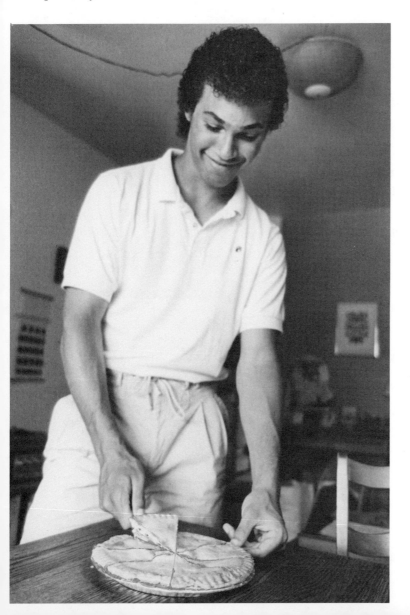

2.1   REVIEW OF TERMS

A *fraction,* or a *common fraction,* is a pair of numbers, one divided by the other.

Examples

$$\frac{3}{4}, \quad \frac{1}{3}, \quad \frac{6}{5}, \quad \frac{5}{8}, \quad \frac{22}{7}, \quad \frac{15}{16}$$

$\frac{3}{4}$ ← numerator
← denominator

A unit of
4 parts

$= \frac{4}{4}$

$= 1$

3 parts of
4 parts

$= 3$ quarters

$= \frac{3}{4}$

2 parts of
4 parts

$= 2$ quarters

$= \frac{2}{4}$

1 part of
4 parts

$= 1$ quarter

$= \frac{1}{4}$

If the numerator is smaller than the denominator, as in $\frac{1}{3}$, $\frac{2}{7}$, and $\frac{4}{9}$, the fraction is called a *proper fraction.*

If the numerator is greater than the denominator, as in $\frac{4}{3}$, $\frac{9}{7}$, and $\frac{3}{2}$, the fraction is called an *improper fraction.*

A *mixed number* is a number made up of a whole number and a fraction, as $3\frac{1}{2}$ and $7\frac{2}{5}$.

Example 1
Express $\frac{32}{5}$ as a mixed number.

Solution
Divide 5 into 32.
There are six 5's in 32 and the remainder is 2.

$$\frac{32}{5} = 6\frac{2}{5}$$

Example 2
Express $7\frac{1}{2}$ as an improper fraction.

Solution
There are 14 halves in 7.
There are 14 + 1 = 15 halves in $7\frac{1}{2}$.

$$7\frac{1}{2} = \frac{15}{2}$$

1. A day is what part of a week?

2. $7\frac{1}{2}$ is what part of 15?

3. What part of 365 is 73?

4. What part of 39 is 13?

5. 8 apples are what part of 1 dozen apples?

6. Change the following to improper fractions.

   (a) $6\frac{7}{8}$ (c) $6\frac{1}{4}$ (e) $8\frac{3}{8}$

   (b) $91\frac{2}{3}$ (d) $5\frac{1}{2}$ (f) $4\frac{3}{4}$

7. Change the following to mixed numbers.

   (a) $\frac{28}{6}$ (c) $\frac{178}{40}$ (e) $\frac{600}{500}$

   (b) $\frac{35}{8}$ (d) $\frac{69}{2}$ (f) $\frac{630}{25}$

Equivalent fractions are fractions that have the same value but different numerators and denominators.

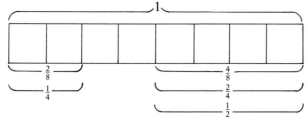

$\frac{1}{2}, \frac{2}{4}, \frac{4}{8}$ are equivalent fractions.

$\frac{1}{4}, \frac{2}{8}$ are equivalent fractions.

If the numerator and denominator of a fraction have no common factor except 1, the fraction is in its *lowest terms*, as $\frac{1}{2}, \frac{1}{3}, \frac{5}{7}, \frac{4}{9}$.

A fraction may be expressed in higher terms by multiplying numerator and denominator by the same number. For example, $\frac{1}{8} = \frac{1 \times 2}{8 \times 2} = \frac{2}{16}$. Multiplying by $\frac{2}{2}$ is the same as multiplying by 1. The form changes but the value remains the same.

Example 3

Express $\frac{3}{8}$ as sixteenths.

Solution

$\frac{3}{8} = \frac{3 \times 2}{8 \times 2} = \frac{6}{16}$ Multiply numerator and denominator by number required to increase denominator to desired number.

Example 4

Express $\frac{3}{5}$ as fortieths.

Solution

$$\frac{3}{5} = \frac{3 \times 8}{5 \times 8} = \frac{24}{40}$$

Example 5

Express $\frac{2}{3}$ and $\frac{5}{8}$ using a common denominator.

Solution

The lowest common multiple of 3 and 8 is 24.

$$\frac{2}{3} = \frac{2 \times 8}{3 \times 8} = \frac{16}{24} \qquad \frac{5}{8} = \frac{5 \times 3}{8 \times 3} = \frac{15}{24}$$

A fraction may be expressed in lower terms by dividing numerator and denominator by the same number.

Example 6

Reduce $\frac{3}{15}$ to its lowest terms.

Solution

$$\frac{3}{15} = \frac{3 \div 3}{15 \div 3} = \frac{1}{5}$$

Divide numerator and denominator by highest number that divides evenly into both.

Example 7

Reduce $\frac{25}{45}$ to its lowest terms.

Solution

$$\frac{25}{45} = \frac{25 \div 5}{45 \div 5} = \frac{5}{9}$$

EXERCISE 2.1

1. Express the following as equivalent fractions in their lowest form.
    (a) $\frac{9}{81}$ (c) $\frac{49}{56}$ (e) $\frac{12}{16}$ (g) $\frac{20}{25}$
    (b) $\frac{27}{36}$ (d) $\frac{96}{144}$ (f) $\frac{1\,575}{1\,995}$ (h) $\frac{36}{66}$

2. For each of the following pairs of fractions, find which is greater by expressing them as equivalent fractions with a common denominator.
    (a) $\frac{1}{3}$ or $\frac{1}{2}$ (d) $\frac{4}{5}$ or $\frac{3}{4}$ (g) $\frac{6}{25}$ or $\frac{9}{35}$
    (b) $\frac{2}{3}$ or $\frac{3}{4}$ (e) $\frac{15}{16}$ or $\frac{29}{30}$ (h) $\frac{23}{25}$ or $\frac{28}{30}$
    (c) $\frac{5}{6}$ or $\frac{7}{8}$ (f) $\frac{7}{9}$ or $\frac{9}{11}$ (i) $\frac{8}{9}$ or $\frac{10}{12}$

3. Find a common denominator for each group of fractions, and express the fractions as equivalent fractions.
    (a) $\frac{3}{2}, \frac{2}{3}, \frac{5}{6}, \frac{1}{2}$ (b) $\frac{5}{8}, \frac{9}{10}, \frac{3}{4}, \frac{3}{5}$ (c) $\frac{9}{10}, \frac{22}{25}, \frac{3}{5}, \frac{8}{15}$

2.2 ADDING AND SUBTRACTING FRACTIONS

To add or subtract fractions
  (i) find the lowest common denominator for all the fractions in the
      question,
 (ii) rewrite each fraction as an equivalent fraction using this denom-
      inator,
(iii) add or subtract the numerators.

Examples

- $\dfrac{2}{3} + \dfrac{4}{5} = \dfrac{10}{15} + \dfrac{12}{15} = \dfrac{22}{15}$

- $\dfrac{3}{4} - \dfrac{2}{3} = \dfrac{9}{12} - \dfrac{8}{12} = \dfrac{1}{12}$

To add or subtract mixed numbers
  (i) add or subtract the whole numbers,
 (ii) add or subtract the fractions,
(iii) add the results of the above.

Example 1

Add $4\frac{1}{2} + 3\frac{5}{8} + 6\frac{3}{4} + 5\frac{1}{16}$.

Solution

  (i) $4 + 3 + 6 + 5 = 18$

 (ii) $\frac{1}{2} + \frac{5}{8} + \frac{3}{4} + \frac{1}{16} = \dfrac{8 + 10 + 12 + 1}{16}$

$$= \frac{31}{16}$$

$$= 1\frac{15}{16}$$

(iii) $18 + 1\frac{15}{16} = 19\frac{15}{16}$

Example 2

Add or subtract as indicated.
(a) $16\frac{2}{3} - 4\frac{1}{2} + 3\frac{5}{6} - 8\frac{3}{4}$
(b) $9\frac{3}{5} - 6\frac{2}{3}$

Solution

(a)   (i) $16 - 4 + 3 - 8 = 7$

     (ii) $\frac{2}{3} - \frac{1}{2} + \frac{5}{6} - \frac{3}{4} = \dfrac{8 - 6 + 10 - 9}{12}$

$$= \frac{3}{12}$$

$$= \frac{1}{4}$$

   (iii) $7 + \frac{1}{4} = 7\frac{1}{4}$

(b)   (i) $8 - 6 = 2$

     (ii) $1\frac{3}{5} - \frac{2}{3} = \frac{8}{5} - \frac{2}{3}$

$$= \frac{24 - 10}{15}$$

$$= \frac{14}{15}$$

   (iii) $2 + \frac{14}{15} = 2\frac{14}{15}$

$\frac{3}{5}$ is too small to subtract $\frac{2}{3}$ from it. Take 1 from the 9. $\frac{8}{5}$ is big enough.

EXERCISE 2.2
Add or subtract as indicated.

1. $\frac{3}{4} + \frac{3}{7}$

2. $\frac{1}{3} + \frac{3}{8} + \frac{1}{4} + \frac{1}{2}$

3. $\frac{2}{3} - \frac{1}{9}$

4. $\frac{5}{5} - \frac{5}{8}$

5. $\frac{3}{5} + \frac{3}{8} - \frac{1}{4}$

6. $\frac{3}{4} + \frac{7}{8} - \frac{6}{9}$

7. $3\frac{1}{6} + 7\frac{1}{8} - 4\frac{3}{8} + 2\frac{3}{4}$

8. $2\frac{5}{6} - 1\frac{20}{21} + 15\frac{2}{3} - 8\frac{4}{7}$

9. $1\frac{2}{7} - 2\frac{5}{8} - 5\frac{7}{8} + 3\frac{1}{4} + 8\frac{1}{2}$

10. $9\frac{3}{7} + 3\frac{4}{21} - 7\frac{1}{3} + 6\frac{4}{7}$

2.3   MULTIPLYING FRACTIONS

To multiply fractions, multiply the numerators and divide by the product of the denominators.

Examples

- $\frac{2}{3} \times \frac{4}{5} = \frac{2 \times 4}{3 \times 5} = \frac{8}{15}$
- $\frac{5}{7} \times \frac{3}{5} = \frac{5 \times 3}{7 \times 5} = \frac{3}{7}$

Reduce numerator and denominator by dividing by a common factor.

To multiply mixed numbers, express the mixed numbers as improper fractions and multiply as you would proper fractions.

Examples

- $1\frac{1}{8} \times \frac{3}{7} = \frac{9}{8} \times \frac{3}{7} = \frac{27}{56}$
- $2\frac{2}{3} \times 4\frac{2}{5} = \frac{8}{3} \times \frac{22}{5} = \frac{176}{15} = 11\frac{11}{15}$
- $10\frac{1}{2} \times \frac{3}{8} \times 2\frac{3}{4} \times \frac{6}{7} = \frac{21}{2} \times \frac{3}{8} \times \frac{11}{4} \times \frac{6}{7} = \frac{3}{1} \times \frac{3}{8} \times \frac{11}{4} \times \frac{3}{1} = \frac{297}{32} = 9\frac{9}{32}$

To multiply a fraction by a whole number, rewrite the whole number as a fraction with denominator 1, and multiply as you would proper fractions.

Examples

- $\frac{5}{8} \times 2 = \frac{5}{8} \times \frac{2}{1} = \frac{10}{8} = 1\frac{2}{8} = 1\frac{1}{4}$
- $6 \times 7\frac{5}{8} = \frac{6}{1} \times \frac{61}{8} = \frac{366}{8} = 45\frac{6}{8} = 45\frac{3}{4}$

EXERCISE 2.3
Multiply.

1. $\frac{1}{3} \times \frac{2}{5}$

2. $\frac{4}{5} \times \frac{10}{13}$

3. $\frac{5}{8} \times \frac{7}{16}$

4. $\frac{2}{3} \times \frac{21}{25}$

5. $\frac{3}{4}$ of $\frac{8}{9}$

6. $\frac{7}{8}$ of $\frac{9}{11}$

7. $\frac{3}{8} \times \frac{7}{8}$

8. $\frac{1}{2} \times \frac{5}{9}$

9. $\frac{9}{10} \times \frac{3}{4} \times \frac{1}{2}$

10. $\frac{2}{3} \times \frac{3}{8} \times 2$

11. $3 \times \frac{5}{6} \times \frac{1}{4}$

12. $8\frac{1}{2} \times 3$

13. $8\frac{1}{2} \times 3\frac{1}{2}$

14. $4\frac{5}{8} \times \frac{3}{7} \times \frac{1}{4}$

15. $4 \times 6\frac{1}{2} \times \frac{3}{4}$

16. $8\frac{1}{3} \times 9\frac{2}{5} \times 3$

17. $3\frac{7}{8} \times 6\frac{3}{7} \times \frac{1}{5}$

18. $\frac{1}{8} \times \frac{2}{9} \times \frac{1}{3} \times \frac{3}{4}$

19. $5\frac{5}{9} \times 9\frac{7}{8} \times 6\frac{2}{5}$

20. $6\frac{1}{7} \times 4\frac{3}{8} \times 5\frac{1}{3}$

2.4 DIVIDING WITH FRACTIONS

Division is the inverse of multiplication.

$$3 \times 4 = 12 \rightarrow 3 = 12 \div 4$$
$$\frac{2}{3} \times \frac{4}{5} = \frac{8}{15} \rightarrow \frac{2}{3} = \frac{8}{15} \div \frac{4}{5}$$
$$\text{but } \frac{2}{3} = \frac{8}{15} \times \frac{5}{4}$$

Thus, dividing by $\frac{4}{5}$ gives the same result as multiplying by $\frac{5}{4}$. We say that $\frac{4}{5}$ and $\frac{5}{4}$ are *reciprocals*. Any 2 numbers whose product is 1 are reciprocals of each other.

$\frac{4}{5}$ is a reciprocal of $\frac{5}{4}$ because $\frac{4}{5} \times \frac{5}{4} = 1$.

$\frac{2}{3}$ is a reciprocal of $\frac{3}{2}$.

To divide by a fraction, multiply by its reciprocal.

Invert and multiply.

Examples

- $\frac{5}{6} \div \frac{2}{5} = \frac{5}{6} \times \frac{5}{2} = \frac{25}{12} = 2\frac{1}{12}$

- $\frac{5}{6} \div 7 = \frac{5}{6} \times \frac{1}{7} = \frac{5}{42}$

- $8 \div \frac{2}{3} = 8 \times \frac{3}{2} = \frac{24}{2} = 12$

- $3\frac{1}{2} \div 6 = \frac{7}{2} \times \frac{1}{6} = \frac{7}{12}$

- $4\frac{3}{4} \div 2\frac{1}{3} = \frac{19}{4} \div \frac{7}{3} = \frac{19}{4} \times \frac{3}{7} = \frac{57}{28} = 2\frac{1}{28}$

EXERCISE 2.4
Divide.

1. $6 \div \frac{2}{3}$

2. $3 \div 1\frac{1}{2}$

3. $\frac{4}{5} \div 2$

4. $3\frac{4}{5} \div \frac{2}{3}$

5. $4\frac{2}{3} \div 6\frac{2}{5}$

6. $\frac{7}{8} \div 1\frac{2}{3}$

7. $9 \div \frac{3}{5}$

8. $\frac{11}{15} \div \frac{3}{8}$

9. $3\frac{4}{5} \div 6$

10. $1\frac{5}{8} \div \frac{7}{8}$

11. $2\frac{7}{10} \div \frac{1}{5}$

12. $3\frac{15}{16} \div 2\frac{3}{16}$

13. $28\frac{7}{8} \div 3\frac{2}{3}$

14. $17\frac{5}{8} \div 2\frac{1}{4}$

15. $16\frac{1}{2} \div 1\frac{3}{8}$

2.5 SIMPLIFYING EXPRESSIONS

An expression involving the four basic operations of addition, subtraction, multiplication, and division must be simplified in a specific order.
- Simplify any expression inside brackets.
- Remove brackets.
- Change "of" to "×".
- Divide and multiply.
- Add and subtract.

Example

Simplify $\frac{3}{4}$ of $\frac{3}{5} - \frac{3}{4} \div \frac{2}{5} + \frac{1}{3}(9 \times \frac{2}{3}) + \frac{4}{5}$.

Solution

$$\frac{3}{4} \text{ of } \frac{3}{5} - \frac{3}{4} \div \frac{2}{5} + \frac{1}{3}(9 \times \frac{2}{3}) + \frac{4}{5} = \frac{3}{4} \times \frac{3}{5} - \frac{3}{4} \div \frac{2}{5} + \frac{1}{3} \times 6 + \frac{4}{5}$$

$$= \frac{9}{20} - \frac{3}{4} \times \frac{5}{2} + 2 + \frac{4}{5}$$

$$= \frac{9}{20} - \frac{15}{8} + 2 + \frac{4}{5}$$

$$= \frac{18 - 75 + 80 + 32}{40}$$

$$= \frac{55}{40}$$

$$= 1\frac{3}{8}$$

BODMAS   *Summary of Steps*

Brackets, Of, Divide, Multiply, Add, Subtract

EXERCISE 2.5

Simplify the following.

1. $\frac{1}{4} \div \frac{2}{3} + \frac{5}{6} - \frac{1}{2} \times \frac{3}{8}$

2. $\frac{1}{4} \div \frac{2}{3} - \frac{1}{3}(\frac{7}{9} - \frac{2}{3}) + \frac{3}{5}$ of 20

3. $\frac{4}{5}(\frac{1}{8} + \frac{2}{3}) + \frac{4}{5}$ of $\frac{7}{8} - 6 \div \frac{4}{5} + \frac{1}{3} \div 2$

2.6 DECIMAL FRACTIONS

A fraction whose denominator is 10, or a power of 10 such as 100, 1 000, or 10 000, is called a *decimal fraction*, or simply, a *decimal*.

Examples

- $\frac{7}{10} = 0.7$

- $\frac{34}{100} = 0.34$

- $\frac{1 \ 29}{1 \ 000} = 0.129$

In each example the number of digits to the right of the decimal point in the decimal fraction indicates the number of zeros after the 1 in the denominator of the equivalent common fraction.

A Conversion of Fractions to Decimals

To express a fraction as a decimal, divide the numerator by the denominator.

Examples

- $\frac{4}{5} = 4 \div 5 = 0.8$

- $\frac{2}{3} = 2 \div 3 = 0.666\,\overline{6}$ a repeating decimal, correct to 4 decimal places
  $= 0.66\overline{6}$ a repeating decimal, correct to 3 decimal places

B Conversion of Decimals to Fractions

To express a decimal fraction as a common fraction, use the number, without the decimal point, as the numerator. The denominator is 1 followed by a number of zeros, the number of zeros being the same as the number of digits to the right of the decimal point.

Examples

- $0.4 = \frac{4}{10} = \frac{2}{5}$

- $0.25 = \frac{25}{100} = \frac{1}{4}$

- $0.625 = \frac{625}{1\,000} = \frac{5}{8}$

- $4.125 = \frac{4\,125}{1\,000} = 4\frac{1}{8}$

EXERCISE 2.6

1. Express each of the following as a decimal fraction correct to 3 decimal places.

    (a) $\frac{1}{2}$ (f) $\frac{2}{7}$ (k) $\frac{1}{12}$ (p) $\frac{11}{85}$

    (b) $\frac{1}{3}$ (g) $\frac{7}{9}$ (l) $\frac{11}{14}$ (q) $4\frac{1}{6}$

    (c) $\frac{2}{3}$ (h) $\frac{5}{6}$ (m) $\frac{15}{22}$ (r) $7\frac{9}{10}$

    (d) $\frac{3}{8}$ (i) $\frac{1}{8}$ (n) $\frac{8}{25}$ (s) $36\frac{2}{3}$

    (e) $\frac{7}{8}$ (j) $\frac{1}{16}$ (o) $\frac{3}{16}$ (t) $41\frac{2}{5}$

2. Express each of the following as a common fraction.

    (a) 0.4   (d) 0.875   (g) 0.5   (j) 8.125

    (b) 0.92   (e) 0.125   (h) 5.25   (k) 3.6

    (c) 0.375   (f) 0.625   (i) 4.42   (l) 6.2

2.7 CONVERSION OF REPEATING DECIMALS TO FRACTIONS

Examples

- $0.33\overline{3} = \frac{1}{3}$

- $0.16\overline{6} = \frac{1}{6}$

In the example above, it is hard to see how $0.33\overline{3}$ could equal $\frac{1}{3}$. $0.33\overline{3}$ is a repeating decimal. Its exact equivalent fraction is $\frac{333\frac{1}{3}}{1000}$, which at first may appear difficult to reduce to lower terms. If we multiply the numerator and the denominator of the fraction by the same number, we will have another equivalent fraction.

Therefore

$$\frac{333\frac{1}{3}}{1000} = \frac{333\frac{1}{3} \times 3}{1000 \times 3}$$

$$= \frac{1000}{3000}$$

$$= \frac{1}{3}$$

Similarly $0.16\overline{6} = \frac{16\overline{6}}{1000}$ by rule

$= \frac{166\frac{2}{3}}{1000}$ because the 6 repeats

$= \frac{166\frac{2}{3} \times 3}{1000 \times 3}$

$= \frac{500}{3000}$

$= \frac{1}{6}$

Note: In this text, fractions having equivalent repeating decimals end with $\frac{1}{3}$ or $\frac{2}{3}$. Examples are $8\frac{1}{3}$ and $66\frac{2}{3}$. For other examples, look at the chart on page 43.

EXERCISE 2.7
Express each of the following as a common fraction.

1. $0.16\overline{6}$ 4. $0.83\overline{3}$ 7. $4.33\overline{3}$

2. $0.08\overline{3}$ 5. $0.58\overline{3}$ 8. $5.66\overline{6}$

3. $0.66\overline{6}$ 6. $2.16\overline{6}$ 9. $0.41\overline{6}$

2.8   ALIQUOT PARTS I

96 brass screws at $12\frac{1}{2}$¢ each

2 dozen hooks at 25¢ each

258 metal rings at $33\frac{1}{3}$¢ each

In these cases you could easily find the total cost by multiplying 96×0.125, 24×0.25, and 258×0.333. There is a quicker way.

Each price is an exact fractional part of $1.

$12\frac{1}{2}$¢ is $\frac{1}{8}$ of $1

25¢ is $\frac{1}{4}$ of $1

$33\frac{1}{3}$¢ is $\frac{1}{3}$ of $1

$96 \times \frac{1}{8}$ of $1 = \frac{96}{8} = 12$

96 brass screws at $12\frac{1}{2}$¢ each cost $12.

$24 \times \frac{1}{4}$ of $1 = \frac{24}{4} = 6$

2 dozen hooks at 25¢ each cost $6.

$258 \times \frac{1}{3}$ of $1 = \frac{258}{3} = 86$

258 metal rings at $33\frac{1}{3}$¢ each cost $86.

A number that divides into another number without a remainder is called an *aliquot part* of the second number. Since these prices divide evenly into $1, they are aliquot parts of $1.

Numbers that are multiples of aliquot parts are also called aliquot parts. For example,

$$37\tfrac{1}{2}¢ = \tfrac{3}{8} \text{ of } \$1 \qquad 50¢ = \tfrac{1}{2} \text{ of } \$1 \qquad 66\tfrac{2}{3}¢ = \tfrac{2}{3} \text{ of } \$1$$

$$62\tfrac{1}{2}¢ = \tfrac{5}{8} \text{ of } \$1 \qquad 75¢ = \tfrac{3}{4} \text{ of } \$1$$

Since unit prices and rates are often quoted as aliquot parts of $1, you can shorten your work by multiplying the number of units by the fractional equivalent of the aliquot part.

Example 1
Find the cost of 83 oranges at 20¢ each.

Solution

$$20¢ = \tfrac{1}{5} \text{ of } \$1$$

$$83 \times \tfrac{1}{5} = 16.60$$

Cost of oranges is $16.60.

Example 2
Find the cost of 75 raisin rolls at $12\tfrac{1}{2}$¢ each.

Solution

$$12\tfrac{1}{2}¢ = \$\tfrac{1}{8}$$

$$75 \times \tfrac{1}{8} = 9.375$$

Cost of rolls is $9.38.

Table of Some Aliquot Parts of 100

Multiples	$\frac{1}{2}$	$\frac{1}{3}$	$\frac{1}{4}$	$\frac{1}{5}$	$\frac{1}{6}$	$\frac{1}{8}$	$\frac{1}{10}$	$\frac{1}{12}$	$\frac{1}{16}$
1	50	$33\frac{1}{3}$	25	20	$16\frac{2}{3}$	$12\frac{1}{2}$	10	$8\frac{1}{3}$	$6\frac{1}{4}$
2	100	$66\frac{2}{3}$	50	40	$33\frac{1}{3}$	25	20	$16\frac{2}{3}$	$12\frac{1}{2}$
3		100	75	60	50	$37\frac{1}{2}$	30	25	$18\frac{3}{4}$
4			100	80	$66\frac{2}{3}$	50	40	$33\frac{1}{3}$	25
5				100	$83\frac{1}{3}$	$62\frac{1}{2}$	50	$41\frac{2}{3}$	$31\frac{1}{4}$
6					100	75	60	50	$37\frac{1}{2}$
7						$87\frac{1}{2}$	70	$58\frac{1}{3}$	$43\frac{3}{4}$
8						100	80	$66\frac{2}{3}$	50
9							90	75	$56\frac{1}{4}$
10							100	$83\frac{1}{3}$	$62\frac{1}{2}$
12								100	75

EXERCISE 2.8
1. State the fractional equivalent of each of the following.

(a)	0.50	(g)	0.25	(m)	0.75
(b)	$0.83\frac{1}{3}$	(h)	$0.91\frac{2}{3}$	(n)	$0.58\frac{1}{3}$
(c)	$0.37\frac{1}{2}$	(i)	0.30	(o)	$0.31\frac{1}{4}$
(d)	$0.16\frac{2}{3}$	(j)	0.10	(p)	$0.33\frac{1}{3}$
(e)	$0.87\frac{1}{2}$	(k)	$0.06\frac{1}{4}$	(q)	$0.62\frac{1}{2}$
(f)	$0.08\frac{1}{3}$	(l)	0.40	(r)	0.80

2. Using fractional parts of a dollar, find the cost of each of the following.

(a) 240 units @ 25¢ = ▆▆▆▆
      66 units @ 50¢ = ▆▆▆▆
     136 units @ 80¢ = ▆▆▆▆
      96 units @ 40¢ = ▆▆▆▆
      32 units @ 60¢ = ▆▆▆▆
            Total = ▆▆▆▆

(d) 144 units @ $8\frac{1}{3}$¢ = ▆▆▆▆
     160 units @ $37\frac{1}{2}$¢ = ▆▆▆▆
     330 units @ $12\frac{1}{2}$¢ = ▆▆▆▆
     480 units @ $18\frac{3}{4}$¢ = ▆▆▆▆
      66 units @ $66\frac{2}{3}$¢ = ▆▆▆▆
            Total = ▆▆▆▆

(b) 136 units @ $33\frac{1}{3}$¢ = ▆▆▆▆
      72 units @ $37\frac{1}{2}$¢ = ▆▆▆▆
     208 units @ $62\frac{1}{2}$¢ = ▆▆▆▆
      56 units @ $66\frac{2}{3}$¢ = ▆▆▆▆
      96 units @ $43\frac{3}{4}$¢ = ▆▆▆▆
            Total = ▆▆▆▆

(e) 165 units @ $91\frac{2}{3}$¢ = ▆▆▆▆
     330 units @ $87\frac{1}{2}$¢ = ▆▆▆▆
      48 units @ $43\frac{3}{4}$¢ = ▆▆▆▆
      28 units @ $6\frac{1}{4}$¢ = ▆▆▆▆
      24 units @ $56\frac{1}{4}$¢ = ▆▆▆▆
            Total = ▆▆▆▆

(c)   18 units @ $16\frac{2}{3}$¢ = ▆▆▆▆
     120 units @ $83\frac{1}{3}$¢ = ▆▆▆▆
     240 units @ $6\frac{1}{4}$¢ = ▆▆▆▆
      64 units @ $12\frac{1}{2}$¢ = ▆▆▆▆
      56 units @ $87\frac{1}{2}$¢ = ▆▆▆▆
            Total = ▆▆▆▆

(f)   69 units @ $66\frac{2}{3}$¢ = ▆▆▆▆
      63 units @ $66\frac{2}{3}$¢ = ▆▆▆▆
      78 units @ $16\frac{2}{3}$¢ = ▆▆▆▆
     160 units @ $87\frac{1}{2}$¢ = ▆▆▆▆
     112 units @ $12\frac{1}{2}$¢ = ▆▆▆▆
            Total = ▆▆▆▆

2.9   ALIQUOT PARTS II

The inverse of the preceding section is to find the number of parts that can be purchased with a given amount at a given rate.

Example 1
How many units can be bought at $12\frac{1}{2}$¢ each if you have $25 to spend?

Solution
$$25 \div 0.125 = 25 \div \tfrac{1}{8} = 25 \times 8 = 200$$
Number of units is 200.

Example 2
How many hair brushes can be bought, at $87\frac{1}{2}$¢ each, for $35?

Solution
$35 \div 87\frac{1}{2}$¢ $= 35 \div \frac{7}{8} = 35 \times \frac{8}{7} = 40$

Number of brushes is 40.

EXERCISE 2.9
Find the number of units that can be bought for the given amounts at the given prices.

	Amount	*Price per Unit*		*Amount*	*Price per Unit*
1.	$50	$0.20	6.	$75	$0.75
2.	$65	$0.35	7.	$56	$0.87\frac{1}{2}$
3.	$76	$0.75	8.	$96	$0.06\frac{1}{4}$
4.	$42	$0.33\frac{1}{3}$	9.	$49	$0.87\frac{1}{2}$
5.	$64	$0.37\frac{1}{2}$	10.	$35	$0.41\frac{2}{3}$

2.10   PERCENT – CHANGING A PERCENT TO A FRACTION

A percent of a number is a hundredth of that number. Therefore five percent of a number is 5 hundredths of that number and may be written as $\frac{5}{100}$ or 0.05 or 5%.

Example
5% of $20 = 0.05 \times$ $20 = $1
People use the terms '5%' or '20%', but in mathematical calculations on a machine you must use either the equivalent common fractions or the equivalent decimals, unless your machine has a percent key.

To change a percent to a fraction, divide by 100 and drop the percent sign.

Examples

- $80\% = \frac{80}{100} = \frac{4}{5}$

- $150\% = \frac{150}{100} = \frac{3}{2} = 1\frac{1}{2}$

- $\frac{1}{2}\% = \frac{1}{2} \times \frac{1}{100} = \frac{1}{200}$

- $8\frac{1}{3}\% = \frac{25}{3} \times \frac{1}{100} = \frac{25}{300} = \frac{1}{12}$

EXERCISE 2.10
Change the following percents to fractions.

1. 40%	4. $33\frac{1}{3}\%$	7. 225%	10. $1\frac{3}{8}\%$	13. $37\frac{1}{2}\%$
2. 60%	5. $16\frac{2}{3}\%$	8. $\frac{1}{4}\%$	11. 75%	14. $62\frac{1}{2}\%$
3. 50%	6. 200%	9. $\frac{1}{8}\%$	12. 90%	15. $6\frac{1}{4}\%$

2.11   PERCENT – CHANGING A FRACTION TO A PERCENT

To change a fraction to a percent, multiply by 100%.

Examples

- $\frac{3}{5} = \frac{3}{5} \times 100\% = 60\%$

- $\frac{1}{3} = \frac{1}{3} \times 100\% = 33\frac{1}{3}\%$

- $1\frac{3}{4} = 1\frac{3}{4} \times 100\% = \frac{7}{4} \times 100\% = 175\%$

EXERCISE 2.11
Express the following fractions as percents.

1. $\frac{1}{2}$ 3. $\frac{3}{4}$ 5. $\frac{3}{8}$ 7. $3\frac{7}{8}$ 9. $\frac{2}{7}$ 11. $2\frac{4}{25}$

2. $\frac{2}{3}$ 4. $\frac{3}{5}$ 6. $\frac{5}{12}$ 8. $\frac{5}{16}$ 10. $1\frac{9}{17}$ 12. $1\frac{35}{38}$

2.12   PERCENT – CHANGING A PERCENT TO A DECIMAL

To change a percent to a decimal, divide the rate percent by 100.

Examples

Note: **To divide by 100, move the decimal point 2 places *left*.**

- $35\% = \frac{35}{100} = 0.35$

- $135\% = \frac{135}{100} = 1.35$

- $35\frac{1}{2}\% = \frac{35\frac{1}{2}}{100} = \frac{35.5}{100} = 0.355$

- $33\frac{1}{3}\% = \frac{33\frac{1}{3}}{100} = \frac{33.\overline{3}}{100} = 0.33\overline{3}$

EXERCISE 2.12
Express the following percents as decimals.

1. 10%   4. $\frac{1}{2}\%$ 7. $4\frac{1}{2}\%$ 10. $8\frac{1}{3}\%$

2. $87\frac{1}{2}\%$ 5. $\frac{2}{3}\%$ 8. $\frac{1}{4}\%$ 11. $6\frac{1}{4}\%$

3. 815%   6. 1 100%   9. $37\frac{1}{2}\%$ 12. $\frac{7}{8}\%$

2.13   PERCENT – CHANGING A DECIMAL TO A PERCENT

This is the reverse of the previous operation. To change a decimal to a percent, multiply the decimal by 100%.

Note: **To multiply by 100, move the decimal point *2* places *right*.**

Examples
- $0.75 = 0.75 \times 100\% = 75\%$
- $1.25 = 1.25 \times 100\% = 125\%$
- $0.375 = 0.375 \times 100\% = 37.5\%$

Table of Some Common Equivalents

Common Fraction	Decimal	Percent	Common Fraction	Decimal	Percent
$\frac{1}{2}$	0.5	50%	$\frac{5}{6}$	$0.83\overline{3}$	$83\frac{1}{3}\%$
$\frac{1}{3}$	$0.33\overline{3}$	$33\frac{1}{3}\%$	$\frac{1}{8}$	0.125	$12\frac{1}{2}\%$
$\frac{2}{3}$	$0.66\overline{6}$	$66\frac{2}{3}\%$	$\frac{3}{8}$	0.375	$37\frac{1}{2}\%$
$\frac{1}{4}$	0.25	25%	$\frac{5}{8}$	0.625	$62\frac{1}{2}\%$
$\frac{3}{4}$	0.75	75%	$\frac{7}{8}$	0.875	$87\frac{1}{2}\%$
$\frac{1}{5}$	0.20	20%	$\frac{1}{10}$	0.10	10%
$\frac{2}{5}$	0.40	40%	$\frac{3}{10}$	0.30	30%
$\frac{3}{5}$	0.60	60%	$\frac{7}{10}$	0.70	70%
$\frac{4}{5}$	0.80	80%	$\frac{9}{10}$	0.90	90%
$\frac{1}{6}$	$0.16\overline{6}$	$16\frac{2}{3}\%$	$\frac{1}{12}$	$0.08\overline{3}$	$8\frac{1}{3}\%$

EXERCISE 2.13

1. Express the following decimals as percents.
   - (a) 0.04
   - (b) 0.125
   - (c) 0.833
   - (d) 0.026 5
   - (e) 0.001 25
   - (f) 2.13
   - (g) 125.25
   - (h) 1.08
   - (i) 1.66
   - (j) 3.75
   - (k) 0.801 25
   - (l) 0.002 5

2. The down payment on a bicycle is 20%. What fraction of the price is the down payment?

3. An antique sofa was sold for 140% of its cost. What percent of the cost is the profit?

4. A bookkeeper finds that expenses are $\frac{3}{5}$ of income. What percent of income are expenses?

5. J. Brown, a farmer, seeded $\frac{5}{8}$ of his hectares in oats and J. Smith, another farmer, seeded 60% of her hectares in oats. Which farmer seeded the larger portion of his/her farm in oats?

2.14   CALCULATING WITH REPEATING DECIMALS

Repeating decimals present a problem when multiplying or dividing. You will always get an accurate answer if you use an equivalent fraction. However, to get an accurate answer with a repeating decimal you must know how many decimal places to use.

Example 1
Find $33\frac{1}{3}\%$ of 62, correct to two decimal places.

Solution
Since $33\frac{1}{3}\% = \frac{1}{3}$, $33\frac{1}{3}\%$ of $62 = \frac{1}{3} \times 62$
$$= 20.67$$
$$0.333\,3 \times 62 = 20.664\,6$$
$$= 20.66$$
$$0.333\,33 \times 62 = 20.666\,46$$
$$= 20.67$$

Example 2
Find $66\frac{2}{3}\%$ of 246, correct to two decimal places.

Solution
$$66\frac{2}{3}\% \text{ of } 246 = \frac{2}{3} \times 246$$
$$= 164$$
$$0.666\,6 \times 246 = 163.983\,6$$
$$= 163.98$$
$$0.666\,66 \times 246 = 163.998\,36$$
$$= 164.00$$

Example 3
Divide 93 by $33\frac{1}{3}\%$, correct to two decimal places.

Solution
$$93 \div 33\frac{1}{3}\% = 93 \div \frac{1}{3}$$
$$= 93 \times 3$$
$$= 279$$

$$\frac{93}{0.333\,3} = 279.027 \qquad \frac{93}{0.333\,33} = 279.002$$
$$= 279.03 \qquad\qquad\qquad = 279.00$$

Example 4
Divide 972 by $8\frac{1}{3}\%$, correct to two decimal places.

Solution
$$972 \div 8\frac{1}{3}\% = 972 \div \frac{1}{12}$$
$$= 972 \times 12$$
$$= 11\,664$$

$$\frac{972}{0.083\,333} = 11\,664.046 \qquad \frac{972}{0.083\,333\,3} = 11\,664.004$$
$$= 11\,664.05 \qquad\qquad\qquad = 11\,664.00$$

More examples

- $728.76 \times \frac{2}{3} = 485.84$

  $728.76 \times 0.666\ 666 = 485.839$
  $\qquad\qquad\qquad\quad\ = 485.84$

- $843.72 \times \frac{1}{12} = 70.31$

  $843.72 \times 0.083\ 33 = 70.307$
  $\qquad\qquad\qquad\ = 70.31$

- $87.4 \div \frac{2}{3} = 87.4 \times \frac{3}{2}$

  $\qquad\qquad = 131.10$

  $\dfrac{87.4}{0.666\ 66} = 131.101$

  $\qquad\qquad = 131.10$

- $573.62 \div \frac{1}{6} = 573.62 \times 6$

  $\qquad\qquad = 3\ 441.72$

  $\dfrac{573.62}{0.166\ 666\ 6} = 3\ 441.72$

To multiply by a repeating decimal, use three decimal places more than the number of digits in the whole number part of the multiplicand. For example, to multiply 384.52 by a repeating decimal, use $3 + 3 = 6$ decimal places.

To divide by a repeating decimal, use four decimal places more than the number of digits in the whole number part of the dividend. For example, to divide 8.632 by a repeating decimal, use $1 + 4 = 5$ decimal places.

Note: You will find that you will *sometimes* get an accurate answer using fewer decimal places. To be sure, use the number of decimal places recommended above.

EXERCISE 2.14

1. Find the following correct to two decimal places.

   (a) $33\frac{1}{3}\%$ of 489   (d) $66\frac{2}{3}\%$ of 542.64

   (b) $58\frac{1}{3}\%$ of 34.56   (e) $16\frac{2}{3}\%$ of 94.86

   (c) $8\frac{1}{3}\%$ of 62   (f) $33\frac{1}{3}\%$ of 4 852.9

2. Divide the following and give your answer correct to two decimal places.

   (a) $75 \div 16\frac{2}{3}\%$ (d) $975 \div 83\frac{1}{3}\%$

   (b) $42.81 \div 33\frac{1}{3}\%$ (e) $3\ 429.73 \div 41\frac{2}{3}\%$

   (c) $1.567\ 83 \div 66\frac{2}{3}\%$ (f) $407.6 \div 33\frac{1}{3}\%$

2.15   BASIC OPERATIONS WITH PERCENTS

A   Addition and Subtraction

Example
A municipality spends 25% of its taxes on secondary education, 33% on elementary education, 16% on local general expenses, and the remainder is contributed to the regional government. What portion does the regional government receive?

Solution
25% + 33% + 16% = 74%
Total taxes = 100%
Taxes to regional government = 100% − 74% = 26%

B   Multiplication and Division

Example 1
Find 20% of 25%.

Solution
$$20\% \text{ of } 25\% = 20\% \times 25\%$$
$$= 0.2 \times 0.25$$
$$= 0.05 = 5\%$$

OR 20% of $25\% = \frac{1}{5} \times 25\%$
$$= 5\%$$

Example 2
Divide 80% by 20%.

Solution
$$\frac{80\%}{20\%} = \frac{0.8}{0.2}$$
$$= 4$$

OR $\dfrac{80\%}{20\%} = \dfrac{4}{5} \div \dfrac{1}{5}$
$$= \frac{4}{5} \times 5 = 4$$

Example 3
Multiply $\frac{1}{4}\% \times 688\%$.

Solution
$$\frac{1}{4}\% \times 688\% = 0.002\,5 \times 688\%$$
$$= 1.72\%$$

OR $\frac{1}{4}\% \times 688\% = \dfrac{1}{400} \times 688\%$
$$= \frac{668\%}{400} = 1.72\%$$

Example 4
Divide $87\frac{1}{2}\%$ by $12\frac{1}{2}\%$.

Solution
$$\frac{87\frac{1}{2}\%}{12\frac{1}{2}\%} = \frac{0.875}{0.125}$$
$$= 7$$

OR $87\frac{1}{2}\% \div 12\frac{1}{2}\% = \dfrac{7}{8} \div \dfrac{1}{8}$
$$= \frac{7}{8} \times 8 = 7$$

EXERCISE 2.15

1. Sally gave a party and estimated that 30% of the salads should be cole slaw. If the boys ate 60% of the cole slaw, what percent of the salads did they eat?

2. Jules Deneau budgeted the earnings from his part-time job as follows: dates, 20%; clothes, 15%; lunches, $12\frac{1}{2}$%; car fare, 5%; sports, 25%; and the rest to savings. What percent of his income did he save?

3. A breakfast cereal has 10.1% protein, 1.4% fat, and 76.7% carbohydrates. What percent of the cereal was composed of other components?

4. On a recent mathematics test, $\frac{1}{4}$ of the students got over 75% and $\frac{1}{3}$ of the remainder earned marks below 55%. What percent of the students earned marks between 55% and 75%?

5. Businesspeople prepare Income Statements every year. Certain items are frequently expressed as a percent of Sales. If Costs are 67% of Sales and Expenses are 23% of Sales, find the percent that Gross Profit and Net Incomes are of Sales.

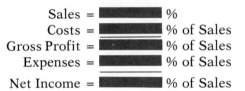

Sales = ▰▰▰ %	
Costs = ▰▰▰ % of Sales	
Gross Profit = ▰▰▰ % of Sales	**Sales – Costs = Gross Profit**
Expenses = ▰▰▰ % of Sales	**Gross Profit – Expenses = Net Income**
Net Income = ▰▰▰ % of Sales	

6. Jose left a will that stated that 60% of his worldly possessions was to go to his immediate family, 25% of the remainder was to go to each of his 3 nieces, and $12\frac{1}{2}$% of the same remainder was to go to each of his 2 nephews. What percent of the total estate did (a) each niece, (b) each nephew receive?

7. What percent of Sales is (a) Gross Profit, (b) Expenses, if costs are 75% of Sales and Net Income is 5% of Sales?

2.16 PERCENT PROBLEMS – FINDING THE AMOUNT

25% of 60 is?
25% more than 60 is?
25% is ?% of 60
25 is ?% smaller than 60
25% of ? is 60
60 is 25% more than?
Each of the above examples asks a different question and requires a different approach to find the answer. Consider the first example.

Base may be identified as following "of," "times", "more than", "as large as".

25% of 60 = 0.25 × 60 = 15

25% is the *rate*.
  60 is the *base*.
  15 is the *amount*.

As shown above, the relationship among these three quantities may be written as

Amount = Rate × Base

The other five examples may also be solved using the formula. The problem in each case is to determine which term is unknown and to which terms the given values correspond.

Example 1
Find 20% of 65.

Solution
20% is the rate.
  65 is the base.

Amount = Rate × Base
       = 20% × 65
       = 0.2 × 65
       = 13

For machine calculations, percent must be expressed as a decimal.

Example 2
What amount is $33\frac{1}{3}$% of 171?

Solution
$33\frac{1}{3}$% is the rate.
  171 is the base.

Machine   Amount = Rate × Base
Instruction   = 0.333 33 × 171
                         = 57

CLEAR

SET DEC 2

Enter 0.333 33

Enter 171

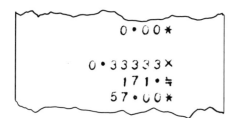

EXERCISE 2.16

Find the amount, correct to 2 decimal places, using the following rates and bases.

	Rate	Base		Rate	Base		Rate	Base
1.	8%	9 400	5.	17%	99	9.	$16\frac{2}{3}\%$	1.6
2.	$6\frac{1}{4}\%$	192	6.	43%	108.50	10.	$33\frac{1}{3}\%$	972
3.	$62\frac{1}{2}\%$	1 550	7.	75%	14	11.	31.25%	456
4.	$37\frac{1}{2}\%$	90	8.	$87\frac{1}{2}\%$	246	12.	78%	462

2.17   PERCENT PROBLEMS – THE 1% METHOD

This method helps to calculate percent quickly and easily when rates are commonly used fractional parts of 1%, such as $\frac{1}{2}\%$, $\frac{1}{4}\%$, and $\frac{1}{3}\%$.

Example 1
Find $\frac{1}{2}\%$ of 680.

Solution
1% of 680 = 6.8

$\frac{1}{2}\%$ of 680 = $6.8 \times \frac{1}{2} = \frac{6.8}{2} = 3.4$

Example 2
Find $1\frac{1}{4}\%$ of 844.

Solution

1% of 844 $\quad = \quad 8.44$

$\frac{1}{4}\%$ of 844 $\; = \frac{8.44}{4} = \; 2.11$

$1\frac{1}{4}\%$ of 844 $\quad = 10.55$

EXERCISE 2.17

Find the following amounts using the 1% method, correct to 2 decimal places.

1. $\frac{1}{5}\%$ of 75

2. 3% of 240

3. 8% of 568

4. $1\frac{1}{2}\%$ of 84

5. $\frac{1}{9}\%$ of 180

6. $3\frac{1}{2}\%$ of $250

7. 12% of 60

8. $2\frac{1}{2}\%$ of 224

9. $\frac{1}{8}\%$ of 420

10. $\frac{7}{8}\%$ of 84

11. $4\frac{1}{2}\%$ of $800

12. $5\frac{1}{2}\%$ of $625

2.18 PERCENT PROBLEMS – FINDING THE BASE

Example 1
12 is 25% of what number?

Solution
25% is the rate.
Since "of" identifies the base, the base is unknown.
12 is the amount.

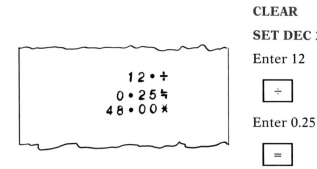

Machine
Instruction

CLEAR

SET DEC 2

Enter 12

$\div$

Enter 0.25

$=$

Amount = Rate × Base

$$\text{Base} = \frac{\text{Amount}}{\text{Rate}}$$

$$= \frac{12}{0.25}$$

$$= 48$$

Example 2
$2.70 is $1\frac{1}{2}$% of what value?

Solution

$$\text{Base} = \frac{\text{Amount}}{\text{Rate}}$$

$$= \frac{2.7}{0.015}$$

$$= 180$$

Value is $180.

EXERCISE 2.18
Give answers correct to 2 decimal places.

1. Of what number does 20% equal 40?

2. 65 is $37\frac{1}{2}$% of what number?

3. If 30% of a number is 210, what is the number?

4. 265 cm are 40% of how many metres?

5. $4.20 is 25% of what amount?

6. Of what sum is $16.35, 15%?

7. 2 dozen oranges represent $12\frac{1}{2}$% of how many oranges?

8. A discount of 32% of what sum equals $22.40?

9. 105% of what number equals 7?

10. 105% of what number equals 5?

11. Of what number is 18, 8%?

12. Of what number is 90, 8%?

13. 28 is 189% of what number?

14. $\frac{1}{4}$ is 75% of what number?

15. How much money must you invest at 16% to earn $500 per year?

16. Pia's mother gave her $45 to make a down payment on a tape recorder. If the down payment was 18%, how much was the recorder?

17. $248.40 is 80% of what price?

18. $81 is 150% of what price?

19. How many dozen eggs do you have to sell to earn $40 if your profit on the selling price is 20% and each dozen sells for $1.10?

20. A decorator receives a 2% rebate when ordering furniture from a manufacturer. If the rebate is $1 450, what was the order worth?

2.19   PERCENT PROBLEMS – FINDING THE RATE

Example 1
12 is what percent of 48?

Solution
Rate is unknown.
Since "of" identifies the base, the base is 48.
12 is the amount.

Machine Instruction	
	Amount = Rate × Base
	Rate $= \dfrac{\text{Amount}}{\text{Base}}$
CLEAR	
SET DEC 2	$= \dfrac{12}{48}$
Enter 12	= 0.25
	= 25%
Enter 48	

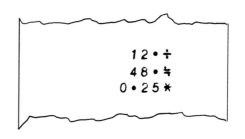

Example 2

2 is what percent of 7?

Solution

$$\text{Rate} = \frac{\text{Amount}}{\text{Base}}$$

$$= \frac{2}{7}$$

$$= 0.285\ 7$$

$$= 28.57\%$$

Remember to express the machine answer as a percent by multiplying the decimal by 100%.

EXERCISE 2.19

1. Find the rate for the following bases and amounts.

	Base	Amount			Base	Amount
(a)	32	6		(f)	16	2
(b)	8	24		(g)	7	14
(c)	105	21		(h)	9	108
(d)	16	1		(i)	56	21
(e)	18	3		(j)	81	27

2. What percent is 150 of 2 500?

3. 16 is what percent of 360?

4. $7 634 is what percent of $76 500?

5. What percent is 505 of 606?

6. What percent is 3 167.35 of 50 800.55?

7. $\frac{1}{4}$ is what percent of $\frac{7}{8}$?

8. What percent is $4.80 of $24?

9. What percent is $480 of $24?

10. $1.75 is what percent of $33.20?

11. Find the percent that $\frac{1}{3}$ is of $\frac{2}{3}$.

2.20   PERCENT PROBLEMS – REVIEW

Now that you have had some practice doing each kind of percent problem, you are ready to try an exercise containing all types.

Remember

$$\text{Amount} = \text{Rate} \times \text{Base}$$

$$\text{Base} = \frac{\text{Amount}}{\text{Rate}}$$

$$\text{Rate} = \frac{\text{Amount}}{\text{Base}}$$

EXERCISE 2.20

Solve the following problems using the appropriate form of the formula Amount = Rate × Base. Remember to identify each item before you start calculating.

1. What is $37\frac{1}{2}$% of 296?

2. Of what sum is $60, 30%?

3. 42% of $785 equals how much?

4. 17 is what percent of 68?

5. What percent of 7.2 is 18?

6. 2.16 is 25% of what number?

7. 0.93 is what percent of $\frac{1}{3}$?

8. $\frac{1}{8}$% of 28 is what number?

9. Of what number is 21, 150%?

10. There are 22 girls and 14 boys in a class.
    (a) What percent are girls?
    (b) What percent are boys?

11. A family with a yearly income of $19 400 allocated 35% for food, 25% for rent, 12% for clothing, 14% for education and reading, 8% for other expenses, and the rest for saving. How much money was allowed for each purpose?

12. If you loaned $1 800 for one year and received $324 in interest, what percent did you charge?

13. Out of a shipment of bicycles, a store sold 170 and had 9 left.
    (a) What percent was left?
    (b) If the original price was $90 and the store offered the remaining 9 bicycles at $75 each, what percent was the discount?

14. If you withdrew 20% of the money in your savings account and spent 60% of the withdrawal on $200 worth of lumber, how much would you have left in your savings account?

2.21   FINDING THE PERCENT OF INCREASE OR DECREASE

"The cost of living has gone up 8%."

"The price of potatoes has dropped by 3%."

These and many similar situations are part of everyday life. It is important to know how to calculate such increase and decrease problems.

Example 1
If 24 is increased to 36, what is the percent of increase?

Solution
Since there is nothing to identify the base, it is necessary to reword the question.

24 increased by what percent of itself equals 36?

Since "itself" refers to 24, the base is 24.
Amount of increase is $36 - 24 = 12$.

$$\text{Rate} = \frac{\text{Amount}}{\text{Base}}$$

$$= \frac{12}{24} = 0.5 = 50\%$$

Example 2
63 is what percent larger than 49?

Solution
Rewording the question:

49 increased by what percent of itself equals 63?

$$\text{Rate} = \frac{\text{Amount}}{\text{Base}}$$

$$= \frac{14}{49} = 0.285\ 7 = 28.57\%$$

Example 3
If 72 is decreased to 60, what is the percent of decrease?

Solution
Rewording the question:
72 decreased by what percent of itself equals 60?

$$\text{Rate} = \frac{\text{Amount}}{\text{Base}}$$

$$= \frac{12}{72} = 0.166\ 7 = 16\tfrac{2}{3}\%$$

Example 4
15 is what percent smaller than 25?

Solution

$$\text{Rate} = \frac{\text{Amount}}{\text{Base}}$$

$$= \frac{10}{25} = 40\%$$

EXERCISE 2.21

1. 16 is what percent greater than 12?

2. 96 increased by what percent of itself will equal 128?

3. 84 is what percent greater than 56?

4. 16 is what percent less than 20?

5. 82 is what percent less than 98?

6. By what rate should 65 be increased to equal 101?

7. By what rate should 256 be decreased to equal 192?

8. $2 560 increased by what rate will equal $3 020.80?

9. By what percent is $\frac{3}{4}$ greater than $\frac{2}{3}$?

10. 1 min is what percent greater than 20 s?

11. 1 h is what percent greater than 5 min?

12. 1 km decreased by what percent equals 6 m?

13. If 24 is increased to 60, and 60 then decreased to 36, what are the percents of increase and decrease?

2.22   FINDING THE AMOUNT OF THE INCREASED OR DECREASED NUMBER

Example 1
60 increased by 15% of itself equals what amount?

Solution
Since "of" identifies the base, and "itself" refers to 60, the base is 60.

(a)   Amount = Rate × Base
                = 0.15 × 60
                = 9

The amount of increase is 9.
The increased number is 69.

(b) $\boxed{\begin{array}{c}100\% \\ \text{of } 60\end{array}}$ + $\boxed{\begin{array}{c}15\% \\ \text{of } 60\end{array}}$ = $\boxed{\begin{array}{c}115\% \\ \text{of } 60\end{array}}$

       Amount = Rate × Base
              = 1.15 × 60
              = 69

To increase a number, multiply by 100% + the percent of increase.

Example 2
80 decreased by 10% of itself equals what number?

Solution
(a) Base = 80   Amount = Rate × Base
        Rate = 10%   = 0.1 × 80
                                              = 8

Amount of decrease is 8.
Amount of decreased number is 72.

To decrease a number, multiply by 100% − the percent of decrease.

(b) $\boxed{\begin{array}{c}100\% \\ \text{of } 80\end{array}}$ − $\boxed{\begin{array}{c}10\% \\ \text{of } 80\end{array}}$ = $\boxed{\begin{array}{c}90\% \\ \text{of } 80\end{array}}$

Base = 80   Amount = Rate × Base
Rate = 90%   = 0.9 × 80
                                        = 72

Example 3
$64.98 increased by $12\frac{1}{2}$% of itself equals what number?

Solution
Base = 64.98
Rate = 100% + $12\frac{1}{2}$% = $112\frac{1}{2}$%

Amount = Rate × Base
             = 1.125 × 64.98
             = 73.10
Amount is $73.10.

Example 4
$34.50 decreased by $37\frac{1}{2}$% of itself equals what number?

Solution
Base = 34.50
Rate = 100% − $37\frac{1}{2}$% = $62\frac{1}{2}$%

Amount = Rate × Base
             = 0.625 × 34.5
             = 21.56
Amount is $21.56.

Sometimes a store will increase a price and later decrease the result.

Example 5
An article priced at $16 was marked up 25% of itself and later marked down 10% of the result. What was the final price?

Solution
(a) Increase: Base = 16
                    Rate = 100% + 25% = 125%

$$\text{Amount} = \text{Rate} \times \text{Base}$$
$$= 1.25 \times 16$$
$$= 20$$

Decrease: Base = 20
$$\text{Rate} = 100\% - 10\% = 90\%$$

$$\text{Amount} = \text{Rate} \times \text{Base}$$
$$= 0.9 \times 20$$
$$= 18$$

Final price is $18.

(b) Combine the steps in (a).
   Base = 16.
   Rate of increase = 125%
   Rate of decrease = 90%

$$\text{Amount} = \text{Rate} \times \text{Base}$$
$$= 1.25 \times 0.9 \times 16$$
$$= 18$$

Final price is $18.

EXERCISE 2.22

1. Find the amount of increase when 82 is increased by 20%.

2. What is the amount of decrease if 144 is decreased by 25%?

3. 82 decreased by what amount equals 68?

4. What is the decrease when 82 is decreased by 25%?

5. 82 decreased by 60% of itself equals what amount?

6. $6.40 increased by $37\frac{1}{2}\%$ equals what amount?

7. $8.60 decreased by $62\frac{1}{2}\%$ of itself equals what amount?

8. 96 is $33\frac{1}{3}\%$ greater than what number?

9. 178 is 50% less than what number?

10. $\frac{1}{4}$ is 25% less than what fraction?

11. 96 increased by 25% of itself and then decreased by 20% of the result will equal what number?

12. A price of $24.68 is increased by $37\frac{1}{2}\%$ of itself, and the result is later decreased by 25%.
    (a) What will the new price be?
    (b) Is the new price an increase or decrease? By how much?

13. Find the net increase when 87 is increased by $66\frac{2}{3}\%$ of itself and the result is decreased by $33\frac{1}{3}\%$.

2.23   FINDING THE BASE

Example 1
What number increased by 20% of itself equals 84?

Solution
The number is increased by 20% of itself.
100% of number + 20% of number = 120% of number

Base = unknown
Rate = 120%
Amount = 84

$$\text{Base} = \frac{\text{Amount}}{\text{Rate}}$$

$$= \frac{84}{1.2}$$

$$= 70$$

Example 2
What number decreased by 25% of itself equals 60?

Solution
Base = unknown
Rate = 100% − 25% = 75%
Amount = 60

$$\text{Base} = \frac{\text{Amount}}{\text{Rate}}$$

$$= \frac{60}{0.75}$$

$$= 80$$

Example 3
What number increased by 40% of itself and the result decreased by 25% equals 165?

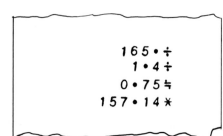

Machine
Instruction
CLEAR
SET DEC 2
Enter 165

÷

Enter 1.4

÷

Enter 0.75

=

Solution
Base = unknown
Rate of increase = 140%
Rate of decrease = 75%
Amount = 165

$$\text{Base} = \frac{\text{Amount}}{\text{Rate}}$$

$$= \frac{165}{1.4 \times 0.75}$$

$$= 157.14$$

EXERCISE 2.23

1. What number increased by 40% of itself equals 68?

2. 72 is 20% greater than what number?

3. 14 is $33\frac{1}{3}$% less than what number?

Remember to use enough decimal places in your repeating decimals.

4. If a number is increased by 20% of itself the amount of increase is 12. Find the increased number.

5. What number increased by $87\frac{1}{2}$% of itself equals $187\frac{1}{2}$?

6. What number decreased by 25% of itself equals 225?

7. What sum decreased by $12\frac{1}{2}$% equals $65.52?

8. What number increased by $12\frac{1}{2}$% of itself equals $\frac{7}{8}$?

9. A price increased by $66\frac{2}{3}$% of itself and then decreased by $33\frac{1}{3}$% of the result equals $246.72. What was the price?

10. What price increased by 25% of itself and the result decreased by 20% equals $9.20?

2.24   RATIO

The *ratio* of two numbers compares the size, or value, of one number with the size, or value, of another number, when both numbers are expressed in the same terms. For example, if there are 20 girls and 10 boys in your class, the ratio of girls to boys is 20 to 10.

20 to 10 may be written as 20 : 10.
20:10 = 2:1

Ratios are often written as fractions. The ratio 20 : 10 may be written $\frac{20}{10}$ or $\frac{2}{1}$. Since a ratio *compares* two numbers, the denominator of the fraction must always be shown.

Example 1
If there are 12 boys and 24 girls in your class, what is the ratio of boys to girls?

Solution
$$\frac{\text{Number of boys}}{\text{Number of girls}} = \frac{12}{24} = \frac{1}{2}$$

The ratio of boys to girls is 1 : 2.
This means that there is 1 boy to every 2 girls.

Example 2
What is the ratio of girls to the total number of students in the class in Example 1?

Solution

$$\frac{\text{Number of girls}}{\text{Number of students}} = \frac{24}{36} = \frac{2}{3}$$

The ratio of girls to total students is 2 : 3.
This means that there are 2 girls for every 3 students.

EXERCISE 2.24
1. Express the following ratios as fractions and then simplify.
   (a) 75 : 125   (f) 75¢ : $3
   (b) 16 : 26   (g) $3.50 : $10.50
   (c) 4 : 6   (h) 30 min : 1 h
   (d) 27 : 81   (i) 2 m : 10 cm
   (e) $\frac{1}{4} : \frac{1}{2}$ (j) 1 d : 8 h

2. (a) Find two numbers whose ratio is 2:3 and whose sum is 40.
   (b) Find two numbers whose ratio is 5:6 and whose sum is 88.

2.25 PROPORTION

Two equal ratios may form a *proportion*. $\frac{1}{2} = \frac{4}{8}$ is a proportion because $\frac{4}{8}$ reduced to its lowest terms equals the ratio $\frac{1}{2}$. Similarly, $\frac{3}{9} = \frac{15}{45}$ and $\frac{3}{4} = \frac{12}{16}$ are proportions.

If two ratios are equal, then the cross-products are also equal.

$$\frac{3}{4} = \frac{12}{16}$$

$$\frac{3}{4} \times \frac{12}{16}$$

$$4 \times 12 = 3 \times 16$$
$$48 = 48$$

If two cross-products are equal, then there is a proportion.

$$\frac{2}{3} \times \frac{4}{6}$$

$$2 \times 6 = 3 \times 4$$
$$12 = 12$$

Therefore $$\frac{2}{3} = \frac{4}{6}$$

Example
Find the missing number in the following proportion.

Solution

$$\frac{4}{5} = \frac{?}{25}$$

$$4 \times 25 = 5 \times \, ?$$
$$100 = 5 \times \, ?$$
$$100 = 5 \times 20$$

The missing number is 20.

EXERCISE 2.25

Find the missing values in the following proportions.

1. $\dfrac{1}{2} = \dfrac{6}{?}$ 6. $\dfrac{32}{8} = \dfrac{?}{4}$

2. $\dfrac{2}{3} = \dfrac{?}{9}$ 7. $\dfrac{9}{81} = \dfrac{7}{?}$

3. $\dfrac{12}{?} = \dfrac{1}{3}$ 8. $\dfrac{64}{8} = \dfrac{16}{?}$

4. $\dfrac{5}{20} = \dfrac{25}{?}$ 9. $\dfrac{10}{?} = \dfrac{125}{625}$

5. $\dfrac{7}{21} = \dfrac{6}{?}$ 10. $\dfrac{?}{18} = \dfrac{3}{36}$

SUMMARY

A *fraction* is a pair of numbers, one divided by the other.

A *proper fraction* is one where the numerator is smaller than the denominator.

An *improper fraction* is one where the numerator is larger than the denominator.

A *mixed number* is made up of a whole number and a fraction.

Equivalent fractions are fractions that have the same value but different numerators and denominators.

A *decimal fraction* is one whose denominator is 10 or a power of 10, such as 100, 1 000, or 10 000.

A number that divides into another number without a remainder is called an *aliquot part* of the second number. Numbers that are multiples of aliquot parts are also called aliquot parts.

A *percent* of a number is a hundredth of that number.

To add or subtract fractions, rewrite each fraction as an equivalent fraction with the lowest common denominator for the set of fractions involved, and add or subtract the numerators.

To multiply a fraction, multiply the numerators and divide by the product of the denominators.

To divide by a fraction, multiply by the reciprocal.

To simplify expressions, remove brackets, change "of" to "×", divide, multiply, add, and subtract.

To express a fraction as a decimal, divide the numerator by the denominator.

To express a decimal as a fraction, remove the decimal point and divide by 1 plus the number of zeroes equal to the number of digits to the right of the decimal point.

To change a percent to a fraction, divide by 100 and drop the percent sign.

To change a percent to a decimal, divide the rate percent by 100 and drop the percent sign.

To multiply by a repeating decimal, use three decimal places more than the number of digits in the whole number part of the multiplicand.

To divide by a repeating decimal, use four decimal places more than the number of digits in the whole number part of the dividend.

To change a decimal to a percent, multiply by 100%.

Amount = Rate × Base

$$\text{Rate} = \frac{\text{Amount}}{\text{Base}}$$

$$\text{Base} = \frac{\text{Amount}}{\text{Rate}}$$

The *ratio* of two numbers compares the size, or value, of one number with the size, or value, of another number, when both numbers are expressed in the same terms.

A *proportion* occurs when two ratios are equal.

REVIEW EXERCISE 2.26

1. Express each of the following common fractions as a decimal and as a percent.

   (a) $\frac{1}{2}$ (c) $\frac{1}{4}$ (e) $\frac{7}{8}$ (g) $\frac{4}{5}$ (i) $\frac{1}{16}$

   (b) $\frac{1}{3}$ (d) $\frac{3}{8}$ (f) $\frac{5}{6}$ (h) $\frac{1}{8}$ (j) $\frac{3}{4}$

2. Simplify the following.

   (a) $\frac{3}{4} \times \frac{1}{2}(\frac{4}{5} + \frac{3}{4}) \div 2 + \frac{1}{2}$

   (b) $\frac{2}{3}$ of $\frac{1}{5}(\frac{1}{3} + \frac{5}{6}) \div \frac{3}{10} \times 4(\frac{1}{2} + \frac{3}{5})$

3. Express each of the following decimals as a fraction or a mixed number and as a percent.

   (a) 0.02   (d) 0.4   (g) 0.375   (j) 0.6

   (b) 0.125   (e) $0.83\overline{3}$ (h) 1.625   (k) 2.875

   (c) 0.75   (f) $0.16\overline{6}$ (i) 320.2   (l) $3.66\overline{6}$

4. 2 weeks increased by what percent equals $1\frac{1}{2}$ years?

5. $\frac{3}{5}$ is what percent of 50?

6. $\frac{1}{4}$ is what percent of 75?

7. 32 increased by $12\frac{1}{2}\%$ of itself equals what number?

8. What number decreased by 20% of itself equals 68?

9. Antonio has a mass of 58 kg. His friend has a mass of 54 kg. Antonio's mass is what percent more than his friend's?

10. $12.50 is what percent of $75?

11. What percent of 146 is 114?

12. A car bought last year for $6 550 is only worth $5 240 this year. What was the rate of depreciation?

13. A stereo was sold at 25% less than its cost. If the selling price was $405, what was its cost?

14. What number increased by $62\frac{1}{2}$% of itself and the result decreased by 20% equals 65?

15. The United Appeal campaign collected $150 000. By what percent would donations have to increase to collect $200 000?

16. What fractional part of a kilometre is 37.5 m?   87.5 hm?   75 dam?

17. What decimal part of a kilolitre is 875 L?

18. What decimal part of an hour is 20 min? 10 s? 25 min?

19. If an item is sold at $44.64 per dozen, there is a profit of $\frac{1}{3}$ of the cost. What would the profit be on each item?

20. A football team lost 12 m on the first play and gained 8 m on the second. How far did they have to go to make a first down? (Assume 10 m for a first down.)

21. In a school of 1 400 students, 0.375 of the total are in Grade 9, 0.333 in Grade 10, and 0.167 in Grade 11. The rest are in Grade 12.
    (a) How many students are in each grade?
    (b) What decimal part of the number of students are in Grade 12?

22. Mr. and Mrs. Alcone budgeted their income as follows: food, 0.20; housing, 0.25; clothing, 0.125; savings, 0.062 5; and the rest for other expenses.
    (a) Find the decimal part of their income budgeted for other expenses.
    (b) If yearly savings were $1 625, what was their yearly income?
    (c) How much money was allocated to food, housing, and clothing?

23. Tom Bailey seeded 0.583 of his farm with oats, 0.166 7 with corn, and left the remaining hectares in pasture.
    (a) If he had 40 ha in corn, how large was his farm?
    (b) How many hectares did he have in oats?

24. Germaine, Claude, and Klaus formed a partnership to operate a bicycle repair business. Germaine was to receive 0.437 5 of the profits, Claude, 0.187 5, and Klaus, the rest.
    (a) What decimal fraction of the profits did Klaus receive?

(b) If their year's profit was $47 400, how much did each partner receive?

25. State the fractional equivalent of the following.
(a) $0.83\overline{3}$ (e) 0.375   (i) 0.312 5
(b) 0.062 5   (f) 0.80   (j) 0.125
(c) 0.875   (g) $0.166\overline{6}$ (k) 0.75
(d) 0.625   (h) $0.333\overline{3}$ (l) $0.66\overline{6}$

26. Without using your machine, find the cost of buying each of the following items.
(a) 160 items @ $12\frac{1}{2}$¢   (f) 18 items @ $8\frac{1}{3}$¢
(b) 28 items @ $87\frac{1}{2}$¢   (g) 35 items @ $33\frac{1}{3}$¢
(c) 165 items @ $91\frac{2}{3}$¢   (h) 75 items @ 60¢
(d) 56 items @ 80¢   (i) 124 items @ $16\frac{2}{3}$¢
(e) 96 items @ $37\frac{1}{2}$¢   (j) 198 items @ $66\frac{2}{3}$¢

27. Without using your machine, find how many items could be bought for the following amounts at the given item price.

	Amount	Price Per Item		Amount	Price Per Item
(a)	$112	20¢	(f)	$108	$87\frac{1}{2}$¢
(b)	$35	40¢	(g)	$64	$16\frac{2}{3}$¢
(c)	$40	$6\frac{1}{4}$¢	(h)	$144	75¢
(d)	$50	$18\frac{3}{4}$¢	(i)	$72	$37\frac{1}{2}$¢
(e)	$92	$41\frac{2}{3}$¢	(j)	$198	6¢

28. Bill Casey worked weekends in a hotel. He earned $56 last week and put 0.375 of it into his savings account.
(a) How much did he save?
(b) What decimal portion did he spend?

29. Divide a class of 30 students into 2 groups having a ratio of 2 : 3.

30. For every $1 of sales, a retailer makes a profit of $0.10. What is the ratio of profit to sales?

31. Find the missing value.
(a) $\frac{3}{4} = \frac{18}{?}$ (b) $\frac{5}{8} = \frac{?}{184}$

UNIT 3

Using Algebra

Throughout this book you will be applying your knowledge of algebra skills to problems of saving, investing, and buying. For example, an article may be priced at $1.00 plus provincial sales tax. If the clerk charges you $1.05, how much tax are you paying? Expressed algebraically

$$\$1.00 + x = \$1.05$$

In this example, x is the unknown amount of tax charged on the article priced at $1.00. It is easy to see that x is $0.05 or 5 cents. But in some other problems, the calculation may not be so easy. This unit, therefore, is intended to help you make more use of your algebra skills.

3.1 POWERS

The product $a \times a \times a \times a$ can be shortened to read a^4, where

> a is the *base*,
> 4 is the *index*,
> a^4 is the *fourth power* of a.

Example

> $3 \times 3 \times 3 \times 3 = 3^4 = 81$
> 3 is the base.
> 4 is the index.
> 81 is the fourth power of 3.

1. Express each of the following products as a power. In each case indicate the base, the index, and the power.
   (a) $m \times m \times m \times m$ (b) $5 \times 5 \times 5$ (c) $4 \times 4 \times 4 \times 4$

2. What is the third power of 2?   the eighth power of x?

3. 216 is what power of 6?

4. 1 000 is the third power of what number?

The product $a^2 \times a^3$ really means $a \times a \times a \times a \times a$, which equals a^5.

To multiply powers having the same base, add the indices.

Similarly, $3a^4 \times 2a^3$ really means

> $3 \times a \times a \times a \times a \times 2 \times a \times a \times a$

which equals

> $3 \times 2 \times a \times a \times a \times a \times a \times a \times a = 6a^7$.

Examples
- $a^3 \times a^5 = a^8$
- $2a^3 \times 4a^6 = 8a^9$
- $2a^2b \times 3a^3b^2 = 6a^5b^3$
- $(a^3b^2) = a^3b^2 \times a^3b^2 = a^6b^4$

Multiply.

1. $m^4 \times m^5$ 3. $2a^2 \times a^3$ 5. $3a^2b \times 4a^3b^2$

2. $a^2 \times a^3 \times a^4$ 4. $2a^2b \times a^3$ 6. $4a^2b^3 \times 6a^3b^4$

The fraction $\dfrac{a^5}{a^3}$ really means $\dfrac{a \times a \times a \times a \times a}{a \times a \times a}$, which equals a^2.

To divide a power by a power having the same base, subtract the indices.

Similarly, $\dfrac{9a^5b^8}{3a^2b^3}$ really means

$$\frac{9 \times a \times a \times a \times a \times a \times b \times b \times b \times b \times b \times b \times b \times b}{3 \times a \times a \times b \times b \times b}$$

which equals

$$\frac{9}{3} \times a^3 \times b^5 = 3a^3b^5.$$

Examples

- $\dfrac{b^7}{b^5} = b^2$

- $\dfrac{9a^5b^8}{3a} = 3a^4b^8$

- $\dfrac{a^5b^8}{a^2} = a^3b^8$

- $\dfrac{8a^5b^8}{2a^2b^3} = 4a^3b^5$

Divide.

1. $\dfrac{a^{10}}{a^8}$ 2. $\dfrac{a^{10}b^6}{a^5}$ 3. $\dfrac{a^{10}b^6}{a^5b^2}$ 4. $\dfrac{25a^{10}b^6}{a^7b^2}$ 5. $\dfrac{25a^{10}b^6}{5a^7b^2}$

EXERCISE 3.1
1. Find the following powers.
   (a) the third power of 5
   (b) the fourth power of 2
   (c) the third power of 2
   (d) the fifth power of 3
   (e) the fourth power of 4
   (f) the fifth power of 5

2. Simplify.
   (a) $a^3b^2 \times 4a^4b^2$
   (b) $(6a^2b)(4ab)(3a^3b^3)$
   (c) $(6a^2b)^2$
   (d) $\dfrac{8a^3b^8}{6a^2b^2}$
   (e) $\dfrac{3(3a^2b^3c^4)(4a^8b^2c^5)}{2(a^2b^3)^2}$

3.2   SQUARE ROOTS

The *square* of a number is the product of a number multiplied by itself. For example,

$$5 \times 5 = 5^2 = 25$$

25 is the square of 5

The *square root* of a given number is the number whose square is equal to the given number.

A number is a *perfect square* when its square root is a whole number. Thus 4, 9, 16, 25, 36, 49, 64, 81, 100 are all perfect squares.

The square roots of some numbers that are perfect squares may be familiar.

$$\sqrt{100} = 10, \quad \sqrt{144} = 12, \quad \sqrt{49} = 7, \ldots$$

Square root of 64
$\sqrt{64} = 8$
Because $8 \times 8 = 8^2 = 64$

Most hand and desk model calculators used today have a square root key $\boxed{\sqrt{}}$

EXERCISE 3.2
Using your square root key, find the following.

1. $\sqrt{5}$ 6. $\sqrt{15}$

2. $\sqrt{75}$ 7. $\sqrt{30}$

3. $\sqrt{62}$ 8. $\sqrt{45}$

4. $\sqrt{8}$ 9. $\sqrt{98}$

5. $\sqrt{12}$ 10. $\sqrt{0.88}$

3.3 FINDING THE SQUARE ROOT OF FRACTIONS

Examples

- $\sqrt{\dfrac{25}{64}} = \dfrac{\sqrt{25}}{\sqrt{64}} = \dfrac{5}{8} = 0.625$

- $\sqrt{\dfrac{27}{49}} = \dfrac{\sqrt{27}}{\sqrt{49}} = \dfrac{5.196\ 2}{7} = 0.742\ 314$

- $\sqrt{\dfrac{36}{56}} = \dfrac{\sqrt{36}}{\sqrt{56}} = \dfrac{6}{7.483} = 0.801\ 817$

EXERCISE 3.3
Find the following square roots.

(a) $\sqrt{\frac{36}{49}}$ (d) $\sqrt{\frac{81}{98}}$ (g) $\sqrt{\frac{1}{2}}$

(b) $\sqrt{\frac{9}{100}}$ (e) $\sqrt{\frac{12}{25}}$ (h) $\sqrt{\frac{1}{4}}$

(c) $\sqrt{\frac{16}{9}}$ (f) $\sqrt{\frac{1}{3}}$

3.4 ADDITION AND SUBTRACTION OF LIKE TERMS

Algebraic terms (terms involving a variable) can only be added or subtracted when they are *like terms*. Like terms have the same variable. For example,

$$2a + 3a = 5a$$
$$2x^2 + 4x^2 = 6x^2$$

$2a$ and $3b$ are unlike terms and cannot be added.

$$2a + 3b = 2a + 3b$$

To simplify algebraic expressions containing two or more terms, collect the like terms, and add or subtract according to the sign.

Examples

• $2a + 7b + 5c - a + 2b - 3c + 3a - 4b - c$
 $= (2a - a + 3a) + (7b + 2b - 4b) + (5c - 3c - c)$
 $= 4a + 5b + c$

• $2a^2 + 3b^2 + 5a^3 + 3a^2 - 2a^3 + b^2$
 $= (2a^2 + 3a^2) + (3b^2 + b^2) + (5a^3 - 2a^3)$
 $= 5a^2 + 4b^2 + 3a^3$

EXERCISE 3.4
Simplify the following.
1. $2x - 3y + 2z + 6x - 2y - 4x + 9y + 5z + 2y - 3z - y$
2. $2ab - 3ac + 3ad + 6ac + 4ab - 2ac - 2ab + 8ac - ab$
3. $4a^2 + 3a^3 + 8b^3 - 2b^2 + 2a^2 + 3b^2 - b^3 + 4a^2b$

3.5 ORDER OF OPERATIONS FOR SIMPLIFYING ALGEBRAIC EXPRESSIONS

B
O
D
M
A
S

To reduce an algebraic expression to its simplest form we follow the same order that we used in simplifying arithmetic expressions in Section 2.5.
• Simplify the expression inside the brackets, and remove the brackets.
• Change "of" to "×".
• Multiply and divide in the order in which these operations occur.
• Add and subtract in the order in which these operations occur.

Example
Simplify the following expressions.

(a) $3a + 2(a + 6a) - \frac{1}{2}$ of $4a$

(b) $3a^4 \div a^2 + 4a(a + 5a - 2a) - \frac{1}{3}$ of $\dfrac{6a^3}{a}$

Solution
(a) $3a + 2(a + 6a) - \frac{1}{2}$ of $4a = 3a + 2(7a) - \frac{1}{2} \times 4a$
$\qquad\qquad\qquad\qquad\qquad = 3a + 14a - 2a$
$\qquad\qquad\qquad\qquad\qquad = 15a$

(b) $3a^4 \div a^2 + 4a(a + 5a - 2a) - \dfrac{1}{3}$ of $\dfrac{6a^3}{a} = 3a^4 \div a^2 + 4a(4a) - \dfrac{1}{3} \times \dfrac{6a^3}{a}$
$\qquad\qquad\qquad\qquad\qquad\qquad\qquad\qquad = 3a^2 + 16a^2 - 2a^2$
$\qquad\qquad\qquad\qquad\qquad\qquad\qquad\qquad = 17a^2$

EXERCISE 3.5

Simplify the following.

1. $16x - 36x^2 \div 3x + 18xy \div 3y$

2. $4(a + b) + 6(4a - b) - 4b$

3. $9xy^2 - 4x(y^2 + 3y^2)$

4. $7(2r + 3r - 4r) + 8r \div 2r \times 3$

5. $(3a + 6a - 4a) \times 2(a - 2a + 3a)$

6. $a^2b + 4a^3b \div 2a + 3a(ab + 2ab)$

7. $8(x + y) \div 4(x + y) + 3x \times 4(2x + 6x - 3x)$

8. $4ab - 3ab \times 2(ab + 5 + ab) \div 10$

9. $18r - \frac{1}{2} \times 12r + \frac{3}{5} \text{ of } 25r - 3r^2 \div r^2$

10. $\dfrac{6x^4y^4}{2} \times 8 \div 4xy(6xy - 4xy + xy)$

3.6 MULTIPLYING A POLYNOMIAL BY A MONOMIAL

A *monomial* is an expression with one term and a *polynomial* is an expression with more than one term. For example,

> $3m$ and $-2a$ are both monomials.
> $4m - 3x$ is a polynomial.

Identify the following as monomials or polynomials.

1. $6x$	6. $a + b$
2. $3ab$	7. $x^2 + 2x + 2$
3. $-7x + 2b$	8. $3a^2b^2$
4. $6x - 3y + 6$	9. 7
5. a	10. $3x^3 - 6x^2$

To multiply a polynomial by a monomial, multiply each term of the polynomial by the monomial, being careful to observe the rules for multiplying positive and negative terms.

A positive term multiplied by a positive term gives a positive term.

A negative term multiplied by a negative term gives a positive term.

A positive term multiplied by a negative term gives a negative term.

Examples
- $a(b + c) = ab + ac$
- $a(b + c + d) = ab + ac + ad$
- $a(b - c - d) = ab - ac - ad$
- $-a(b + c - d) = -ab - ac + ad$

EXERCISE 3.6
Expand and simplify the following.

1. $3(a + b) + a(4 + b)$

2. $-3(a + 2b) + 6a(4 - b) - 4(a + 3b)$

3. $2a(a - 3b + 4c) + 2b(4a - b)$

3.7   DIVIDING A POLYNOMIAL BY A MONOMIAL

To divide a polynomial by a monomial, divide each term in the polynomial by the monomial. Be sure to give each term in the quotient its proper sign.

Examples

- $$\frac{6ax + 9bx}{3x} = 2a + 3b$$

- $$\frac{4a^3 + 10a^2 - 6a}{2a} = 2a^2 + 5a - 3$$

EXERCISE 3.7
Simplify.

1. $\dfrac{2a + 2b}{2}$

2. $\dfrac{3x + 4xy}{x}$

3. $\dfrac{6a^3 - 3a^2 + a}{a}$

4. $\dfrac{8x^3 + 12x^2 - 4x}{2x}$

5. $\dfrac{3a^2b + 15ab^2 - 18a^2b^2}{3ab}$

3.8   FACTORING AN EXPRESSION FOR A COMMON FACTOR

To factor a polynomial for a common factor
- Find the largest number that is a factor of the numerical part of each term.
- Find the highest power of each letter that is present in every term.
- Divide each term by the product of the above steps.
- Write the monomial factor allowed by the second factor in brackets.

Examples
- $ab + ac = a(b + c)$
- $P + Prt = P(1 + rt)$
- $2a + 4b = 2(a + 2b)$
- $3a^3 + 6a^2b + 12ab^2 = 3a(a^2 + 2ab + 4b^2)$

Note that factoring is the inverse operation to multiplying a polynomial by a monomial in order to remove brackets.

EXERCISE 3.8
Factor.

1. $2a + 4b$

2. $rV + rA$

3. $2ab + 4ac + 8a$

4. $2a + 8ab + 12c - 8ac$

5. $C + \frac{1}{4}CP$

6. $30a^3b + 42a^2b^2 + 12ab^3$

3.9   SUBSTITUTION

Substitution is a procedure that replaces the variables in an algebraic expression by assigned numerical values.

Example
$a = 2, b = 3, c = -4$

$$\begin{aligned} 2a + 6b + c &= 2(2) + 6(3) + (-4) \\ &= 4 + 18 - 4 \\ &= 18 \end{aligned}$$

EXERCISE 3.9
If $x = 2, y = 3, z = 0$, and $w = -1$, find the value of each of the following.

1. $3x + 2y$
2. $wx - 6z + 3xy$
3. $x^2 + 2y^2 + z$
4. $4x - 7yz + 3yw - 4z$

5. $\dfrac{x^2 - 2wy}{3xy}$

6. $\dfrac{6x - 2x^2y^2 - wz}{x^2 - y^2}$

3.10   SOLVING AN EQUATION IN ONE UNKNOWN

Businesspeople must deal with many problems involving pricing, commission, insurance, taxes, and profit and loss. Business machines are tools they use for speed and accuracy.

Algebra is another tool. Learning the basic algebraic rules and their applications enables you to solve similar business and personal problems quickly and easily.

Many of the business applications are solved with the aid of formulas such as interest equals principal times rate times time. Written algebraically this formula is the equation $I = Prt$, where t represents the time in years. An equation is a mathematical sentence composed of two expressions connected by an equal sign. If the equation is true, the two sides of the equation are said to be in balance.

Examples
- $5 + 3 = 8$
- $a - 2 = 6$
- $2m^2 - 3mn = 12$
- $x^2 + 2xy + y^2 = 0$
- $x^2 + y^2 = 25$

Rule of Addition
If the same number is added to each side of an equation, the equation is still in balance.

$$a - 2 = 6$$
$$a - 2 + 2 = 6 + 2$$
$$a = 8$$

+

Rule of Subtraction
If the same number is subtracted from each side of an equation, the equation is still in balance.

$$a + 2 = 6$$
$$a + 2 - 2 = 6 - 2$$
$$a = 4$$

—

Rule of Division
If both sides of an equation are divided by the same number, the equation is still in balance.

$$4a = 16$$
$$\frac{4a}{4} = \frac{16}{4}$$
$$a = 4$$

÷

$$50\% \text{ of Sales} = \$16.$$
$$0.5 \times \text{Sales} = \$16.$$
$$\frac{0.5 \times \text{Sales}}{0.5} = \frac{\$16.}{0.5}$$
$$\text{Sales} = \$32.$$

Rule of Multiplication
If both sides of an equation are multiplied by the same number, the equation is still in balance.

✕

$$\frac{2a}{3} = 6$$
$$\frac{3}{2} \times \frac{2a}{3} = \frac{3}{2} \times 6$$
$$a = 9$$

Note: **The application of the rule of multiplication removes fractions from the equation.**

Transposition in an equation is a term used to describe short-cuts in applying the rules of addition and subtraction.

Example 1
Solve the equation $a - 2 = 16$.

Solution

$$a - 2 = 16$$
$$a = 16 + 2 \qquad \textbf{Rule of Addition}$$
$$a = 18$$

Example 2
Solve the equation $2a = 16$.

Solution

$$2a = 16$$

Transpose $a = \dfrac{16}{2}$ **Rule of Division**

$$a = 8$$

Example 3
Solve the equation $4p + 5 = 9$.

Solution

$$4p + 5 = 9$$

Transpose $4p = 9 - 5$ **Rule of Subtraction**

$$4p = 4$$
$$p = 1$$

Example 4
If 25% of the cost of an article is $16, how much does the article cost?

Solution

$$25\% \text{ of cost} = 16$$
$$0.25 \times \text{cost} = 16$$

Transpose $\text{cost} = \dfrac{16}{0.25}$

$$\text{cost} = 64$$

The article costs $64.

EXERCISE 3.10
Solve the following equations.

1. $3a + 4 = 28$

2. $3(x + 2) = 2x - 6$

3. $8a - a = 12 - a$

4. $11b + 2 = 26 + 7b$

5. $6a - (a - 3) - 11 = a + 5 - (a - 7)$

6. $3a(a - 10) = a(3a - 4) - 14$

7. $2a^2(a^2 + 1) - 2a^4 = 32$

8. 40% of $C = \$80$

9. 25% of $\$160 = A$

10. $\$1\ 800 = \dfrac{R}{2 \times 0.08}$

3.11   MULTIPLE OPERATIONS

In this section you will perform some calculations with multiple operations.

Example

Find the value of $\dfrac{2560 \times 148}{0.125 \times 365}$, correct to two decimal places.

Solution
Machine
Instruction

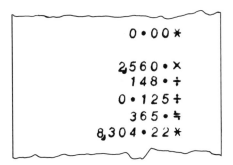

CLEAR

SET DECIMAL 2

Enter 2 560

Press ×

Enter 148

Press ÷

Enter 0.125

Press ÷

Enter 365

Press =

This is the danger spot. Many students want to multiply here but 365 is part of the denominator and you must divide.

On Your Computer

Machine Ready

] ☐

Type   PRINT   2560*148/0.125/365

] PRINT 2560*148/0.125/365
8304.21917
] ☐

Press **RETURN**

Remember to divide.

EXERCISE 3.11
Perform the following calculations.

1. $\dfrac{420 \times 62}{0.13 \times 96}$

2. $\dfrac{380 \times 142}{0.142\,5 \times 365}$

3. $\dfrac{4\,800}{0.165 \times 4.5}$

4. $\dfrac{336.72 \times 85}{0.0975 \times 365}$

5. $\dfrac{39 \times 672.5 \times 48}{63 \times 248.3}$

3.12   REARRANGING FORMULA TERMS

The formula for finding simple interest is

$I = Prt$

Finding the interest is relatively simple when you know the numerical values of the variables P, r, and t.

If the unknown quantity is P, it is easier to find its value by rearranging the formula to isolate the variable P. To do this apply the rules for solving simple equations in one unknown.

$I = Prt$

Divide both sides by rt.

$$\frac{I}{rt} = P$$

It is usually preferable to place the unknown variable on the left side of the equation.

$$P = \frac{I}{rt}$$

Example
If $S = 8$ and $M = 2$, find C in the equation $S = C + M$.

Solution
$S = C + M$
$C = S - M$
$C = 8 - 2$
$C = 6$

EXERCISE 3.12
1. $I = Prt$ is the formula for finding interest, where t represents the time in years, r = rate, and P = principal.
   (a) Find P when   (i) $I = \$18$, $r = 15\%$, $t = 2$ years
                         (ii) $I = \$31.83$, $r = 15.5\%$, $t = 6$ months
   (b) Find r when   (i) $P = \$800$, $t = 3$ years, $I = \$384$
                         (ii) $P = \$575$, $t = 73$ d, $I = \$19.50$

(c) Find t when (i) $I = \$185$, $P = \$500$, $r = 18.5\%$
  (ii) $I = \$244.38$, $P = \$8\,500$, $r = 17.5\%$

2. $T = Ar$ is the formula for finding taxes (T), when the assessment is represented by A dollars and the rate is r mills. ($\$1 = 1\,000$ mills)
  (a) Find A when (i) $T = \$1\,800$, $r = 60$ mills
    (ii) $T = \$125\,000$, $r = 45$ mills
  (b) Find r when (i) $T = \$680$, $A = \$17\,000$
    (ii) $T = \$36\,000$, $A = \$500\,000$

3. $P = S - (C + E)$ is the formula for finding profit (P), when sales are
represented by S, costs by C, and expenses by E.
  (a) Find S when (i) $P = \$10\,000$, $C = \$15\,000$, $E = \$3\,000$
    (ii) $P = \$2.64$, $C = \$5.40$, $E = \$1.50$
  (b) Find E when (i) $P = \$5.10$, $S = \$37.50$, $C = \$28.00$
    (ii) $P = \$6.75$, $S = \$48.90$, $C = \$39.00$

4. $P = \dfrac{A}{1 + rt}$ is the formula for finding the principal that amounts to A
dollars at the rate r in t years.

  (a) Find A when (i) $P = \$1\,000$, $r = 16\%$, $t = 2$ years
    (ii) $P = \$1\,000$, $r = 15.4\%$, $t = 6$ months
  (b) Find r when $P = \$1\,000$, $A = \$1\,900$, $t = 5$ years
  (c) Find t when $P = \$12\,000$, $A = \$12\,495$, $r = 16.5\%$

5. $A = L + OE$ is the basic accounting equation where assets are represented by A, liabilities by L, and owner's equity by OE.
  (a) Find L when $A = \$35\,800$, $OE = \$18\,000$
  (b) Find OE when $A = \$1\,350\,000$, $L = \$400\,800$

6. $S = C + M$ is the formula for finding the selling price (S) when cost is
represented by C and markup by M.
  (a) Find C when $M = 25\%$ of S, $S = \$6.40$
  (b) Find C when $M = 25\%$ of C, $S = \$8.20$
  (c) Find M when $S = \$10.50$, $C = \$6.75$

7. $D = r(C - A)$ is the formula for finding depreciation (D) when the rate
of depreciation is r, the original cost of the asset is C, and the depreciation accumulated to date is A.
  (a) Find C when $r = 30\%$, $D = \$661.50$, $A = \$2\,295$
  (b) Find r when $D = \$160$, $C = \$1\,000$, $A = \$200$
  (c) Find A when $D = \$2\,707.50$, $r = 5\%$, $C = \$60\,000$

8. $P = F(1 - nd)$ is the formula for finding the proceeds (P) of a promissory note that has a face value of F and is discounted at the rate d.
n represents the discount time in years.
  (a) Find F when $P = \$880.20$, $d = 17\%$, $n = 73$ d
  (b) Find d when $P = \$466$, $F = \$500$, $n = 146$ d

3.13 SOLVING WORD PROBLEMS

Do you have difficulty solving word problems? Many students do. While doing Exercise 3.9, you found the unknown quantity when you were given the values of the other parts of the equation.

Example 1
If $P = \$1000$, $r = 16\%$, and $t = 2$, find I using the equation $I = Prt$.

Solution
$I = Prt$
$ = 1000 \times 0.16 \times 2$
$ = 320$
The interest is $320.

The difficulty in solving word problems lies in selecting the correct value for each part of the equation. You will find it easier to solve these problems if you follow a few simple rules.

1. Read the problem carefully. This sounds very elementary but many students have difficulty because they start to solve the problem before reading it thoroughly.

2. List the known facts.

3. Write down the unknown fact.

4. Write an equation showing the relationship between the known facts and the unknown fact.

5. Substitute the known values in your equation.

6. Solve the equation.

Example 2
Sarah deposited $500 in a savings account paying interest at 14% per year. How much money did Sarah earn the first two years?

Solution
Known facts: Deposit (Principal) = $500
 Interest rate = 14% per year
 Time = 2 years
Unknown fact: Interest earned
Equation: Interest earned = deposit × rate × time
$$I = 500 \times 0.14 \times 2$$
$$= 140$$
Sarah earned $140.

Example 3
Shaku bought 200 boxes of berries to sell at a roadside stand. He paid 75¢ for each box. His expenses totalled $45.50. If he sold his berries for $1.25 per box, how much was his profit?

Solution
Known facts: Cost = 200 × 0.75
                Expenses = $45.50
                Sales = 200 × 1.25
Unknown fact: Profit
Equation: Profit = Sales − Cost − Expenses
                = (200 × 1.25) − (200 × 0.75) − 45.50
                = 54.50
Shaku earned $54.50.

   Some problems can be solved by simply translating the word sentence into an arithmetic sentence. An equation is simply an arithmetic sentence.

Example 4
               Sixteen increased by 25% equals what number?

Translation: 16   × 1.25   =   N

Solution   20   =   N

Example 5
               What number increased by 25% and the result decreased by 10% equals 731.25?

Translation: $N × 1.25 × 0.9 = 731.25$

Solution $N = \dfrac{731.25}{1.25 × 0.9}$
                = 650

EXERCISE 3.13

1. 960 increased by 42% equals what number?

2. Zina bought a $100 bond that paid interest at the rate of 12% per year. How much interest did she receive in one year?

3. Guenther expected to earn $25 every three months from his $1000 bond. What rate of interest did he receive?

4. What number increased by 30% and the result decreased by 20% equals 249.6?

5. A certain business sold $19 600 worth of merchandise last month. The cost of the goods sold was $14 900. The owner paid $224 in taxes and insurance, $130 for utilities, $110 for heat, and $1 350 for wages. How much profit was earned?

6. The owner of Bits 'N Pieces raised the price of a $4.00 dish by 25%. When the dish did not sell, the new price was marked down by 30%. What was the final selling price of the dish?

7. Sal's pay cheque was $392.00. She had worked 40 h at her regular pay rate and 6 h overtime at time-and-a-half. What was her regular pay rate per hour?

SUMMARY OF RULES

(1) To multiply powers having the same base, add the indices.

(2) To divide powers having the same base, subtract the indices.

(3) The order of operations used to reduce an algebraic expression to its simplest form is brackets, of, divide, multiply, add, and subtract.

(4) To multiply a polynomial by a monomial, multiply each term of the polynomial by the monomial.

(5) To divide a polynomial by a monomial, divide each term of the polynomial by the monomial.

(6) To factor a polynomial, find the highest common factor of each term in the polynomial and divide the polynomial by that factor. Write the monomial factor followed by the second factor in brackets.

(7) If the same number is added to or subtracted from each side of an equation, the equation is still in balance.

(8) If both sides of an equation are multiplied by or divided by the same number, the equation is still in balance.

SUMMARY OF DEFINITIONS

(1) The square of a number is the product of a number multiplied by itself.

(2) The square root of a given number is the number whose square is equal to the given number.

(3) A perfect square is a number whose square root is a whole number.

(4) An algebraic term is a term containing one or more variables.

(5) Like terms have the same variable.

(6) A monomial is an expression of one term.

(7) A polynomial is an expression containing two or more terms.

REVIEW EXERCISE 3.14

1. Simplify.

    (a) $\dfrac{2(4a^3bc^2)\,(3a^5b^2c^3)}{3a(a^2b^3)^2}$

    (b) $\frac{3}{4}$ of $\frac{7}{8} - \frac{4}{5} \div \frac{2}{3} \times \frac{1}{2}(\frac{3}{4} \times \frac{2}{3}) + \frac{4}{5} \times \frac{1}{3}$

    (c) $3ax + 4a^2 + 9ab - 2ax + 2a^2 + 6ax - 3ab + 4ax + 4ab$

2. Factor.

    (a) $3a^2b + 6ab^3 + 12ab$

    (b) $4mr^2 + 12m^3r + \dfrac{8m^2}{3}$

3. Solve for a.

    (a) $3(a + 2) = 2a - 6$

    (b) $5(5 - 2a) - 3(8 - 2a) = 0$

    (c) $\dfrac{a - 1}{10} - \dfrac{2 - a}{5} - \dfrac{5 - a}{2} = 0$

4. Using the formula $P = \dfrac{A}{1 + rt}$ find A when $P = 1\,000$, $r = 14\%$, $t = 2$.

5. Using the formula $T = Ar$, find A when $T = \$850$ and $r = 0.065$ dollars.

CUMULATIVE REVIEW 1

1. Express $\frac{3}{8}$ as a percent.

2. Express 0.875 as a percent.

3. Express $\frac{5}{8}$ as a decimal.

4. Express $0.83\overline{3}$ as a proper fraction.

5. Simplify $\frac{3}{8} \times \frac{4}{5}(\frac{3}{5} + \frac{1}{4}) \div 2$.

6. 20 is what percent of 80?

7. 84 is what percent of 336?

8. 40 increased by $12\frac{1}{2}\%$ of itself equals what number?

9. What number increased by 30% of itself equals 179.4?

10. The area of one room is 14 m². Another room is 21 m². The second room is what percent larger than the first?

11. $\frac{3}{5}$ is what percent of 75?

12. What number increased by 40% of itself and the result decreased by 25% equals 630?

13. Find 48% of $650.

14. Add horizontally.
    (a) 36 + 462.3 + 38.124 + 3.921
    (b) 342.684 + 78.2 + 936.55

15. Use your subtotal key to add the following.

    (a) 364
         382
         691
         ███S
         482
         783
         ███S
          38
         920
         720
         ███T

    (b) 972.6
           3.42
          72.08
         464.62
         ████S
         891.02
          77.98
          49.62
         ████S
         896.14
         ████T

16. Multiply mentally.
    (a) 36 × 25
    (b) 128 × 125

17. Divide mentally.
    (a) 4 875 ÷ 25
    (b) 16 750 ÷ 125

UNIT 4

Earnings and Deductions

Have you ever received a pay cheque and wondered why the amount you received was not the same as the amount you had earned? It is important to know how earnings are calculated and how deductions are determined.

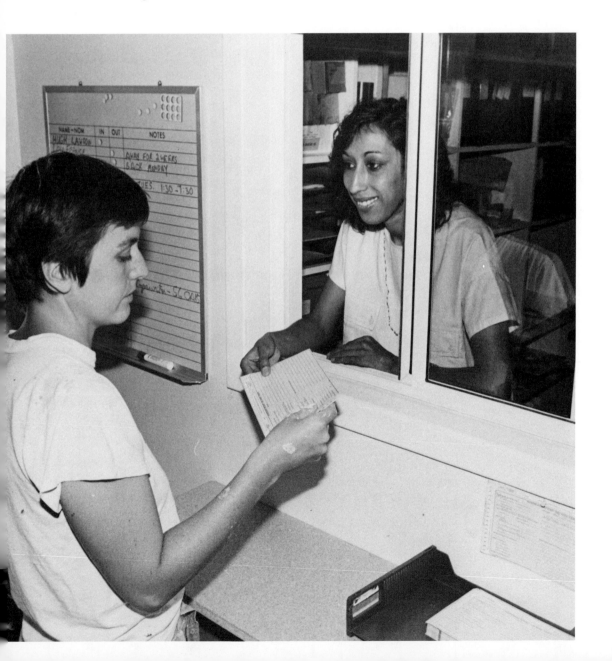

4.1   CALCULATING EARNINGS – STRAIGHT COMMISSION

Many salespeople earn a commission on sales instead of a monthly salary, a wage, or an hourly rate. The Avon salesperson, for example, might work on a 30% commission basis. In such a case, from an order totalling $24.65 for Avon products, the salesperson would receive 30% of $24.65 as commission.

Machine
Instruction

CLEAR

SET DEC 3

24.65

$\boxed{\times}$

0.3

$\boxed{=}$

```
0•000*

24•65×
  0•3=
7•395*
```

Net sale	$24.65
× commission rate	0.30
Equals $ commission	$7.395 (round off to $7.40)

EXERCISE 4.1
1. Find the amount of commission the salesperson would earn in each of the following.

	Net Sale	Commission Rate	$ Amount of Commission
(a)	$ 46.95	30%	▇▇▇▇
(b)	152.80	25%	▇▇▇▇
(c)	946.51	20%	▇▇▇▇
(d)	4 423.50	10%	▇▇▇▇
(e)	3 692.75	15%	▇▇▇▇

Net Sale: There were no goods returned and it does not include sales tax.

2. If a salesperson sells a used car for $2 625 (before sales tax) and is working for 20% commission, how much is earned on the sale?

3. A vacuum cleaner salesperson is told that he will earn 40% of his net sales. In his first week, he sells 2 vacuum cleaners that retail at $199.95 each. How much does he earn?

4. A commissioned salesperson earns 25% of her net sales. Her net sales for her first week are $142.92, for the second week $78.65, for the third week $87.90, and for the fourth week $103.65. How much does she earn for her first four weeks?

5. Sales representatives hired by a newspaper are told that they should earn $20 000 a year for selling newspaper advertising on a 20% commission basis. One representative's sales for a year are:

January	$ 8 010
February	6 905
March	5 850
April	7 910
May	7 560
June	7 790
July	8 255
August	8 485
September	8 080
October	9 445
November	10 975
December	9 860

Does she/he earn more or less than the $20 000 she/he is told she/he should earn? By how much?

6. Maria Miczek is a broker selling bonds. Her commission rate is 5%. Find her earnings on the following sales.
   (a) 6 $100 bonds selling at 73
   (b) 4 $100 bonds selling at $87\frac{1}{2}$
   (c) 7 $100 bonds selling at $94\frac{3}{8}$
   (d) 5 $100 bonds selling at 102
   (e) 3 $100 bonds selling at $68\frac{1}{2}$

4.2   CALCULATING EARNINGS – SALARY PLUS COMMISSION

Example
Luc Renoie has a part-time job in a men's wear store. He is to earn $50 a month salary plus 10% commission on net sales. In his first month Luc makes net sales of $1 050. Calculate his total earnings for the month.

Solution

Net sales	$1 050
× % commission	0.10
Equals $ commission	$105.00
Plus salary	50.00
Month's earnings	$155.00

Some salespeople are given a monthly salary plus a percent commission on net sales *over a certain amount*. For example, Debbie Tuik works part-time as a sales clerk. She earns $60 a month salary plus 20% commission on net sales over $1 000. In Debbie's first month she makes net sales of $2 080. To calculate Debbie's total earnings for the month:

Machine
Instruction

CLEAR	Net sales	$2 080
	Less basic sales	1 000
SET DEC 2	Equals net sales for commission	$1 080
2 080	× % commission	0.20
⬚ +	Equals $ commission	$216.00
	Plus salary	60.00
1 000	Equals salary for month	$276.00

2 080

⬚ +

1 000

⬚ −

⬚ M+

⬚ RM

⬚ ×

⬚ CM

0.2

⬚ M+

⬚ RM

⬚ +

60

⬚ +

⬚ *

⬚ CM

```
             0 • 0 0 *

         2,0 8 0 • 0 0 +
         1,0 0 0 • 0 0 −
         1,0 8 0 • 0 0 ◊
         1,0 8 0 • 0 0 ᴙᴹ
         1,0 8 0 • 0 0 ×
         1,0 8 0 • 0 0 ᴧ

             0 • 2 =
         2 1 6 • 0 0 ◊

         2 1 6 • 0 0 ᴙᴹ
         2 1 6 • 0 0 +
          6 0 • 0 0 +
         2 7 6 • 0 0 *

         2 1 6 • 0 0 ᴄᴹ
```

EXERCISE 4.2

1. Betty Marrie has agreed to work for $150 a month plus 5% of net sales over $1 000. During the month of December she has net sales of $13 045. How much does she earn in December?

2. Bill Fraser sold goods for Smith Belting Ltd. at a commission rate of 8% on net sales over $5 000 plus a monthly salary of $250. During the month of April he had net sales of $17 000. How much did he earn for April?

3. Rob Holland, an author, agrees to write a book for a publisher for 10% commission (royalty) on sales up to 10 000 books and 12% royalty on sales over 10 000. The book sells for $9.95.
   (a) During the first six months 8 500 books are sold.
   How much royalty does Rob receive from the publisher?
   (b) By the end of the first year, 12 000 books are sold.
   How much does Rob receive for the whole year?

4. The Road Runners cut an LP for a recording company. The Road Runners are to receive 5% on sales up to 50 000, 8% on sales from 50 001 to 100 000, and 12% on sales over 100 000. The LP sells for $5.95.
   (a) During the first six months 42 000 records are sold. How much do the Road Runners receive?
   (b) During the second six months, total sales rise to 87 450. How much do the Road Runners receive *for the second six months*? What is their total for the year?
   (c) Over a period of two years, the record sells 650 000 copies. What is the total received by the Road Runners for two years?

4.3 CALCULATING EARNINGS – REAL ESTATE COMMISSIONS

A *real estate broker* is a person who is licensed to sell property and receive a commission for doing so. A *real estate agent* is a person licensed to work for a real estate broker. If a broker signs an agreement to sell a home (called a listing) and personally sells the home, the broker is entitled to receive the commission.

For example, if the home sells for $60 000 and the listing is at 5%, the commission is calculated as follows.

Sale	$60 000
× commission as per listing	0.05
Equals $ commission	$ 3 000
Sale	$60 000
Less commission	3 000
Equals proceeds for the owner	$57 000

If, however, the broker obtains the listing and the agent sells the house, they split the commission on a previously agreed upon basis: perhaps the broker gets 3% and the agent gets 2%.

For example, if the home sells for $59 500 and the listing is at 5%, the commission is as follows.

Sale	$59 500
× commission as per listing	0.05
Equals $ commission	$ 2 975

$$\begin{array}{rl}
\text{Sale} & \$59\ 500 \\
\text{Less commission} & \underline{\quad 2\ 975} \\
\text{Equals proceeds for owner} & \$56\ 525
\end{array}$$

Broker's Commission + Agent's Commission = Commission
           3%   2%   5% as per listing

Broker's Commission = $\frac{3}{5}$, or 60%, of total commission

Agent's Commission = $\frac{2}{5}$, or 40%, of total commission

Broker's Commission = 60% of $2 975 = $ _____

Agent's Commission = 40% of $2 975 = $ _____

Total Commission as per listing $2 975

EXERCISE 4.3

1. Broker lists house; agent sells house. Calculate the following if the broker gets 3% and the agent gets 2%.

	House Sold For	% Comm. as per Listing	$ Comm. as per Listing	$ Comm. for Broker	$ Comm. for Agent
(a)	$59 500	5%			
(b)	48 700	5%			
(c)	69 900	5%			
(d)	75 500	5%			
(e)	46 700	5%			

2. Agent lists house; agent sells house. Calculate the following if the broker gets $1\frac{1}{2}$% and the agent gets $3\frac{1}{2}$%.

	House Sold For	% Comm. as per Listing	$ Comm. as per Listing	$ Comm. for Broker	$ Comm. for Agent
(a)	$44 900	5%			
(b)	52 700	5%			
(c)	64 850	5%			
(d)	74 900	5%			
(e)	88 700	5%			

3. An agent went to work for a real estate broker on an agreement that if the agent listed and sold the same home, the agent would get 55% of the $ commission as per listing, and the broker would get 45% of the $ commission as per listing. How much would the agent get if he/she listed a home at 6% commission and sold it for $48 500? How much would the broker get?

4. A real estate broker and an agent have an agreement whereby the broker gets 60% and the agent gets 40% of the $ commission as per listing if the broker lists the property but the agent sells it. The broker lists a variety store at 5% commission and the agent sells it for $145 000. How much does the broker get? How much does the agent get?

4.4   CALCULATING EARNINGS – PIECEWORK

Many farm workers and factory workers are paid by the number of items or "pieces" they produce or the number of containers of fruit or vegetables they pick. This method provides an incentive for the workers to produce more.

Example 1
The X-Tel factory pays on a straight piecework basis. The factory rate for a particular part is 80¢ a piece. Jackie Hall finished the following number of pieces in a recent week: Monday 52, Tuesday 58, Wednesday 66, Thursday 67, and Friday 54. What were her total earnings?

Solution
Number of pieces = 52 + 58 + 66 + 67 + 54 = 297
Earnings = 297 × $0.80 = $237.60

Example 2
Another factory offers a bonus for pieces completed over a minimum quota. In one department the rate was 90¢ per piece up to a quota of 40 items and a bonus of 20¢ per piece for pieces over the quota. Tom Cooper produced the following in one week: Monday 38, Tuesday 44, Wednesday 52, Thursday 51, and Friday 35. Find his weekly earnings.

Solution

Monday	38 × $0.90
Tuesday	44 × $0.90 + 4 × $0.20
Wednesday	52 × $0.90 + 12 × $0.20
Thursday	51 × $0.90 + 11 × $0.20
Friday	35 × $0.90

Total = 220 × $0.90 + 27 × $0.20
= $198.00 + $5.40
= $203.40

EXERCISE 4.4

1. Find the weekly earnings for the following employees who work in different departments.

Name	Pieces Produced					Rate per Piece
	M	T	W	T	F	
P. Pauluk	82	90	97	95	90	$0.65
S. Smith	30	34	49	38	35	1.12
R. Reytag	40	40	48	50	45	0.85
C. Collins	76	78	62	83	78	0.70
S. Storey	92	106	110	78	105	0.64

2. Stavros Manikas receives 45¢ for every unit he produces up to 100 and a bonus of 16¢ per unit for all units over 100 each day. His weekly production is as follows: Monday 98, Tuesday 110, Wednesday 123, Thursday 115, and Friday 102. Find his weekly earnings.

3. Lori Jones receives 46¢ per unit for the first 80 units she produces, 56¢ per unit for the next 20, and 70¢ per unit for all over 100. Find her earnings if she produced 90 units on Monday, 98 on Tuesday, 100 on Wednesday, 113 on Thursday, and 102 on Friday.

4. Michelle worked on an assembly line and earned 20¢ each time she fitted two parts together. She completed 120 fittings on Monday, 130 on Tuesday, 160 on Wednesday, 165 on Thursday, and 140 on Friday. How much did she earn?

5. Luigi and Maxine picked strawberries for a week in July. They were paid 12¢ per box for the first 50 boxes picked each day, and 15¢ per box for all boxes over 50. Find their earnings for the week.

	Luigi	Maxine
Monday	35	42
Tuesday	53	59
Wednesday	58	70
Thursday	72	69
Friday	65	70

4.5 CALCULATING EARNINGS – HOURLY WAGES

Most employers who pay hourly wages use a *time clock* and a *time card* to keep a record of the number of hours each employee works. The employee puts a card into the clock to be stamped when he/she arrives at work and again when he/she leaves.

Each company uses its own rules to determine time worked, late penalties, and overtime. The set of rules that D. Allen's employer used are as follows:

(1) A regular day is from 08:00 to 12:00 and 13:00 to 17:00.

(2) There is a one hour lunch break at 12:00.

A quarter hour is the first, second, third, or fourth 15 min in the hour.

(3) There is a penalty of $\frac{1}{4}$ h for every $\frac{1}{4}$ h or part thereof that an employee is late or leaves early.

(4) Payment is made only for full quarter hours worked. For example, an employee who left at 16:55 would be credited with 1 quarter hour after 16:30 (16:30 to 16:45).

(5) There is no payment for time worked before 08:00.

(6) Time worked over 40 h per week in paid at overtime rates. Note that in the diagram, the overtime rate = 1.5 × 6.35 = \$9.525, *not* \$9.53.

(7) Time worked on Sundays and holidays is paid at double the regular rate.

NAME D. Allen					EMPLOYEE NO. 62		
SOCIAL INSURANCE NO. 622-110-565							
WEEK ENDING JANUARY 20							
CLOCK CARD							
	REGULAR						
DAYS	In	Out	In	Out	In	Out	Hours
Monday	7:50	12:00	12:58	17:01			8
Tuesday	8:00	12:07	12:59	16:40			$7\frac{1}{2}$
Wednesday	8:10	12:01	13:00	17:00			$7\frac{3}{4}$
Thursday	9:00	12:00	13:00	16:30	17:55	19:00	$7\frac{1}{2}$
Friday	7:55	12:05	12:56	17:09	17:40	21:01	$11\frac{1}{4}$
Saturday							
Sunday							
		Hours		*Rate*		*Earnings*	
REGULAR		40		6.35		\$254.00	
OVERTIME		2		9.525		19.05	
TOTAL HOURS		42		Gross Earnings		\$273.05	

This is an example of a completed time card. D. Allen punched in each day as he arrived and punched out when he left. The payroll clerk completed the calculations.

EXERCISE 4.5

1. State the number of hours worked in each case using the rules applying to the above example.

	In	Out	In	Out
(a)	7:56	12:01	13:05	15:52
(b)	8:01	12:02	12:59	16:36
(c)	8:17	12:00	13:02	16:15

2. Compute the overtime rate for the following regular rates.
   (a) \$5.52   (b) \$6.15   (c) \$8.79   (d) \$7.95

3. Rule time cards similar to that shown and calculate the gross earnings for each of the following employees.

(a) Josh Graham   Employee No. 8
SIN 530 674 482

	In	Out	In	Out
Mon.	8:14	12:00	12:51	17:03
Tues.	7:58	11:38	13:30	16:30
Wed.	8:35	12:00	12:51	17:01
Thurs.	7:59	12:00	12:58	17:10
Fri.	7:53	12:02	12:54	17:10

Regular rate: $6.25

(b) Kai Cheong Wing   Employee No. 9
SIN 643 786 573

	In	Out	In	Out
Mon.	7:56	12:01	12:59	17:01
Tues.	8:12	12:00	13:00	17:10
Wed.	8:00	12:01	13:14	17:04
Thurs.	7:58	11:48	12:59	17:06
Fri.	8:00	12:00	12:51	16:48

Regular rate: $6.40

(c) Paul Jones   Employee No. 10
SIN 478 080 783

	In	Out	In	Out	In	Out
Mon.	7:52	12:00	12:58	17:00	17:30	21:20
Tues.	8:00	12:01	12:59	16:10		
Wed.	8:10	12:05	12:55	17:02	17:25	20:50
Thurs.	7:51	11:48	12:50	17:01		
Fri.	8:00	12:00	12:59	17:00		

Regular rate: $10.35

(d) Nicolae Dezso   Employee No. 11
SIN 987 654 345

	In	Out	In	Out	In	Out
Mon.	8:00	12:05	12:59	17:02		
Tues.	7:55	11:50	13:00	17:01		
Wed.	8:10	12:00	12:07	16:45		
Thurs.	7:59	12:03	13:18	17:01	17:30	19:05
Fri.	8:09	12:09	12:58	16:00		
Sat.	7:59	11:15				

Regular rate: $7.08

(e) Regina Gamm   Employee No. 12
SIN 987 090 878

	In	*Out*	*In*	*Out*
Mon.	8:00	12:00	12:49	17:00
Tues.	8:35	12:04	12:51	17:02
Wed.	7:58	12:05	12:56	17:04
Thurs.	7:55	12:02	13:00	17:10
Fri.	7:57	11:50	13:15	17:00

Regular rate: $8.60

(f) Blaine White   Employee No. 13
SIN 672 438 901

	In	*Out*	*In*	*Out*
Mon.	8:00	12:02	13:00	17:00
Tues.	7:58	12:01	12:57	16:00
Wed.	7:59	12:00	13:00	17:03
Thurs.	8:25	12:02	12:55	17:01
Fri.	8:10	11:32	12:52	17:00

Regular rate: $6.80

(g) Des Sobring   Employee No. 14
SIN 983 400 620

	In	*Out*	*In*	*Out*	*In*	*Out*
Mon.	9:00	12:02	12:59	17:00	17:30	20:35
Tues.	7:52	12:01	12:59	16:48		
Wed.	8:01	12:04	12:57	17:03	17:28	21:20
Thurs.	7:48	12:01	13:00	17:00		
Fri.	7:42	11:53	12:58	17:02		
Sat.	7:56	11:30				

Regular rate: $8.60

(h) Giovanni Silva   Employee No. 15
SIN 732 040 562

	In	*Out*	*In*	*Out*	*In*	*Out*
Mon.	7:56	12:00	12:58	17:02		
Tues.	8:00	12:01	13:00	16:50	18:00	20:16
Wed.	7:58	11:49	12:59	17:02	17:30	21:10
Thurs.	8:00	12:06	13:10	17:30		
Fri.	7:55	12:00	13:00	16:36		

Regular rate: $8.50

4.6   PAYROLL DEDUCTIONS – CANADA PENSION PLAN

Maximum CPP contributions change each year according to changes in the cost of living.

All employees between 18 and 70, and earning over $2000 per year, except those in the province of Quebec, which has its own pension plan, are required to contribute to the Canada Pension Plan (CPP). Each employee contributes 1.8% of his/her pensionable earnings up to a maximum of $338.40. Employers contribute an equal amount. A self-employed person contributes double the amount of an employed person. Quebec Pension Plan (QPP) rates are the same as CPP rates.

Deductions are made according to tables prepared by Revenue Canada-Taxation. Failure to deduct and remit contributions on the part of the employer may result in a fine or imprisonment. The employer must also pay his/her required contribution.

Figure 4.1 is an excerpt from the *Canada Pension Plan and Unemployment Insurance Premium Tables* for a weekly pay period. To find the weekly deduction, look down the column headed remuneration until you find the gross earnings, then look across to the column headed C.P.P. and note the deduction.

Example
Find the CPP deduction for gross earnings of $300.

Solution
300 lies between 299.85 and 300.40.
The CPP deduction is $4.71 per week.

EXERCISE 4.6
Find the CPP deduction for the following gross weekly earnings.

1. $290.70
2. $292.50
3. $289.67
4. $293.78
5. $310.92

6. $354.95
7. $293.87
8. $346.21
9. $405.40
10. $412.93

4.7   PAYROLL DEDUCTIONS – UNEMPLOYMENT INSURANCE

Deductions from pay for unemployment insurance are compulsory for all employees under 70 years of age except a few exempt classes of persons. The earnings of students working part time are usually not high enough to require contributions.

When you begin work you should obtain a *Social Insurance Number*, which you will keep for the rest of your life. The Unemployment Insurance Commission will keep a record of all your present and future employment.

When you leave a job you will receive a *separation certificate*, which must be presented to your local Unemployment Insurance Commission

CANADA PENSION PLAN CONTRIBUTIONS　　　**COTISATIONS AU RÉGIME DE PENSIONS DU CANADA**

WEEKLY PAY PERIOD — *PÉRIODE HEBDOMADAIRE DE PAIE*

Remuneration / *Rémunération* From-*de*	To-*à*	C.P.P. R.P.C.	Remuneration / *Rémunération* From-*de*	To-*à*	C.P.P. R.P.C.	Remuneration / *Rémunération* From-*de*	To-*à*	C.P.P. R.P.C.	Remuneration / *Rémunération* From-*de*	To-*à*	C.P.P. R.P.C.
278.19	278.73	4.32	318.19	318.73	5.04	358.19	358.73	5.76	398.19	398.73	6.48
278.74	279.29	4.33	318.74	319.29	5.05	358.74	359.29	5.77	398.74	399.29	6.49
279.30	279.84	4.34	319.30	319.84	5.06	359.30	359.84	5.78	399.30	399.84	6.50
279.85	280.40	4.35	319.85	320.40	5.07	359.85	360.40	5.79	399.85	400.40	6.51
280.41	280.95	4.36	320.41	320.95	5.08	360.41	360.95	5.80	400.41	405.40	6.56
280.96	281.51	4.37	320.96	321.51	5.09	360.96	361.51	5.81	405.41	410.40	6.65
281.52	282.07	4.38	321.52	322.07	5.10	361.52	362.07	5.82	410.41	415.40	6.74
282.08	282.62	4.39	322.08	322.62	5.11	362.08	362.62	5.83	415.41	420.40	6.83
282.63	283.18	4.40	322.63	323.18	5.12	362.63	363.18	5.84	420.41	425.40	6.92
283.19	283.73	4.41	323.19	323.73	5.13	363.19	363.73	5.85	425.41	430.40	7.01
283.74	284.29	4.42	323.74	324.29	5.14	363.74	364.29	5.86	430.41	435.40	7.10
284.30	284.84	4.43	324.30	324.84	5.15	364.30	364.84	5.87	435.41	440.40	7.19
284.85	285.40	4.44	324.85	325.40	5.16	364.85	365.40	5.88	440.41	445.40	7.28
285.41	285.95	4.45	325.41	325.95	5.17	365.41	365.95	5.89	445.41	450.40	7.37
285.96	286.51	4.46	325.96	326.51	5.18	365.96	366.51	5.90	450.41	455.40	7.46
286.52	287.07	4.47	326.52	327.07	5.19	366.52	367.07	5.91	455.41	460.40	7.55
287.08	287.62	4.48	327.08	327.62	5.20	367.08	367.62	5.92	460.41	465.40	7.64
287.63	288.18	4.49	327.63	328.18	5.21	367.63	368.18	5.93	465.41	470.40	7.73
288.19	288.73	4.50	328.19	328.73	5.22	368.19	368.73	5.94	470.41	475.40	7.82
288.74	289.29	4.51	328.74	329.29	5.23	368.74	369.29	5.95	475.41	480.40	7.91
289.30	289.84	4.52	329.30	329.84	5.24	369.30	369.84	5.96	480.41	485.40	8.00
289.85	290.40	4.53	329.85	330.40	5.25	369.85	370.40	5.97	485.41	490.40	8.09
290.41	290.95	4.54	330.41	330.95	5.26	370.41	370.95	5.98	490.41	495.40	8.18
290.96	291.51	4.55	330.96	331.51	5.27	370.96	371.51	5.99	495.41	500.40	8.27
291.52	292.07	4.56	331.52	332.07	5.28	371.52	372.07	6.00	500.41	505.40	8.36
292.08	292.62	4.57	332.08	332.62	5.29	372.08	372.62	6.01	505.41	510.40	8.45
292.63	293.18	4.58	332.63	333.18	5.30	372.63	373.18	6.02	510.41	515.40	8.54
293.19	293.73	4.59	333.19	333.73	5.31	373.19	373.73	6.03	515.41	520.40	8.63
293.74	294.29	4.60	333.74	334.29	5.32	373.74	374.29	6.04	520.41	525.40	8.72
294.30	294.84	4.61	334.30	334.84	5.33	374.30	374.84	6.05	525.41	530.40	8.81
294.85	295.40	4.62	334.85	335.40	5.34	374.85	375.40	6.06	530.41	535.40	8.90
295.41	295.95	4.63	335.41	335.95	5.35	375.41	375.95	6.07	535.41	540.40	8.99
295.96	296.51	4.64	335.96	336.51	5.36	375.96	376.51	6.08	540.41	545.40	9.08
296.52	297.07	4.65	336.52	337.07	5.37	376.52	377.07	6.09	545.41	550.40	9.17
297.08	297.62	4.66	337.08	337.62	5.38	377.08	377.62	6.10	550.41	555.40	9.26
297.63	298.18	4.67	337.63	338.18	5.39	377.63	378.18	6.11	555.41	560.40	9.35
298.19	298.73	4.68	338.19	338.73	5.40	378.19	378.73	6.12	560.41	565.40	9.44
298.74	299.29	4.69	338.74	339.29	5.41	378.74	379.29	6.13	565.41	570.40	9.53
299.30	299.84	4.70	339.30	339.84	5.42	379.30	379.84	6.14	570.41	575.40	9.62
299.85	300.40	4.71	339.85	340.40	5.43	379.85	380.40	6.15	575.41	580.40	9.71
300.41	300.95	4.72	340.41	340.95	5.44	380.41	380.95	6.16	580.41	585.40	9.80
300.96	301.51	4.73	340.96	341.51	5.45	380.96	381.51	6.17	585.41	590.40	9.89
301.52	302.07	4.74	341.52	342.07	5.46	381.52	382.07	6.18	590.41	595.40	9.98
302.08	302.62	4.75	342.08	342.62	5.47	382.08	382.62	6.19	595.41	600.40	10.07
302.63	303.18	4.76	342.63	343.18	5.48	382.63	383.18	6.20	600.41	605.40	10.16
303.19	303.73	4.77	343.19	343.73	5.49	383.19	383.73	6.21	605.41	610.40	10.25
303.74	304.29	4.78	343.74	344.29	5.50	383.74	384.29	6.22	610.41	615.40	10.34
304.30	304.84	4.79	344.30	344.84	5.51	384.30	384.84	6.23	615.41	620.40	10.43
304.85	305.40	4.80	344.85	345.40	5.52	384.85	385.40	6.24	620.41	625.40	10.52
305.41	305.95	4.81	345.41	345.95	5.53	385.41	385.95	6.25	625.41	630.40	10.61
305.96	306.51	4.82	345.96	346.51	5.54	385.96	386.51	6.26	630.41	635.40	10.70
306.52	307.07	4.83	346.52	347.07	5.55	386.52	387.07	6.27	635.41	640.40	10.79
307.08	307.62	4.84	347.08	347.62	5.56	387.08	387.62	6.28	640.41	645.40	10.88
307.63	308.18	4.85	347.63	348.18	5.57	387.63	388.18	6.29	645.41	650.40	10.97
308.19	308.73	4.86	348.19	348.73	5.58	388.19	388.73	6.30	650.41	655.40	11.06
308.74	309.29	4.87	348.74	349.29	5.59	388.74	389.29	6.31	655.41	660.40	11.15
309.30	309.84	4.88	349.30	349.84	5.60	389.30	389.84	6.32	660.41	665.40	11.24
309.85	310.40	4.89	349.85	350.40	5.61	389.85	390.40	6.33	665.41	670.40	11.33
310.41	310.95	4.90	350.41	350.95	5.62	390.41	390.95	6.34	670.41	675.40	11.42
310.96	311.51	4.91	350.96	351.51	5.63	390.96	391.51	6.35	675.41	680.40	11.51
311.52	312.07	4.92	351.52	352.07	5.64	391.52	392.07	6.36	680.41	685.40	11.60
312.08	312.62	4.93	352.08	352.62	5.65	392.08	392.62	6.37	685.41	690.40	11.69
312.63	313.18	4.94	352.63	353.18	5.66	392.63	393.18	6.38	690.41	695.40	11.78
313.19	313.73	4.95	353.19	353.73	5.67	393.19	393.73	6.39	695.41	700.40	11.87
313.74	314.29	4.96	353.74	354.29	5.68	393.74	394.29	6.40	700.41	705.40	11.96
314.30	314.84	4.97	354.30	354.84	5.69	394.30	394.84	6.41	705.41	710.40	12.05
314.85	315.40	4.98	354.85	355.40	5.70	394.85	395.40	6.42	710.41	715.40	12.14
315.41	315.95	4.99	355.41	355.95	5.71	395.41	395.95	6.43	715.41	720.40	12.23
315.96	316.51	5.00	355.96	356.51	5.72	395.96	396.51	6.44	720.41	725.40	12.32
316.52	317.07	5.01	356.52	357.07	5.73	396.52	397.07	6.45	725.41	730.40	12.41
317.08	317.62	5.02	357.08	357.62	5.74	397.08	397.62	6.46	730.41	735.40	12.50
317.63	318.18	5.03	357.63	358.18	5.75	397.63	398.18	6.47	735.41	740.40	12.59

Voir indications à la page 3　　　　　　　　　　See instructions on page 3

Figure 4.1

UNEMPLOYMENT INSURANCE PREMIUMS　　　　PRIMES D'ASSURANCE-CHÔMAGE

WEEKLY PAY PERIOD — *PÉRIODE HEBDOMADAIRE DE PAIE*

288.05 — 413.25

Remuneration *Rémunération*		U.I. Premium *Prime d'a.-c.*	Remuneration *Rémunération*		U.I. Premium *Prime d'a.-c.*	Remuneration *Rémunération*		U.I. Premium *Prime d'a.-c.*	Remuneration *Rémunération*		U.I. Premium *Prime d'a.-c.*
From-*de*	To-*à*		From-*de*	To-*à*		From-*de*	To-*à*		From-*de*	To-*à*	
299.79 –	300.21	6.90	331.09 –	331.51	7.62	362.39 –	362.82	8.34	393.70 –	394.12	9.06
300.22 –	300.64	6.91	331.52 –	331.95	7.63	362.83 –	363.25	8.35	394.13 –	394.56	9.07
300.65 –	301.08	6.92	331.96 –	332.38	7.64	363.26 –	363.69	8.36	394.57 –	394.99	9.08
301.09 –	301.51	6.93	332.39 –	332.82	7.65	363.70 –	364.12	8.37	395.00 –	395.43	9.09
301.52 –	301.95	6.94	332.83 –	333.25	7.66	364.13 –	364.56	8.38	395.44 –	395.86	9.10
301.96 –	302.38	6.95	333.26 –	333.69	7.67	364.57 –	364.99	8.39	395.87 –	396.30	9.11
302.39 –	302.82	6.96	333.70 –	334.12	7.68	365.00 –	365.43	8.40	396.31 –	396.73	9.12
302.83 –	303.25	6.97	334.13 –	334.56	7.69	365.44 –	365.86	8.41	396.74 –	397.17	9.13
303.26 –	303.69	6.98	334.57 –	334.99	7.70	365.87 –	366.30	8.42	397.18 –	397.60	9.14
303.70 –	304.12	6.99	335.00 –	335.43	7.71	366.31 –	366.73	8.43	397.61 –	398.04	9.15
304.13 –	304.56	7.00	335.44 –	335.86	7.72	366.74 –	367.17	8.44	398.05 –	398.47	9.16
304.57 –	304.99	7.01	335.87 –	336.30	7.73	367.18 –	367.60	8.45	398.48 –	398.91	9.17
305.00 –	305.43	7.02	336.31 –	336.73	7.74	367.61 –	368.04	8.46	398.92 –	399.34	9.18
305.44 –	305.86	7.03	336.74 –	337.17	7.75	368.05 –	368.47	8.47	399.35 –	399.78	9.19
305.87 –	306.30	7.04	337.18 –	337.60	7.76	368.48 –	368.91	8.48	399.79 –	400.21	9.20
306.31 –	306.73	7.05	337.61 –	338.04	7.77	368.92 –	369.34	8.49	400.22 –	400.64	9.21
306.74 –	307.17	7.06	338.05 –	338.47	7.78	369.35 –	369.78	8.50	400.65 –	401.08	9.22
307.18 –	307.60	7.07	338.48 –	338.91	7.79	369.79 –	370.21	8.51	401.09 –	401.51	9.23
307.61 –	308.04	7.08	338.92 –	339.34	7.80	370.22 –	370.64	8.52	401.52 –	401.95	9.24
308.05 –	308.47	7.09	339.35 –	339.78	7.81	370.65 –	371.08	8.53	401.96 –	402.38	9.25
308.48 –	308.91	7.10	339.79 –	340.21	7.82	371.09 –	371.51	8.54	402.39 –	402.82	9.26
308.92 –	309.34	7.11	340.22 –	340.64	7.83	371.52 –	371.95	8.55	402.83 –	403.25	9.27
309.35 –	309.78	7.12	340.65 –	341.08	7.84	371.96 –	372.38	8.56	403.26 –	403.69	9.28
309.79 –	310.21	7.13	341.09 –	341.51	7.85	372.39 –	372.82	8.57	403.70 –	404.12	9.29
310.22 –	310.64	7.14	341.52 –	341.95	7.86	372.83 –	373.25	8.58	404.13 –	404.56	9.30
310.65 –	311.08	7.15	341.96 –	342.38	7.87	373.26 –	373.69	8.59	404.57 –	404.99	9.31
311.09 –	311.51	7.16	342.39 –	342.82	7.88	373.70 –	374.12	8.60	405.00 –	405.43	9.32
311.52 –	311.95	7.17	342.83 –	343.25	7.89	374.13 –	374.56	8.61	405.44 –	405.86	9.33
311.96 –	312.38	7.18	343.26 –	343.69	7.90	374.57 –	374.99	8.62	405.87 –	406.30	9.34
312.39 –	312.82	7.19	343.70 –	344.12	7.91	375.00 –	375.43	8.63	406.31 –	406.73	9.35
312.83 –	313.25	7.20	344.13 –	344.56	7.92	375.44 –	375.86	8.64	406.74 –	407.17	9.36
313.26 –	313.69	7.21	344.57 –	344.99	7.93	375.87 –	376.30	8.65	407.18 –	407.60	9.37
313.70 –	314.12	7.22	345.00 –	345.43	7.94	376.31 –	376.73	8.66	407.61 –	408.04	9.38
314.13 –	314.56	7.23	345.44 –	345.86	7.95	376.74 –	377.17	8.67	408.05 –	408.47	9.39
314.57 –	314.99	7.24	345.87 –	346.30	7.96	377.18 –	377.60	8.68	408.48 –	408.91	9.40
315.00 –	315.43	7.25	346.31 –	346.73	7.97	377.61 –	378.04	8.69	408.92 –	409.34	9.41
315.44 –	315.86	7.26	346.74 –	347.17	7.98	378.05 –	378.47	8.70	409.35 –	409.78	9.42
315.87 –	316.30	7.27	347.18 –	347.60	7.99	378.48 –	378.91	8.71	409.79 –	410.21	9.43
316.31 –	316.73	7.28	347.61 –	348.04	8.00	378.92 –	379.34	8.72	410.22 –	410.64	9.44
316.74 –	317.17	7.29	348.05 –	348.47	8.01	379.35 –	379.78	8.73	410.65 –	411.08	9.45
317.18 –	317.60	7.30	348.48 –	348.91	8.02	379.79 –	380.21	8.74	411.09 –	411.51	9.46
317.61 –	318.04	7.31	348.92 –	349.34	8.03	380.22 –	380.64	8.75	411.52 –	411.95	9.47
318.05 –	318.47	7.32	349.35 –	349.78	8.04	380.65 –	381.08	8.76	411.96 –	412.38	9.48
318.48 –	318.91	7.33	349.79 –	350.21	8.05	381.09 –	381.51	8.77	412.39 –	412.82	9.49
318.92 –	319.34	7.34	350.22 –	350.64	8.06	381.52 –	381.95	8.78	412.83 –	413.25	9.50
319.35 –	319.78	7.35	350.65 –	351.08	8.07	381.96 –	382.38	8.79	413.26 –	413.69	9.51
319.79 –	320.21	7.36	351.09 –	351.51	8.08	382.39 –	382.82	8.80	413.70 –	414.12	9.52
320.22 –	320.64	7.37	351.52 –	351.95	8.09	382.83 –	383.25	8.81	414.13 –	414.56	9.53
320.65 –	321.08	7.38	351.96 –	352.38	8.10	383.26 –	383.69	8.82	414.57 –	414.99	9.54
321.09 –	321.51	7.39	352.39 –	352.82	8.11	383.70 –	384.12	8.83	415.00 –	415.43	9.55
321.52 –	321.95	7.40	352.83 –	353.25	8.12	384.13 –	384.56	8.84	415.44 –	415.86	9.56
321.96 –	322.38	7.41	353.26 –	353.69	8.13	384.57 –	384.99	8.85	415.87 –	416.30	9.57
322.39 –	322.82	7.42	353.70 –	354.12	8.14	385.00 –	385.43	8.86	416.31 –	416.73	9.58
322.83 –	323.25	7.43	354.13 –	354.56	8.15	385.44 –	385.86	8.87	416.74 –	417.17	9.59
323.26 –	323.69	7.44	354.57 –	354.99	8.16	385.87 –	386.30	8.88	417.18 –	417.60	9.60
323.70 –	324.12	7.45	355.00 –	355.43	8.17	386.31 –	386.73	8.89	417.61 –	418.04	9.61
324.13 –	324.56	7.46	355.44 –	355.86	8.18	386.74 –	387.17	8.90	418.05 –	418.47	9.62
324.57 –	324.99	7.47	355.87 –	356.30	8.19	387.18 –	387.60	8.91	418.48 –	418.91	9.63
325.00 –	325.43	7.48	356.31 –	356.73	8.20	387.61 –	388.04	8.92	418.92 –	419.34	9.64
325.44 –	325.86	7.49	356.74 –	357.17	8.21	388.05 –	388.47	8.93	419.35 –	419.78	9.65
325.87 –	326.30	7.50	357.18 –	357.60	8.22	388.48 –	388.91	8.94	419.79 –	420.21	9.66
326.31 –	326.73	7.51	357.61 –	358.04	8.23	388.92 –	389.34	8.95	420.22 –	420.64	9.67
326.74 –	327.17	7.52	358.05 –	358.47	8.24	389.35 –	389.78	8.96	420.65 –	421.08	9.68
327.18 –	327.60	7.53	358.48 –	358.91	8.25	389.79 –	390.21	8.97	421.09 –	421.51	9.69
327.61 –	328.04	7.54	358.92 –	359.34	8.26	390.22 –	390.64	8.98	421.52 –	421.95	9.70
328.05 –	328.47	7.55	359.35 –	359.78	8.27	390.65 –	391.08	8.99	421.96 –	422.38	9.71
328.48 –	328.91	7.56	359.79 –	360.21	8.28	391.09 –	391.51	9.00	422.39 –	422.82	9.72
328.92 –	329.34	7.57	360.22 –	360.64	8.29	391.52 –	391.95	9.01	422.83 –	423.25	9.73
329.35 –	329.78	7.58	360.65 –	361.08	8.30	391.96 –	392.38	9.02	423.26 –	423.69	9.74
329.79 –	330.21	7.59	361.09 –	361.51	8.31	392.39 –	392.82	9.03	423.70 –	424.12	9.75
330.22 –	330.64	7.60	361.52 –	361.95	8.32	392.83 –	393.25	9.04	424.13 –	424.56	9.76
330.65 –	331.08	7.61	361.96 –	362.38	8.33	393.26 –	393.69	9.05	424.57 –	424.99	9.77
									425.00 –	AND UP *ET PLUS*	9.78

Figure 4.2

(UIC) office if you wish to collect unemployment insurance. If you have contributed for the required length of time and are willing and able to work but cannot find suitable employment, you will receive benefits. The amount of unemployment insurance benefits will depend on the rate of your contributions and the length of time you have been contributing to the fund.

Figure 4.2 is another excerpt from the *Canada Pension Plan and Unemployment Insurance Premium Tables* for a weekly pay period.

Example
Find the UIC deduction for gross earnings of $300.

Solution
300 lies between 299.79 and 300.21.
The UIC deduction is $6.90 per week.

EXERCISE 4.7
Find the UIC deduction for the following gross weekly earnings.

1. $362.85
2. $415.62
3. $299.78
4. $386.43
5. $319.77

6. $423.86
7. $428.92
8. $351.16
9. $381.97
10. $402.33

4.8   PAYROLL DEDUCTIONS – INCOME TAX

It is compulsory for employers to deduct income tax from all employees' pay, except those whose yearly taxable income falls below the minimum taxable income. Most people in this category are students working part time. When a person begins working for a new employer, he/she completes a TD1 form showing his/her claim for personal exemptions. These exemptions are now being adjusted every year to reflect the increase in the cost of living.

Table of Net Claim Codes 1984 *Table des codes de demande nette*			
Net Claim – *Demande nette* Exceeding – Not exceeding *Excédant – N'excédant pas*	Net Claim Code *Code de demande nette*	Net Claim – *Demande nette* Exceeding – Not exceeding *Excédant – N'excédant pas*	Net Claim Code *Code de demande nette*
$3,959 — 4,010	1	$ 7,410 — 8,130	8
4,010 — 4,640	2	8,130 — 8,890	9
4,640 — 5,330	3	8,890 — 9,720	10
5,330 — 5,920	4	9,720 — 10,540	11
5,920 — 6,690	5	10,540 — 11,320	12
6,690 — 7,050	6	11,320 — 11,920	13
7,050 — 7,410	7	11,920 and up – *et plus*	X
Exemption from Tax Deduction as claimed below — *Exemptions des retenues d'impôt demandées ci-dessus*			0

Figure 4.3

Figure 4.3 is an excerpt from the TD1 form. It shows the net claim codes necessary to use the Income Tax Deduction Tables. The net claim is the total personal exemption of the taxpayer. This means that earnings up to the amount of the net claim are not taxed. For example, a person having a net claim of $3 170 is taxed according to Code 1. Column 1 in Figure 4.4 shows the weekly tax deduction for Code 1.

Figure 4.4 is an excerpt from the Income Tax Deduction Tables for weekly pay periods. Since CPP contributions and UI premiums paid are not taxable, the weekly contribution to the Canada Pension Plan and unemployment insurance must be deducted from the weekly pay to determine the pay for income tax purposes.

Steps to find income tax deduction:

(1) Deduct CPP contributions and UI premiums from weekly pay.

(2) Determine personal exemptions.

(3) Look down column headed Weekly Pay to figure obtained in (1).

(4) Look straight across page to figure in column headed with the applicable net claim code.

Example

Franz Gerhard earns $275 per week. His personal exemption is $5 560, his CPP contribution is $4.47 per week, and his UP premium $4.95 per week. What is his weekly tax deduction?

Solution

Gross earnings − CPP − UI = Earnings for tax purposes
$275 − $4.47 − $4.95 = $265.58

Franz's total personal exemption of $5 560 lies between $5 330 and $5 920. According to Figure 4.3, his net claim code is 4. Looking down the Weekly Pay column in Figure 4.4 you find $265.58 on line 3. Looking straight across to column 4, you find his weekly tax deduction is $30.40.

EXERCISE 4.8

Find the income tax deduction for the following employees.

Employee	Weekly Earnings	CPP Cont.	UI Prem.	Personal Exemptions
1. A. Aylsworth	$306.60	$4.83	$7.05	$3 960
2. B. Buta	299.79	4.70	6.90	8 140
3. C. Crawley	372.45	6.01	8.57	8 790
4. D. Donut	385.78	6.25	8.87	4 670
5. E. Everly	406.10	6.65	9.34	9 500

ONTARIO
WEEKLY TAX DEDUCTIONS
Basis — 52 Pay Periods per Year

TABLE 2

ONTARIO
RETENUES D'IMPÔT PAR SEMAINE
Base — 52 périodes de paie par année

IF THE EMPLOYEE'S "NET CLAIM CODE" ON FORM TD1 IS — SI LE «CODE DE RÉCLAMATION NETTE» DE L'EMPLOYÉ SELON LA FORMULE TD1 EST DE

DEDUCT FROM EACH PAY — RETENEZ SUR CHAQUE PAIE

WEEKLY PAY / PAIE PAR SEMAINE	1	2	3	4	5	6	7	8	9	10	11	12	13	See note p.23 / Column A
255.00 - 259.99	36.70	34.70	31.05	27.60	24.10	21.15	19.25	16.45	12.80	8.85	4.80			
260.00 - 264.99	38.15	36.15	32.50	28.95	25.45	22.50	20.60	17.80	14.05	10.15	6.10	1.35		
265.00 - 269.99	39.55	37.55	33.95	30.40	26.80	23.85	21.95	19.15	15.35	11.45	7.35	3.45		
270.00 - 274.99	41.00	39.00	35.35	31.85	28.15	25.20	23.35	20.50	16.65	12.70	8.65	4.70		
275.00 - 279.99	42.40	40.40	36.80	33.25	29.55	26.55	24.70	21.85	18.00	14.00	9.95	6.00	2.60	2.60
280.00 - 284.99	43.85	41.85	38.20	34.70	30.95	27.90	26.05	23.20	19.35	15.25	11.20	7.25	3.90	3.35
285.00 - 289.99	45.30	43.25	39.65	36.15	32.40	29.30	27.40	24.60	20.70	16.60	12.50	8.55	5.15	3.40
290.00 - 294.99	46.70	44.70	41.05	37.55	33.80	30.70	28.75	25.95	22.10	17.95	13.75	9.85	6.45	3.40
295.00 - 299.99	48.15	46.15	42.50	39.00	35.25	32.15	30.15	27.30	23.45	19.30	15.05	11.10	7.70	3.40
300.00 - 304.99	49.55	47.55	43.95	40.40	36.70	33.55	31.60	28.65	24.80	20.65	16.35	12.40	9.00	3.40
305.00 - 309.99	51.00	49.00	45.35	41.85	38.10	35.00	33.00	30.05	26.15	22.00	17.70	13.65	10.25	3.40
310.00 - 314.99	52.40	50.40	46.80	43.25	39.55	36.45	34.45	31.50	27.50	23.35	19.05	14.95	11.55	3.40
315.00 - 319.99	53.85	51.85	48.20	44.70	40.95	37.85	35.90	32.90	28.85	24.70	20.40	16.25	12.85	3.40
320.00 - 324.99	55.30	53.25	49.65	46.15	42.40	39.30	37.30	34.35	30.25	26.05	21.75	17.60	14.10	3.50
325.00 - 329.99	56.75	54.70	51.05	47.55	43.80	40.70	38.75	35.75	31.70	27.40	23.10	18.95	15.40	3.55
$ 330.00 - 334.99	58.25	56.15	52.50	49.00	45.25	42.15	40.15	37.20	33.15	28.75	24.45	20.30	16.70	3.60
335.00 - 339.99	59.75	57.65	53.95	50.40	46.70	43.55	41.60	38.65	34.55	30.20	25.85	21.65	18.05	3.60
340.00 - 344.99	61.25	59.15	55.35	51.85	48.10	45.00	43.00	40.05	36.00	31.60	27.20	23.00	19.40	3.60
345.00 - 349.99	62.75	60.65	56.80	53.25	49.55	46.45	44.45	41.50	37.40	33.05	28.55	24.35	20.80	3.60
350.00 - 354.99	64.25	62.15	58.30	54.70	50.95	47.85	45.90	42.90	38.85	34.50	29.95	25.70	22.15	3.60
355.00 - 359.99	65.75	63.65	59.80	56.15	52.40	49.30	47.30	44.35	40.30	35.90	31.35	27.05	23.50	3.60
360.00 - 364.99	67.25	65.15	61.35	57.60	53.80	50.70	48.75	45.75	41.70	37.35	32.80	28.45	24.85	3.60
365.00 - 369.99	68.75	66.65	62.85	59.15	55.25	52.15	50.15	47.20	43.15	38.75	34.25	29.85	26.20	3.65
370.00 - 374.99	70.25	68.15	64.35	60.65	56.70	53.55	51.60	48.65	44.65	40.20	35.65	31.25	27.55	3.70
375.00 - 379.99	71.75	69.65	65.85	62.15	58.20	55.00	53.00	50.05	46.00	41.60	37.10	32.70	28.90	3.80
380.00 - 384.99	73.25	71.15	67.35	63.65	59.70	56.45	54.45	51.50	47.40	43.05	38.50	34.10	30.35	3.80
385.00 - 389.99	74.75	72.65	68.85	65.15	61.20	57.95	55.90	52.90	48.85	44.50	39.95	35.55	31.75	3.80
390.00 - 394.99	76.30	74.15	70.35	66.65	62.70	59.45	57.35	54.35	50.30	45.90	41.35	37.00	33.20	3.80
395.00 - 399.99	77.80	75.65	71.85	68.15	64.20	60.95	58.85	55.75	51.70	47.35	42.80	38.40	34.60	3.80
400.00 - 404.99	79.30	77.20	73.35	69.65	65.70	62.45	60.35	57.25	53.15	48.75	44.25	39.85	36.05	3.80
405.00 - 409.99	80.80	78.70	74.85	71.15	67.25	63.95	61.85	58.75	54.55	50.20	45.65	41.25	37.45	3.80
410.00 - 414.99	82.30	80.20	76.35	72.65	68.75	65.45	63.40	60.25	56.00	51.60	47.10	42.70	38.90	3.80
415.00 - 419.99	83.80	81.70	77.85	74.15	70.25	66.95	64.90	61.75	57.50	53.05	48.50	44.10	40.35	3.80
420.00 - 424.99	85.35	83.20	79.35	75.65	71.75	68.45	66.40	63.25	59.00	54.50	49.95	45.55	41.75	3.80
425.00 - 429.99	87.10	84.70	80.90	77.20	73.25	69.95	67.90	64.75	60.50	55.90	51.40	47.00	43.20	3.80
430.00 - 434.99	88.85	86.40	82.40	78.70	74.75	71.50	69.40	66.25	62.00	57.40	52.80	48.40	44.60	3.60
435.00 - 439.99	90.85	88.15	83.90	80.20	76.25	73.00	70.90	67.80	63.50	58.90	54.25	49.85	46.05	3.60
440.00 - 444.99	92.30	89.85	85.45	81.70	77.75	74.50	72.40	69.30	65.00	60.40	55.65	51.25	47.45	3.80
445.00 - 449.99	94.00	91.60	87.20	83.20	79.25	76.00	73.90	70.80	66.50	61.90	57.15	52.70	48.90	3.80
450.00 - 454.99	95.75	93.30	88.95	84.70	80.75	77.50	75.40	72.30	68.00	63.40	58.65	54.10	50.35	3.60

Figure 4.4

4.9 PREPARING THE PAYROLL

At the end of each pay period a payroll clerk will summarize the earnings, deductions, and net or take-home pay for each employee. There are some additional deductions a payroll clerk might have to consider.

Group insurance
Provincial hospitalization
Credit Union payments or deposits
Union dues
Private pension plans
Bond purchases
Charitable donations

This summary is then used to prepare the pay cheques or the cash payments, whichever method is used to pay employees. Examine carefully the completed payroll register that follows.

Payroll Register
For the week Beginning 19-- 02 01 and Ending 19-- 02 07

	EMPLOYEE DATA				EARNINGS			DEDUCTIONS								
NO	SIN NO	NAME	TAX EXEMP	HOURS	REG	O/T	TOTAL	CPP	UIC	INC TAX	GROUP INS	HOSP	UNION DUES	TOTAL	NET PAY	CH NO
1	293 490 768	Fox F.	8790	40	298		298.00	4.67	6.85	20.70	3.85	59.50	14.90	110.47	187.53	22
2	782 453 752	Day D.	3960	40	364		364.00	5.86	8.37	62.75	4.70	29.75	18.20	129.63	234.37	23
3	857 748 838	Aron A.	8140	46	278	40.05	318.05	5.03	7.32	26.15	3.60	59.50	13.90	115.50	202.55	24
4	750 090 765	Bay B.	7430	43	358	17.78	375.78	6.07	8.64	45.75	4.65	59.50	17.90	142.51	233.27	25
5	984 888 750	Glass G.	8850	38	360		360.00	5.79	8.28	37.40	4.65	59.50	18.00	133.62	226.38	26
					1 658	57.83	1 715.83	27.42	39.46	192.75	21.45	267.75	82.90	631.73	1 084.10	

Figure 4.5

Note:

(1) Income tax deductions are based on Figure 4.4.

(2) CPP and UIC deductions are based on Figures 4.1 and 4.2.

(3) Other deductions are examples only.

(4) To find Net Pay, subtract Total Deductions from Total Earnings.

(5) The total of the Net Pay column = total of Total Earnings – total of Total Deductions.

(6) Each employee does not have the same amount of group insurance.

(7) The employees who pay $23 for hospitalization are single; the others are married.

(8) Voluntary deductions are deducted once a month. They are sometimes deducted in part each week.

EXERCISE 4.9

1. Prepare a payroll register similar to the one given for the week of February 1 for the following employees.

Giselle Brunet No. 110 SIN 354 567 754   Group insurance $3.00
Exemption for income tax: $3 960   Union dues $12.98
Hours worked: regular 40; overtime 5   Hospitalization $29.75
Rate: $8.65/h; overtime at time-and-a-half   Credit Union $2.00
Income tax (See Figure 4.4)
Canada Pension Plan (See Figure 4.1)
Unemployment insurance (See Figure 4.2)

Terry O'Hara No. 111 SIN 777 654 652   Group insurance $3.00
Exemption for income tax: $4 460   Union dues $13.35
Hours worked: regular 40; overtime $2\frac{1}{2}$ Hospitalization $59.50
Rate: $8.90/h; overtime at time-and-a-half   Credit Union $20.00
Income tax, CPP, and UIC as for Giselle Brunet

Nasser Ramji No. 112 SIN 846 399 288   Union dues $11.40
Exemption for income tax: $4 280   Hospitalization $59.50
Hours worked: regular 40; overtime 6   Credit Union $17.50
Rate: $7.60/h; overtime at time-and-a-half
Income tax, CPP, and UIC as for Giselle Brunet

2. Prepare a payroll register for the week of January 24 to January 31 for the following employees.

Name	Status	Exempt.	Reg.	O/T	Rate	SIN	Ins.	Bonds
M. Baie	M	$8 790	40	$5\frac{1}{2}$	$6.75	782 111 325	1.50	2.00
S. Hamid	S	3 960	40	3	6.90	338 287 852	1.50	2.00
B. Chu	M	5 320	38		7.62	334 765 762	0.75	3.00
C. Rivers	M	8 850	40	4	7.35	782 000 265	2.00	2.50

Hospitalization is $29.75 per month for single employees and $59.50 per month for married employees. One quarter of the monthly payment is deducted each week. Each employee contributes $0.25 per week to the local United Appeal. Calculate CPP, UIC, and income tax according to Figures 4.1, 4.2, 4.3, 4.4.

3. Prepare a payroll register for the week of March 18 for the following employees who are paid on a piecework basis.

No.	SIN	Pers. Exempt	Pieces Completed	Hosp.
1	378 982 000	$3 960	118	$ 7.44
2	090 287 339	3 960	115	7.44
3	937 883 265	3 960	124	7.44
4	352 039 376	8 790	132	14.88

Employees are paid $2.60 per piece for the first 100 pieces and $2.70 for all pieces over 100. Calculate CPP, UIC, and income tax as in Question 2.

4.10   VACATION PAY

It is compulsory to give certain groups of employees in most provinces at least two weeks vacation with pay after one year of employment. In most cases, the vacation pay must be a minimum of 4% of the employee's yearly wages.

Generally the employee receives his/her usual cheque just prior to going on vacation. Construction workers and other employees who, because of the nature of their jobs often work at several different jobs in one year, usually received their accumulated vacation pay when they leave a job or take a vacation. In cases like these, employers calculate the vacation pay each week, add it to the hourly wages to find gross earnings for income tax purposes, and then deduct the vacation pay with the other deductions to find net or take-home pay. When a worker leaves his/her employment he/she is given the accumulated vacation pay with the last regular pay cheque. When this method is used, two columns must be added to the payroll register.

Payroll Register

EARNINGS			DEDUCTIONS										
TOTAL	VAC PAY	GROSS EARN- INGS	CPP	UIC	INCOME TAX	GRP- INS	HOSP	UNION DUES	VAC PAY	TOTAL	NET PAY	CH NO
366.58	14.66	381.24	6.17	8.77	68.75	0.75	29.75	10.05	14.66	138.90	242.34	45
374.00	14.96	388.96	6.31	8.95	70.25	1.00	29.75	10.28	14.96	141.50	247.46	46
365.00	14.60	379.60	6.14	8.73	57.60	1.00	29.75	9.94	14.60	127.76	251.84	47
358.50	14.34	372.84	6.02	8.58	63.65	0.75	29.75	9.68	14.34	132.77	240.07	48
1 464.08	58.56	1 522.64	24.64	35.03	260.25	3.50	119.00	39.95	58.56	540.93	981.71	

Figure 4.6

EXERCISE 4.10

The DeClair Construction Company adds 4% of the weekly wages to each employee's earnings to accumulate vacation pay. Using the following information, calculate the net pay for each of the employees.

1. Darcy McGee   Employee No. 41
   Exemption for income tax $3 960
   Weekly earnings $358.75; vacation pay 4%
   Income tax deduction (See Figure 4.4)
   CPP and UIC deductions (See Figures 4.1, 4.2)
   Hospitalization $7.44

2. Mae Yen   Employee No. 42
   Exemption for income tax $6 460
   Weekly earnings $296.40; vacation pay 4%
   Income tax deduction (See Figure 4.4)
   CPP and UIC deductions (See Figures 4.1, 4.2)
   Hospitalization $14.88

3. James Joycer   Employee No. 43
   Exemption for income tax $5 440
   Weekly earnings $295.92; vacation pay 4%
   Income tax deduction (See Figure 4.4)
   CPP and UIC deductions (See Figures 4.1, 4.2)
   Hospitalization $14.88

4. Olga Hrynick   Employee No. 44
   Exemption for income tax $3 960
   Weekly earnings $353.50; vacation pay 4%
   Income tax deduction (See Figure 4.4)
   CPP and UIC deductions (See Figures 4.1, 4.2)
   Hospitalization $7.44

4.11 PAYING THE PAYROLL

Most employers pay their employees by cheque or by transferring the funds to a bank or to the employee's bank. Some small businesses may pay part-time or regular employees in currency. When currency is used it is necessary to know how many of each denomination of bills and coins each employee should receive, and the total of each denomination required, so that the correct currency can be withdrawn from the bank.

To do this the payroll clerk prepares a *payroll currency memorandum* and a *currency requisition*. These forms may be called by different names.

Payroll Currency Memorandum 19- 02 07

		Bills					Coins			
Employee	*Net Pay*	*$20*	*$10*	*$5*	*$2*	*$1*	*25¢*	*10¢*	*5¢*	*1¢*
A. Allen	$ 324.56	16			2		2		1	1
B. Bard	$ 317.17	15	1	1	1			1	1	2
C. Coll	$ 338.45	16	1	1	1	1	1	2		
D. Dawe	$ 357.69	17	1	1	1		2	1	1	4
E. Eichler	$ 329.86	16		1	2		3	1		1
Totals	1 667.73	80	3	4	7	1	8	5	3	8

Currency Requisition

Denomination	Quantity	Amount
$20	80	$1 600.00
$10	3	30.00
$ 5	4	20.00
$ 2	7	14.00
$ 1	1	1.00
25¢	8	2.00
10¢	5	0.50
5¢	3	0.15
1¢	8	0.08
Total		$1 667.73

EXERCISE 4.11

Prepare a payroll currency memorandum and a currency requisition for the following groups of employees.

1. T. Smith $226.78
    R. Fong   248.23
    S. Tallak   279.69
    V. Vale   214.87

2. B. Tomasi $287.63
    W. McBey   243.33
    M. Rosen   219.17
    K. Kolk   257.94

4.12 EMPLOYEE RECORDS

Each employer keeps an individual record of each employee's earnings, deductions, and net pay. From this record the payroll clerk can quickly calculate the accumulated amounts at any given date.

Individual Employee's Earnings Record for Year 19--

NAME	Fox, Frank G.	EMPLOYEE	No. 1
ADDRESS	141 Main St. S.	SOCIAL INSURANCE NO.	293 490 768
TELEPHONE	388 4278	MARITAL STATUS	M
DATE OF BIRTH	1955 08 01	TAX EXEMPTIONS	$8 790
		POSITION	Stockroom clerk
		DATE EMPLOYED	1974 12 10

PAY PD. END.	RATE PER HOUR	HOURS	EARNINGS			DEDUCTIONS							NET PAY	ACC. EARNINGS
			REG.	O/T	TOTAL	CPP	UIC	INC. TAX	GR. INS.	HOSP	UNION DUES	TOTAL		
Jan. 31														1296
Feb. 7	$7.45	40	298		298	4.67	6.85	20.70	3.85	59.50	14.90	110.47	187.53	1594

Note: This is the individual employee's record of Employee No. 1 as shown on the payroll register in Section 4.9, page 104.

After the payroll is completed, the payroll clerk transfers the information on the payroll register to each employee's individual record.

EXERCISE 4.12

1. Rule individual employee's earnings record forms and transfer the information you recorded on your payroll register in Question 1, Exercise 4.9. Include the following personal information for each employee:

   Giselle Brunet, 38 Willo Crescent, telephone 345 6782
   Born 1960 01 01, single
   Receiving clerk
   Taken on strength, 1984 05 04
   Terry O'Hara, 387 Lundie Lane, Apt. 2, telephone 387 5455
   Born 1947 04 17, married
   Stock Room Supervisor
   Taken on strength, 1975 07 15
   Nasser Ramji, 789 Avenue Road E., telephone 428 6767
   Born 1941 10 03, married
   Invoice clerk
   Taken on strength, 1959 10 29

2. Prepare employee's earnings records for the month of February for the following employees.
   (a) Allen Blake   single
      SIN 456 764 009
      Personal exemptions $3 960
   (b) Frances Deluca   married
      SIN 980 995 023
      Personal exemptions $7 430
   (c) Suzanne Ferris   married
      SIN 433 092 472
      Personal exemptions $8 140

Earnings:	Blake	Deluca	Ferris
First week	$ 309.00	$ 327.81	$ 363.00
Second week	309.00	323.92	360.00
Third week	312.50	338.40	362.73
Fourth week	309.00	335.00	366.50
Accumulated to January 31	$1 160.92	$1 290.93	$1 271.00
Deductions:			
Bonds	10.00	8.00	5.00
Union Dues	13.45	13.75	18.00
Group Insurance	6.00	7.00	6.50

   Employees pay one quarter of their monthly hospitalization premium per week.
   Single employees pay $29.75 per month and married employees pay $59.50 per month.
   Group insurance premiums are deducted in the fourth week.
   Union dues are deducted in the third week.
   Payments on bonds are deducted in the second week.

SUMMARY

Commission is a percent of sales paid to salesmen instead of, or combined with, a salary.

Piecework rates are a form of earnings paid according to the number of items produced.

Steps in Preparing the Payroll

(1) Calculate the number of regular and overtime hours worked from the employee's time card.

(2) Calculate the regular, overtime, and total gross earnings.

(3) Using the tables prepared by Revenue Canada Taxation, find the amount to be deducted from gross earnings for Canada Pension Plan contributions and unemployment insurance premiums.

(4) Subtract the Canada Pension Plan contribution and the unemployment insurance premium from gross earnings.

(5) Use the amount obtained in Step (4), the employee's personal exemptions, and the Income Tax Deduction tables to find the amount to be deducted from gross earnings for income tax.

(6) Add the deductions for Canada Pension Plan contribution, unemployment insurance, income tax, and any other deductions such as OHIP premium or union dues.

(7) Subtract the amount obtained in Step (6) from gross earnings to find net pay.

REVIEW EXERCISE 4.13

1. (a) A car sales manager told her sales staff that they would earn $125 for each car sold, but she could not approve an offer less than 82% of the list price. On his first day, a sales representative was offered $5 450 for a sports car listed at $6 800. Would the sales manager approve this offer. Why or why not?
   (b) What percent commission would the sales representative earn if the car sold at the full list price?
   (c) What percent commission would the sales representative earn if the car sold at 86% of the list price?

2. Joan Roberts, a life insurance sales representative is told that she will earn a 10% commission on each premium that the insured pays. (The premium is the amount paid each month, quarterly, or yearly by the person insured.)
   (a) Joan sells life insurance to a client who is required to pay a premium of $29.45 quarterly. How much commission does Joan earn if the client pays for one year?

(b) Later, Joan sells to a client who is to pay premiums of $18.95 per month. How much commission will Joan earn if the client pays for one year?

(c) Before the end of her second week, Joan sells insurance to a client who is to pay premiums of $48.25 quarterly. How much will Joan earn if the client pays for one year?

(d) Assuming that the three insured pay their premiums for 20 years, how much will Joan have earned over the 20 years for only two weeks work?

3. Mario Datlani received $500 per month plus a 3% commission on all sales over $1 000. Find his monthly earnings if his sales amounted to $82 800.

4. The following employees are paid on a piecework basis. They receive $2.54 for the first 50 pieces completed, $2.74 for the next 25 pieces, and $2.94 for any pieces completed over 75. Calculate the weekly gross earnings for each employee.

    Employee A   73 pieces
    Employee B   92 pieces
    Employee C   87 pieces

5. Using the following information prepare
   (a) a payroll register showing the net pay of the four employees,
   (b) a payroll currency memorandum and a currency requisition.

Employee No. 1   John Adam   SIN 573 555 908
                        Gross pay $365.78
                        Exemption for income tax $7 430
                        Income tax (See Figure 4.4)
                        CCP (See Figure 4.1)
                        Unemployment insurance
                          (See Figure 4.2)
                        Group insurance $1.50
                        Bond payment $2.00
                        Hospitalization $59.50

Employee No. 2   Gila Alalouf   SIN 477 834 867
                        Gross pay $373.56
                        Exemption for income tax $5 320
                        Income tax, CPP, and UIC
                          as for John Adam
                        Group insurance $2.40
                        Bond payment $2.00
                        Hospitalization $59.50

Employee No. 3   Wendy Colico   SIN 548 574 879
Gross pay $368.97
Exemption for income tax $3 960
Income tax, CPP, and UIC
   as for John Adam
Group insurance $2.50
Bond payment $2.50
Hospitalization $29.75

Employee No. 4   Doug Prado   SIN 439 203 208
Gross pay $362.67
Exemption for income tax $9 500
Income tax, CPP, and UIC
   as for John Adam
Group insurance $1.50
Hospitalization $29.75

6. Find the gross earnings for the following employees.
   (a) Employee A

	In	Out	In	Out	In	Out
M	8:01	12:00	12:59	17:30	19:00	21:18
T	7:55	12:01	12:58	17:01		
W	7:58	12:01	13:00	17:10	18:30	21:10
T	7:48	11:50	13:10	17:15	18:20	20:00
F	7:59	12:00	12:59	17:02		

Rate $6.65/h, time-and-a-half for overtime

   (b) Employee B

	In	Out	In	Out	In	Out
M	7:50	12:01	12:59	17:00	18:10	21:15
T	7:59	12:02	13:10	17:10		
W	7:59	11:45	12:50	17:03	19:30	20:31
T	7:58	12:00	12:56	16:27	18:39	20:40
F	8:10	12:01	13:05	17:02		

Rate $7.35/h, time-and-a-half for overtime

   (c) Employee C

	In	Out	In	Out	In	Out
M	8:06	12:01	12:59	17:00		
T	7:48	12:02	12:59	17:01		
W	7:58	12:05	12:57	17:30	18:25	21:30
T	7:56	11:48	13:01	17:02	18:10	21:10
F	8:05	12:03	12:50	17:02		

Rate $7.25/h, time-and-a-half for overtime

7. Prepare a payroll register for the following employees for the week of March 6. Vacation pay is calculated at 4% of gross earnings.

Employee	Personal Exemptions	Hours	Rate
1	$8 790	$42\frac{1}{2}$	$7.95
2	3 960	$36\frac{3}{4}$	8.60
3	7 430	$44\frac{1}{4}$	7.10
4	8 140	41	8.05

CUMULATIVE REVIEW 2

1. $\frac{5}{6}$ of what price equals $240?

2. $582 increased by $\frac{1}{3}$ of itself and the result decreased by $\frac{1}{4}$ gives what amount?

3. $2.25 is what percent less than $3.00?

4. A salesperson sold $825 worth of goods on Friday and $924 worth on Saturday. What was the percent increase or decrease in sales?

5. $81.30 is 25% of what amount?

6. An employee changed jobs from one paying $4.40/h to one paying $208 per week for a 40 h week. What is the percent increase or decrease in pay correct to 2 decimal places?

7. Find 0.05% of $750.

8. 68 is what percent of 544?

9. 392 is what percent of 147?

10. Factor.
    (a) $4a^2b + 8ab^3 + 16ab$
    (b) $5mr^2 + 15m^3r + \dfrac{10m^2}{3}$

11. Express $\frac{3}{8}$ as a decimal.

12. Express $\frac{1}{16}$ as a percent.

13. Express $\frac{5}{12}$ as a percent.

14. Solve for a.
    (a) $6(a + 2) = 4a - 6$
    (b) $10(10 - 4a) - 6(16 - 4a) = 0$
    (c) $\dfrac{a - 2}{10} - \dfrac{4 - a}{5} - \dfrac{10 - a}{2} = 0$

15. Using the formula $T = Ar$, find the following.
    (a) T when $A = \$10\,560$ and $r = \$0.085$
    (b) A when $T = \$1\,700$ and $r = \$0.065$

16. Find $12\frac{1}{2}\%$ of 984.

17. Multiply mentally.
    (a) 410×25 (b) 99×316

18. Divide mentally.
    (a) $3825 \div 25$ (b) $14\,250 \div 125$

19. Find $\frac{1}{2}\%$ of 360.

20. What number increased by 40% and the result decreased by 25% equals 504?

UNIT 5

Savings

A couple won $500 000 in the Provincial Lottery. They decided to deposit the winnings in a bank and collect 10% interest per annum. By doing this they reasoned they would never have to spend any of the $500 000 (*principal*), but could live very well off the interest for the rest of their lives. How can the bank afford to pay the couple so much interest every year?

As a consumer you also can deposit your savings with various institutions and receive interest on your deposit(s). Chartered banks are the most widely known savings institutions.

Although the chartered banks are the best known of the savings institutions, they do not always give you the *highest rate of interest* on your deposits. Trust companies often give a higher rate of interest on deposits than do chartered banks. Are there any trust companies in your community? Usually, the savings institution that will give you the highest rate of interest is the credit union. Most credit unions are associated with companies where people work, or with groups of people employed in a similar profession, such as a teachers' credit union. There are, however, independent credit unions for general membership. An important distinction between the credit union and the chartered banks and trust companies is that the credit union is a non-profit organization and generally is able, therefore, to offer higher rates of interest on deposits.

There are, of course, other avenues to explore before investing your money. Bonds, such as Canada Savings Bonds, usually yield a competitive rate of interest. Why does our government want you to invest your savings with them?

Another way to collect interest on your deposit or investment is to buy shares in a Canadian company. The rate of interest, called a *dividend*, depends on the success of the company. Why would companies want you to invest your money with them?

Before deciding where to deposit or invest your money, you have several decisions to make.

"If I need to have my money returned, how quickly can I get it?"

"Can I have small parts of my money returned if needed?"

"Where can I get the highest amount of interest?"

5.1   SIMPLE INTEREST

Interest is the price paid for the use of money. If you deposit cash in a bank, the bank will use your money and pay you interest. Interest can be expressed as the number of dollars earned but is more usually expressed as a rate or percent. For example, you can earn 8% on your savings. To compute *simple interest*, the factors are principal, rate, and time.

The *principal* is the amount deposited.
The *rate* is an annual rate unless expressed otherwise.
The *time* is expressed in years.

If the length of time is thirty days, it is shown as $\frac{30}{365}$. If the length of time is one year, it is shown as 1.

The formula for finding interest is

$I = Prt$

Machine Instruction	*Example 1* Find the interest on $600 at 12% for 2 a.

CLEAR

SET DEC 2

600

$\boxed{\times}$

0.12

$\boxed{\times}$

2

$\boxed{=}$

Solution

$I = Prt$
$\quad = 600 \times 0.12 \times 2$
$\quad = 144.00$

The interest is $144.

```
      600•×
      0•12×
        2•=
    144•00*
```

CLEAR

500

$\boxed{\times}$

0.115

$\boxed{\times}$

63

$\boxed{\div}$

365

$\boxed{=}$

Example 2
Find the interest on $500 at $11\frac{1}{2}$% for 63 d.

Solution
$I = Prt$
$\quad = 500 \times 0.115 \times \frac{63}{365}$
$\quad = $ ▆▆▆▆

```
      0•00*

      500•×
    0•115×
       63•÷
     365•=
     9•92*
```

CLEAR

800

$\boxed{\times}$

0.18

$\boxed{\times}$

13

$\boxed{\div}$

52

$\boxed{=}$

Example 3
Find the interest on $800 at 18% for 13 weeks.

Solution
$I = Prt$
$\quad = 800 \times 0.18 \times \frac{13}{52}$
$\quad = $ ▆▆▆▆

```
      0•00*

     800•×
     0•18×
      13•÷
      52•=
    36•00*
```

EXERCISE 5.1

1. Find the simple interest.

	Principal	Rate	Time
(a)	$ 1 500	18%	3 a
(b)	1 250	17%	146 d
(c)	675	$7\frac{1}{2}\%$	102 d
(d)	1 550	$12\frac{3}{4}\%$	7 months
(e)	1 600	$11\frac{1}{4}\%$	90 d
(f)	2 225	$8\frac{1}{4}\%$	6 months
(g)	3 450	$13\frac{3}{4}\%$	5 a
(h)	6 280	$10\frac{1}{8}\%$	219 d
(i)	10 560	19%	4 months
(j)	6 780	$9\frac{1}{2}\%$	185 d

2. Tom loaned $75 to his friend who promised to pay Tom back in six months plus interest at 10%. How much did Tom earn on his investment?

3. Revenue Canada was late sending Judy her rebate of $324.62 so interest at 6% was added to compensate for the rebate being 60 d late. How much did Judy receive?

4. What was the monthly simple interest earned on a promissory note for $1 200 if the rate was $9\frac{1}{2}\%$?

5. Nancy's mother gave her a $100 bond for her birthday. The bond paid interest semi-annually at the rate of $10\frac{3}{4}\%$ per annum. How much interest did Nancy earn the first six months?

Machine
Instruction

CLEAR

SET DEC 2

13

$\boxed{\times}$

12

$\boxed{\div}$

600

$\boxed{\div}$

2

$\boxed{\%}$

5.2   FINDING THE RATE

The formula for finding the rate at which the interest is earned is

$$r = \frac{I}{Pt}$$

Example
At what annual rate will $600 earn interest of $13.00 in 2 months?

Solution

$$r = \frac{I}{Pt}$$

$$= \frac{13}{600 \times \frac{2}{12}}$$

$$= 0.13$$

$$= 13\%$$

```
            0•00*

           13•×
           12•÷
          600•÷
            2•%
         13•00*
```

EXERCISE 5.2

1. Find the rate at which interest is earned, correct to 2 decimal places.

	Principal	Interest Earned	Time
(a)	$3 500	$1 890.00	4 a
(b)	1 800	46.60	90 d
(c)	500	16.00	73 d
(d)	2 340	6.83	1 month
(e)	3 560	1 080.00	2 a
(f)	6 820	595.20	219 d
(g)	4 220	151.92	146 d
(h)	675	4.25	1 month
(i)	2 890	1 560.00	5 a
(j)	3 240	279.45	6 months

2. Jason's bank added $5.92 interest to his account on April 1 based on his minimum quarterly balance of $364. What was the interest rate?

3. Susan's $1 000 bond paid her $52.50 every six months. What was the rate of the bond?

4. Gino received $95.20 in repayment of a load of $85 made one year ago.
   (a) how much interest did Gino earn?
   (b) What was the rate of interest?

5. Ella's bank added $18.65 interest to her account on October 1 based on her minimum quarterly balance of $785.32. What was the interest rate?

5.3 FINDING THE TIME

The formula for finding the time in which the interest is earned is

$$t = \frac{I}{Pr}$$

Example
In how many days will $800 earn $10.78 interest at 12% per annum?

Solution

$$t = \frac{I}{Pr}$$

$$= \frac{10.78}{800 \times 0.12}$$

= 0.11 (correct to 2 decimal places)

Machine Instruction

CLEAR

SET DEC 2

10.78

$\boxed{\div}$

800

$\boxed{\div}$

0.12

$\boxed{=}$

```
10•78÷
800•÷
0•12=
0•11✳
```

Remember that in our simple interest formula, *t* is expressed in years.

0.11 a = 0.11 × 365 d = 41 d (to the nearest day)

EXERCISE 5.3

1. Find the time in which interest is earned to the nearest day.

		Principal	Rate	Interest
	(a)	$4 250	17%	$ 360.00
	(b)	895	$14\frac{1}{2}$%	32.50
	(c)	1 725	$9\frac{1}{2}$%	550.00
	(d)	2 560	12%	92.50
	(e)	3 450	$9\frac{1}{4}$%	1 219.67
	(f)	5 700	$10\frac{1}{2}$%	985.50
	(g)	1 250	$16\frac{3}{4}$%	61.75
	(h)	375	$11\frac{1}{2}$%	26.80
	(i)	655	$17\frac{3}{4}$%	52.60
	(j)	2 120	$8\frac{3}{4}$%	324.90

2. Sean received $537.50 interest earned on his $5 000 savings bond. If the rate was $10\frac{3}{4}$%, what was the time?

3. A friend of René paid back the $200 René had lent him plus $18 in interest. If René aked for 10% interest how long was the loan outstanding?

4. When Sherrie examined her passbook some time after making her opening deposit of $500, she noticed that $8.13 interest had been added on July 1. Sherrie knew that the interest rate was $6\frac{1}{2}$%, but what was the period of time?

5. Interest at $11\frac{1}{2}$% on a $1 500 promissory note came to $43.95. What was the time of the note?

Machine
Instruction

CLEAR

SET DEC 2

55

×

365

÷

0.14

÷

146

=

5.4   FINDING THE PRINCIPAL

The formula for finding the principal that will earn the interest is

$$P = \frac{I}{rt}$$

Example
What principal at 14% per annum will earn $55 in 146 d?

Solution

$$P = \frac{I}{rt}$$

$$= \frac{55}{0.14 \times \frac{146}{365}}$$

$$= \frac{55 \times 365}{0.14 \times 146}$$

$$= 982.14$$

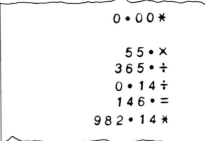

EXERCISE 5.4

1. Find, to the nearest dollar, the principal that will earn interest at the rate and in the time given.

	Interest	Rate	Time
(a)	$ 422.00	17%	2 a
(b)	19.50	9%	3 months
(c)	62.25	12%	219 d
(d)	1 592.50	10%	3 a
(e)	42.25	$16\frac{1}{4}$%	146 d
(f)	560.00	$9\frac{3}{4}$%	6 months
(g)	32.80	$14\frac{1}{2}$%	90 d
(h)	2 340.00	$13\frac{1}{4}$%	5 a
(i)	255.00	$8\frac{3}{4}$%	186 d
(j)	68.70	$9\frac{1}{2}$%	292 d

2. A ten month investment earned $52.50 at $12\frac{1}{2}$%. How much was the investment?

3. How much did Mary lend Aaron three years ago if Aaron repaid her in full plus interest of $399 at 14%?

4. The latest entry in Marylou's passbook was $12.86 interest on her deposit made one month earlier. If the bank interest rate was $8\frac{3}{4}$%, how much was Marylou's deposit?

5. Kellie wanted to buy a bond giving her a regular income of $300 every six months. If the going rate was 12%, what value of a bond should she buy?

5.5   FINDING A FUTURE AMOUNT

Sometimes you want to know how much you should invest now in order to have a certain sum at some time in the future.

Example
What principal will amount to $1 773.75 if invested at 15% for 146 d?

Solution
Amount (A) = Principal (P) + Interest (I)

$$A = P + I$$
$$= P + Prt$$
$$A = P(1 + rt)$$

$I = Prt$

In this case we want to find the principal.

Machine
Instruction

CLEAR

SET DEC 3

0.15

146

$\boxed{\div}$

365

$\boxed{\text{M}+}$

1

$\boxed{\text{M}+}$

1 773.75

$\boxed{\div}$

$\boxed{\text{RM}}$

$\boxed{=}$

$\boxed{\text{CM}}$

$$P = \frac{A}{1 + rt}$$

$$= \frac{1\ 773.75}{1 + (0.15 \times \frac{146}{365})}$$

$$= \frac{1\ 773.75}{1 + (0.06)}$$

$$= \frac{1\ 773.75}{1.06}$$

$$= 1\ 673.35$$

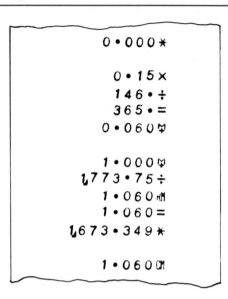

EXERCISE 5.5

1. Given an amount (principal + interest), find the principal when you also know the rate and time.

	Amount	Rate	Time
(a)	$8 640.50	$8\frac{3}{4}\%$	146 d
(b)	5 225.00	$9\frac{1}{2}\%$	90 d
(c)	1 465.50	12%	2 months
(d)	560.00	$11\frac{3}{4}\%$	1 a
(e)	985.75	14%	219 d

2. A bank passbook showed that $83.18 was added to Kim's account on October 20. The last balance in the account was dated April 20 and was $1 752.20. What was the rate of interest Kim was receiving?

3. An amount of $1 500 is left on deposit to earn interest at the rate of 13% per annum. Calculate the interest earned if the money is deposited in full on November 20 and is left until February 20.

4. Bond interest amounted to $157.50 when a coupon was cashed one year after the bond was purchased. If the bond bore interest at $15\frac{3}{4}\%$, what was the principal amount of the bond?

5. How long will it take for a $1 500 deposit to earn $200 interest at 9% per annum?

6. Mrs. Kostiuk decided to auction her house and contents and move into a rest home. Because of income tax entanglements she did not receive the proceeds of the auction until one year later. At that time she received a cheque for $46 906.50 and was told this included interest for one year at 12% per annum. How much did she receive from the auction?

5.6   COMPOUND INTEREST

The interest discussed up to now is called simple interest. If you deposit $100 in a savings account paying interest at 12%, calculated quarterly, the first interest payment of $3 is simple interest. That $3 is then added to your account balance and the next time interest is calculated it will be $3.09 ($103 × 0.12 × $\frac{1}{4}$).

When interest is calculated and added to a previous balance at regular intervals we say it is *compounded*. The total interest earned is the *compound interest*. The total amount, after interest is calculated and added, is the *compound amount*.

Compound Amount = Original Principal + Compound Interest

If you invested $100 at 12% per annum for ten years, your money would earn $120 simple interest. Your investment would be worth $220 in ten years.

$100 × 0.12 × 10

However, if you invested your $100 at 12% per annum compound interest, your investment would amount to $310.58 in ten years. The interest of $210.58 is 75% more than the $120 earned at simple interest. This is a significant increase. Let's see how it is done.

Example 1
If $1 is invested at 12% per annum, and the interest due at the end of each interest period is added to the principal, and the interest for the next interest period is calculated on that new principal, what will be the amount at the end of ten years?

Solution
Principal at start of 1st year = $1.00
Interest on $1 at 12% for 1 a =   0.12

Amount at end of 1st year   =   1.12 $(1 + 0.12)$
Interest on $1.12 for 1 a   =   0.134 4

Amount at end of 2nd year =   1.254 4 $(1 + 0.12)(1 + 0.12)$ **$(1 + 0.12)^2$**
Interest on $1.254 4 for 1 a =   0.150 528

Amount at end of 3rd year =   1.404 928 $(1 + 0.12)^3$
Similarly
Amount at end of four years = $(1 + 0.12)^4$
Amount at end of five years = $(1 + 0.12)^5$
Amount at end of ten years = $(1 + 0.12)^{10}$

There are prepared tables to help us calculate these amounts. Look at Table 1 in the back of the book. This is a table giving the amounts to which $1 will accumulate at i rate of interest per interest period in n interest periods. The *interest period* is the time used to calculate interest. For example, if interest is calculated semi-annually, the interest period is 6 months and there are 2 interest periods in 1 year. The letter n is used to represent the number of interest periods.

Since interest in Example 1 is calculated annually, $n = 10$. Find 10 in the column headed n and go across the row to the column headed 12%. The number is 3.105 84, which is the amount that $1 will accumulate to if compounded annually for ten years at 12%.

Since the amount of $1 at the end of ten years is 3.105 84, the amount of $100 compounded annually for ten years is $100 \times 3.105\ 84$, which equals $310.58.

Example 2

$(1 + 0.06)^{20}$

Interest compounded semi-annually at 12% for ten years would have 20 interest periods and the rate per interest period would be 6%.

Example 3

$(1 + 0.03)^{40}$

Interest compounded quarterly at 12% for ten years would have 40 interest periods and the rate per interest period would be 3%.

EXERCISE 5.6

State the value for n and i in each of the following cases.

	Compounded	Annual Interest Rate	Time
1.	Annually	10%	6 a
2.	Semi-annually	12%	5 a
3.	Semi-annually	11%	$3\frac{1}{2}$ a
4.	Quarterly	14%	11 a
5.	Quarterly	10%	4 a, 3 months

5.7 NOMINAL AND EFFECTIVE RATES FOR COMPOUND INTEREST

The *nominal* rate is the quoted rate.

The *effective* rate is the true rate.

When the nominal rate is calculated more than once a year, the effective rate is higher. For example, 12% calculated quarterly results in more interest earned than 12% calculated yearly.

Example

Find the effective rate of interest when the nominal rate of 12% is compounded quarterly.

Solution

From Table 1, the amount of $1 compounded quarterly at 12% for one year is 1.125 51.

The interest on $1 is $0.125 51 or 12.55%.

The nominal rate of 12% per annum becomes 12.55% when compounded quarterly.

EXERCISE 5.7

Find the effective rate of interest for the following nominal rates.

	Nominal Rate	*Compounded*
(a)	12%	Semi-annually
(b)	12%	Quarterly
(c)	12%	Monthly
(d)	10%	Quarterly
(e)	16%	Semi-annually
(f)	16%	Quarterly
(g)	8%	Semi-annually
(h)	9%	Semi-annually

5.8 AMOUNT

$$A = P(1 + i)^n$$

This is the formula used for calculating the amount (A) that the principal (P) will accumulate to at i rate of interest per interest period for n interest periods.

Example 1

Find the amount of $600 compounded semi-annually for 5 a at 12%.

Machine Instruction

Solution

$P = \$600$

$i = 0.06$ (12% per year = 6% per half year)

$n = 10$ (5 × 2)

$A = P(1 + i)^n$

$\quad = 600(1.06)^{10}$

$\quad = 600 \times 1.790\ 85$ (Table 1)

$\quad = \$1\ 074.51$

CLEAR

SET DEC 2

600

1.790 85

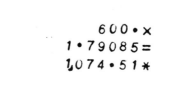

Example 2

Find the amount of $750 compounded annually for $6\frac{1}{2}$ a at 18%.

Solution

$P = \$750$

$i = 18\%$

$n = 6\frac{1}{2}$

Since the tables do not give the amount for $6\frac{1}{2}$ a, we must find the amount for 6 a and multiply that figure by the rate for $\frac{1}{2}$ a. Since the rate per year is 18%, the rate per half year is 9%.

$A = 750(1.18)^6(1.09)$

$\quad = 750(2.699\ 55) \times 1.09$

$\quad = \$2\ 206.88$

Example 3
Find the accumulated amount when $1 000 is invested at 12% compounded annually for 5 a and 2 months.

Solution
Rate for 2 months = rate for $\frac{1}{6}$ a

$$= \frac{12\%}{6} = 2\%$$

$$\begin{aligned}
A &= P(1 + i)^n \\
&= 1\ 000(1.12)^5 \times (1.02) \\
&= 1\ 000(1.762\ 34) \times (1.02) \\
&= 1\ 762.34 \times 1.02 \\
&= \$1\ 797.59
\end{aligned}$$

EXERCISE 5.8
1. Find the accumulated amount for each of the following.

	Principal	Rate per Annum	Compounded	Time
(a)	$4 000	16%	annually	8 a
(b)	6 000	9%	semi-annually	7 a
(c)	2 000	10%	quarterly	10 a
(d)	3 000	16%	annually	$15\frac{1}{2}$ a
(e)	5 000	12%	quarterly	12 a
(f)	2 000	18%	annually	20 a, 3 months
(g)	8 650	10%	quarterly	3 a, 9 months

2. Sally Silverstein invested $800 at $1\frac{1}{2}$% per month. How much did she have at the end of two years?

3. Jack Boudreau deposited $850 in an account that paid 18% interest calculated every half year. If Jack left his money, including interest, in the account, what would his balance be at the end of $8\frac{1}{2}$ a?

4. When Martine Van Doo died she bequeathed $700 000 to her favorite university to be used for a new science building. Since that sum was not enough, the university invested it at 12% compounded annually to raise additional funds. Three years later the university was ready to begin construction. To how much had Martine's bequest amounted?

5.9   PRESENT VALUE

You now know how to find the amount to which a given sum of money, or principal, will accumulate. This principal is called the *present value* (*PV*). It is the value *now* as compared to the amount of future value.

Example 1
Mr. Stalker wants to invest a sum of money now so that he will have $4 000 in ten years time to help pay for his child's college courses. If the money is compounded at 12% per annum, how much must Mr. Stalker invest?

Solution
Since $A = P(1 + i)^n$, then $P = \dfrac{A}{(1 + i)^n}$

$$PV = \frac{A}{(1 + i)^n}$$

$$= A \times \frac{1}{(1 + i)^n}$$

$\dfrac{1}{(1 + i)^n}$ is the present value of \$1 compounded for n interest periods at i rate of interest per interest period. This value is given in Table 2 in the back of this book.

$$PV = A \times \frac{1}{(1 + i)^n}$$

$$= 4\,000 \times \frac{1}{(1.12)^{10}}$$

$$= 4\,000 \times 0.321\,97$$

$$= \$1\,287.88$$

```
0•00✶

4,000•×
0•32197=
1,287•88✶
```

Mr. Stalker must invest \$1 287.88 now to have \$4 000 in ten years time.

Example 2
What principal will amount to \$2 500 if compounded semi-annually for eight years at 9% per annum?

Solution
$A = 2\,500$
$i = 0.045$ (9% per year $= 4\frac{1}{2}$% per half year)
$n = 16$ (twice a year for 8 a)
$$PV = A \times \frac{1}{(1.045)^{16}}$$

$$= 2\,500 \times 0.494\,47$$

$$= \$1\,236.18$$

Example 3
What principal compounded annually at 12% will amount to \$3 000 at the end of $7\frac{1}{2}$ a?

Solution
To find PV for $7\frac{1}{2}$ a, first find the PV for 7 a, and then multiply by the PV for $\frac{1}{2}$ a. Since the rate per year is 12%, the rate per half year is 6%.

$$PV = A \times \frac{1}{(1 + i)^n}$$

$$= 3\,000 \times \frac{1}{(1.12)^7} \times \frac{1}{(1.06)}$$

$$= 3\,000 \times 0.452\,35 \times 0.943\,4$$

$$= \$1\,280.24$$

EXERCISE 5.9

1. Find the present value for each of the following.

	Amount	Rate per Annum	Compounded	Time
(a)	$10 000	18%	annually	5 a
(b)	500	9%	annually	6 a
(c)	3 500	16%	annually	$10\frac{1}{2}$ a
(d)	3 000	12%	monthly	4 a
(e)	9 800	10%	quarterly	3 a

2. Brenda Wilco wants to be able to pay her mortgage in full when it comes up for renewal in five years time. She figures that she will owe $8 700. How much should she invest now if money is compounded semi-annually at 12%?

3. Alice Sims has borrowed a sum of money from her bank. She must repay $800 in six years. What is the present value of the loan if money is compounded quarterly at 10%?

4. James Blakey has promised to give each of his children $1 000 on their 21st birthdays. His children will be 8, 10, and 12 this year. What is the total amount he will have to invest this year if money is worth 12% compounded semi-annually?

5. Mr. and Mrs. de Vries plan to take a world cruise in $12\frac{1}{2}$ years time. How much will they have to invest now if they plan to spend $14 000 and money is compounded quartly at 14%?

6. Dagmar wants to have $100 to spend on a gift for her parents' 25th wedding anniversary in six years time. How much will she have to invest now if she can get interest at 15% compounded semi-annually.

5.10 ANNUITIES

Many people plan regular savings so that they can avoid making purchases on credit. A series of equal payments or deposits made at equal intervals of time is called an annuity. For example, a deposit of $100 at the end of each month for five years is an ordinary annuity. We will be concerned with ordinary annuities only in this unit.

Examples
- Deposits made at the end of each month for a trip in five years
- Pension payments received at the end of each month for life
- A scholarship received at the end of each year for four years

The *payment period* of an annuity is the time between equal payments. The *rent* is the amount of each regular payment. The *term* is the time from the beginning of the first payment period to the end of the last payment period.

To find the amount to which an ordinary annuity will accumulate, first consider the amount to which a series of payments of $1 paid at the end of each year for three years accumulate if compounded annually at 12% per annum.

Now	End of one year	End of two years	End of three years

Amount of last payment _____ = $1.00

Amount to which $1 will accumulate in 1 a at 12% _____ $(1.12)^1 =$ 1.12

Amount to which $1 will accumulate in 2 a at 12% _____ $(1.12)^2 =$ 1.254 4

The amount to which a series of payments of $1 at the end of each year for 3 a will accumulate _____ = $3.374 4

Amount for three years = $(1.12)^2 + (1.12)$ + 1
Amount for four years = $(1.12)^3 + (1.12)^2 + (1.12)$ + 1
Amount for ten years = $(1.12)^9 + (1.12)^8 \ldots (1.12)$ + 1
Amount for n years = $(1.12)^{n-1} + (1.12)^{n-2} \ldots (1.12)$ + 1

The amounts $(s_{\overline{n}|i})$ of an ordinary annuity of $1 at i rate per interest period for n interest periods can be found in Table 3 at the back of the book.

Using Table 3, find the amount of an ordinary annuity of $1 at i rate for n periods for each of the following.

	Regular Payment	Rate per Annum	Compounded	Time
1.	$1	8%	annually	8 a
2.	$1	16%	annually	15 a
3.	$1	12%	semi-annually	14 a
4.	$1	12%	quarterly	7 a
5.	$1	14%	quarterly	11 a

To find the amount (A_n) to which an ordinary annuity greater than $1 will accumulate at i rate per interest period for n interest periods, simply multiply the amount of an ordinary annuity of $1 by the regular payment or rent (R).

$A_n = Rs_{\overline{n}|i}$

Example 1
Juno Martini deposited $600 at the end of every year for ten years. What is the accumulated amount if interest was compounded annually at 12%?

Solution

$R = \$600$
$i = 0.12$
$n = 10$

$A_n = R(s_{\overline{n}|i})$
$ = 600(s_{\overline{10}|0.12})$
$ = 600 \times 17.548\ 67$
$ = 10\ 529.202$
$ = \$10\ 529.20$

Example 2

If Juno had deposited $300 at the end of every six months, how much would she have in ten years?

Solution

$R = \$300$

$i = 0.06$ (12% per year = 6% per half year)

$n = 20$ (twice a year for 10 a)

$A_n = R(s_{\overline{n}|i})$

$\quad = 300\,(s_{\overline{20}|0.06})$

$\quad = 300 \times 36.785\ 59$

$\quad = 11\ 035.677$

$\quad = \$11\ 035.68$

EXERCISE 5.10

1. Find the amount to which the following annuities will accumulate.

	Payment	Frequency of Payments	Annual Rate	Compounded	Time
(a)	$100	yearly	8%	annually	6 a
(b)	350	half-yearly	12%	semi-annually	13 a
(c)	50	yearly	16%	annually	12 a
(d)	100	half-yearly	18%	semi-annually	10 a
(e)	200	quarterly	10%	quarterly	$10\frac{1}{2}$ a

2. Hendrik Schievink wishes to leave some money to his college when he dies. He invests $2 500 at the end of each year until his death occurs eighteen years later. How much will his college receive if money is worth 8% compounded annually?

3. Karen deposits $400 every six months with her credit union, which pays 16% compounded semi-annually. How much will she have accumulated in thirteen years?

4. Ken and Judy May receive $266.80 every month from a four year mortgage they hold. If they invest this money every month at 12% compounded monthly, how much will their investment be worth when the mortgage is fully paid?

5. When Lucia was 9, her mother began depositing $100 every three months in an account paying interest at 18% compounded quarterly. How much money will be in the account when Lucia starts university at age 18?

6. Bert and Katrina are just married. They plan to live in an apartment for five years and then buy a house. In order to have a down payment they decide to invest $400 every three months in an account paying 12% compounded quarterly. How much money will they have for their down payment?

5.11   ANNUITIES – FINDING THE PAYMENT

In the preceding section you found the amount to which an ordinary annuity would accumulate. Here, you will find the reverse, the ordinary annuity (R) that will accumulate to a given amount (A_n) at i rate per interest period for n interest periods.

$$A_n = R(s_{\overline{n}|i})$$

Therefore

$$R = \frac{A_n}{s_{\overline{n}|i}} \text{ or } R = A_n \times \frac{1}{s_{\overline{n}|i}}$$

The values for $\frac{1}{s_{\overline{n}|i}}$ are found in Table 4.

Example
Jacqueline LeBlanc wishes to deposit a sum of money every year so as to have \$20 000 in ten years. How much will she have to deposit if interest is compounded annually at 12%.

Solution

$A_n = \$20\ 000$

$n = 10$

$i = 0.12$

$R = A_n \times \frac{1}{s_{\overline{n}|i}}$

$ = 20\ 000 \times \frac{1}{s_{\overline{10}|0.12}}$

$ = 20\ 000 \times 0.56\ 98$

$ = \$1\ 139.60$

EXERCISE 5.11

1. Find the annuity that will accumulate to a given amount at the rate and term specified.

	Amount	Annual Rate	Compounded	Term
(a)	\$ 1 000	14%	quarterly	10 a
(b)	1 450	12%	semi-annually	6 a
(c)	25 000	12%	quarterly	8 a
(d)	1 500	16%	semi-annually	$6\frac{1}{2}$ a
(e)	700	9%	annually	30 a

2. The town of Endsville has to redeem bonds valued at \$30 000 in fifteen years. How much would they have to invest at the end of each year if money is worth 9% compounded annually?

3. What amount of money should be invested at the end of every six months for $7\frac{1}{2}$ a to amount to \$9 350 if money is compounded semi-annually at 16%?

4. Olif has promised to pay a creditor \$950 at the end of two years. How much should he deposit monthly in an account paying 12% per year compounded monthly?

5. Mr. and Mrs. Sawyer will be retiring in eight years. They plan to spend $10 000 on a cruise at that time. How much should they invest every six months if money is worth 12% compounded semi-annually?

6. In a certain investment institution money is worth 18% compounded quarterly. How much should be deposited every three months in order to accumulate $6 500 at the end of twelve years and three months?

5.12   ANNUITIES – FINDING THE PRESENT VALUE

Since an annuity is a *series* of payments, we must first find the amount to which the annuity will accumulate and then we can easily find the present value of that amount.

Example
Find the present value of an ordinary annuity of $100 paid at the end of each year for six years if interest is compounded at 12% annually.

Solution
(a) To find the amount of an annuity of $100 compounded at 12% per year for six years.

$$A_n = R(s_{\overline{n}|i})$$
$$= 100 \times s_{\overline{6}|0.12}$$
$$= 100 \times 8.115\ 17$$
$$= \$811.517$$

(b) To find the present value of $811.517 when interest is compounded at 12% for six years.

$$PV = A \times \frac{1}{(1 + i)^n}$$
$$= 811.517 \times \frac{1}{(1.12)^6}$$
$$= 811.517 \times 0.506\ 63$$
$$= \$411.14$$

The calculation of present value of an ordinary annuity is made easier by using Table 5 at the back of the book. This table gives the values for the present value of an annuity of $1 at i rate of interest per interest period for n interest periods and is represented by $a_{\overline{n}|i}$.

$$PV = Ra_{\overline{n}|i}$$
$$= 100a_{\overline{6}|0.12}$$
$$= 100 \times 4.111\ 42$$
$$= \$411.14$$

This answer is the same as the one obtained in Example 4, part (b).

EXERCISE 5.12

1. Find the present value of the ordinary annuities listed below with their rates and times.

	Rent	Annual Rate	Paid and Compounded	Terms in Years
(a)	$ 80	8%	annually	10
(b)	100	16%	semi-annually	12
(c)	50	14%	quarterly	9
(d)	3 500	12%	semi-annually	15
(e)	300	10%	quarterly	11

2. Eileen Baker has just learned that she will receive $2 500 every six months for 25 years as a bequest from her late father. If interest is compounded semi-annually at 16% per annum, how much is the bequest worth now?

3. Clare Brussells wishes to provide a scholarship of $500 per year for twenty years. How much must she put into the fund now if it will earn interest at 10% per year compounded annually?

4. Eugene has a choice of two annuities. Annuity A pays $500 each month for three years. Annuity B pays $1 000 each half year for twenty-two years. If money is worth 12%, which annuity would cost less now? (In each case, money is compounded at the end of each payment period.)

5. Cawley sells a house to Burns who promises to pay $5 000 down and $1 500 including interest and principal at the end of every six months for eighteen years. If money is worth 16% compounded semi-annually, what is the purchase price of the house?

6. Denise borrowed a sum of money from her parents so that she could buy a new motorcycle. She promised to pay her parents $100 at the end of each month for ten months. If money is worth 18% compounded monthly, how much did Denise borrow?

5.13 ANNUITIES – FINDING AN ORDINARY ANNUITY GIVEN ITS PRESENT VALUE

If you ever win a sum of money in a lottery you might want to invest it in a fund that would pay you a fixed amount of money at regular intervals. To find the amount of the regular payment (R) you rearrange the formula for finding present value of an ordinary annuity at i rate of interest per interest period for n periods.

$$PV = R\,(a_{\overline{n}|i})$$

Therefore

$$R = \frac{PV}{a_{\overline{n}|i}} \quad \text{or} \quad R = PV \times \frac{1}{a_{\overline{n}|i}}$$

Table 6 gives the value of an annuity that $1 will buy at i rate of interest per interest period for n interest periods and is represented by $\frac{1}{a_{\overline{n}|i}}$.

Example
Vito Roselli invested $30 000 to provide a pension for twenty years. If money was worth 12% compounded annually, how much did Vito receive at the end of each year?

Solution
PV = $30 000
n = 20
i = 0.12

$$R = PV \times \frac{1}{a_{\overline{n}|i}}$$

$$= 30\ 000 \times \frac{1}{a_{\overline{20}|0.12}}$$

$$= 30\ 000 \times 0.133\ 88$$

$$= \$4\ 016.40$$

EXERCISE 5.13

1. Find the ordinary annuity that would be provided for by the following present values at the rates and times indicated.

	Present Value	Annual Rate	Paid and Compounded	Time in Years
(a)	$50 000	10%	annually	13
(b)	3 000	9%	semi-annually	20
(c)	2 500	14%	quarterly	10
(d)	10 000	16%	semi-annually	15
(e)	400	12%	quarterly	10

2. Francine planned to rent a house to a tenant and pay off the $18 500 mortgage out of the rent she received over a period of $11\frac{1}{2}$ years. What portion of quarterly rent will Francine use to increase her investment if money is worth 14% compounded quarterly?

3. How much would Jerry James receive each month from his investment of $5 000 if interest was compounded monthly at 12% and he took $3\frac{1}{2}$ years to withdraw all the money?

4. Mr. and Mrs. Chen invested $63 000 in a pension that would provide a regular quarterly payment for twelve years. What would be the amount of each payment if money was worth 16% compounded quarterly?

5. Sam Allistair invested $5 000 to provide an athletic prize for his favorite high school. If the prize was to be awarded at the end of each year for 35 years, and money was worth 10% compounded annually, how much would each winner receive?

6. An investment of $8 500 bearing interest at 14% per annum, is to be repaid in equal instalments at the end of each half year for 17 years. What is the amount of the half-yearly income?

5.14   BANKS AND OTHER FINANCIAL INSTITUTIONS

Chartered banks, trust companies, and credit unions compete for your savings dollar by offering a wide variety of accounts and services. It is wise to investigate before you decide where to open an account. Sometimes the extra services offered will outweigh a slight difference in how much your money will earn in interest.

There are three basic types of consumer accounts and all others are variations or combinations of these three. Different financial institutions may use different names for these accounts.

A   Personal Chequing Account

This is a popular account for persons who pay most of their bills by cheque and write quite a few cheques every month.

Features
- No interest is earned on your deposits.
- You receive a monthly statement showing the increases and decreases in your account.
- Your cancelled cheques are returned with the statement.
- You receive a free personal record book.
- You receive plain personalized cheques free of charge.
- The charge for these services is a flat monthly fee or a small charge for each cheque written depending on the institution.

B   Chequing Savings Account

This account is for people who write very few cheques each month and wish to have only one account.

Features
- Interest is calculated daily and added to your account monthly, or calculated monthly on either your average monthly balance or your lowest monthly balance and added to your account semi-annually.
- You receive a monthly statement.
- No cancelled cheques are returned with the statement.
- You receive a free personal record book.
- There is usually a charge for your blank cheques.
- Service charges may be a fixed monthly fee or a charge for each cheque issued.
- Some institutions offer a limited number of free cheques if a minimum balance is maintained in the account.

Example

Southvale Bank allows chequing savings customers to write one free cheque for every $100 in their lowest balance per month. The charge for each additional cheque is 29¢. In addition, the bank pays interest at the rate of 4% per annum calculated monthly on the lowest balance of the month. Here is the latest page from Russ Petrovic's personal record book.

CHEQUE NO.	DATE 19--		PARTICULARS	AMOUNT OF CHEQUE		✓	AMOUNT OF DEPOSIT		BALANCE	
									572	60
42	June	21	Eaton's	14	95				557	65
43		24	July rent	295	00				262	65
44		25	Spending money	125	00				137	65
		28	Weekly pay				310	00	447	65
45		29	Phone bill	32	60				415	05
		30	Interest					46	415	51
		30	Service charges		87				414	64

Note that Russ adds deposits to the previous balance and subtracts cheques.

The interest on June 30 was 4% of $137.65, which was the lowest balance during the month. Russ was allowed one free cheque because he had one $100 in his lowest balance. He was charged 29¢ each for the other three cheques.

1. The following shows cheques and deposits for July. Fill in the balance column, interest, and service charges for Russ.

CHEQUE NO.	DATE 19--		PARTICULARS	AMOUNT OF CHEQUE		✓	AMOUNT OF DEPOSIT		BALANCE	
									414	64
46	July	15	Visa	58	93					
47		24	August rent	295	00					
		28	Weekly pay				310	00		
48		29	Phone bill	42	65					
		31	Interest							
		31	Service charges							

C Savings Account

This type of account is for people who want a higher rate of interest than they would receive on a chequing savings account and who do not intend to use the account for chequing.

Features
- You receive a passbook showing increases and decreases in your account.
- The passbook is updated by the bank after each transaction.
- All withdrawals are made in person.
- Interest may be calculated on your lowest monthly balance or on your average monthly balance and added to your account monthly or semi-annually.
- Interest may be calculated on your daily balance at a slightly lower rate and added monthly. For example, a bank might offer 9% calculated monthly and $8\frac{1}{2}$% calculated daily.

Example
Karen Paige's bank pays interest semi-annually, calculated monthly on the lowest monthly balance, at the rate of 10% per annum. Below is a page from Karen's passbook.

DATE		WITHDRAWALS	DEPOSITS/ INTEREST	BALANCE
19--				
April	2			1 400 00
	10		200 00	1 600 00
May	10		200 00	1 800 00
	18	50 00		1 750 00
June	9		100 00	1 850 00
July	15	350 00		1 500 00
	30		80 00	1 580 00
Aug.	10		200 00	1 780 00
Sept.	10		200 00	1 980 00
	17	100 00		1 880 00
Oct.	1		80 08	1 960 08

After each transaction, the bank teller inserts the passbook, with the transaction information, into a machine. The machine prints the amount of the deposit or withdrawal and prints the new balance. As in the personal record book of Russ Petrovic, the deposits are added to the previous balance and the withdrawals are subtracted.

Interest calculation

April	$1\ 400 \times 0.1/12 =$	$11.67
May	$1\ 600 \times 0.1/12 =$	13.33
June	$1\ 750 \times 0.1/12 =$	14.58
July	$1\ 500 \times 0.1/12 =$	12.50
August	$1\ 580 \times 0.1/12 =$	13.17
September	$1\ 780 \times 0.1/12 =$	14.83
		$80.08

1. Complete Karen's passbook for the next six months.

DATE		WITHDRAWALS		DEPOSITS/ INTEREST		BALANCE	
19--							
Oct.	1					1 960	08
	15			150	00		
Nov.	19	25	00				
	23	18	00				
Dec.	8	50	00				
	10	35	00				
Jan.	20			100	00		
Feb.	6			100	00		
Mar.	15	50	00				
Apr.	1						

D   Combination or Multi-Level Accounts

Some financial institutions are offering accounts that combine the features of the basic three. These are very popular with people who want chequing privileges and interest on their savings in just one account. The name of the account varies from bank to bank but all have similar features.

Features
- No charge chequing.
- Low daily interest if your average monthly balance is less than a stated minimum, usually $1 000 or $2 000.
- Higher daily interest if your average monthly balance is over the minimum.
- Choice of record keeping options
  - (a) • No statement and no return of cancelled cheques
    - Small charge for any cancelled cheques retrieved from storage by the bank for your inspection
  - (b) • Monthly statement
    - Return of cancelled cheques
    - Small fee for returning the cheques
  - (c) • Descriptive monthly statement identifying cheques so that there is no need for the return of cancelled cheques
    - Fee for retrieval of cancelled cheques

E   Special Accounts

These accounts offer customers additional banking services for a fixed monthly fee. Some examples are the Commerce Key Account, the Bank of Nova Scotia's Scotia Club and Royal Trust's Select Card. Services offered include some or all of the following:

- unlimited chequing
- monthly statement and return of cancelled cheques
- free or reduced cost safety deposit box
- no charge for purchase of traveller's cheques
- overdraft protection to a stated maximum, usually $100
- no charge for payment of utility and gasoline charge card bills
- access to your account through any branch

INTEREST RATES PAID ON ACCOUNTS

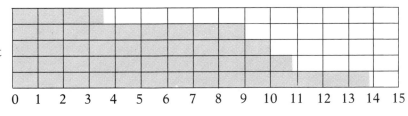

Account

Chequing Savings
Straight Savings
30 d Term Deposit
1 a Term Deposit
5 a Term Deposit

0   1   2   3   4   5   6   7   8   9   10   11   12   13   14   15

Interest Rate

EXERCISE 5.14

1. The Stoney Creek bank pays interest semi-annually, calculated at 9% monthly on the lowest monthly balance. Jim Schwartz had a balance of $2 540.63 including interest on April 2. Jim deposited $100 on April 30, $150 on May 25, $100 on June 30, $200 on July 25, and $100 on September 30. His withdrawals were $50 on June 10, $50 on July 15, and $400 on August 14. Write the entries in Jim's passbook including interest on October 1.

2. On April 30, Mila opened a new account paying $8\frac{1}{2}$% daily interest added on the first day of every month. If she deposited $1 000 and made no further deposits or withdrawals during May, how much did she have in her bank account at the end of the business day June 1?

3. If Mila in Question 2 made no further withdrawals or deposits for six months, how much would she have in her account at the close of business on November 1?

4. Pierre opened an account paying 9% interest calculated on the lowest monthly balance and paid semi-annally. If he started his account on the same day that Mila did, with a deposit of $1 000, how much would he have in his account at the close of business on November 1?

5. Joan has a personal chequing account. Last month she wrote 16 cheques. Find her service charge if her bank charges 30¢ per cheque.

6. Harry's bank charges only 28¢ per cheque. During April he wrote 24 cheques. How much was his service charge?

7. Brian has a chequing saving account. Interest is paid semi-annually and calculated on the lowest monthly balance at the rate of 4% per annum. There is a service charge of 29¢ per cheque deducted monthly. After the last interest payment on April 1, Brian had a balance of $342.78. He made regular deposits of $100 at the end of every month. In addition he deposited $35 on May 14 and $82 on August 10. He also wrote a cheque for $135 on June 13 and for $98 on July 2. What was the balance in Brian's account at the close of business on October 1?

8. Rudi has a personal chequing account. He writes an average of 16 cheques per month. If his service charges average $4.48, how much does his bank charge for each cheque written?

9. Rhonda has a personal chequing account and wrote 14 cheques last month. If her trust company charges 32¢ per cheque, how much will her service charge be?

10. Jill has a chequing savings account that pays $4\frac{1}{2}$% per annum calculated monthly on the lowest monthly balance. Her bank charges 30¢ for every cheque written over the free number of cheques of one for every $100 in her lowest monthly balance. Last month her lowest monthly balance was $342.68. During the month Jill made three deposits and wrote six cheques.
(a) How much interest did Jill's money earn?
(b) How much was Jill's service charge?

5.15   TERM DEPOSITS

Term deposits, sometimes called guaranteed investment certificates (G.I.C.), pay higher interest rates than savings accounts. This is because the depositor guarantees to leave the money on deposit for a specific period of time and the bank or trust company guarantees to pay interest at a certain rate for that time. You may choose a 30 d, 60 d, 90 d, one, two, three, four, five, or six year term. If you invest in a five year term deposit at $13\frac{1}{2}$%, you will receive $13\frac{1}{2}$% on your investment every year for five years even if savings account rates drop to 6%. Of course, if savings account rates rise to 14%, you will still get $13\frac{1}{2}$% on your term deposit.

A minimum deposit is usually required. This minimum ranges from $500 to $5 000 depending on the term, rate of interest, and time of interest period that you choose.

Interest may be calculated at maturity, monthly, semi-annually, or annually, and added to your bank or trust account or mailed to your home.

Term deposits are locked in to maturity or redeemable for a penalty. This means that once you have invested your savings in a term deposit you must leave it there for the time of the term or pay a penalty.

Term deposits are a safe investment and you have the advantage of always knowing exactly how much your investment is earning.

Example

James Pawley invested $5 000 in a 60 d term deposit paying $11\frac{1}{2}\%$ per annum calculated at maturity. How much interest did James earn?

Solution

Interest = $5 000 × 0.115 × $\frac{60}{365}$

       = $94.52

EXERCISE 5.15

Calculate the interest earned on the following term deposits.

	Deposit	*Term*	*Rate*	*Calculated*
(a)	$5 000.00	60 d	$10\frac{1}{2}\%$	at maturity
(b)	600.00	5 a	$13\frac{1}{2}\%$	annually
(c)	2 500.00	2 a	13%	semi-annually
(d)	1 750.00	90 d	$11\frac{1}{2}\%$	at maturity
(e)	873.00	5 a	$10\frac{3}{4}\%$	semi-annually
(f)	8 000.00	4 a	$12\frac{3}{4}\%$	monthly

5.16   OTHER WAYS TO INVEST YOUR SAVINGS

Some people prefer to invest their savings in a form other than savings accounts or term deposits. We will examine some of these ways briefly.

A   Bonds

A bond is a printed promise to pay a certain sum of money at a certain future date together with interest at a stated rate at regular intervals. When you buy a bond you are actually lending money to the government or to a corporation and you become a creditor or bondholder.

The face value is the value printed on the bond or its *denomination*. It is usually $100 or some multiple of $100.

Bond interest is a percent of the face value and may be paid quarterly, semi-annually, or annually.

Example 1

Find the semi-annual interest on a $1 000, $10\frac{1}{2}\%$ bond.

Solution

Interest = 1 000 × 0.105 × 0.5

       = $52.50

The *maturity date* is the date the borrower will pay the face amount of the bond.

The *market price* is the price the bond is selling at. Prices are quoted per $100 of face value.

Example 2

A $1 000 bond selling at 98 means that the price is $98 for every $100 of $1 000. The price is 0.98 × 1 000 or $980 and we say that this bond is selling at a discount.

Example 3

A $1 000 bond selling at 102 means that the price is $102 for every $100 in $1 000. The price is 1.02 × 1 000 or $1 020 and we say that this bond is selling at a premium.

Canada Savings Bond are a very popular form of investment with Canadians. You may buy them through a bank or through a payroll deduction plan. They may be redeemed at any bank at any time for their full face value plus any accrued interest. *Accrued interest* is the interest from the last interest date to the date of redemption. You cannot sell these bonds to another individual.

Corporation bonds and government bonds other than Canada Savings Bonds can be bought from and sold to other individuals, usually through the services of a broker.

1. Alma owned $2 000 worth of bonds and was to receive $12\frac{1}{2}$% paid annually. How much would Alma receive annually?

2. If bond interest is $11\frac{1}{4}$% paid semi-annually, how much would Marty receive for semi-annual interest on a $500 bond?

3. Pheroza wanted to sell $5 000 worth of bonds. The price quoted to her was $97\frac{1}{2}$.
   (a) Would Pheroza be selling for a premium or a discount?
   (b) How much would Pheroza receive?

B Stocks

When you buy a share of stock, you buy a share in the issuing company and you become a *shareholder* or part owner of the company.

Each shareholder receives a *share certificate* indicating the number of shares owned. The invester may keep these shares and share in the profits the company makes. If the price, or market value rises, the owner may decide to sell the shares and realize a capital gain on the investment.

The *market price* is the price at which shares are bought and sold. It is quoted as so many dollars per share. For example, a quotation of $15\frac{1}{4}$ means $15\frac{1}{4}$ or $15.25.

As an owner, you will receive a share of the profits of the corporation. This share of profits is called a *dividend* and may be paid quarterly, semi-annually, or annually.

There are two main classes of stock, *preferred* and *common*. Preferred shares pay a fixed dividend, which is a percent of the face value, and this dividend is paid before any common share dividend is paid. A common share dividend will be declared if the corporation has enough profits. It is found by dividing the profits to be shared by the total number of common shares outstanding.

Example 1
A corporation has sold 100 000 common shares and has $2 400 000 in profits available for distribution to common shareholders. What dividend would an invester receive for each common share owned?

Solution

$$\text{common share dividend} = \frac{\text{profits available for distribution to common shareholders}}{\text{number of common shares}}$$

$$= \frac{\$2\ 400\ 000}{100\ 000}$$

$$= \$24$$

Example 2
How much would it cost you to buy 25 shares of Gulf Oil Canada at $26\frac{7}{8}$ if the brokerage fee is ignored?

Solution
Cost = number of shares × price per share
$$= 25 \times 26.875$$
$$= \$671.88$$

Example 3
What is the quarterly dividend on 100 shares of an 8% preferred stock having a face value of $50?

Solution

$$\text{Dividend} = \frac{100 \times 50 \times 0.08}{4}$$

$$= \$100$$

1. A corporation has sold 50 000 common shares and has $1 420 000 in profits available for distribution to common shareholders. What dividend could the corporation give for each common share?

2. How much would you receive if you sold 75 shares of Intersel at $33\frac{5}{8}$? (Ignore brokerage fee.)

3. What would the semi-annual dividend be on 150 shares of $9\frac{1}{2}$% preferred stock having a face value of $75?

C   Real Estate

Another way to invest your savings is to purchase a house and rent it to a tenant.

If the rental received exceeds the total of all the costs of owning the house, you will make a profit, which could be considered as interest on your investment.

Example

André bought a house for $60 000, which he rents for $600 per month. He pays $1 200 in property taxes per year, $280 in insurance per year, and estimates maintenance and repairs at $500. Calculate the rate of return on his investment.

Solution

Gross Income: $600 × 12		$7 200.00
Expenses:		
Taxes	$1 200.00	
Insurance	280.00	
Maintenance & repairs	500.00	1 980.00
Net Profit		$5 220.00

$$\text{The rate of return} = \frac{\text{Net Profit}}{\text{Investment}} = \frac{5\ 220}{60\ 000} = 8.7\%$$

1. Carol and Frank bought a house for $55 000. They rented the upper and lower floors for a total of $700 per month. Over their first year they paid out a total of $4850. Calculate Carol and Frank's rate of return on their investment.

   Mortgages are another form of real estate investment. If you invest in a mortgage, you will receive a fixed income for a stated number of years. However, if you want to use your money for something else, you may find it difficult to sell the mortgage and may be forced to suffer a loss.

D   Gold and Silver

You can invest in gold or silver by buying bars of the precious metal from your bank. If the value rises, you can sell the bars and profit from your investment. On the other hand, the price may drop and you will incur a loss if you sell.

E   Art and Antiques

Some people invest part of their savings in objects of art and antiques. It is, however, a risky form of investment. The value of these items is very often determined by the individual taste and preference of the buyer. You need expert knowledge if you are to make a profit.

EXERCISE 5.16

1. Larry Jones bought a $1 000, $13\frac{1}{2}$% seven year Canada Savings Bond bearing semi-annual interest coupons. If Larry keeps the bond to maturity find the following.
   (a) the value of each semi-annual coupon
   (b) the total interest earned
   (c) the maturity value

2. Gabriele bought a $5 000 bond at 89 ($89 per $100 of face value).
   (a) How much did Gabriele pay for the bond?
   (b) How much did Gabriele receive at maturity?
   (c) Did Gabriele buy at a premium or at a discount?

3. How much is the annual dividend on 150 shares of a 5% preferred stock having a par value of 40?

4. Helen bought 200 shares of CIL at $21\frac{3}{4}$. How much did she pay?

5. Jason would like to invest in gold. He investigated and settled on three alternatives.
   (i) To buy a gold Krugerrand coin would cost him $450 plus a 3.5% premium and 7% sales tax on the total.
   (ii) To buy a gold Canadian Maple Leaf coin would cost him the same but there would be no provincial sales tax.
   (iii) To buy a wafer would cost $450 plus a $3 "bar charge" per wafer.
   Find the following.
   (a) the cost of each alternative
   (b) the profit on each alternative if he sold them some time later at $500 and, in the case of the coins, received a refund of $2\frac{1}{2}$% of the purchase price
   (c) the percent return on each investment

6. Mae and Ng decided to invest $70 000 in a duplex, which they rented for $800 per month. They estimated that their taxes would be $1 400 per year, insurance would be $295 per year, and repairs and maintenance would be 2% of the value of the building. Find
   (a) Mae and Ng's net profit,
   (b) the rate of return on Mae and Ng's investment.

SUMMARY

Simple interest formulas

$$I = Prt \quad \text{OR} \quad P = \frac{A}{1 + rt}$$

$$r = \frac{I}{Pt} \qquad t = \frac{I}{Pr} \qquad P = \frac{I}{rt}$$

Saving and Investing – Credit Unions
                 – Trust Companies
                 – Banks
                 – Stocks and Bonds

Term Deposit – money deposited for a specific period of time

Nominal rate – the quoted rate

Effective rate – the true rate

Compound amount – the total amount after interest has been calculated and added to the previous balance

Compound interest – the difference between the original principal and the compound amount

To find the amount at compound interest:

$$A = P(1 + i)^n$$

To find the present value of an amount:

$$PV = \frac{A}{(1 + i)^n}$$

To find the amount of an ordinary annuity:

$$A_n = R(s_{\overline{n}|i})$$

To find the payment for an ordinary annuity that will accumulate to a given amount:

$$R = \frac{A_n}{s_{\overline{n}|i}}$$

To find the present value of an ordinary annuity:

$$PV = R(a_{\overline{n}|i})$$

To find the ordinary annuity, given the present value:

$$R = \frac{PV}{a_{\overline{n}|i}}$$

Where A = amount PV = present value
        R = rent (equal payment) n = number of interest periods
        P = principal i = rate per interest period

REVIEW EXERCISE 5.17

1. Find the simple interest.

	Principal	Rate	Time
(a)	$4 820	$9\frac{1}{4}\%$	36 d
(b)	2 550	$8\frac{3}{4}\%$	73 d
(c)	4 760	$10\frac{1}{4}\%$	55 d
(d)	3 860	$15\frac{3}{4}\%$	86 d
(e)	5 860	$14\frac{1}{2}\%$	65 d

2. Find the rate at which interest is earned for each of the following.

	Principal	Interest Earned	Time
(a)	$2 200	$690.00	3 a
(b)	1 600	82.50	6 months
(c)	1 580	79.00	146 d
(d)	1 640	541.20	2 a
(e)	2 490	59.76	219 d

3. Find the time in which interest is earned to the nearest day.

	Principal	Rate	Interest
(a)	$3 750	$12\frac{1}{2}$%	$ 281.25
(b)	2 890	$13\frac{3}{4}$%	97.98
(c)	3 220	$9\frac{1}{8}$%	1 028.39
(d)	1 560	$8\frac{3}{4}$%	22.43
(e)	6 250	$15\frac{1}{2}$%	460.00

4. Find to the nearest dollar the principal that will earn the given interest, at the rate and in the time given.

	Interest	Rate	Time
(a)	$452	$12\frac{1}{4}$%	4 months
(b)	98	$8\frac{1}{2}$%	1 a
(c)	165	$13\frac{3}{4}$%	186 d
(d)	220	$11\frac{1}{8}$%	90 d
(e)	415	$9\frac{3}{8}$%	6 months

5. How long will it take for a deposit of $2 000 to earn $350 interest at $8\frac{1}{2}$% per annum?

6. Bond interest amounted to $187.50 when a coupon was cashed one year after the bond was issued. If the bond bore interest at $9\frac{3}{8}$%, what was the principal amount of the bond?

7. If you invest $50 at the end of each month in an account that pays 12% per annum compounded monthly, how much will you have in four years?

8. Find the compound interest on $2 700 for $7\frac{1}{2}$ a compounded half yearly at 9% per annum.

9. Yung-Lin Lee has won a prize that pays him $1 000 at the end of each half year for fifteen years. He plans to invest the money as soon as he receives it in a fund paying 16% per annum compounded semi-annually. How much will the fund be worth in fifteen years?

10. On her daughter's 21st birthday, Dora Dibblee invested a sum of money, at 10% compounded quarterly, that would pay her daughter $10 000 on her thirtieth birthday. How much did Dora invest?

11. Sally bought a $1 000 $11\frac{3}{4}$% bond having interest payable quarterly. How much was her annual income from this bond?

12. Santo owned 100 shares of a $6\frac{1}{2}$% preferred stock having a face value of $50. What was his annual income from these shares?

CUMULATIVE REVIEW 3

1. State the equivalent percent for the following fractions.

(a) $\frac{1}{2}$ (b) $\frac{3}{8}$ (c) $\frac{3}{4}$ (d) $\frac{4}{5}$ (e) $\frac{1}{10}$ (f) $\frac{1}{12}$ (g) $\frac{2}{3}$ (h) $\frac{7}{8}$ (i) $\frac{1}{3}$

2. 350 m are what percent of 5 km?

3. Sheila has a mass of 48 kg and Kerrie has a mass of 60 kg. Sheila's mass is what percent less than Kerrie's?

4. Find $\frac{1}{4}$% of 3 964.

5. Find $\frac{1}{8}$% of 468.

6. Simplify.
$\frac{3}{4} \times \frac{2}{3}(\frac{1}{2} + \frac{3}{4}) \div \frac{5}{8} + 2$

7. Solve for *a*.
(a) $6a + 2 = 4a + 8$ (b) $2a(a + 6) = 4a + 8 + 2a^2$

8. 25 is what percent greater than 20?

9. Find the total number of hours worked by Akira Kuramochi.

	In	Out	In	Out	In	Out	Hours
Monday	8:00	12:01	12:55	17:02			
Tuesday	7:42	12:02	12:58	17:01			
Wednesday	7:49	12:01	13:10	17:02	17:58	19:02	
Thursday	8:03	12:04	12:52	17:10	18:40	19:35	
Friday	7:56	12:02	12:56	16:15			

10. Akira Kuramochi receives $9.50/h for the first 40 h worked and time-and-one-half for all hours over 40. Using the results of the time card in Question 9, find Akira's gross pay for the week.

11. Nicola works as a salesperson. She receives a salary of $500 per month plus a commission of 5% of all sales over $3 000. Last month her sales totaled $24 600. Find Nicola's earnings for the month.

12. 32 is what percent of 186?

13. 60 increased by 40% and the result decreased by 20% equals what number?

14. What number increased by 25% and the result decreased by 10% equals 1 080?

15. Multiply mentally.
(a) 432×25 (b) 680×125

16. Divide mentally.
(a) $1\ 675 \div 25$ (b) $3\ 625 \div 125$

17. Perform the operations indicated.
(a) $\dfrac{362.6 \times 48}{13.04 \times 1.632}$ (b) $\dfrac{962.75 \times 365}{0.087\ 5 \times 14}$

18. Using aliquot parts find the cost of the following.
(a) 832 items at $12\frac{1}{2}$¢ each   (c) 927 items at $33\frac{1}{3}$¢ each
(b) 632 items at 25¢ each

UNIT 6

Personal Finance

Although it is very wise to save money and *earn* interest, there are times or circumstances when it is necessary to borrow money. In this case you will *pay* interest to the person or institution who lends you the money. Just as it was recommended in Unit 5 to obtain the *highest* rate of interest for deposits and investments, it is also wise and intelligent to shop around for the *lowest* rate of interest to pay for borrowing money. There are many factors to consider when shopping for the lowest rate of interest.

(a) Is the loan life insured? If the loan is life insured, and the person borrowing the money happens to die before the loan is fully repaid, insurance will cover the balance owing. Also whether the borrower or the lender pays for the insurance should be made clear.

(b) How much collateral is required? Personal property, such as furniture or a car, life insurance policies, bonds, and shares of stock are all usually acceptable collateral. If the borrower is unable to repay the loan, the lender has the right to sell the collateral to satisfy the balance owing on the loan. (Provincial laws differ as to the amount of time "extension" allowed to make up for missed payments before collateral may be sold by the lender.) Credit rating can also affect the amount of collateral required for a loan. For persons under 18 who have yet to establish a credit rating, or have very little collateral, a responsible adult's signature to guarantee payment of the loan if the minor defaults in payments may be required.

(c) How long do I have to repay the loan? Generally speaking, the longer the time you have to repay a loan, the smaller your individual (usually monthly) payments will be and vice versa. However, it is important to realize that the *longer* the time to repay a loan, the *more* interest you pay.

(d) Can I repay the loan in full at *any* time without charge or penalty? (Why would this factor be important when considering obtaining a loan?)

The federal government helps consumers in borrowing money in the following ways.

(a) The lender must clearly show the borrower the exact rate of interest that will be charged.

(b) The lender must clearly show the borrower the total dollar amount of interest that the borrower will be required to pay.

With this much help from the government, it is not too difficult for us to compare and decide from which lending institution to borrow. Generally, the credit union loans money at the lowest rate of interest. The next lowest rate of interest for loans can be obtained from banks and trust companies.

Although the retailer does not loan actual money, you are allowed the use of merchandise when you are making regular payments toward the full price. The retailer charges the next highest rate of interest (for credit purchases). With a few exceptions, the finance company charges the highest rate of interest for loans.

Schedule 1. A Typical Schedule for Personal Loans from a Chartered Bank

Repayment Period	Amount Required	Cost of Borrowing	Amount to be Repaid	Monthly Payments
12 months	$ 500	$ 37.24	$ 537.24	$ 44.77
	1 000	74.60	1 074.60	89.55
	2 500	186.56	2 686.56	223.88
18 months	$ 500	$ 55.12	$ 555.12	$ 30.84
	1 000	110.24	1 110.24	61.68
	2 500	275.60	2 775.60	154.20
24 months	$1 000	$146.48	$1 146.48	$ 47.77
	2 500	366.56	2 866.56	119.44
	3 500	513.04	4 013.04	167.21
30 months	$1 000	$183.50	$1 183.50	$ 39.45
	2 500	459.20	2 959.20	98.64
	4 000	734.90	4 734.90	157.83
36 months	$1 000	$221.48	$1 221.48	$ 33.93
	2 500	553.88	3 053.88	84.83
	4 000	886.64	4 886.64	135.74

Cost of borrowing expressed as a nominal annual percentage rate: $13\frac{1}{2}\%$
Cost of borrowing includes insurance.

Schedule 2. A Typical Schedule for Personal Loans from a Trust Company

Repayment Period	Loan Amount	Monthly Payment	Cost of Loan	Annual Interest Rate
12 months	$ 500	$ 45.13	$ 41.56	15%
	1 000	90.26	83.12	15%
	1 500	135.39	124.68	15%
	2 000	180.52	166.24	15%
	2 500	225.65	207.80	15%
24 months	$1 000	$ 48.49	$ 163.67	15%
	1 500	72.74	245.76	15%
	2 000	96.98	327.52	15%
	2 500	121.23	409.52	15%
36 months	$2 000	$ 69.34	$ 496.24	15%
	2 500	86.68	620.48	15%
	3 000	103.27	717.72	$14\frac{1}{2}\%$
	4 000	137.69	956.84	$14\frac{1}{2}\%$
48 months	$3 000	$ 82.74	$ 971.52	$14\frac{1}{2}\%$
	4 000	110.32	1 295.36	$14\frac{1}{2}\%$

Cost of loan includes insurance.

6.1   SHOPPING FOR A LOAN – BANKS AND TRUST COMPANIES

Chartered banks and trust companies in Canada compete with one another for consumer deposits and loans. Although each bank and each trust company may have its own name variations for loans, basically the loans are of three types:
- Personal Loans
- Demand Loans
- Mortgage Loans – This type of loan is discussed in detail in another text by the same author.

The chartered banks in Canada are very competitive and there is little difference among them with regard to the rate of interest charged for personal loans. Trust companies usually charge a slightly higher rate of interest than the chartered banks. Compare the illustrated schedules of personal loans.

EXERCISE 6.1
Compare the two schedules.

1. What are the different rates of interest charged for loans up to $3 000? Over $3 000?

2. (a) If you wanted to borrow $1 000 from a chartered bank and repay the loan in 12 months, what is the total amount you would repay? (Refer to Schedule 1.)
    (b) Schedule 2 does not show the total amount to be repaid. Calculate as follows:

    Loan Amount $1 000
    Add: Cost of Loan ▬▬▬▬
    Amount to be Repaid ▬▬▬▬

3. (a) If you wanted to borrow $2 500 and repay the loan in 24 months, what is the total amount you would repay from Schedule 1? From Schedule 2?
    (b) Why would a consumer want to repay the loan in more than a 12 month period?

6.2   INTEREST RATES WHEN LOAN IS PAID IN MONTHLY INSTALMENTS

It is important for the borrower to realize that although the interest rate is expressed as an annual percentage rate, interest is calculated on the decreased balance each month.

Example
A loan of $1 000 is to be repaid in 24 months, at $145 per month, at an annual interest rate of $21\frac{3}{4}\%$. Find the interest paid each month.

Solution

For the first month, interest is calculated as follows.

$I = Prt$

$\quad = 1\,000 \times 0.217\,5 \times \dfrac{1}{12}$

$\quad = 18.13$

Payment	**$ 145.00**
Less interest	**18.13**
Payment on principal	**$ 126.87**

The $145 payment, therefore, pays $18.13 in interest and $126.87 of principal.

For the second month, interest is calculated as follows.

$I = Prt$

$\quad = 873.13 \times 0.217\,5 \times \dfrac{1}{12}$

$\quad = 15.83$

Original	**$1 000.00**
Less Pay	**126.87**
Present principal	**$ 873.13**

If we were to continue to calculate the interest per month on the decreasing principal for the 24 month period, we would have computed an amortized schedule of payments for the length of the loan. This information is very important if it is an *open* loan, that is, the unpaid balance may be paid any time before the loan becomes due.

EXERCISE 6.2

(a) Compute the amortized schedule of payments for the first six months for a loan of $2 500 with a repayment period of 24 months using Schedule 2. Use the given format for your schedule.

End of	Monthly Payment	Interest for Month	Amount Applied to Principal	Loan Balance
				$2500
First Month	▬	▬	▬	▬
Second Month	▬	▬	▬	▬
Third Month	▬	▬	▬	▬
Fourth Month	▬	▬	▬	▬
Fifth Month	▬	▬	▬	▬
Sixth Month	▬	▬	▬	▬

(b) Repeat the calculation of part (a) for a loan of $2 500, and repayment period of 30 months, but use Schedule 1.

6.3 CALCULATING INTEREST RATES ON LOANS PAID ON INSTALMENTS: ANNUAL EFFECTIVE RATE OR TRUE ANNUAL INTEREST RATE

To calculate the interest rate on an instalment loan, the formula $r = \dfrac{I}{Pt}$ cannot easily be computed because of the decreased principal each month.

A more efficient method of calculating is to use the following formula.

$$r = \frac{2Nc}{A(n + 1)}$$

where r = the annual interest rate
N = the number of payments in one year
c = the cost of borrowing
A = the amount borrowed
n = the number of payments to pay the loan in full

Example
A loan of $2 500 is to be repaid in 18 months under Schedule 1. What is the effective annual interest rate?

Solution

Machine
Instruction

$$r = \frac{2Nc}{A(n + 1)}$$

CLEAR

$$= \frac{2 \times 12 \times 275.60}{2\ 500(18 + 1)}$$

SET DEC 2

$$= 13.9\%$$

2

12

275.6

÷

2 500

÷

19

%

```
2 • X
12 • X
275 • 6 ÷
2500 • ÷
19 • %
13 • 92 *
```

But Schedule 1 specifically states that the rate of interest is 13.5%!

Banks and trust companies normally express the annual interest rate as *nominal* interest. They arrive at this rate by multiplying the monthly rate of interest of $1\frac{1}{8}\%$ by the number of months in a year. Hence $12 \times 1\frac{1}{8}\% = 13\frac{1}{2}\%$ (nominal interest rate).

As we saw from our example, a borrower actually pays a higher rate than the nominal rate. The 13.9% is called the *annual effective rate* or the *true annual interest rate*.

EXERCISE 6.3
Compute the effective interest rate per annum on the following.
1. Use Schedule 1.
   (a) Borrow $4 000 for 30 months
   (b) Borrow $1 000 for 24 months
   (c) Borrow $2 500 for 36 months
2. Use Schedule 2.
   (a) Borrow $1 500 for 24 months
   (b) Borrow $3 000 for 36 months
   (c) Borrow $3 000 for 48 months

6.4   PERSONAL LOANS

A   Promissory Notes

One requirement of almost every personal loan is that the borrower sign a *promissory note*. This *promise to pay* is held by the lender until the note is paid in full. A common form of promissory note is illustrated below.

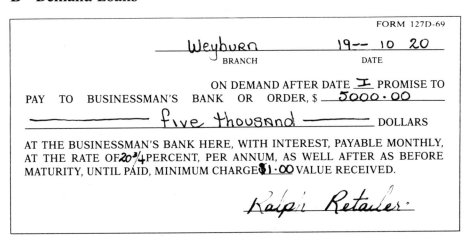

$ _2500.00_ DUE ___1988 10 17___ Winnipeg ___ 1986 10 14 ___
PLACE   DATE

INT. _1075.00_
$ _3575.00_ ___24 Months___ AFTER DATE _I_ PROMISE TO PAY TO
CONSUMER'S BANK   OR ORDER

~ three thousand, five Hundred and seventy-five °⁰⁄₁₀₀ DOLLARS

WITH INTEREST AT THE RATE OF 21½ PERCENT, PER ANNUM, AS WELL AFTER AS BEFORE MATURITY UNTIL PAID MINIMUM CHARGE, $1·00 AT THE CONSUMERS' BANK HERE, VALUE RECEIVED.

John G. Borrower

This promissory note is called an *interest added* note because interest is added to the amount borrowed.

(a) What is the amount being borrowed?
(b) How much interest is being added to the amount borrowed?
(c) What is the rate of interest being charged?
(d) Who is giving the loan?
(e) Who is receiving the loan?
(f) When is the loan due to be paid in full?

Note that, although the loan is for 24 months, the due date is three days after a 24 month period. This is called three *days of grace*. Also, months are considered to be of equal length of time. If there is no corresponding date in the due month, the last day of that month is used. For example, if a loan is taken on August 30 for 6 months, the due date is March 3. (February 28 plus 3 days of grace equals March 3, except for leap years.)

B Demand Loans

FORM 127D-69

___Weyburn___ ___19-- 10 20___
BRANCH   DATE

ON DEMAND AFTER DATE _I_ PROMISE TO
PAY TO BUSINESSMAN'S BANK OR ORDER, $ ___5000·00___
___ five thousand ___ DOLLARS

AT THE BUSINESSMAN'S BANK HERE, WITH INTEREST, PAYABLE MONTHLY, AT THE RATE OF 20¾ PERCENT, PER ANNUM, AS WELL AFTER AS BEFORE MATURITY, UNTIL PAID, MINIMUM CHARGE $1·00 VALUE RECEIVED.

Ralph Retailer

Note that the typical promissory demand note shown differs from the promissory interest added note in the following ways.

(a) The demand note has no due date, but rather is payable *on demand* of the bank or trust company. Days of grace do not apply to demand notes.

(b) Interest on the demand loan is payable monthly, but there is no fixed amount to be paid on the principal as there is with a personal loan.

(c) The rate of interest is lower than it is for a personal loan.

Because there is no due date, demand loans are for short periods of time. If payment is not made within a short period of time, the bank or trust company may demand that the loan be repaid at their discretion. Payment is almost 100% guaranteed because collateral such as bonds or equipment would have to have been signed over to the bank or trust company in order to obtain such a loan. Collateral is almost 100% of the loan itself.

Usually with demand loans there are no instalment payments on the principal borrowed. The interest is paid monthly, and the rate of interest is lower than for personal loans. This type of loan is a *preferred loan* because of the above factors. As well, these loans are normally for businesses rather than consumers. Can you think of reasons why consumers are not able to obtain demand loans? Why do businesses need to borrow money for only short periods of time?

The calculation of interest for a demand loan is made using an exact number of days, rather than monthly as a personal loan. Also, because the principal is not reduced in instalments, the formula used is $I = Prt$.

EXERCISE 6.4

1. A businessperson took out a demand loan on October 25 of one year for $3 500 bearing interest at $19\frac{3}{4}\%$ per annum. How much interest would have been charged if the loan was repaid on January 16 of the following year?

2. A demand loan was taken out on May 27 of one year for $1 025 at $20\frac{3}{4}\%$. How much interest would have been charged if the loan was repaid on April 30 of the following year?

3. Calculate the interest to be paid on a demand loan, for $5 500 at $19\frac{1}{4}\%$, taken out on January 15 on the following dates (not a leap year).
   (a) February 15   (b) March 15   (c) April 15

4. The following payments were made on a demand note, date January 27, for $3 500 at $20\frac{1}{2}\%$: February 27, $100.00; March 27, $100.00; and April 27, $100.00. Prepare a schedule of payments and interest.

6.5   SHOPPING FOR A LOAN – THE CREDIT UNION

"Keen Credit Union announces 15% rebate."

If the credit union ends its fiscal (accounting) year with a surplus, then, depending on how large the surplus is, the directors of the credit union may declare a rebate to loan accounts. Although the borrower pays interest each month on the unpaid balance of the loan, some of it is returned when the rebate is announced.

Assume that a borrower paid interest of $460 for one year on a loan of $2 000, at the rate of 23%, and received a rebate of $60. Although the borrower paid interest at the rate of 23% during the year, the effective rate of interest was much lower. Using the simple interest formula, and assuming again that the principal amount did not decrease with monthly payments, we can find the effective rate of interest.

Assuming the principal did not decrease

$$
\begin{array}{ll}
\text{Interest paid during the year } \$460 \\
\qquad\qquad \text{Rebate for the year } \underline{\quad 60} \\
\qquad \text{Actual interest paid } \$400
\end{array}
\qquad
\begin{aligned}
r &= \frac{I}{Pt} \\[4pt]
&= \frac{400}{2\ 000 \times 1} \\[4pt]
&= 20\%
\end{aligned}
$$

Although you cannot know the amount or rate of rebate in advance, investigate a local credit union's past rebates in order to estimate the effective rate of interest on a loan. Generally, you will find the credit union's rate of interest for loans is the lowest of most sources. Also, all loans are life insured.

Normally, the credit union does not allow the borrower to pay monthly interest and not decrease the principal with the monthly payment. To calculate the effective rate of interest when the principal decreases with monthly payments, set up a schedule like the one shown to answer the following questions.

Loan Account

Date	Interest Paid	Decrease of Principal	Balance Owing

Note: Treat all months as equal units of time.

EXERCISE 6.5

1. Calculate the amount of interest paid and the effective rate of interest for the following (assume the principal does not decrease with monthly payments).

	Principal	Int. Paid	Rate of Int. Paid	Time	Rebate	Annual Effective Rate of Int.
(a)	$3 000		$21\frac{3}{4}\%$	1 year	$55	
(b)	2 500		$20\frac{3}{4}\%$	1 year	40	
(c)	4 500		$21\frac{1}{4}\%$	1 year	90	
(d)	3 500		$20\frac{3}{4}\%$	1 year	80	
(e)	1 500		$22\frac{1}{4}\%$	1 year	35	

2. The board of directors of a credit union announced a rebate of 15% of interest paid on loan accounts. Calculate the effective rate of interest if a borrower had a loan of $4 200 and had paid interest totalling $950 in one year.

3. Frank Vormittag took out a loan at his credit union for $1 500 on January 1 and was to make monthly payments of $150. He was to be charged interest at the rate of 20% per annum.
   (a) How long will it take to pay off the loan? How much is the last payment?
   (b) Calculate the effective rate of interest if Frank received a rebate of $42 at the end of the year.

4. Cathy Hutton was to pay $205 monthly for interest and principal on a loan of $1 000 at the rate of 21% per annum taken out on March 1.
   (a) How long will it take to pay off the loan? What is the last payment?
   (b) Calculate the effective rate of interest if Cathy received a 16% rebate.

6.6   SHOPPING FOR A LOAN – FINANCE COMPANIES

Finance companies generally charge the highest rate of interest of lending institutions for personal loans.

As with banks and trust companies, finance companies usually have the borrower pay back in equal monthly payments, and the interest is calculated on the diminished monthly balance. Persons shopping for a loan from a finance company should check on whether the loan is life insured and whether the loan may be repaid at any time without penalty.

$$r = \frac{2Nc}{A(n + 1)}$$

The formula previously used for calculating interest rates on loans repaid by monthly payments, where the interest is computed on the diminished monthly balance, is also used here.

EXERCISE 6.6

1. Maria Santarelli borrowed $1 800 to buy a used car. The finance company suggested 24 monthly payments of $91.50. Compute the annual interest rate.

2. Compute the effective annual interest rate for each of the following.
   (a) John Stone investigated borrowing from a finance company. He found that to borrow $3 850, he would make monthly payments of $185.95 for 24 months.
   (b) Paul Lumley, a classmate of John, investigated a chartered bank and found that to borrow $3 850, he would make monthly payments of $181.59 for 24 months.
   (c) Fatima Aljoudi investigated a trust company loan and found that to borrow $3 850, she would make monthly payments of $183.79 for 24 months.

(d) Mohan Gursa investigated a local credit union and fond that to borrow $3 850, he would make monthly payments of $250 until the loan was paid off. He was to pay interest on the unpaid balance at the rate of $2\frac{1}{4}$% per month. Mohan projected a rebate of 12% of interest paid for the end of the first year, and a rebate of 15% of interest paid for the end of the second year. Prepare a schedule of payments that Mohan would show to his class.

6.7 RETAILER'S CREDIT

Although the consumer cannot borrow a sum of money from a retailer, money can be borrowed by using a charge plan or retailer's credit.

Harry Finley was in need of a new washing machine. He investigated whether he should use the retailer's charge plan or borrow the money from his credit union and pay the retailer in cash. The results of his investigation follow.

On shopping for the best price for the model he wanted, Harry found the washing machine had a retail price of $375. The retailer offered Harry the machine with no down payment and showed him the following schedule of monthly payments and services charges.

Note: **The retailer's 'service charge' is the same as interest charged for a loan.**

Retailer's Monthly Payment Schedule

Amounts	Monthly Payment
Balance up to $55	Pay $5
$ 55.01 to $75	6
75.01 to $100	7
100.01 to $125	8
125.01 to $165	9
165.01 to $195	10
195.01 to $225	11
225.01 to $245	12
245.01 to $260	13
260.01 to $275	14
275.01 to $295	15
295.01 to $315	16
315.01 to $340	17
340.01 to $360	18
360.01 to $375	19
375.01 to $400	20
Over $400	5%

The service charge for the washing machine was to be $1\frac{1}{2}$% per month and would be added to Harry's account each month based on his previous month's balance.

If his month end balance was	His service charge would be
$ 50	$0.75
100	1.50
200	3.00
400	6.00
600	9.00

According to the monthly payment schedule, Harry would make monthly payments of $19. The retailer told Harry he would be required to make 24 payments. Using the formula

$$r = \frac{2Nc}{A(n + 1)}$$

calculate the effective annual interest rate charged by the retailer.

Machine Instruction

CLEAR

SET DEC 2

2

$\boxed{\times}$

12

$\boxed{\times}$

81

$\boxed{\div}$

375

$\boxed{\div}$

25

$\boxed{\%}$

$$r = \frac{2 \times 12 \times 81}{375(24 + 1)}$$

$$= 20.73\%$$

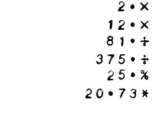

Harry's credit union informed him that they would charge him $1\frac{1}{4}\%$ per month on the unpaid balance for a loan of $375. At the end of the year, the credit union would give him a rebate, the amount of which would depend on the decision of the Board of Directors. If Harry wished to make the same monthly payments as he would for the retailer ($19) he would be required to make 22 payments. Using the formula

$$r = \frac{2Nc}{A(n + 1)}$$

calculate the effective annual interest rate charged by the credit union if Harry were to receive a $10 rebate at the end of the first year and a $5 rebate at the end of the second year.

$$r = \frac{2 \times 12 \times 28}{375(22 + 1)}$$

$$= 7.79\%$$

EXERCISE 6.7

1. A low-price department store advertises credit terms as follows:
   A minimum payment of 10% of any balance owing at the end of any
   fiscal month shall be made provided that in no event shall any payment
   be less than $7.00. A service charge of 2% per month is to be added to
   any unpaid balance owing at the end of each fiscal month.
   (a) Adam Csonka buys a digital clock radio for $65 with no down pay-
       ment. Prepare a schedule showing Adam's payments until the radio
       is fully paid for, if he makes the minimum monthly payment.
   (b) Calculate the annual effective rate of interest.

2. (a) A local television dealer advertises monthly rates of $1\frac{3}{4}$% per month
       on the unpaid balance and monthly payments of 10% of the pur-
       chase price. If Heather Klaasen buys a television for $695, prepare
       a schedule of her payments until the television is fully paid for. There
       is a 10% down payment.
   (b) What is the annual effective interest rate?

3. Carlos wanted to give Angela her diamond on her birthday but could
   not afford payments of more than $20 per month. The diamond that he
   wanted to give her retailed at $500 and the retailer offered Carlos the
   ring at monthly payments of $17.86 for 36 months. What would the
   annual effective interest rate be?

4. Sharon argued that since the monthly interest rate was 1%, the effective annual interest would be $1 \times 12 = 12$% per annum. Is she correct?
   Why or why not?

5. Marcel agrees to purchase a stereo-type component for $485 at monthly
   payments of $15.90 for three years. What would the annual effective
   rate of interest be?

SUMMARY

Borrowing – Credit Unions
          – Banks
          – Trust Companies
          – Retailers
          – Finance Companies

Calculating the interest on the decreasing monthly balance, expressed as
an annual effective rate or true annual interest rate.

$$r = \frac{2Nc}{A(n + 1)}$$

REVIEW EXERCISE 6.8

1. Find the simple interest.

	Principal	Rate	Time
(a)	$4 820	$21\frac{1}{4}\%$	36 d
(b)	2 550	$22\frac{1}{2}\%$	73 d
(c)	4 760	$20\frac{3}{4}\%$	55 d
(d)	3 860	$20\frac{1}{4}\%$	86 d
(e)	5 860	$21\frac{3}{4}\%$	65 d

2. Find the rate at which interest is paid for each of the following.

	Principal	Interest Paid	Time
(a)	$4 400	$1 380.00	3 a
(b)	3 200	165.00	6 months
(c)	1 580	85.60	146 d
(d)	1 640	650.00	2 a
(e)	2 490	89.60	219 d

3. Find the time, to the nearest day, in which interest is paid for each of the following.

	Principal	Rate	Interest
(a)	$3 750	$20\frac{3}{4}\%$	$185
(b)	2 890	$21\frac{3}{4}\%$	320
(c)	3 220	$22\frac{1}{4}\%$	640
(d)	1 560	$21\frac{1}{2}\%$	120
(e)	6 250	19%	1 200

4. Find to the nearest dollar the principal that will cost the given interest, at the rate and in the time given.

	Interest	Rate	Time
(a)	$452	$20\frac{3}{4}\%$	3 months
(b)	98	$21\frac{3}{4}\%$	1 a
(c)	165	$22\frac{1}{4}\%$	186 d
(d)	220	$21\frac{1}{2}\%$	90 d
(e)	415	19%	6 months

5. How long will it take for a loan of $2 000 to cost $700 interest at $20\frac{1}{2}\%$ per annum?

6. Interest on a promissory note amounted to $355 one year after the note was signed. If the note bore interest at $19\frac{3}{4}\%$, what was the principal amount of the note?

7. Compute the schedule of payments for the first six months for a loan of $2 500 where the monthly payment is $200.44. Interest is $21\frac{1}{2}$% per annum.

8. Compute the effective interest rate per annum of each of the following.

	Amount Borrowed	*Monthly Payment*	*Loan to be Repaid in*
(a)	$4 000	$135.74	36 months
(b)	2 500	121.23	24 months
(c)	4 500	105.89	60 months
(d)	4 500	124.11	48 months
(e)	2 000	180.52	12 months

9. A demand loan was taken out on May 15 for $3 500 at $22\frac{1}{4}$% per annum. How much interest would have been charged if the loan was repaid 15 d later?

10. The Board of Directors for a local credit union announced a 12% rebate of interest paid for the year. Set up a schedule of payments until the end of the first year if Barbara Kruger borrowed $1 500 at $1\frac{1}{8}$% per month and was to pay $115 per month.

11. Debbie Olds had borrowed $1 000 from a local credit union. At the end of the year she had paid $120 interest but then received a 15% rebate of interest paid. What was the effective rate of interest for the year if the loan was repaid in the year by regular monthly payments?

12. O. C. Scott bought a pair of skis for $314.95. He was to pay back $36 per month and the interest was to be $1\frac{1}{2}$% per month. Set up a schedule to determine the following.
    (a) How many months it would take O. C. to fully pay for the skis
    (b) The total interest O. C. would pay
    (c) The effective annual interest rate

CUMULATIVE REVIEW 4

1. Simplify the following.

$$\tfrac{2}{5} \times \tfrac{1}{2}(\tfrac{3}{4} + \tfrac{4}{5}) \div \tfrac{6}{5}$$

2. If Tom has a mass of 65 kg and Sandy has a mass of 58 kg, Tom's mass is what percent more than Sandy's?

3. What fractional part of a kilometre is 150 m? 6 hm? 55 dam?

4. What number increased by 55% of itself equals 310?

5. State the fractional equivalent of each of the following.
   (a) 0.166 $\overline{6}$ (d) 0.75
   (b) 0.031 25   (e) 0.125
   (c) 0.625

6. What number is 22% smaller than 50?

7. 58% of what number equals 520?

8. 155 cm are 60% of how many metres?

9. Factor $12x^2y^2 + 4x^4y + \dfrac{16x^2y}{2}$.

10. Solve the following equations.
    (a) $10x + 52 = 43$
    (b) $4y(y + 3) - 3y = 108 + 4y^2$
    (c) $4b(b - 8) = 2b(2b - 2) - 56$

11. A waterless cooking ware set was to be sold by a door-to-door sales representative for $259.95. The sales representative was to receive 35% commission. Over a period of two months, the sales representative sold 6 sets. How much was earned in two months?

12. Brad McQuarrie was to earn a basic salary of $125 per week and a 10% commission on sales over $3 000 per week. In his first week Brad had sales of $4 500, and he had $6 200 for his second week. What were his total earnings for the two weeks?

13. Dale Dowson earned $10.50/h for the first 40 h worked per week and time-and-one-half for overtime. Calculate his gross earnings if he worked $44\frac{1}{2}$ h.

14. Rupa received $450.80 for a 44 h week at the same factory as Dale. What was Rupa's hourly pay rate?

15. Bob's bond interest amounted to $662.50 one year after the bond was issued. If the interest rate was $13\frac{1}{4}$%, what was the face value of the bond?

16. How much will an investment of $500 amount to in one year if money is worth 16% compounded semi-annually?

17. Helen wrote 13 cheques last month. If the service charge was 28¢ per cheque, how much did her chequing privilege cost her?

UNIT 7

Personal Income Tax

Author's Note: The information and illustrations in this unit are based on income tax regulations in effect in 1984 for 1983 earnings. Since some regulations are changed every year and certain amounts (for example, personal exemptions) are tied to the cost of living, the authors strongly recommend that students obtain copies of the current income tax forms and do the exercises according to the latest information. Copies of Individual Income Tax Return forms may be obtained free of charge from your local District Tax Office. However, the basic procedures outlined here have been in effect for several years and are unlikely to change in the near future.

Many centuries ago a Sumerian writer engraved the proverb "You can have a lord, you can have a king, but the man to fear is the tax collector." on a stone tablet. Paying taxes today is no more popular than it was then. However, most people agree that taxation is a "necessary evil". Every person living in Canada is subject to income tax. When we pay taxes we are really paying ourselves. Tax revenue is used to provide the increasingly numerous services that we demand, such as education, health services, highways, and welfare, to name only a few.

The Canadian tax system is based on self-assessment. Personal information about income and expenses are volunteered by the taxpayer when the tax to be paid is calculated. Payment is made easier by requiring employers to deduct income taxes from wages or salaries. This spreads payments over the whole year. Since the money is taken from our pay before we get it, the process seems less painful.

Early in the year employers prepare T4 slips for each employee. These slips show total earnings and deductions for the year past. A taxpayer who works for more than one employer receives a T4 slip from each employer. The employer sends one copy of the T4 to the District Taxation Office, two to the employee, and keeps one on file as a record. The taxpayer submits one copy with the tax return and keeps one copy.

It is the responsibility of each taxpayer to see that his/her taxes are paid. At the end of the year each taxpayer prepares a tax return form for the whole year giving him/her an opportunity to reassess personal tax status each year. This Individual Income Tax Return form and any money owing must be mailed on or before April 30 of each year.

A   Penalties

The penalty for late filing is 5% of the unpaid tax and 5% of Canada Pension Plan contributions on self-employed earnings still owing. Interest is charged on late payments of tax and/or Canada Pension Plan contributions (if greater than $40) on self-employed earnings.

B   Tax Evasion

To detect tax evaders, Revenue Canada employs a variety of procedures ranging from an audit of the tax returns of members of a particular profession or trade, to a field audit when a representative of the taxation office examines an individual's or firm's books in detail.

C   Collection of Tax

The federal government collects personal federal income tax from taxpayers in all provinces. It also collects Canada Pension Plan contributions for all provinces except Quebec, personal income tax for all provinces except Quebec, and all unemployment insurance premiums. Quebec has an independent pension plan similar to the Canada Pension Plan. Taxpayers in Quebec fill out two tax forms: one for the federal and one for the provincial government. Provincial Income Tax on the Individual Income Tax Return forms is the amount levied by all provinces, except Quebec, and collected for them by the federal government.

D   Canada Pension Plan

Most working Canadians between the ages of 18 and 70 contribute to the Canada Pension Plan. Employees contribute 1.8% of all earnings over a basic exemption and up to a maximum contribution. The exemption and the maximum contribution change yearly. The employer contributes an equal amount.

E   Unemployment Insurance

Canadians pay unemployment insurance premiums on earnings from insurable employment. Excepted employment may be found in the *Canada Pension Plan and Unemployment Insurance Premium Tables* prepared by Revenue Canada. Copies of this booklet may be obtained on request from your District Taxation Office. Taxpayers covered by the Unemployment Insurance Act pay a percent of their insurable earnings up to a maximum, which is subject to change each year. The employer contributes 1.4 *times* the employee's premium. For example, if the employee's contribution is $414 for the year, the employer contributes $579.60 ($414 × 1.4).

7.1   INDIVIDUAL INCOME TAX RETURN

Completing the individual income tax return involves seven steps.

(1) Identify yourself by means of personal information.

(2) Calculate your total income.

(3) Calculate your net income.

(4) Calculate your taxable income.

(5) Calculate your federal and provincial tax payable.

(6) Calculate your provincial tax credit (if applicable).

(7) Calculate the amount of tax you still owe or the amount of refund you are claiming.

We will examine each step in turn and prepare a complete return for a fictitious taxpayer.

(1)   Identification

Personal information such as name, address, job, social insurance number, and marital status, is supplied here. If you do not have a social insurance number, you must apply for one by submitting a completed form S-1, which you can obtain from your District Taxation office.

(2)   Total Income

Income From Employment includes the amount of gross earnings from employment shown in Box C of the T4 slip, commissions shown in Box L, adult training allowances, net research grants, tips, and gratuities. Net research grants are research grants less any expenses of the research. With certain exceptions, each employee may deduct 20% of employment income up to a maximum of $500 for employment expense. For example, if your income from employment is $17 000, you deduct $500. If your income is $2 250, you deduct $450.

Pension Income includes income from the Old Age Security Pension, Canada Pension Plan, and private pension plans.

Income From Other Sources includes taxable family allowance payments, dividends from taxable Canadian corporations, interest and other investment income, rental income, and taxable capital gains.

Income From Self-Employment includes business, professional, commission, farming, and fishing income.

Not to be Included as Income for tax purposes are the following items:
    Workmen's Compensation Payments
    War Disability Pensions
    Blind Persons' Allowances
    Guaranteed Income Supplement
    Mother's Allowances
    Lottery Winnings
Old Age Assistance Payments made to some individuals who do not qualify for the Old Age Security Payments are not taxable.

Example
Complete the Identification and Total Income sections of the Individual Income Tax Return for John Doe. Use the following information.

John is single and lives at 72 West 18th Street, Ourtown L0R 1T0. He works in the warehouse at X Company Ltd., 32 East Street. He was born on 1965 10 10. His social insurance number is 672 004 326 and he filed a tax return last year.

John's T4 slip shows earnings from employment $14 480, Canada Pension Plan contribution $228.24, unemployment insurance premium $333.04, registered pension plan contribution $868.80, and union dues deducted $240.

John has a T5 slip showing his investment income. He used the information on this slip to fill out Schedule 4, which is a complete statement of his investment income.

Schedule 4 shows that his interest and other investment income was $216.83, and the cost of renting his safety deposit box in the bank was $12.50.

Trace this example, item by item, on the completed portions of the tax return that follows. Note on line 05 that the maximum $500 for employment expenses has been claimed since 20% of $14 480 is greater than $500.

The forms used for John's tax return are the same for all provinces and territories except Quebec and except when stated otherwise.

02-057-143

Revenue Canada Taxation	**Revenu Canada** Impôt	**T4-1983** Supplementary - *Supplémentaire*				**STATEMENT OF REMUNERATION PAID** *ÉTAT DE LA RÉMUNÉRATION PAYÉE*		

(C) TOTAL EARNINGS BEFORE DEDUCTIONS	**(D)** EMPLOYEE'S PENSION CONTRIBUTION CANADA PLAN / QUEBEC PLAN	**(E)** U.I. PREMIUM	**(F)** REGISTERED PENSION PLAN CONTRIBUTION	**(G)** INCOME TAX DEDUCTED	**(H)** U.I. INSURABLE EARNINGS	**(I)** C.P.P. PENSIONABLE EARNINGS ★	**(J)** EXEMPT CPP QPP / U.I.
14480 00	228 24	333 04	868 80	1708 20	14480 00		RPC RRQ / A-C
GAINS TOTAUX AVANT DÉDUCTIONS	*DU CANADA / DU QUÉBEC COTISATION DE PENSION (EMPLOYÉ)*	*PRIME D.A.-C.*	*COTISATION RÉGIME ENREGISTRÉ DE PENSIONS*	*IMPÔT SUR LE REVENU RETENU*	*GAINS ASSURABLES A-C*	*GAINS OUVRANT DROIT À PENSIONS POUR R.P.C.* ★	*EXONÉRATION*

BOX (C) AMOUNT INCLUDES ANY AMOUNTS IN BOXES (H), (I), (K) AND (L) *LE MONTANT DE LA CASE (C) COMPREND TOUS MONTANTS FIGURANT AUX CASES (H), (I), (K) ET (L)*	**(K)** TAXABLE ALLOWANCES AND BENEFITS	**(L)** EMPLOYMENT COMMISSIONS	**(M)** PENSION PLAN REGISTRATION NUMBER	★ If different from Box (C) - *S'ils sont différents de la Case (C)*
	186 20		4261	
	ALLOCATIONS ET PRESTA-TIONS IMPOSABLES	*COMMISSIONS D'EMPLOI*	*Nº D'ENREGISTREMENT DU RÉGIME DE PENSIONS*	UNION DUES $240.00

EMPLOYEE - *EMPLOYÉ:*
SURNAME FIRST (in capital letters) USUAL FIRST NAME AND INITIALS AND FULL ADDRESS
NOM DE FAMILLE D'ABORD (en capitales) PRÉNOM USUEL ET INITIALES ET ADRESSE COMPLÈTE

(A) PROVINCE OF EMPLOYMENT *PROVINCE D'EMPLOI*	**(B)** SOCIAL INSURANCE NUMBER *Nº D'ASSURANCE SOCIALE*	**(N)** EMPLOYEE NO *Nº DE L'EMPLOYÉ*
ONTARIO	672 004 326	14

→ DOE JOHN
72 West 18th Street
Ourtown

NAME AND ADDRESS OF EMPLOYER - *NOM ET ADRESSE DE L'EMPLOYEUR*

X Company Limited
32 East Street
Ourtown

- **Attach to your 1983 Income Tax Return SEE INFORMATION ON REVERSE**
- *Annexer à votre déclaration d'impôt sur le revenu de 1983 VOIR LES RENSEIGNEMENTS AU VERSO*

2

Figure 7.1

Revenue Canada Taxation	**Revenu Canada** Impôt	**T5** Supplementary – *Supplémentaire*	**STATEMENT OF INVESTMENT INCOME** *ÉTAT DES REVENUS DE PLACEMENTS*	

		Dividends from Taxable Canadian Corporations *Dividendes de corporations canadiennes imposables*		Rev 83			
Year	**(A)** Actual Amount of Eligible Dividends	**(B)** Taxable Amount of Eligible Dividends	**(C)** Federal Dividend Tax Credit	**(D)** Eligible Interest from Canadian Sources	**(I)** Capital Gains Dividends	**(J)** Gross Foreign Income
1983	*Montant réel des dividendes admissibles*	*Montant imposable des dividendes admissibles*	*Crédit d'impôt fédéral pour dividendes*	216.83 *Intérêts admissibles de source canadienne*	*Dividendes sur gains en capital*	*Revenus étrangers bruts*
	(E) Actual Amount of Ineligible Dividends	**(F)** Taxable Amount of Ineligible Dividends	**(G)** Royalties from Canadian Sources	**(H)** Other Income from Canadian Sources	**(K)** Foreign Tax Paid	**(L)** Amount Eligible for Pension Deduction
Année	*Montant réel des dividendes non admissibles*	*Montant imposable des dividendes non admissibles*	*Redevances de sources canadiennes*	*Autres revenus de source canadienne*	*Impôt étranger payé*	*Montant admissibles à la déduction de pensions*

RECIPIENT: SURNAME FIRST, AND FULL ADDRESS
BÉNÉFICIAIRE: NOM DE FAMILLE D'ABORD, ET ADRESSE COMPLÈTE

Social Insurance Number
Numéro d'assurance sociale

672 004 326

→ Doe John
72 West 18th Street
Ourtown

NAME AND ADDRESS OF PAYER (Must appear on each slip)
NOM ET ADRESSE DU PAYEUR (À inscrire sur chaque feuillet)

Bank of Nova Scotia
West End Shopping Centre
Ourtown

- **For Recipient Attach to your Income Tax Return SEE INFORMATION ON REVERSE**
- *Pour le bénéficiaire - Annexer à votre déclaration d'impôt sur le revenu VOIR LES RENSEIGNEMENTS AU VERSO*

2

Figure 7.2

14

■◆ Revenue Canada   Revenu Canada
Taxation   Impôt

1983
T1 GENERAL

Federal and Ontario
Individual Income Tax Return
Identification

Name (Please print)
Mr. ~~Mrs. Miss Ms.~~

J O H N _ _ D O E

Social Insurance Number

6 7 2 0 0 4 3 2 6

Spouse's Social Insurance Number

Usual First Name and Initial   Surname, Family or Last Name

Your Date of Birth

Present Address (Please print)

7 2 _ W e s t _ 1 8 T h _ S t r e e t

Number, Street and Apt. No., or P.O. Box No. or R.R. No.

O U R T O W N

City

O N T A R I O   L O R _ 1 T O

Province or Territory   *Postal Code*

Day	Month	Year
1 0	1 0	1 9 6 5

Marital Status on December 31, 1983

Married 1 ☐   Widow(er) 2 ☐
Divorced 3 ☐   Separated 4 ☐
Single 5 ☒

Name of Spouse

Have you filed an Income Tax Return before?   YES 1 ☑   NO 2 ☐
If 'YES', please indicate for what year: 19 **8 2**
Name on last return: same as above ☑ or _____
Address on last return: same as above ☑ or _____

Type of work or occupation in 1983 *WAREHOUSE WORKER*
Name of present employer *X COMPANY LIMITED*
Address of Spouse: same as mine ☐ or _____

Your Province or Territory of Residence on December 31, 1983, was:
ONTARIO

If self-employed in 1983, please state province of self-employment:
_____

If you became or ceased to be a resident of Canada in 1983, give:

	Day	Month		Day	Month
Date of Entry			or Departure		

If taxpayer is deceased, Day   Month   Year
please give date of death:

Please do not
use this area

Calculation of Total Income

Income from Employment	Total Earnings Before Deductions from Box (C) on all T4 slips (attach copy 2 of T4 slips)	01	14 480 00 ⊙
	Commissions from Box (L) on all T4 slips, included in above total 02		
	Other employment income including training allowances, tips and gratuities, etc.		
	(please specify)	03	⊙
	Total employment earnings (add lines 01 and 03) 04		14 480 00
	Subtract: Employment expense deduction - If line 04 above is $2,500.00		
	or more, claim $500.00. If less, claim 20% of line 04. 05	500 00	⊙
	Other allowable expenses (please specify)		
	_____ 06		⊙
	Total employment expenses (add lines 05 and 06) 07	500 00 ▷	500 00
	Net employment earnings (subtract line 07 from line 04) 08		13 980 00
Pension Income	Old Age Security Pension (attach copy of T4A(OAS) slip) 09		⊙
	Canada or Quebec Pension Plan benefits (attach copy 2 of T4A(P) slip) 10		⊙
	Other pensions or superannuation (attach copy 3 of T4A slips) 11		⊙
Income from Other Sources	Taxable Family Allowance payments (attach copy of TFA1 slip) 12		⊙
	Unemployment Insurance benefits (attach copy 2 of T4U slip) 13		⊙
	Taxable amount of dividends from taxable Canadian corporations (attach completed Schedule 4) 14		⊙
	Interest and other investment income (attach completed Schedule 4) 15		216 83 ⊙
	Rental income (Schedule 7) Gross 03 Net 16		⊙
	Taxable capital gains (Allowable capital losses) - complete and attach Schedule 2 17		
	Indexed Security Investment Plan taxable capital gains (allowable capital losses)		
	(attach copy of form T5-ISIP) 915		⊙
	Other income (please specify) 18		⊙
Self-Employed Income	Business income Gross 84 Net 19		⊙
	Professional income Gross 85 Net 20		⊙
	Commission income Gross 86 Net 21		⊙
	Farming income Gross 87 Net 22		⊙
	Fishing income Gross 88 Net 23		⊙

Total Income (add lines 08 to 23 inclusive - please enter this amount on line 24 on page 2) 24 | 14 196 83 ▷ | 14 196 83

14

Please do not use this area 82

Please do not use this area 900

Figure 7.3

(3)   Net Income

Net income is determined by subtracting certain deductions from total income. These deductions are portions of your income that are not taxable. Deductions may be made for Canada or Quebec Pension Plan contributions, unemployment insurance premiums, registered pension plan and retirement savings plan payments, and union and professional dues. Tuition fees may be deducted by students only, whether they have been paid by the student or by someone else. Allowable child care expenses are also deducted in this section.

(4)   Taxable Income

Taxable income equals net income (calculated on page 1 of the tax return) less personal exemptions, deductions for medical expenses and charitable donations, and other deductions as listed at the bottom of page 2 of the income tax return.

   Personal exemptions represent the portion of income on which no tax is levied. Since 1973, personal exemptions have been adjusted to the Consumer Price Index. The average Consumer Price Index for the twelve month period ending 1972 09 30 was selected as the base amount. Hence, personal exemptions from taxation rise as the index rises. The total amount of your exemptions depends on the number, age, and net income of your dependents. Your dependents' net income is the figure they arrive at when they complete the net income section of the tax form.

   Trace carefully, item by item, the following example showing John Doe's calculation of net income and taxable income.

Example
(a) John has medical receipts of $232 and charitable donation receipts for $180.
(b) John's Statement of Investment Income (Schedule 4) shows that he may claim $216.83 as an interest and dividend income deduction under other deductions from net income.
(c) John can claim the cost of his safety deposit box under other deductions, line 39.
(d) The net amount eligible for interest, dividends, and capital gains deduction (E) on Schedule 4 is transferred to line 51 on page 2.

(5)   Federal and Provincial Tax Payable

There are two methods of tax calculation: the tax table method and the detailed calculation method. A tax table is provided in the tax guide for taxpayers who
• have taxable income below a specified amount subject to yearly change
• have no Tax Adjustment, Dividend Tax Credit, or Foreign Tax Credit
• have no self-employed income from a business with a permanent establishment outside the province in which they reside.

Schedule 4 – **Statement of Investment Income** (See "Line 14" and "Line 15" in Guide)

State names of payers in appropriate areas and enclose any information slips received. If space below is insufficient attach statements.

I – Taxable Amount of Dividends from Taxable Canadian Corporations
Include amounts credited through banks, trust companies, brokers and estates.
  1. Dividends Eligible for Interest, Dividends and Capital Gains Deduction
  (from Box (H) on T3 slips or Box (B) on T5 slips) – *do **not** include dividends received from a corporation not dealt with at arm's length*

Total dividends eligible for interest, dividends and capital gains deduction *(area V below)* ◊ _____ (A)

  2. Dividends Not Eligible for Interest, Dividends and Capital Gains Deduction
  (from Box (I) on T3 slips, Box (F) on T5 slips or Box (E) on T5-ISIP) – *include dividends received from a corporation not dealt with at arm's length*

Total dividends not eligible for interest, dividends and capital gains deduction ◊

Taxable Amount of Dividends from Taxable Canadian Corporations *(Enter this amount on line 14 on page 1 of return)*

II – Interest from Canadian Sources Eligible for Interest, Dividends and Capital Gains Deduction
Interest from Canada Savings Bonds,   BANK OF NOVA SCOTIA   216 83
Other Bonds, and Trust, Bank or
other Deposits (specify)
Interest from Mortgages, Notes and other
Securities *(except interest received from a related*
person and from a partnership by a partner)
Eligible Annuity Payments (See item D under "Line 15" in Guide)

Total Interest from Canadian Sources Eligible for Interest, Dividends and Capital Gains Deduction *(area V below)*   216 83 ◊   216 83 (B)

III – Other Investment Income Not Eligible for Interest, Dividends and Capital Gains Deduction
Other Canadian Investment Income (specify)

Interest and Other Investment
Income from Foreign Sources

Total Other Investment Income Not Eligible for Interest, Dividends and Capital Gains Deduction ◊

Total Interest and Other Investment Income *(Enter on line 15 on page 1 of your return)*

IV – Carrying Charges (See item A under "Line 39" in Guide)
Interest on money borrowed to earn Investment Income eligible for Interest, Dividends and Capital Gains Deduction
Interest on money borrowed to earn other Investment Income
Management or Safe Custody Fees
Safety Deposit Box Charges   12 50
Accounting Fees
Investment Counsel Fees
Other *(please specify)*

Total Carrying Charges *(Enter this amount as 'Other deductions' on line 39 on page 2 of your return)*   12 50 (C)

V – Calculation of Interest, Dividends and Capital Gains Deduction (See "Line 51" in Guide)
Total dividends eligible for interest, dividends and capital gains deduction *(amount (A) above)*
Total interest from Canadian sources eligible for interest, dividends and capital gains deduction *(amount (B) above)*   216 83
Eligible Taxable Capital Gains – One-half of the Gains included in the amounts on lines 978, 980 and 989 on
  Schedule 2 – *(for the purpose of this calculation, capital losses should be excluded from these amounts)*

Total of above three amounts   (D)

Subtract: Interest on money borrowed to earn income eligible for this deduction
(See item A under "Line 39" in Guide)

Net amount eligible for interest, dividends and capital gains deduction   216 83 (E)

Interest, Dividends and Capital Gains Deduction *(Enter $1,000.00 or amount (E), whichever is less, on line 51 on page 2 of your return)*

Figure 7.4

2 Calculation of Taxable Income

Total Income (from line 24 on page 1) 24   14 196 83

Deductions from Total Income			
Canada or Quebec Pension Plan contributions			
Contributions through employment from Box (D) on all T4 slips (maximum $300.60)	25	228 24	
Contribution payable on self-employed earnings (from page 3)	26		
Unemployment Insurance premiums from Box (E) on all T4 slips (maximum $460.72)	29	333 04	
Registered pension plan contributions	32	868 80	
Registered retirement savings plan premiums (attach receipts)	33		
Registered home ownership savings plan contributions (attach receipts)	34		
Annual union, professional or like dues (attach receipts)	35	240 00	
Tuition fees - claimable by student only (attach receipts)	36		
Child care expenses (complete and attach Schedule 5)	37		
Allowable business investment losses	38		
Other deductions (please specify) SAFETY DEPOSIT BOX	39	12 50	

Add lines 25 to 39 inclusive 40   1682 58   ▷   1682 58

Net Income (subtract line 40 from line 24) 41   12 514 25

Add: Accumulated Forward Averaging Amount Withdrawal (from form T581)   **917**
                                                        41(a)

Claim for Personal Exemptions

Basic Personal Exemption	Claim $3,770.00	3770 00	
Age Exemption - If you were born in 1918 or earlier	Claim $2,360.00		
If you did not receive the Old Age Security Pension, attach a letter giving reasons.			

Married Exemption - If applicable, please check ✓ box 1. or 2.

Married on or before December 31, 1983, and supported spouse in 1983

1. whose net income in that year, while married, was not over $570.00   1. ☐   Claim $3,300.00   **42**

2. whose net income in that year, while married, was over $570.00

but not over $3,870.00   2. ☐   3,870 00

Subtract: spouse's net income while married

If your marital status changed   Claim

in 1983, please give date of change

Exemption for Wholly Dependent Children - Provide details below and claim according to child's age and net income. *See Guide if child's net income exceeds limit.*
Children born in 1966 or later - Claim $710.00 for each child whose net income was not over $2,450.00
Children born in 1965 or earlier - Claim $1,300.00 for each child whose net income was not over $2,570.00 and who, if born in 1961 or earlier, was in full-time attendance at a school or university or was infirm.

Name of child (attach list if space insufficient)	Relationship to you	Date of birth of child Day Month Year	If born in 1961 or earlier state whether infirm or school attended	Net income in 1983 $	Claim

Total claim for wholly dependent children **43**   ▷

Additional Personal Exemptions from Schedule 6 attached   **44**

Total Personal Exemptions (add above items)   **45**   3770 00   ▷   3770 00

Subtract line 45 from line 41(a) 46   8 744 25

Other deductions from Net Income

Standard deduction - Claim $100.00 (no receipts required) **or** total at line 50 below, **but not both**   47   180 00

Medical expenses - (attach receipts and complete Schedule 9)	48	232 00	
Subtract: 3% of 'Net Income' (line 41 above)		375 43	
Allowable portion of medical expenses		0	
Add: **Charitable donations** (attach all receipts)	49	180 00	
Total (If this amount is greater than $100.00, enter on line 47 above)	50	180 00	

Interest, dividends and capital gains deduction (attach completed Schedule 4)	51	216 83	
Pension income deduction	52		
Deduction for blind persons or persons confined to a bed or wheelchair			
Claim relates to: Self ☐ or dependant other than spouse (specify)	53		
Education deduction (attach completed form T2202 or T2202A)	54		
Deductions transferred from spouse (attach completed Schedule 3)	55		
Gifts to Canada or a province (attach receipts)	56		
Unemployment Insurance benefit repayment payable from page 3	58		
Non-capital losses of other years	59		
Capital losses of other years (1972 to 1982)	60		

Add lines 47, 51 to 60 inclusive   61   396 83   ▷   396 83

Subtract line 61 from line 46   61(a)   8 447 42

Subtract: **Forward Averaging Elective Income Deduction** from form T540   **911**

Taxable Income (enter this amount on page 4)   **62**   8 447 42

Figure 7.5

Since John Doe has no Dividend Tax Credit, Foreign Tax Credit, or Tax Adjustment, and earns less than $30 000, he can use the tax table method and complete Schedule 1 to calculate his income tax payable. The first step is to transfer the amount of taxable income from line 62 on the tax return page 2 to page 4. Total federal tax is found by using the rates given at the bottom of Schedule 1.

1983 FEDERAL AND ONTARIO TAX TABLE

(1) Taxable Income over — not over	(2) Federal Tax	(3) Ontario Tax Payable
$ 8400– 8410	$ 1138	$ 655.50
8410– 8420	1140	656.40
8420– 8430	1142	657.30
8430– 8440	1144	658.30
8440– 8450	1145	659.20
8450– 8460	1147	660.10
8460– 8470	1149	661.10
8470– 8480	1151	662.00
8480– 8490	1153	662.90
8490– 8500	1155	663.90

Figure 7.6

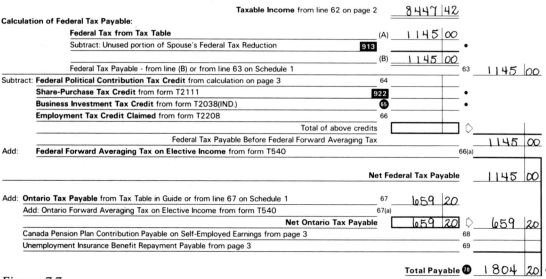

4 Summary of Tax and Credits There are two methods of tax calculation (see Guide).

Taxable Income from line 62 on page 2 —— 8447 42

Calculation of Federal Tax Payable:

Federal Tax from Tax Table   (A) 1145 00

Subtract: Unused portion of Spouse's Federal Tax Reduction   **913**   •

                                                                            (B) 1145 00

Federal Tax Payable - from line (B) or from line 63 on Schedule 1   63   1145 00

Subtract: **Federal Political Contribution Tax Credit** from calculation on page 3   64

Share-Purchase Tax Credit from form T2111   **922**   •

Business Investment Tax Credit from form T2038(IND.)   **65**   •

Employment Tax Credit Claimed from form T2208   66

Total of above credits   [   ] ◇

Federal Tax Payable Before Federal Forward Averaging Tax   1145 00

Add: **Federal Forward Averaging Tax on Elective Income** from form T540   66(a)

Net Federal Tax Payable   1145 00

Add: **Ontario Tax Payable** from Tax Table in Guide or from line 67 on Schedule 1   67   659 20

Add: Ontario Forward Averaging Tax on Elective Income from form T540   67(a)

Net Ontario Tax Payable   [659 20] ◇   659 20

Canada Pension Plan Contribution Payable on Self-Employed Earnings from page 3   68

Unemployment Insurance Benefit Repayment Payable from page 3   69

Total Payable **70**   1804 20 •

Figure 7.7

If John Doe lived in a province other than Ontario or Quebec, he would calculate his provincial tax payable as follows:

Newfoundland: 60% of Basic Federal Tax = $687.00
Prince Edward Island: 52.5% of Basic Federal Tax = $601.13
Nova Scotia: 56.5% of Basic Federal Tax = $646.93
New Brunswick: 58% of Basic Federal Tax = $664.10
(Note: Basic Federal Tax is $1 145.)

Basic Manitoba Income Tax—54% of **'Basic Federal Tax'**	618 30
Add: Manitoba Surtax—20% of ('Basic Manitoba Income Tax' in excess of $2,675.00)	0
Adjusted Manitoba Income Tax	618 30
Subtract: Provincial Foreign Tax Credit from calculation on form T2036	
Manitoba Tax	618 30
Subtract: Manitoba Tax Reduction—If your Taxable Income is greater than $3,620.00, enter zero at this line. Otherwise, see Guide.	0
MANITOBA TAX PAYABLE 67 ✱	618 30

Figure 7.8

Basic Saskatchewan Tax Payable – from Tax Table in Guide or 51% of 'Basic Federal Tax' on Schedule 1	583 95
Add: Saskatchewan Surtax – 12% of (Basic Saskatchewan Tax Payable in excess of $4,000.00)	0
Adjusted Saskatchewan Tax Payable *(if amount is $160.00 or less, do not proceed; simply enter zero on line (F))* (A)	583 95

Subtract: Saskatchewan Tax Reductions

1. Basic Tax Reduction 1.   160 00

2. Child Tax Reduction – Claim $50.00 for each dependent child resident in Canada, born in 1966 or later and claimed by you

       Number of children **905**   X $50.00 *(maximum $300.00)*   2.

      ⊙

3. Senior Citizens Tax Reduction – Claim $50.00 if you were born in 1918 or earlier   3.

                        Sub-total (B)

Subtract: Enter Amount (A)
            minus Amount (B)

                        X 30% *(if negative, enter zero)*   (C)

Total of Saskatchewan Tax Reductions (Amount (B) Minus Amount (C))
                               (if negative, enter zero)   ►(D)   0

Reduced Saskatchewan Tax Payable (Amount (A) minus Amount (D)); *(if negative, enter zero)*	(E)	583 95
Subtract: Provincial Foreign Tax Credit from calculation on form T2036		
Net Saskatchewan Tax Payable – Enter this amount on line 67 on your return	(F)	583 95

Figure 7.9

Basic Alberta Income Tax—38.5% of **'Basic Federal Tax'**		440 83
Subtract: Royalty Tax Rebate applied (from line (H) on form T79)		0
Alberta Income Tax after rebate	(A)	440 83

Subtract: Alberta Selective Tax Reduction:

Basic claim		300 00	
Subtract ½ of Alberta Income Tax after rebate (Amount (A) above)		220 42	
Total *(if negative, there is no reduction, enter zero)*	(B)	79 58	
Subtract Amount (A) or Amount (B), whichever is less, as the tax reduction			79 58
Reduced Alberta Income Tax			361 25
Subtract: Provincial Foreign Tax Credit from calculation on form T2036			
ALBERTA TAX PAYABLE 67 ✱			361 25

Figure 7.10

Basic British Columbia Income Tax—44% of ['Basic Federal Tax'] _____ 503|80

Subtract: Provincial Foreign Tax Credit from calculation on form T2036

Adjusted British Columbia Tax Payable _____ 503|80

Add: British Columbia Surtax—10% of ('Adjusted British Columbia Tax Payable' in excess of $3,500.00)

BRITISH COLUMBIA TAX PAYABLE 67 * _____ 503|80

Figure 7.11

(6) Provincial Tax Credit

If you live in Ontario, Manitoba, or Alberta, you may be able to reduce your tax payable by completing the provincial tax credit page.

John paid $2 880 in rent last year. The sales tax credit is found by taking 1% of John's personal exemption, $3 770 as shown on page 2 of the tax return. The 2% of taxable income is based on the amount calculated on page 2.

ONTARIO TAX CREDITS

T1C (ONT.)

Basic guidelines for claiming Ontario Tax Credits appear on the reverse side of this form.
The Ontario Ministry of Revenue administers a separate grant program for persons 65 years of age and older.
Persons eligible to claim these grants are not entitled to claim the Property or Sales Tax Credits, or the Temporary Home Heating Credit on this form.

Calculation of Ontario Property and Sales Tax Credits for 1983

PROPERTY TAX CREDIT – *See item 1 on the Reverse Side and Complete the Declaration Below.*

Total Rental Payments in 1983	910	$2 880|00 ×20% = $576|00	
Property Taxes paid in 1983	920		
College Residence – claim $25.00 – *see item 1(f)*	930		
Occupancy Cost (total of above three lines) – *see item 1(d)*	940	$576|00	

Enter $180.00 or 'Occupancy Cost' (line 940), whichever is *less* $180|00

Add: 10% of 'Occupancy Cost' (line 940) 57|60

Total Property Tax Credit 237|60 $237|60

SALES TAX CREDIT – 1% of 'Total Personal Exemptions' (line 45 on page 2 of your return) – *see item 2* 37|70

Total of above credits (A) $275|30

ENTER 2% of 'Taxable Income' (line 62 on page 2 of your return) or if Taxable Income is $1,986.00 or less, enter "NIL". (B) $168|95

NET PROPERTY AND SALES TAX CREDITS – Subtract Amount (B) from Amount (A).
If Amount (B) is greater than Amount (A), enter "NIL". (C) $106|35

ENTER Amount (C) or $500.00, whichever is *less*, on line (D) (D) $106|35

Calculation of Ontario Temporary Home Heating Credit for 1983 *(See item 3 on Reverse Side)*

Basic Heating Credit for 1983 20|00

ENTER 1% of 'Taxable Income' (line 62 on page 2 of your return) or if Taxable Income is $1,986.00 or less, enter "NIL". (E) _____

NET TEMPORARY HOME HEATING CREDIT – Subtract Amount (E) from $20.00. If Amount (E) is greater than $20.00, enter "NIL". (F) _____

NET PROPERTY AND SALES TAX CREDITS AND TEMPORARY HOME HEATING CREDIT – Add Amounts (D) and (F). (G) _____

Calculation of Ontario Political Contribution Tax Credit for 1983

Attach official receipts to this form *otherwise your claim will be rejected.*

Total Ontario Political Contributions in 1983 950 _____

Allowable credit – 75% of first $100.00 of Total Contributions is _____

50% of next $450.00 of Total Contributions is _____

33⅓% of amount of Total Contributions exceeding $550.00 is _____

Total allowable credit *(maximum $500.00)* (i) _____

Ontario Tax Payable (from line 67 on your return) _____

SUBTRACT: Ontario Property and Sales Tax Credits and Temporary Home Heating Credit (Amount (G) above)

Ontario Tax Payable in excess (ii) _____

ALLOWABLE ONTARIO POLITICAL CONTRIBUTION TAX CREDIT –
Enter Amount (i), or Amount (ii), whichever is *less* (H) _____

Ontario Tax Credits – Total of Amounts (G) and (H) – Enter this amount on line 74 on your return. _____

Declaration (If Property Tax Credit claimed)

I hereby declare that the address(es) of my principal residence(s) in Ontario during the 1983 taxation year was (were):

Address(es) of Principal Residence(s)		No. of Months Resident in 1983	Rent/Property Tax Paid in 1983	Name of Landlord/Municipality
1	Rent ☐ Own ☐		$	
2	Rent ☐ Own ☐		$	

If you had more than 2 principal residences, continue on a separate sheet. *See item 1(c).*

Certification

I certify that the information in this document is true and correct and if I am claiming the Property and Sales Tax Credits or Temporary Home Heating Credit, that I was not 65 years of age or older on December 31, 1983.

Date _____ Sign here _____

Figure 7.12

If John Doe lived in Manitoba or Alberta, he would calculate his provincial tax credit as shown in Figures 7.13, 7.14.

MANIT☘BA   TAX CREDIT PROGRAMS   T1C (MAN.)

Calculation of Family Income (If single, or spouse has no net income, enter zero at line 2 below)

My Net Income (line 41 on page 2 of my return)	1	12 514 25	
My spouse's Net Income (line 41 on my spouse's return – *if negative, enter zero,* **931**	2		
Family Income (Add lines 1 and 2)	3	12 514 25	

Calculation of Manitoba Cost of Living Tax Credit for 1983

For All Claimants: Basic Credit: 3% of total of amounts on lines 45, 53 and 54 on page 2 of your return   113 10 (A)

Additional Credit for Married Persons: If you are a married person at the end of 1983 **and** your spouse has agreed that only you will claim the Manitoba Cost of Living Tax Credit, enter 3% of the total of the amounts that are claimable by your spouse on lines

45, 53 and 54 on page 2 of a separate return (whether it is filed or not)	**969**	4		
Subtract: 3% of the amount claimed, if any, on line 42 on page 2 of your return		5		
Additional Credit		6	➥	0 (B)
Total of above amounts (A) and (B)				113 10 (C)
Subtract: 1% of 'Family Income' (line 3 above)				125 14 (D)
Manitoba Cost of Living Tax Credit – *if negative, enter zero*				0 (E)

Calculation of Manitoba Property Tax Credit for 1983

Total Rental Payments for 1983 in Manitoba	**910** 2880	X 20% = 7	576 00	
Net Property Taxes *paid* for 1983 in Manitoba	**920**	8	0	
Add: Resident Homeowner Tax Assistance (see instruction on back) – *if not received, enter zero*	**930**	9	0	
Occupancy Cost (total of lines 7, 8 and 9)	**940**	10	576 00 (F)	

Basic Credit of $525.00	11	525 00	
Senior Citizens – Add $100.00 if you were born in 1918 or earlier	12		
Sub-total (Add lines 11 and 12)		525 00	
Subtract: 1% of 'Family Income' (line 3 above)		125 14	
Total (minimum $325.00)		399 86 (G)	

Total Manitoba Property Tax Credit – Enter Amount (F) or Amount (G), whichever is less   13   399 86

Subtract: (a) Resident Homeowner Tax Assistance if received (line 9 above)

(b) Shelter Allowance Program benefits received during 1983 *(see reverse)* **951**

14   0

Net Manitoba Property Tax Credit (line 13 minus line 14)   399 86 ➥ 399 86 (H)
(If claimed, complete Declaration on reverse)

Manitoba Cost of Living and Property Tax Credit – Add Amounts (E) and (H). If you did not have a Manitoba Political Contribution in 1983, enter this amount on line 74 of your return.   399 86 (I)

Figure 7.13

To claim the Alberta Tax Credits: *See reverse side for Basic Eligibility Rules.*

* complete all requested information shown on this form for the tax credits you are claiming and attach one signed copy of this form to your income tax return.
* file a completed Individual Income Tax Return, even if you have no taxable income but are claiming Alberta tax credits

Calculation of Alberta Renter Assistance Credit for 1983
Note: The Renter Assistance Credit is not applicable to persons aged 65 and over (see reverse).
Receipts for rental payments are not required to be filed with the return but must be retained for examination on request

Total Rental Payments in 1983 in Alberta   **910**   2880 00

Basic Credit Allowance of $200.00	200 00
Add: 5% of the above 'Total Rental Payments in 1983 in Alberta' (line 910 above)	144 00
Total Basic Credit Allowance (maximum $500.00)	344 .00
Deduct: 1% of 'Taxable Income' (line 62 on page 2 of your return)	125 14
Enter the **greater of this amount or $50.00** on line (A) below	218 86

Alberta Renter Assistance Credit – If you did not have an Alberta Political Contribution for 1983, sign this form and enter Amount (A) on the 'Alberta Tax Credits' line 74 on your return.   (A)   50 00

Calculation of Alberta Political Contribution Tax Credit for 1983
Attach official receipts to this form otherwise your claim will be rejected.

Total Alberta Political Contributions in 1983   **960**

Allowable credit - 75% of first $150.00 of Total Contributions is	
50% of next $675.00 of Total Contributions is	
33¹⁄₃% of amount of Total Contributions exceeding $825.00 is	
Total allowable credit *(maximum $750.00)*	(i)

Alberta Tax Payable (from line 67 on your return)   (ii)

ALLOWABLE ALBERTA POLITICAL CONTRIBUTION TAX CREDIT – Enter Amount (i), or Amount (ii), whichever is *less*   (B)

Alberta Tax Credits – Total of Amounts (A) and (B) – Enter this amount on line 74 on your return.   50 00

Figure 7.14

(7)   Balance Due or Refund Claimed

Total Federal Political Contributions
`960` _____

Tax Adjustments
`961` _____ •

Foreign Taxes Paid
`962` _____ •

Net Foreign Income
`963` _____

`975` _____

Total tax deducted per information slips	**71**	1708 20 • ⊙
Ontario Tax Credits	**74**	106 35 •
Canada Pension Plan Overpayment	**75**	•
Unemployment Insurance Overpayment	**76**	•
Amounts paid by instalments	**77**	•
Child Tax Credit (from Schedule 10)	**78**	•
Forward Averaging Tax Credit (from form T581)	**923**	• ⊙
Refund of Business Investment Tax Credit (from form T2038-IND.)	**924**	• ⊙

Total Credits 1814 55 ▷ 1814 55

Please enter this difference in applicable space below. 10 35
A difference of less than $1.00 is neither charged nor refunded.

IMPORTANT: The inside front cover of your guide tells you when to expect your refund.

Refund 79 ___ 10 35 •   **Balance Due 80** _____ •

Amount Enclosed _____ •

Please attach cheque or money order **payable to the Receiver General. Do not mail cash.**
Payment is due not later than April 30, 1984.

Name and address of any individual or firm, other than the taxpayer, who has prepared this return for compensation.
Name _____
Address _____
Telephone _____

I hereby certify that the information given in this return and in any documents attached is true, correct and complete in every respect and fully discloses my income from all sources.

Please sign here *John Doe*
Date *April 28, 1984* Telephone 679-1389

It is a serious offence to make a false return.

Privacy Act Personal Information Bank number RC-T-P20

Form authorized and prescribed by order of the Minister of National Revenue for purposes of Part I of the Income Tax Act, Part I of the Canada Pension Plan and Part VIII of the Unemployment Insurance Act, 1971.

Figure 7.15

(8)   Income Tax in Quebec

Taxpayers in the province of Quebec must complete two sets of income tax forms.

The *Federal Individual Income Tax Return* for residents of Quebec on December 31 must be completed to determine federal income tax payable. It is submitted to Revenue Canada. This form is very similar to the Federal and Provincial Individual Income Tax Return for all other Canadian taxpayers. The section on page 3 for calculation of Canada Pension Plan contributions for self-employed workers is replaced by a section enabling residents of Quebec who were employed outside the province of Quebec during the taxation year, to transfer to the province of Quebec a percent of the tax deducted by an employer in another province.

Transfer of Tax Deducted - Quebec Residents Employed Outside the Province

- Residents of Quebec on December 31, 1983 employed outside the province during 1983 may transfer income tax deducted on T4 slips issued by your employers outside Quebec.
- Your employer deducted income tax for the province where you worked. However, your provincial tax is payable to the province where you resided on December 31.
- When filing your return you may transfer to Quebec 45% of the tax deducted by your employer outside the Province of Quebec.

Calculate the transfer as follows:

Total 'Income Tax Deducted' on T4 slips from employers outside Quebec _____

Transfer of Tax Deducted - 45% of the above amount. Enter this amount on line 72 on page 4. Claim this amount on your 1983 Quebec Income Tax Return. _____

Note: Include all tax deducted on line 71 'Total tax deducted per information slips' on page 4.

If you do not have a federal taxable income, no transfer is necessary. All the deductions of tax made by your employer outside Quebec will be refunded to you when your federal return is assessed.

of Part I of the Income Tax Act, Part I of the Canada Pension Plan and Part VIII of the Unemployment Insurance Act, 1971.

Privacy Act Personal Information Bank number RC-T-P20

Figure 7.16

On page 4, province of Quebec taxpayers deduct any tax deducted transferred, from total tax deducted per information slips, to find tax deducted applicable to federal tax. They then add the refundable Quebec abatement (a percent of Basic Federal Tax) to find total credits.

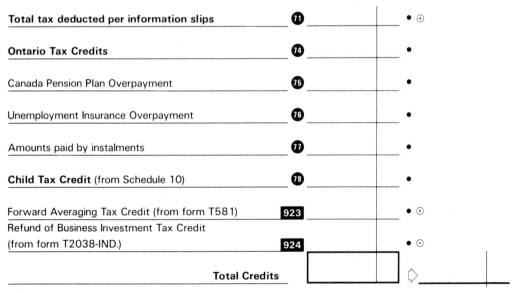

Total tax deducted per information slips	**71**	• ⊙
Ontario Tax Credits	**74**	•
Canada Pension Plan Overpayment	**75**	•
Unemployment Insurance Overpayment	**76**	•
Amounts paid by instalments	**77**	•
Child Tax Credit (from Schedule 10)	**78**	•
Forward Averaging Tax Credit (from form T581)	**923**	• ⊙
Refund of Business Investment Tax Credit (from form T2038-IND.)	**924**	• ⊙
Total Credits		

Figure 7.17

The *Provincial Return of Income*, which does not include family allowances or unemployment insurance benefits in the calculation of net income, must be completed and submitted to the Minister of Revenue for Quebec.

The calculations for Quebec Pension Plan contributions for employed and self-employed taxpayers, and for overpayments of Quebec Pension Plan, are included in this Return of Income. Quebec Health Insurance Plan contributions are calculated and added to income tax to find the total payable.

If you live in the province of Quebec, you should calculate the income tax for the situations in Exercise 7.1 using your Provincial Return of Income and the Federal Income Tax Return for residents of Quebec on December 31 of the taxation year.

EXERCISE 7.1
Prepare individual income tax returns for the following people.

1. Steve Haché lives at 48 Pine Street and was born May 3. He is 18 years old, lives with his parents, goes to high school, and has a social insurance number 473 992 537. During the past year he worked as a short-order cook at Tasty Foods and as a waiter at the Sunny Diner. His T4 slips give the following information.
Total earnings, $4 525
Canada Pension Plan contributions, $49.05
Unemployment insurance premiums, $104.08
Income tax deducted, $102.50
Steve has one T5 slip showing $98.52 earned on his bank savings account and another T5 showing $127.50 earned on his Canada Savings Bonds. He pays $14 per year for a safety deposit box.

2. Teresa Bronson, 21 years old, lives at 38 Graham Avenue, and attends a community college. Last summer she worked for J.B. Black, 142 Centre Street. During the rest of the year she did some part-time bookkeeping for Bradford Hardware, 91 Centre Street. She paid $2 160 in rent last year and donated a total of $120 to charity. Teresa's T4 slips showed the following.
Total earnings, $7 475
Canada Pension Plan contributions, $102.15
Unemployment insurance premiums, $171.93
Income tax deducted, $307.10
She has a T5 slip showing earnings of $163.98 on her bank savings account and a receipt from her school showing that her parents paid $550 in tuition fees on her behalf. Teresa's social insurance number is 673 000 485.

3. Rick Stacey has been working as a sales clerk at Barker's Pharmacy. He is 23 years old, has his own apartment at 27 Brock Street, which he rents

for $260 per month, and his social insurance number is 619 000 483.
Rick's T4 slip shows the following.
Total earnings, $16 400
Canada Pension Plan contributions, $262.80
Unemployment insurance premiums, $377.20
Income tax deducted, $2 200.20
Registered retirement savings plan premiums, $1 000.00
Last year he paid out $538 for medical and dental expenses and donated
$110 to charity. He also has T5 slips showing that he earned $206.93 on
his bank savings account and $155 on his Canada Savings Bonds.

1983 FEDERAL AND ONTARIO TAX TABLE

(1) Taxable Income over / not over	(2) Federal Tax	(3) Ontario Tax Payable	(1) Taxable Income over / not over	(2) Federal Tax	(3) Ontario Tax Payable
$ 2100– 2110	$ 19	$ 68.70	$10100–10110	$ 1461	$ 814.40
2110– 2120	21	74.50	10110–10120	1463	815.30
2120– 2130	22	80.20	10120–10130	1465	816.30
2130– 2140	24	86.00	10130–10140	1467	817.20
2140– 2150	26	91.80	10140–10150	1468	818.10
2150– 2160	27	97.50	10150–10160	1470	819.10
2160– 2170	29	103.30	10160–10170	1472	820.00
2170– 2180	30	109.10	10170–10180	1474	820.90
2180– 2190	32	111.40	10180–10190	1476	821.90
2190– 2200	34	112.10	10190–10200	1478	822.80
$ 2200– 2210	$ 35	$ 112.90	$10200–10210	$ 1480	$ 823.70
2210– 2220	37	113.70	10210–10220	1482	824.70
2220– 2230	38	114.50	10220–10230	1484	825.60
2230– 2240	40	115.30	10230–10240	1486	826.50
2240– 2250	42	116.10	10240–10250	1487	827.50
2250– 2260	43	116.90	10250–10260	1489	828.40
2260– 2270	45	117.60	10260–10270	1491	829.30
2270– 2280	46	118.40	10270–10280	1493	830.30
2280– 2290	48	119.20	10280–10290	1495	831.20
2290– 2300	50	120.00	10290–10300	1497	832.10
$ 2300– 2310	$ 51	$ 120.80	$10300–10310	$ 1499	$ 833.10
2310– 2320	53	121.60	10310–10320	1501	834.00
2320– 2330	54	122.40	10320–10330	1503	835.00
2330– 2340	56	123.20	10330–10340	1505	835.90
2340– 2350	58	123.90	10340–10350	1506	836.80
2350– 2360	59	124.70	10350–10360	1508	837.80
2360– 2370	60	125.20	10360–10370	1510	838.70
2370– 2380	62	126.10	10370–10380	1512	839.60
2380– 2390	64	126.90	10380–10390	1514	840.60
2390– 2400	65	127.70	10390–10400	1516	841.50

CUMULATIVE REVIEW 5

1. Multiply mentally.
   (a) 36 × 25   (b) 96 × 125

2. Using the 1% method find
   (a) $\frac{1}{2}$% of 456   (b) 2% of 264

3. Find the value of x if $4x + 6 = 10$.

4. 40% of 372 equals what number?

5. What number increased by 25% of itself equals 80?

6. Divide mentally.
   (a) $120 \div 8$ (b) $1\,625 \div 125$

7. If $a = 3$, $b = 2$, and $c = 1$, find the value of
   (a) $3ab + 2ac - 6ac$ (b) $4a^2 + 2b^2 - 3c^2$

8. Find $\frac{1}{2}\%$ of 4 864.

9. 75 increased by what rate equals 90?

10. 364 increased by 30% of itself and the result decreased by 10% equals what number?

11. What would be the commission rate if a salesperson earned $2 288 on sales of $28 600?

12. What number increased by 40% of itself and the result decreased by 20% equals 560?

13. Sam earned $640 last week. If he received 5% commission on all sales, how much were his sales?

14. How much interest would you earn for the month of May if your investment was $5 000 and the interest rate was 9%?

15. How long would it take to earn $80 from an investment of $1 000 if the rate is 8% per annum?

16. State the value for n and i for each of the following.

	Rate of Interest	Compounded	Time
(a)	10%	Quarterly	12 a
(b)	9%	Semi-annually	18 a

17. Find the weekly earnings for a 44 h week if the rate for regular hours is $10.40/h and the rate for all time over 40 h/week is time-and-one-half.

18. June earned $186.80 for a 40 h week. What was her rate per hour?

19. What rate of interest should you look for if you want to earn $281.25 on an investment of $2 500 in one year?

20. Using your knowledge of aliquot parts find the cost of buying 392 items at $12\frac{1}{2}$¢ each.

UNIT 8

Buying Merchandise

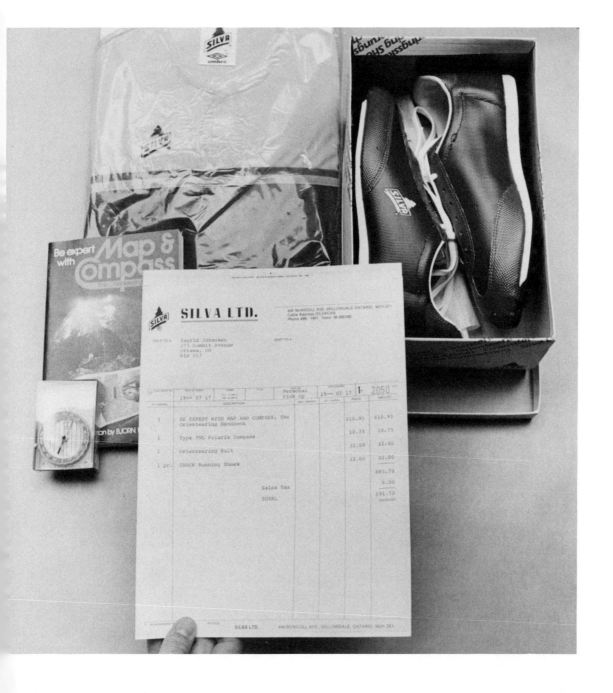

8.1 CONSUMER PURCHASES

A   Using Cash

When you go to a store to buy a record, jeans, or a bottle of pop, or to have your hair cut, you are a consumer. Every person who buys a product or service for his/her personal use is considered to be a consumer, a person who uses or consumes goods and services. Anyone who sells to consumers is called a retailer. When a consumer buys and pays for a product or service, the retailer gives either a cash register tape or a sales receipt to the customer.

```
~~~~~~~~~~~~~~~~~~~~
19-- 04 11
$29.95   I
  9.95   II
 39.90   Subtotal
  2.79   Sales Tax
 42.69   TOTAL

       Thank you
       Jones Ltd.
~~~~~~~~~~~~~~~~~~~~
```

Cash Register Tape

Jones Ltd.			
18 Palmer St.			
Amherst, NS B4H 1Z5			

Sold to: John Manson
16 Birch St.
Bedford, NS B4A 2W6

Date: 19-- 04 11   Terms: 30 d

QUANTITY	ITEM	UNIT PRICE	AMOUNT
1 pr.	jeans	$29.95 pr.	$29.95
1	T-shirt	9.95 ea.	9.95
			39.90
		Sales Tax	2.79
		TOTAL	42.69

2% per month on overdue accounts

Why is it important for consumers to receive either a cash register tape or a sales receipt from retailers? Why do some retailers give only cash register tapes and other retailers give sales receipts?

B   Using Credit

In the above example the consumer paid cash for the goods received from Jones Ltd. If the consumer had chosen to defer payment, he might have used the retailer's credit and charged it, or he might have used a credit card such as VISA. What is the difference on the business form to indicate cash or charge? Which would be more expensive to the retailer? Why?

Retailers' credit cards may be used only when buying from the issuing company. For example, a Sears card may be used only in a Sears store in Canada and in a Sears Roebuck store in the United States. A Texaco credit card may be used only at a service station selling Texaco products.

There is no service charge for the use of these cards but you pay a high rate of interest if you do not pay your bill promptly. Department stores allow you to pay a minimum amount each month depending on your balance and you pay a credit charge (interest) based on your previous month's balance.

Following is an excerpt from a department store charge card statement.

"IF YOU PAY YOUR ACCOUNT IN FULL WITHIN 25 DAYS OF THE BILLING DATE SHOWN ON THE STATEMENT, THERE IS NO CREDIT CHARGE.

A credit charge is added to your account monthly based on the previous month's balance, calculated at the rate of 2.40% per month (28.8% per annum).

If payment of 50% or more of your previous balance is received within the current billing period, the payment will be deducted before credit charge is calculated."

General purpose credit cards such as VISA, MasterCard, or American Express may be used at participating establishments all over the world. VISA charges a yearly user fee or a fee for each transaction. Consumers who use the card only a few times a year save money by selecting the transaction fee rather than the yearly fee. The yearly fee may be paid monthly as part of the monthly charge for a special bank account such as the Bank of Nova Scotia's SCOTIACLUB. At the present time MasterCard does not charge a user fee but the interest rate for payments made after the due date is higher than VISA's. American Express charges a relatively large user fee and you must pay the total amount shown on your statement each month.

In all cases, the interest charged for bills not paid on or before the due date is higher than you would pay if you borrowed the money from a chartered bank or trust company.

Example

Pam charged several purchases totalling $267.45 during April. The due date was May 22 and the charge for overdue payments was 18.6%/a calculated daily.
(a) How much would Pam pay on May 22?
(b) How much interest would appear on Pam's next statement if she paid her account on June 3?
(c) Pam paid a $12 annual user fee. What percent would the monthly portion of the fee be of her month's charges?

Solution

(a) Pam would pay the amount shown on the statement, $267.45.
(b) Interest $= \$267.45 \times 0.186 \times \frac{12}{365}$

$\qquad = \$1.64$
(c) The monthly portion of the fee would be $\frac{\$1}{\$267.45}$ or 0.37% of her April charge purchases.

EXERCISE 8.1

1. Joan's department store credit card statement dated May 28 showed a balance owing of $250. She could pay the whole sum at once or pay the $6 minimum payment and be charged 2.4%/month on the $250.
   (a) How much interest would Joan be charged on her June statement if she paid the minimum amount on May 28?
   (b) What annual rate would she be paying?
   (c) How much would she save if she borrowed the $250 from the bank at $15\frac{1}{2}$%?

2. Santiago's statement showed an amount owing of $48.65 payable on or before October 12. If he forgot to pay the bill until October 28, and the rate was 0.050 957%/d, how much interest would appear on his next statement?

3. What annual rate would Santiago be paying?

4. The balance owing on or before March 18 on Sue's credit card account was $485. She paid her bill on April 10. Find the amount of interest charged if the rate was
   (a) 18.6%/a calculated daily,
   (b) 28.8%/a calculated for one month.

5. Ng-Hem had a department store credit card and a general purpose card. He paid a $12 user fee for the general purpose card and no fee for the other. All his accounts were paid on time. He liked the general purpose card because he could use it at so many places but wondered what per cent it cost him.
   (a) If he charged $1 500 during the year, what percent of this would the fee be?
   (b) If he charged $300 during the year, what percent of this would the fee be?
   (c) Would the fee increase or decrease as a percent of his charge purchases as his use of the card increased?

8.2 INVOICES

Consumers buy from retailers and receive either a cash register receipt business form or a sales receipt business form. Just as consumers buy from retailers, retailers must purchase their goods from someone. Retailers who purchase in very large quantities usually purchase their goods directly from the person or company who makes the goods, the manufacturer.

MANUFACTURER → RETAILER → CONSUMER

Not all retailers, however, are able to purchase in large quantities since they are not able to sell that many goods. Those retailers who purchase small quantities must buy from the wholesaler. The wholesaler's function is to buy in large quantities from manufacturers and then sell in smaller quantities to retailers.

MANUFACTURER → WHOLESALER → RETAILER → CONSUMER

Why do you think one arrow goes directly to the retailer and misses the wholesaler?

The business form the consumer receives is either the ■■ or the ■■ The business form the retailer receives from the wholesaler or the manufacturer is called an *invoice*. Examine the invoice below.

Trottier Électrique 72 Rue Abbot Montreal, PQ H4M 1W6 Date: 19-- 07 10		Sold To: Corbett Hardware 781 Hess St. Winnipeg, MB R3E 1V2	
QUANTITY	ITEM	UNIT PRICE	AMOUNT
3	#6295 adapters	5.95 ea.	
50 m	#73AB electric wire	4.29 m	
6 rolls	#22 electrical tape	0.99 roll	
12	#43c clamps	3/1.00	_____
		TOTAL	══════

Which business prepared the invoice?

What is the unit price for #6295 adapters?

Calculate the figure that will be inserted in the AMOUNT column for #6295 adapters. This process of multiplying the quantity times the unit price and entering the product in the amount column is called *extending*. Calculate the extensions for the remaining items on the invoice and then total the invoice. If your province has provincial sales tax, why is there no provincial sales tax on the invoice?

EXERCISE 8.2
Extend and total the following.

	Quantity	*Item*	*Unit Price*	*Amount*
1.	20 L	#2462 Fabric Softener	1.79 L	■■
	50 kg	#4265 Salt	0.69 kg	■■
	424	#3578 Light Bulbs	0.74 ea.	■■
2.	25 m	#408 Perm. Press Cloth	0.98 m	■■
	150	#622 Drapery Hooks	0.06 ea.	■■
	50 m	#410 Perm. Press Cloth	1.06 m	■■

3.	Quantity	Unit	Item	Unit Price	Amount
	16	ea.	Maxim 415 Towel	3.69	■■■■
	110	ea.	Novelty Hat	0.89	■■■■
	20	L	Detergent	0.95	■■■■
	35	L	Floor Wax	2.79	■■■■

4.	Quantity	Unit	Item	Unit Price	Amount
	250	L	Relish	2.25	■■■■
	65	doz.	Eggs	1.45	■■■■
	425	g	Mustard	0.002 9	■■■■
	2 250	g	Wieners	0.006 5	■■■■
	875	g	Mozzarella Cheese	0.008 7	■■■■

8.3   CASH DISCOUNTS

Most consumers are bargain hunters. You want to buy merchandise at a lower than regular selling price. The difference between what you actually pay and what the merchandise regularly sells for (the catalogue price or retail price) is called a discount. A new car, for example, might retail for $11 445. If you bargain with the car dealer and buy the car for $10 845, then you have obtained a $600 discount. Why do you think the car dealer would do this?

Retailers, wholesalers, and manufacturers also watch for suppliers who offer a discount. One reason a supplier will offer a discount is to encourage prompt payment. When goods are bought and sold between the manufacturer and the wholesaler, or between the wholesaler and the retailer, a cash payment is seldom made. Terms for payment, such as 30 d, is the usual practice. To encourage payment before 30 d, however, terms such as 2/10, n/30 are common. 2/10, n/30 means that if payment is made within 10 d of the invoice date, a 2% cash discount may be subtracted from the total of the invoice and the remaining 98% accepted as full payment. If 100% payment is not received by 30 d from the invoice date, then interest will be added.

Explain the following terms.

(a) 1/10, n/30   (b) 2/15, n/30   (c) 1/15, n/60   (d) 2/10, 1/20, n/30

Trottier Électrique 72 Rue Abbot Montreal, PQ H4M 1W6		Sold To: Corbett Hardware 781 Hess St. Winnipeg, MB R3E 1V2	
Date: 19-- 06 10		Terms: 2/10,n/30	
QUANTITY	ITEM	UNIT PRICE	AMOUNT
3	#6295 adapters	5.95 ea.	17.85
50 m	#73AB electric wire	4.29 m	214.50
6 rolls	#22 electrical tape	0.99 roll	5.94
		TOTAL	238.29

From the invoice we see that, if Corbett Hardware wants to take advantage of the 2% discount, they must pay within 10 d of the invoice date, that is, by July 20.

Invoice date   July 10
Plus 10 d   10

Date by which payment must   July 20
be made to receive discount

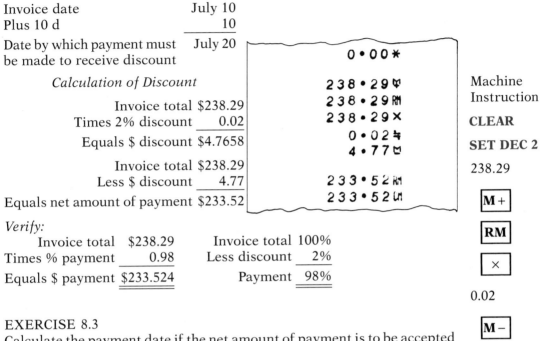

Machine
Instruction

CLEAR

SET DEC 2

238.29

$\boxed{M+}$

$\boxed{RM}$

$\boxed{\times}$

0.02

$\boxed{M-}$

$\boxed{RM}$

$\boxed{CM}$

Calculation of Discount

Invoice total $238.29
Times 2% discount   0.02
Equals $ discount $4.7658

Invoice total $238.29
Less $ discount   4.77
Equals net amount of payment $233.52

Verify:

Invoice total $238.29   Invoice total 100%
Times % payment   0.98   Less discount   2%
Equals $ payment $233.524   Payment   98%

EXERCISE 8.3
Calculate the payment date if the net amount of payment is to be accepted and calculate the other two columns.

	Invoice Total	Terms	Invoice Date	Payment Date	Cash Discount	Net Amount of Payment
(a)	$ 846.50	1/10, n/30	July 23			
(b)	962.75	1/15, n/30	Jan. 4			
(c)	6 203.41	2/10, n/30	Aug. 28			
(d)	8 526.10	2/15, n/60	Mar. 20			
(e)	495.26	1/10, n/30	June 30			
(f)	5 240.65	2/15, n/30	Sept. 6			
(g)	467.80	1/8, n/15	Apr. 10			
(h)	3 625.92	2/10, n/30	Oct. 15			
(i)	2 469.58	1/10, n/20	Nov. 12			
(j)	3 976.83	3/10, n/30	June 28			

8.4   TRADE DISCOUNTS

It is common for manufacturers to produce catalogues illustrating their products. Spalding, for example, has catalogues for sports equipment. A customer in a retail store that sells Spalding golf clubs may wish to examine the catalogue for clubs the retailer does not have on hand. The price the consumer sees in the catalogue is the manufacturer's suggested retail price or catalogue price. The consumer does not know how much the retailer has to pay for the clubs because the retailer has discount sheets that give discounts on the catalogue prices, in a separate file.

Catalogue –
What the
customer sees }

#8259 – 5 piece Knudson model includes 3, 5, 7, 9 irons and putter. Flexi-whip shafts for balanced swing. $129.95

Discount Sheet –
What the retailer sees }

Item No.	Description	Catalogue Price	Trade Disc.	Quantity 10	Disc. 20
8259	5 pc. Knudson Model	$129.95	50%	5%	10%

If the retailer orders only 1 set of No. 8259 golf clubs, the discount received is 50% of catalogue price.

Catalogue price	129.95		Catalogue price	129.95
Times % discount	0.50		Less $ discount	64.98
Equals $ discount	64.9750		Retailer's cost	64.97

This retailer pays $64.97 per set of clubs for any number of sets up to 9.

If the retailer orders 10 sets of No. 8259 golf clubs, the 50% trade discount and a further 5% quantity discount for buying in a larger quantity is received. The 5% quantity discount is calculated after the trade discount is subtracted from the list price. The quantity discount is *not* calculated on the list price.

64.97
0.05
─────
3.2485

Catalogue price	$129.95
Less trade discount (50% of $129.95)	64.98
	$ 64.97
Less quantity discount (5% of $64.97)	3.25
Retailer's cost	$ 61.72

If the retailer orders 20 sets of No. 8259 golf clubs, the 50% trade discount and a further 10% quantity discount is received. In your notebook calculate the missing figures.

64.97
0.10
─────

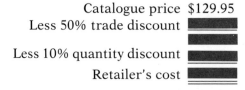

Catalogue price	$129.95
Less 50% trade discount	▅▅▅▅
	▅▅▅▅
Less 10% quantity discount	▅▅▅▅
Retailer's cost	▅▅▅▅

The small independent retailer has a hard time competing with large chain stores. Why do you think that it is so difficult for the small independent retailer?

EXERCISE 8.4
Calculate the net amount of payment for each of the following.

1.

	Catalogue Price	Trade Discount	Quantity Discount	Net Amount of Payment
(a)	$485.00	50%	10%	
(b)	549.00	40%	5%	
(c)	79.95	25%	2%	
(d)	65.95	55%	20%	
(e)	49.95	45%	15%	

2.

	Catalogue Price	Trade Discount	Quantity Discount	Net Amount of Payment
(a)	$ 59.95	50%	10%	
(b)	89.00	50%	15%	
(c)	495.00	40%	5%	
(d)	349.95	45%	15%	
(e)	82.95	25%	5%	

3. Luci Bléau is a buyer for the sporting goods department in a large store and wants to purchase a quantity of tennis racquets. Supplier A offers her the racquets at a catalogue price of $36.95 less 50% and 10%. Supplier B offers the racquets at a catalogue price of $36.95 less 55% and 5%. Is there any difference in the retailer's cost price?

4. Marion Holland is a buyer in the lingerie department for a retail store and wants to purchase panty hose in large quantities. Supplier A offers her hose at a catalogue price of $3.79 a pair less 40% and 10%. Supplier B offers the same hose catalogued at $3.79 a pair less 45% and 5%. Which is the better buy?

5. A buyer for sandals has an opportunity to buy from a new supplier sandals that are listed in the catalogue at $18.99 a pair less 50% and 5%. The regular supplier offers the same sandals but listed at $19.29 a pair less 55% and 10%. Should the purchase be made from the regular supplier or the new supplier?

8.5 SINGLE EQUIVALENT DISCOUNT

When more than one discount is available, it is more convenient for calculations and comparisons if a single equivalent discount is used.

Example 1
Recording Artist Ltd. offers a local retailer a quantity of LP's, many with different catalogue prices, but all with the same discount of 50% and 5%. The Fifth Wheel's "Collection" has a catalogue price of $10.95. What is the price of "Collection" to the retailer?

Solution

If we let the list price equal 100%, we can calculate the single equivalent discount.

Catalogue price = 100%		Catalogue price =	100%
Less 50% discount =	50	Less retailer's cost price =	47.5
	50	Equals discount =	52.5%
Less 5% discount =	2.5		

Equals retailer's cost price = 47.5%

A series of discounts of 50% and 5% equals the single equivalent discount of 52.5%.

10.95
× 0.525
―――――
5.748 75

"Collection", therefore, has a cost price to the retailer of

Catalogue price = $10.95
Less 52.5% discount = 5.75

Equals retailer's cost price = $ 5.20

Using the single equivalent discount above, you can find the cost price of all the LP's from Recording Artist Ltd. If "Hits of the 50's" has a list price of $8.95, how do you calculate the retailer's cost price using the single equivalent discount?

Calculate the retailer's cost price of the following standard selections from Recording Artists Ltd.

Catalogue Prices		*Retailer's Cost Prices*	
Album	*Tape*	*Album*	*Tape*
$10.98	$15.95	▬▬▬	▬▬▬
8.49	12.89	▬▬▬	▬▬▬

There is a faster method of finding the single equivalent discount and the retailer's cost price if the catalogue price and the series of discounts are known.

Catalogue price (100%) = $49.95
Discounts = 55%, 10%

Since the first discount is 55% of the catalogue price, the retailer's cost price is 45% of 49.95. Therefore, the retailer's cost price, after first discount, is

100% − 55% = 45%   49.95 × 0.45 = 22.477 5

Since the second discount is 10% of 22.477 5, the retailer's cost price is 90% of 22.477 5. The retailer's cost price, after second discount, is

100% − 10% = 90%   22.477 5 × 0.90 = 20.229 75

Therefore, the retailer's cost price, after all discounts are deducted, is $20.23. In short form, both discounts are put together.

Retailer's cost price = $49.95 × 0.45 × 0.90
= $20.23

As a formula

Retailer's Cost Price = Catalogue Price × (100% − Discount Rate)

Example 2
Find the retailer's cost price of an article listed in the catalogue at $150 if discounts of 20% and 10% are offered.

Solution
Retailer's Cost Price = Catalogue Price × (100% − Discount Rate)
                      = $150 × (100% − 20%)(100% − 10%)
                      = $150 × 0.8 × 0.9
                      = $108

Machine
Instruction

CLEAR

SET DEC 2

150

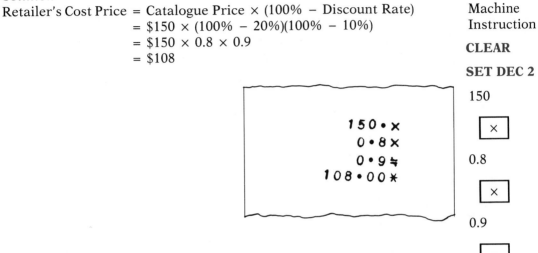

$\boxed{\times}$

0.8

$\boxed{\times}$

0.9

$\boxed{=}$

EXERCISE 8.5

1. Find the single equivalent discount of the following series of discounts.
   (a) 45%, 10%
   (b) 55%, 15%
   (c) 50%, 10%
   (d) 55%, 5%
   (e) 55%, 10%

2. Find the retailer's cost price for the following catalogue prices if they have the same discounts of 50% and 5%.
   (a) $259.95
   (b)   89.50
   (c)   98.99
   (d) 157.50
   (e)   49.95

3. Using the shortcut method, find the retailer's cost price for the following.

	Catalogue Price	Trade Discount	Quantity Discount
(a)	$ 59.95	45%	10%
(b)	68.49	50%	5%
(c)	299.50	55%	10%
(d)	385.95	60%	15%
(e)	499.99	55%	15%
(f)	79.95	45%	5%
(g)	459.95	50%	10%

4. Using the shortcut method, find the retailer's cost price and the total amount of discount to be deducted for the following.

	Catalogue Price	Trade Discount	Quantity Discount
(a)	$ 65.50	35%	5%
(b)	298.00	55%	15%
(c)	489.50	50%	15%
(d)	345.95	45%	10%
(e)	98.00	55%	10%

SUMMARY

To extend an invoice is to multiply the quantity of goods by the unit price of the goods. To obtain the total of the invoice, you add all the extensions.

Sometimes a cash discount is given if the invoice is paid within a short period of time.

If the price on the invoice is a catalogue or retail price, then a trade discount(s) may be given.

REVIEW EXERCISE 8.6

1. Extend and total the following invoice.

Quantity	No. and Description	Unit Price	Amount
6	563 Vacuum Cleaner bags	$ 0.99	▬
22	22F – Fits 285 g Thermos	2.59	▬
3 pk.	102 Tennis balls	1.73	▬
15 pr.	Poly skate guard #12	2.79	▬
16 pk.	502 lambs wool pads	3.29	▬
4	1266 elect. can opener	29.98	▬

2. An invoice dated August 28, with terms of 3/10, n/30, totals $1 096.55. By what date would we have to pay to take advantage of the discount? How much would we pay then?

3. An invoice totals $6 840.62, has terms of 2/10, 1/20, n/30, and is dated March 15. How much would we save by paying on March 24 rather than April 14? How much would we save by paying on March 24 rather than March 26?

4. An invoice with a total amount of $8 756.92 allows trade discounts of 45% and 10%. What amount do we pay?

5. We receive an invoice with a total amount of $6 289.56 and are allowed trade discounts of 55%, 15%, and 5%. How much do we pay? What is the single equivalent discount? (Do not round off in calculations.)

6. The total amount of an invoice is $7 685.29. The invoice is dated May 22, has terms of 3/10, n/30, and allows us trade discounts of 45% and 15%. What is the last day payment would be accepted before interest is added? How much would we pay then? How much would we pay on or before June 1?

7. Find the single equivalent discount on an article listed in the catalogue at $42.50, whose cost to the buyer was $34.

CUMULATIVE REVIEW 6

1. Express each of the following common fractions as a decimal and as a percent.

   (a) $\frac{2}{25}$ (b) $\frac{2}{3}$ (c) $\frac{6}{16}$ (d) $\frac{5}{8}$ (e) $\frac{3}{5}$

2. Express each of the following decimals as a fraction or mixed number and as a percent.

   (a) 0.05 (b) 4.652 (c) 3.75 (d) 0.005 (e) 0.875

3. 56 increased by 40% of itself equals what number?

4. Simplify the following.

   (a) $\dfrac{4(3a^5bc^3)(4a^4b^3c^5)}{6a(a^3b^2)^2}$

   (b) $\frac{5}{7}$ of $\frac{2}{3} - \frac{2}{3} \div \frac{1}{2}(\frac{7}{8} \times \frac{2}{3}) + \frac{1}{2} \times \frac{2}{3}$

   (c) $4ab - 5b^2 + 3ab - 4ax + 6a^2 - 2ax - b^2$

5. Factor the following.
   (a) $12ab + 6a^3b + 8ab^2$
   (b) $33a^2b^3 + 8ab^2 + 7a^3b$

6. Solve for b.

   (a) $\dfrac{b-4}{10} - \dfrac{5-b}{15} - \dfrac{10-b}{2} = 0$

   (b) $5(b + 6) = 3b - 8$

   (c) $4(4 - 3b) - 7(6 - 2b) = 0$

7. Using the formula $B = Kt$, find K when $B = \$985$ and $t = \$42$.

8. Find the interest on a one year loan of $960 at $13\frac{3}{4}\%$.

9. How long did it take to pay back a loan of $1 250 at 16% if the total interest paid was $49.31?

10. Zeta earned $58.19 on her 60 d term deposit. If the rate was $14\frac{3}{4}\%$, how much was the deposit?

11. Ahmad worked $45\frac{3}{4}$ h for $10.25/h for the first 40 h and time-and-one-half for overtime. How much did he earn?

12. Find the weekly Canada Pension Plan contributions and unemployment insurance premiums for the following earnings.
    (a) $382.48   (b) $299.85   (c) $312.47   (d) $406.70

13. Using your knowledge of aliquot parts, find the cost of the following.
    (a) 48 items at $16\frac{2}{3}$¢ each   (c) 63 items at $33\frac{1}{3}$¢ each
    (b) 584 items at 25¢ each   (d) 75 items at 40¢ each

14. $500 will amount to how much in 18 months if money is calculated at 14% compounded semi-annually?

15. Derek earned $534.38 for a 45 h week. If he received regular rates for the first 40 h and time-and-one-half for overtime, what was his regular rate of pay?

16. When is the Individual Income Tax Return due?

17. Who may claim tuition fees as a deduction, the parent or the student?

UNIT 9

Retail Sales

Many Canadians look in awe at the way the Russians have developed such strong hockey teams in only a few short years. When Russian coaches are asked how they accomplished such a task, they reply very simply.

"We looked at Canadian hockey players, the best in the world, and learned what their strongest features were, then developed a training progam based on what we learned."

Retailers in Canada can do something very similar. They can look at successful retailers, learn what their strongest features are, then follow a program or policy based on this learning. Throughout Canada it is not unusual to find "Out of Business" signs on storefronts along the streets of cities and towns. One of the biggest reasons for these failures is that the retailers did not price their goods properly.

9.1   MARKUP ON COST

Imagine that you are the owner of Johnston's Sporting Goods. As you remember from Unit 8, you must purchase the goods that you have in your store from either the manufacturer or a wholesaler before you can offer them to your customers.

MANUFACTURER → WHOLESALER → RETAILER → CONSUMER

Can you think of items that are staple goods in a grocery store?

Many items are in great demand by consumers. For these items a retailer can afford to pay whatever price the supplier asks because it is known that the items will sell. Items that must be carried in a store because of high consumer demand are called *staple goods*.

As the owner of Johnston's Sporting Goods, you consider canvas shoes to be a staple item and you seek out a supplier of them. After locating a supplier, you find that each pair of shoes is going to cost you $6.50. This seems very expensive. You must carry a large number of sizes and styles in order to have a proper selection and supply in your store. You know, however, that you can sell the shoes to your customers for $10.00 a pair.

Consider the following. You have purchased canvas shoes for $6.50 a pair. You have raised (or marked up) this price to $10.00 (the price your customers will pay). You have thus marked up the cost price by $3.50.

Notice that this percent is expressed using the amount the shoes cost the retailer as a base, not the retail price the customers will pay for them.

The shoes cost you	6.50	(Cost Price)
You marked them up	+ 3.50	
Your customers will pay you	$10.00	(Retail Price)

This markup can be expressed as a percent.

$$\frac{\$Markup}{\$Cost\ Price} \times 100\% = \frac{3.50}{6.50} \times 100\% = 53.846\%$$

Verify: Cost price $6.50
      Times markup % 0.53846
      Equals $ markup 3.4999

As you can see, there are two prices mentioned:

- the price you must pay your supplier for the shoes – *cost price*,

- the price your customers must pay you for the shoes – *retail price*.

It is important to keep these prices separate in your mind. Many times a retail store advertises a special sale of goods at 20% off. Does it make a difference which price (cost or retail) is used in calculating a reduction of 20%? Why?

EXERCISE 9.1

1. Find the $ markup on cost for each of the following.

	Cost of Goods	% Markup on Cost	$ Markup on Cost
(a)	$ 0.70	50%	
(b)	1.60	45%	
(c)	22.43	55%	
(d)	79.85	60%	
(e)	142.39	42%	
(f)	175.50	40%	
(g)	642.90	38%	
(h)	489.72	35%	
(i)	326.41	75%	
(j)	1 010.25	125%	

2. Find the % markup on cost for each of the following.

	Cost of Goods	$ Markup on Cost	% Markup on Cost
(a)	$152.80	$36.20	
(b)	84.50	40.49	
(c)	34.70	16.30	
(d)	18.25	6.25	
(e)	6.13	2.46	
(f)	12.80	4.15	
(g)	0.90	0.49	
(h)	2.16	0.79	
(i)	2.00	0.99	
(j)	4.81	2.38	

3. A belt costing $5.50 is to be given a markup of 45% on cost. What will the retail be?

4. The % markup on cost is $37\frac{1}{2}$% and $ markup is $15.00. Find the cost.

5. A store wishes to offer panty hose at $0.95 a pair retail. The buyer needs markup of 65% on cost. How much can the buyer afford to pay?

6. Find the retail price of goods costing $42.50 if the markup on cost is 30%.

7. Goods costing $385 sold for $519.75. What was the % markup on cost?

9.2 MARGIN OF RETAIL

As the owner of Johnston's Sporting Goods, you consider many items not to be staple goods. You must, therefore, make a decision on whether or not to carry them. Naturally, you want to carry the items that have the greatest difference between the cost price and the retail price, that is, the greatest *margin*.

$ Margin = Retail Price − Cost Price

You need a standard to follow, to help determine what is, and what is not, an acceptable margin. Although you can easily find the $margin, this is not an acceptable standard because each item in the store is different in terms of cost price, retail price, and the speed at which it sells.

Therefore you need a standard by which you can compare all of these different products. Expressing your margin as a percent of retail accomplishes this.

Let us examine a simplified income statement of a small but successful retailer in Canada and analyse the strong features.

Johnston's Sporting Goods
Income Statement
for the year ending 19-- 12 31

INCOME
Net Sales $100 000.00

COST OF GOODS SOLD
Less: Cost of Goods Sold   55 000.00

Equals: Gross Profit (or Margin) $ 45 000.00

EXPENSES
Less: Total Expenses   25 000.00

Equals: Net Income $ 20 000.00

What does this statement say? Basically it says that through Johnston's cash register was rung a total of $100 000 in net sales for the year. That is, Johnston's customers paid $100 000 for goods received during the year. Obviously, if Johnston's bought the goods for the same amount of money, the store would not have been in business for a year.

The goods sold to the customers cost Johnston's $55 000. This leaves a gross profit or *margin* of $45 000 ($100 000 − $55 000). From the margin of $45 000 is subtracted the total expenses (wages, utilities, advertising, etc.), leaving Johnston's Sporting Goods a final net income of $20 000 ($45 000 − $25 000).

What can we learn from this income statement? Perhaps we can express the information here in a form that would give us a better basis for comparison.

Let net sales = 100%.

$$\text{Net sales} \quad \$100\ 000 = 100\% \text{ of sales}$$
$$\text{Cost of goods sold} \quad 55\ 000 = 55\% \text{ of sales}$$
$$\text{Gross profit or margin} \quad \$\ 45\ 000 = 45\% \text{ of sales}$$

Verify: $\quad \dfrac{\text{Margin}}{\text{Net Sales}} = \dfrac{45\ 000}{100\ 000} \times 100\%$

$$= 45\%$$

Johnston's Sporting Goods is a small but successful business. Operating on a 45% margin of sales may be one key to its success. Consider the following situations.

Bev Avey, a buyer for a sporting goods store, wants to buy children's running shoes for his store. One particular brand of shoes will cost him $7.50 a pair. Bev knows his customers will not pay more than $11.95 a pair.

In terms of our previous example, net sales in this case is the retail price.

$$
\begin{aligned}
\text{Retail price (net sales)} &= \$11.95 \\
\text{Less cost of goods sold} &= \underline{7.50} \\
\text{Margin} &= \$\ 4.45
\end{aligned}
$$

$$
\begin{aligned}
\%\ \text{Margin of Retail} &= \frac{\text{Margin}}{\text{Retail}} \times 100\% \\
&= \frac{4.45}{11.95} \times 100\% \\
&= 37.66\%
\end{aligned}
$$

Using the standard of Johnston's Sporting Goods, should Bev buy the shoe? Why or why not?

Connie Kay is a buyer for women's sportswear. She knows that her customers will not pay more than $95.87 for a down-filled ski jacket. Using Johnston's Sporting Goods margin of retail as her policy, how much can she afford to pay the manufacturer of the jacket?

$$
\begin{aligned}
\text{Retail} \quad &\$95.87 \\
\text{Times \% margin of retail} \quad &\underline{0.45} \\
\text{Equals \$ margin} \quad &\underline{\underline{\$43.14}}
\end{aligned}
$$

Calculate the cost price.

To Calculate the $ Margin

Retail Price − Cost of Goods Sold = Margin

Example 1
Find the margin on goods retailing for $10.50 and costing $7.40.

Solution
$$
\begin{aligned}
\text{Margin} &= \text{Retail price} - \text{Cost of goods} \\
&= \$10.50 - \$7.40 \\
&= \$3.10
\end{aligned}
$$

To Calculate the % Margin of Retail

$$
\%\ \text{Margin of Retail} = \frac{\$\,\text{Margin}}{\$\text{Retail}} \times 100\%
$$

Machine
Instruction

CLEAR

SET DEC 2

4

18

%

Remember:
**Margin is based
on retail, mark-
up is based on
cost.**

Example 2
Find the rate of margin of retail on goods selling at $18 when the margin is $4.

Solution

$$\text{\% Margin of Retail} = \frac{\$\text{Margin}}{\$\text{Retail}} \times 100\%$$

$$= \frac{4}{18} \times 100\%$$

$$= 22.22\%$$

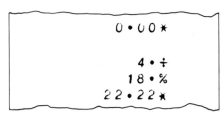

EXERCISE 9.2

1. Calculate the $ margin and the % margin of retail for each of the following, correct to 2 decimal places.

	Retail Price	Cost of Goods	$ Margin	% Margin of Retail
(a)	$ 1.00	$ 0.50		
(b)	4.99	3.20		
(c)	69.95	51.80		
(d)	149.50	132.29		
(e)	249.95	189.62		
(f)	24.95	16.27		
(g)	265.00	191.92		
(h)	34.50	18.67		
(i)	129.95	93.40		
(j)	359.95	244.50		

2. In each of the following situations, calculate the top cost price that the buyer should pay.

	Retail Price	% Margin of Retail	Cost of Goods
(a)	$ 89.95	40%	
(b)	125.00	$33\frac{1}{3}\%$	
(c)	449.95	25.5%	
(d)	61.50	32.5%	
(e)	99.95	$43\frac{1}{3}\%$	
(f)	695.00	28.6%	
(g)	389.49	31.5%	

3. Jacques Trudeau is a buyer for women's wear in a large department store. He has been told that his margin on sales would be 38%. On a buying trip to Montreal he examines blouses and determines what his customers would pay for them, as well as how many of each he should buy. How much should he pay for the whole order if he is to make the 38% margin?

Quantity to Buy	Retail Each
24	$ 6.95
16	7.50
12	9.49
6	12.95
6	15.95

4. (a) June Lindo is a buyer for a new camera department in a large store in Saskatoon. She is told by the store manager that her department is expected to sell $125 000 worth of merchandise for the year and that the department should operate at a margin of 42% of sales. How much merchandise should June purchase over the year?

(b) If her plan for the year is as follows, how much should she purchase each month? Verify your answer.

January	2%
February	3%
March	4%
April	7%
May	11%
June	12%
July	8%
August	6%
September	4%
October	18%
November	20%
December	5%
	100%

5. (a) Find the % margin of sales for each of the following departments and also find the % margin of sales for the whole store.

Meat Department
Sales   = $130 000
Cost of Goods Sold =   85 900

Produce Department
Sales   = $ 26 750
Cost of Goods Sold =   21 000

Grocery Department
Sales   = $325 000
Cost of Goods Sold = 282 050

Dairy Department
Sales   = $ 87 500
Cost of Goods Sold =   76 250

(b) Which department has the lowest % margin of sales? Which has the highest?

(c) Why do you think there are different % margins of sales for different departments?

9.3   MARGIN AND MARKUP

The $ Margin of Retail = The $ Markup on Cost

Does it follow that % margin of retail = % markup on cost?

Example 1

An item costing $1.20 was sold for $1.50. Find (a) the % markup on cost,
(b) the % margin of retail.

Solution

Machine
Instruction

CLEAR

SET DEC 2

0.3

| ÷ |

1.5

| × |

100

| = |

(a) Markup = Retail – Cost
$$= \$1.50 - \$1.20$$
$$= \$0.30$$

$$\% \text{ Markup on Cost} = \frac{\text{Markup}}{\text{Cost}} \times 100\%$$

$$= \frac{0.30}{1.20} \times 100\%$$

$$= 25\%$$

(b) $$\% \text{ Margin of Retail} = \frac{\text{Margin}}{\text{Retail}} \times 100\%$$

$$= \frac{0.30}{1.50} \times 100\%$$

$$= 20\%$$

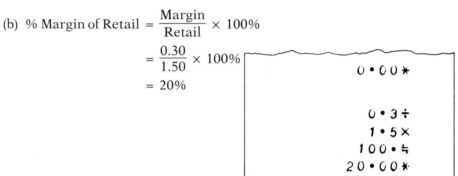

```
0 • 00 *

0 • 3 ÷
1 • 5 ×
100 • ÷
20 • 00 *
```

Because % margin is *of retail*, and % markup is *on cost*, they do not equal
the same percent, even though they have the same dollar value.

Example 2

Find the % margin of retail that is equivalent to a 40% markup on cost.

Solution

Let cost = 100%

Retail   = Cost + Markup
= 100% of cost + 40% of cost
= 140% of cost

$$\% \text{ Margin of Retail} = \frac{\text{Margin}}{\text{Retail}} \times 100\%$$

$$= \frac{40\% \text{ of cost}}{140\% \text{ of cost}} \times 100\%$$

$$= 28.57\%$$

EXERCISE 9.3

1. Copy the chart and fill in the blanks.

	Cost of Goods	Retail	% Margin of Retail	% Markup on Cost
(a)	$4.58	$ 6.79		
(b)		11.95	25%	
(c)	8.53			55%
(d)	1.79	2.98		
(e)		4.59	40%	
(f)	3.97			60%
(g)	2.17	3.25		
(h)		5.79	38%	
(i)	5.89			75%
(j)	8.60	11.49		

2. A toy motorcycle is quoted by a manufacturer at $1.20, and the markup a buyer needs to realize a fair profit is 40% margin of retail. What will the retail price have to be?

3. A book costing $6.50 is to be given a markup of 45% of retail. What will be the retail price?

4. If the percent margin of retail is 40% and the margin is $15.00, find the cost.

5. A buyer needs a markup of 45% on cost. How much should the buyer pay if the goods are to be sold at $4.50?

9.4 TRANSPORTATION COSTS

Transportation cost, or *freight-in*, is the amount charged the store for delivery of goods. This charge may be made by the manufacturer or wholesaler, in which case the transportation cost is added to the invoice the retailer receives. Or the charge may be made by the transportation company directly to the retailer. The transportation costs could be for truck, railway, express or freight, or mail. Can you think of any other ways of transporting goods?

When the retailer is billed for transportation costs, it is the usual practice to consider these costs as part of the cost of goods. Before a markup on cost is calculated therefore, freight-in or transportation costs are added to the invoice cost to find the cost of goods received.

Machine Instruction		

Example

Invoice cost	$1 320.00
Add Freight-in	26.00
Cost of goods	$1 346.00
Add 50% Markup on cost	673.00
Retail	$2 019.00

```
          0 • 0 0 *
    1,320 • 0 0 ✦
       26 • 0 0 ✦
    1,346 • 0 0 ♥
    1,346 • 0 0 ×
        0 • 5 ✦
      673 • 0 0 ✦
    2,019 • 0 0 ℞
    2,019 • 0 0 ✦
```

CLEAR

SET DEC 2

1320

M +

26

M +

RM

×

0.5

M +

RM

CM

EXERCISE 9.4

1. Calculate the missing figures in each of the following.

	Invoice Cost	Freight-in	Cost of Goods	% Markup on Cost	Retail
(a)	$4 250.70	$ 43.80	▮	45%	▮
(b)	2 589.75	25.62	▮	50%	▮
(c)	967.58	33.41	▮	55%	▮
(d)	1 476.92	16.87	▮	42%	▮
(e)	18.95	4.26	▮	65%	▮
(f)	3 541.38	126.85	▮	38%	▮
(g)	5 267.42	424.80	▮	44%	▮
(h)	2 985.89	126.75	▮	55%	▮
(i)	22.50	2.25	▮	34%	▮
(j)	175.50	15.80	▮	62%	▮

2. (a) If goods cost $24.50 for 10 items, with $2.50/10 transportation cost, and are marked $3.50 each retail, what is the % markup on cost?
   (b) What is the % margin of retail?

3. An article costs $8 and transportation to the store is $0.85. If a margin of retail of 35% is needed, what should the retail price be?

4. If goods cost $15 for 10 items plus $0.20/10 for freight, and you need 42% margin of retail, what retail price per unit do you mark on the goods?

9.5   COST OF GOODS SOLD

So far in this unit we have studied the markup or profit on a single item. Businesspeople must know the margin of profit on the total goods sold. They do this by first calculating the *cost of goods sold*.

At the end of the year the books of Eisen's Sport Shop show the following items of information.

Cost of goods on hand January 1 $30 000	Cost of goods purchased during the year $15 000	Cost of goods on hand December 31 $25 000

From these figures, Ms. Eisen knew that the total cost of the sports equipment she had offered for sale was $45 000. She found this by adding the cost of goods on January 1 ($30 000) and the cost of purchases during the year ($15 000). Since she had $25 000 worth of goods left in stock at the end of the year, the cost of the goods she had sold was $45 000 – $25 000 or $20 000.

Another word for goods on hand is *inventory*. Therefore,

$$\text{Cost of Goods Sold} = \text{Beginning Inventory} + \text{Purchases} - \text{Ending Inventory}$$

Example 1

Prepare a Statement of Cost of Goods Sold for the year 19-- for Kampus Korner if the inventory on January 1 was $2 500, purchases during the year were $3 000, and the inventory on December 31 was $1 800.

Solution

Kampus Korner	
Statement of Cost of Goods Sold	
For the Year Ending 19-- 12 31	
Inventory 19-- 01 01	$2 500
Add: Purchases	3 000
Cost of Goods Available for Sale	$5 500
Less: Inventory 19-- 12 31	1 800
	$3 700

Machine Instruction

CLEAR

SET DEC 2

2 500

+

3 000

+

◊

1 800

−

*

```
      0 • 0 0 *

  2,5 0 0 • 0 0 +
  3,0 0 0 • 0 0 +
  5,5 0 0 • 0 0 ◊
  1,8 0 0 • 0 0 −
  3,7 0 0 • 0 0 *
```

Find the cost of goods sold for each of the following situations.

Name	Beginning Inventory	Purchases	Ending Inventory
1. Kool Music	$ 6 500	$ 4 200	$ 5 900
2. Jean's Jean Shop	5 400	6 300	4 500
3. Boutique Five	2 300	2 900	1 600
4. Bill's Sports	22 000	36 000	19 500

When the operator of a business wants to find the net profit or income for the year, the cost of goods sold and the operating expenses must be subtracted from the sales for the year.

$$\text{Net Income} = \begin{matrix} \text{Sales} \\ \text{Revenue} \end{matrix} - \begin{matrix} \text{Cost of} \\ \text{Goods Sold} \end{matrix} - \begin{matrix} \text{Operating} \\ \text{Expenses} \end{matrix}$$

Example 2
Kampus Korner's sales for the year were $6 400, and the expenses of operating the business were $500 for salaries, $1 000 for rent, and $300 for miscellaneous. Prepare an Income Statement for the year using the information given in the previous example.

Solution

Kampus Korner
Income Statement
For the Year Ended 19-- 12 31

Revenue from Sales		$6 400
Cost of Goods Sold		
Inventory 19-- 01 01	$2 500	
Add: Purchases	3 000	
Cost of Goods Available for Sale	$5 500	
Less: Inventory 19-- 12 31	1 800	
Cost of Goods Sold		3 700
Gross Margin or Profit		$2 700
Expenses		
Salaries	$ 500	
Rent	1 000	
Miscellaneous	300	
Total Operating Expenses		1 800
Net Income for the Year		$ 900

EXERCISE 9.5

1. Prepare an Income Statement for the following for the year ended
   19-- 12 31

   (a) Bette's Boutique:
       Sales to Customers $4 100
       Rent Expense $900
       Salaries Expense $1 200
       Advertising Cost $240
       Utilities Expense $320

   (b) Koski's Bicycle Repair Service:
       Repair Service Revenue $21 900
       Rent Expense $1 200
       Salaries Expense $9 800
       Utilities Expense $1 100
       Advertising Expense $350
       Telephone Expense $90
       Miscellaneous Expense $500

   (c) April Sales Company:
       Revenue from Sales $124 000
       Merchandise Inventory January 1 $50 000
       Purchases during year $45 000
       Merchandise Inventory December 31 $52 000
       Advertising Expense $320
       Miscellaneous Expense $820
       Office Expense $1 000
       Insurance Expense $400
       Supplies Expense $600
       Utilities Expense $320
       Salaries Expense $21 000

2. Find the missing amounts.

	Sales	Beginning Inventory	Purchases	Ending Inventory	Gross Margin	Expenses	Net Income
(a)	7 200	2 000	6 000	▮	2 200	1 800	▮
(b)	100 000	75 000	▮	85 000	75 000	▮	57 000
(c)	92 000	▮	35 000	65 000	▮	15 000	7 000
(d)	72 000	32 000	40 000	2 000	▮	3 500	▮
(e)	▮	5 000	4 955	4 600	5 800	▮	2 900

SUMMARY

Retail is the price at which goods are offered for sale.

Cost price is the price the retailer or wholesaler pays for goods.

Freight-in should be added to the billed cost of goods before a markup is calculated.

$ Retail − $ Markup = $ Cost

$ Cost + $ Markup = Retail

$$\frac{\$ \text{ Markup}}{\$ \text{ Cost}} \times 100\% = \% \text{ Markup on Cost}$$

$$\frac{\$ \text{ Margin}}{\$ \text{ Retail}} \times 100\% = \% \text{ Margin of Retail}$$

Cost of Goods Sold = Beginning Inventory + Purchases − Ending Inventory

Net Income = Revenue − Cost of Goods Sold − Expenses

REVIEW EXERCISE 9.6
Give answers correct to 2 decimal places where applicable.

1. (a) The retail price of an article is $1.45 and the cost price is $0.55. Calculate the % markup on cost.
   (b) What is the % margin of retail?

2. (a) A retailer plans to sell $45 000 worth of goods at retail and wants to operate on a 45% margin of retail. How much does he/she have to spend on purchasing merchandise?
   (b) If he/she estimates freight-in to be $585, how much will have to be spent on purchasing merchandise?

3. If a retailer has just purchased goods for $10 520, and operates a store on a 52% margin of retail, how much will the goods sell for?

4. (a) If a sporting goods department plans to sell $49 000 worth of goods at retail, and wants to maintain a 55% markup on cost, how much money will there be to purchase merchandise?
   (b) If the sporting goods department had an opening inventory of goods valued at a cost of $15 000, how much should be spent on the purchase of merchandise?

5. The $ markup on an item is $7.50 and this is a 55% markup on cost. How much does the item sell for?

6. An article will sell for $11.95 and freight will cost $0.55 to deliver it to the store. Can the retailer buy the article and still maintain a 55% markup on cost when the invoice cost is $6.52?

7. A retailer received an invoice totalling $1 468.75 for 25 electric hedge clippers. As well, the express company sent a bill for $48.95 express charges. The retailer wants to maintain a 54% margin of retail. How much will each unit sell for?

8. Prepare a Statement of Cost of Goods Sold for the month of January for Syd's Cycle Shop, if the inventory on January 1 was $1 800, purchases made during the month were $3 900, and the inventory on January 31 was $2 100.

9. Prepare an Income Statement for the Bay City Brothers for the month of February from the following information.
    Sales, $18 500
    Inventory February 1, $2 200
    Purchases, $14 000
    Inventory February 28, $3 000
    Advertising, $200
    Property Taxes, $150
    Salaries paid, $1 200
    Utilities Expense, $65
    Miscellaneous Expense, $350

CUMULATIVE REVIEW 7

1. What number increased by 25% equals 75?

2. What percent of 155 is 25?

3. Kilometres for Kids collected $175 000. By what percent would they have to increase their collections to achieve their aim of $250 000?

4. Sales for one year were $45 000 and for the next year were $52 000. What was the rate of increase in sales?

5. State the decimal equivalent of each of the following.
   (a) $12\frac{1}{2}$ (b) $91\frac{2}{3}$ (c) $37\frac{1}{2}$ (d) $60\frac{1}{4}$ (e) $8\frac{2}{5}$

6. Norbert Loc deposited $25.50 in a bank account on September 1. On December 1 his passbook showed that he received 45¢ interest. What was the rate of interest he received for the three months?

7. What percent is 13 of $33\frac{1}{3}$?

8. Simplify the following.
   (a) $15pq - 6pq + 15pr - 4pr - 5pq$
   (b) $2(a + 4b) + 5(6a - b) + 4a$
   (c) $2x(5p + 3r) - 7xr + x(3p - 2r)$
   (d) $11xy + 17xy - 5xy - 4xy$
   (e) $\dfrac{x^8 \times x^5}{x^4}$
   (f) $x^2 + 3y^2 + 7x^2 + 5x^2 + 8y^2 - 2x^2$

9. Collect the like terms and simplify.
   (a) $2(x + 6) + (x + 6)$
   (b) $(x + 7) + (x + 4) + (6x - 1) - (x + 4)$
   (c) $2(x - 4) - 4(3x - 2) + (2x + 2)$
   (d) $3(p + 5) - (5p + 6)$
   (e) $4(x + 3) - 3(x + 3)$

10. A customer wishes to make 4 children's dresses. Each dress requires $3\frac{1}{2}$ m of material costing $2.98/m.
    (a) How much material does she have to buy?
    (b) How much does she have to pay?

11. An employee worked $7\frac{3}{4}$ h a day for $5\frac{1}{2}$ d and received $185.50 for one week's work. What was the hourly rate of pay?

12. An invoice for $1 540 is subject to a discount of 6% if paid within 10 d. If the bill is paid on time, how much should be remitted?

13. Trade discounts of 15% and 10% are offered on merchandise having a list price of $70. What is the net price?

14. What is the single equivalent discount of the following?
    (a) 8%, 3%, 1%
    (b) 55%, 10%, 5%
    (c) 60%, 15%, 1%
    (d) 40%, 5%, 1%
    (e) 35%, 5%, 2%

15. A list price of $150 is subject to trade discounts of 10%, 5%, 2%, and a cash discount of 3/10, n/30. If payment is made in 10 d, how much should be remitted?

16. The list price of an invoice is $75. Trade discounts are 20%, 10%, and 5%. A cash discount is offered of 2/10, n/30. If the bill is paid in 10 d, how much should be remitted?

17. A salesperson sold $2 000 worth of goods per week and received a salary of $175 a week plus 5.2% of sales over $700 per week. How much did the salesperson earn?

18. A salesperson received $194.50 for commission on sales. How much was sold if he/she was working on 5% commission?

19. Emil Sikorski received an invoice dated April 10 for $176.42 plus sales tax of 12%. The terms of sale were 2/15, n/30.
    (a) How much would Emil pay on April 15?
    (b) How much would he pay on April 26?

20. Name two common deductions that taxpayers may make from their total income.

UNIT 10

You and Your Automobile

The decision to purchase a car – be it new or used – should not be made hastily. The decision to buy should be made only after all the costs have been examined. For example, how much is it going to cost to fill the tank each week? The costs of owning a car and leasing a car should also be compared. If a car is needed only for a matter of days or weeks, leasing may be the answer. Most people decide to buy a car, however, because they want to own it.

The price of an automobile depends on the year, the size, and the condition of the car. For example, a brand new full-size car could cost up to $30 000, whereas a six-year-old compact car might cost only $4 000 plus some minor repairs.

When purchasing a brand new automobile, make sure you know exactly what you are getting for your money, and make sure you are completely satisifed.

When purchasing a used automobile, check to see if the car has been in any accidents (Front: grill, headlight rims, bumpers; back: tail-light rims, bumper; any noticeable dents), or if body fill has been used to fill in rust spots temporarily. It is important to look for these areas because they will be the cause of minor repairs in the future.

In all cases, take the auto for a test run, listen to the engine, check the condition of the seats, floors, dash, trunk, etc. When talking about the price of an auto, always try to negotiate and bring the price lower. This is an accepted practice in Canada.

10.1   FINANCING THE PURCHASE OF AN AUTOMOBILE

There are many ways to finance an automobile. Most people do not have enough cash on hand to buy a car outright, so they take out a personal bank loan or set up monthly payments with the car dealer. In either case, payments are usually geared to income.

In the chapter on borrowing, you examined the costs of borrowing from banks, trust companies, and credit unions. Another source of financing is the automobile dealer. There are three main ways of financing the purchase of a car through the dealer. Each way goes through a bank, and each way is just a little different.

A   Conditional Sales Contract

This contract has fixed interest, which is predetermined and which does not change even if the interest rate at the bank does. It provides fifteen days interest free and can run for as long as 60 months, although 36 months is the average time. This contract is open, so besides the monthly payment, extra money can be put on it with no penalty. The vehicle (car) is used as security. That is, if payments are not made, the bank takes the car as settlement of the debt.

B   Chattel Mortgage

This contract differs greatly from the conditional sales contract. The interest, for instance, is calculated daily, so every time the interest rate changes, the interest changes also. This contract also uses more than just the vehicle for security and can include furniture and other household items. Why do you think this would be necessary?

C   Promissory Demand Note

This type of contract is very simple. It is a demand note that states that you owe the bank so much money, and when the bank demands payment, you have seven days to pay the money back. This type of deal usually carries interest 1% to 3% higher than the prime interest rate, but is given only to preferred customers.

Simple interest is used for the conditional sales contract and the promissory demand note

Reference:
Unit 5

$$I = Prt$$

A chattel mortgage, because interest is calculated daily, involves compound interest.

To calculate the effective annual interest rate:

$$r = \frac{2Nc}{A(n + 1)}$$

N = number of payments in one year
c = cost of borrowing
A = amount borrowed
n = number of payments to pay the loan in full

EXERCISE 10.1

1. Find the simple interest.

	Principal	Rate	Time
(a)	$4 820	$21\frac{1}{4}\%$	36 d
(b)	2 550	$22\frac{1}{2}\%$	73 d
(c)	4 760	$20\frac{3}{4}\%$	55 d
(d)	3 860	$20\frac{1}{4}\%$	86 d
(e)	5 860	$21\frac{3}{4}\%$	65 d

2. A loan of $2 500 is to be repaid in 18 months under Schedule 1, page 151. What is the effective annual interest rate?

3. Joyce needs $3 150 to purchase a used car. She has decided to take out a conditional sales contract from the car dealer. If interest is $15\frac{1}{4}\%$ and she wants to take the loan out for 36 months, find the amount of interest she pays on the loan.

4. Stefan wishes to buy a car that sells for $13 600. If he takes out a promissory demand note, how much interest would he have to pay for 34 d if the interest rate is 15%?

5. If Tracie borrows $2 500 to buy a car, and repays it in 12 months, what is the effective annual interest rate? (Schedule 1, page 151)

6. Dawn Lee needs $4 125 to purchase a small car. She wants 24 months to pay back the loan, which has interest of 15%. If Dawn Lee takes out a conditional sales contract, how much interest will she pay?

7. Steve wants to buy a used car worth $475. If he takes out a promissory demand note, how much interest would he have to pay for 60 d if the interest rate is $15\frac{1}{4}\%$?

8. If Rashmi borrows $4 000 to buy a car and plans to repay it in 36 months, what is the effective annual interest rate? (Schedule 1, page 151)

9. Sarah wishes to buy a car worth $2 500. She is not sure which kind of loan to take. She works as a nurse and so gets paid regularly. Sarah is single, living on her own. She would like to pay the loan back in 12 months.
    (a) Find out how much interest Sarah would pay if she takes out a conditional sales contract, interest at 15%.
    (b) Find the effective annual interest rate if Sarah takes out a chattel mortgage. (Schedule 1, page 151)

10. Joe decides to buy a six-year-old car worth $2 650. If he takes out a promissory demand note for 45 day at $14\frac{3}{4}\%$, how much interest would he have to pay?

10.2 COST TO MAINTAIN AN AUTOMOBILE

As the owner of an automobile you must do certain things to keep your car running smoothly besides feeding it gas. For example, the oil should be checked regularly and added or changed as necessary.

Cost to Drive a Car in Ontario*

Size of Car	24 000 km/a	Cost/km
Compact	$5 038	21¢
Medium	5 504	22.9¢
Full-size	6 100	25.4¢

*From C.A.A. 1983 car costs

This chart shows approximately how much it would cost to run a car based on the assumption that the car would travel 24 000 km in a year. The cost per kilometre includes such things as gas, oil, general maintenance, tires, snow tires, and insurance.

EXERCISE 10.2

1. Find the cost/km to drive the following cars.
    (a) A compact Chevrolet Chevette for 150 km
    (b) A full-size Gran Torino station wagon for 3 015 km
    (c) A medium size Buick for 578 km

2. Boris Schacht drove his compact car 20 km on Monday, 50 km on Tueday, 35 km on Wednesday, 10 km on Thursday, and 15 km on Friday. How much did it cost Boris to drive his car that week?

3. Sandra Graham drives her large station wagon to school and back every day. She lives approximately 3 km from the school.
   (a) How much would it cost to drive back and forth for a week?
   (b) How much would it cost to drive back and forth for a month?

4. Sue Cook drives a medium-size car 25 km to work each day. She works five days a week. She drives approximately 35 km every weekend.
   (a) How much does it cost for one week?
   (b) how much does it cost for one month?

5. Steve Kotnjek drives 68 km daily to work.
   (a) Find the cost for a week if Steve drives a compact car.
   (b) Find the cost for a month if Steve drives a full-size station wagon.
   (c) If public transit costs $4.80 one way, what is the cheapest way for Steve to go to work each day?

6. Gino owns a medium-size Ford Mustang that he drives 15 km to school and 15 km home each day.
   (a) How much does it cost for one week?
   (b) How much does it cost for one month?

7. Kim lives 30 km from school. In order to get there, she can either take her mother's compact car or take the city bus.
   (a) Find out how much it would cost per kilometre for Kim to drive to school and back for a week.
   (b) If it costs 85¢ to travel one way on the bus, how much would it cost Kim to take the bus to and from school for a week?
   (c) Which is the least expensive way for Kim to travel?

8. Beverly has just landed a job in the city. The only problem is that she lives in a small town 70 km away from her job. She does own a compact car and is assured of ample parking, but would like to travel the cheapest way possible.
   (a) Find out how much it would cost Beverly to drive back and forth for a week.
   (b) If public transit cost $4.80 one way, find the total cost for one week.
   (c) Which is the least expensive way for Beverly to travel back and forth to work? Which is more convenient?

9. Lui owns a compact Toyota. Niki owns a compact Pontiac. Cheryl owns a full-size station wagon. Donna owns a medium-size Plymouth. Each one works at the same plant and must drive approximately 53 km to work each day, five days a week.
   (a) Calculate the cost for each person for one week.
   (b) Compare the costs. Which person has the most cost? the least cost? Is this logical?

10. David owns a medium-size Plymouth. He also owns a full-size station wagon. If David has to drive 35 km to work each day, and then drives 30 km on the weekend, what is the cheapest way for David to use each car?

10.3   AUTOMOBILE INSURANCE

It is not unusual for courts to award very large sums of money (damages) when making a decision in cases regarding automobile accidents. Personal pain and suffering, medical payments, and past and future loss of earnings are perhaps the major factors the courts consider when arriving at a total sum of money to be paid by the person at fault. Sums such as $75 000, $150 000, and even $300 000 are not uncommon damages reported in Canadian newspapers. Large sums of money such as these are obviously beyond the capacity of the majority of individuals to pay.

Some provinces have government automobile insurance plans. Other provinces require the car owner to use private insurance companies.

As a result, when driving an automobile, it is compulsory in Canada to carry insurance against liability for loss caused to other persons. Standard automobile policies contain a section for Third Party Liability, which insures against public liability (P.L.) for bodily injury to, or death of any person, or damage to property (P.D.).

Payments for P.L. and P.D. insurance are called premiums. Rates for premiums depend on many factors.

- Age, sex, and marital status of driver: Do you think premiums would be different for teenagers and middle-aged drivers? Why? Do you think premiums would be different for male and female drivers? Why? Do you think premiums would be different for married drivers and unmarried drivers? Why?
- Previous driving convictions: in past two and three years
- Previous accident claims: in past two and three years
- Province of residence? Why do you think premiums differ from province to province?
- Place of residence in the province: Why should premiums be different in urban and rural areas?
- Drive to work
- Drive for business or pleasure, or both
- Kind of car

The above factors are some of many that determine what rate of premium drivers pay for their P.L. and P.D. insurance. Again, P.L. and P.D. insurance is carried in the event of injury and/or damage to the other person(s) and his/their property.

How do young drivers rate as insurance risks?
Young drivers (16-25) have a high accident rate, out of proportion to their percentage of the driving population. Their premiums are higher than those paid by older, more experienced drivers, because the cost, as well as the frequency, of their accidents is greater. The figures on page 219 give an idea of the accident rate of young drivers, compared to that of other age categories.*

Figure 10.1 is an example of Third Party Liability (P.L. & P.D.) rates for private passenger cars. These rates apply in the city of London, and the towns and villages surrounding the city.

*Compiled from figures for liability insurance submitted by insurance companies across Canada

	Claims per 100 cars in urban areas
Pleasure drivers over 25 who do not drive to work	7.8
Pleasure drivers over 25 who drive to work	9.7
Cars owned or principally operated by single men under 19 with less than one year's experience or a claim in the past 12 months	37.6
Cars owned or principally operated by single women under 21 with less than one year's experience	16.9
Cars owned or principally operated by married men under 21 with less than one year's experience	22.8

Under the heading INCLUSIVE LIMITS is listed the amount of Third Party Liability insurance you are buying.

FACILITY ASSOCIATION

PAGE 34   PRIVATE PASSENGER

SCHEDULE OF RATES – ONTARIO – TERRITORY 4

THIRD PARTY LIABILITY   (INCL. LIMITS IN 000'S)

CLASS		200	300	500	1000	CLASS		200	300	500	1000	CLASS		200	300	500	1000
	5	136	138	142	149		5	89	91	93	98		5	403	410	422	444
	3	205	209	215	226		3	135	137	142	149	10	3	611	621	640	672
01	2	253	257	265	278	06	2	166	169	174	183	11	2	752	764	787	827
	1	296	301	310	325		1	195	198	204	214		1	880	894	921	968
	0	351	357	368	386		0	231	235	242	254		0	1045	1062	1094	1150
	5	165	168	173	182		5	184	186	192	202		5	265	269	277	291
	3	250	254	262	276		3	278	282	291	306		3	401	407	420	441
02	2	308	313	323	339	07	2	342	347	358	376	12	2	493	501	516	542
	1	361	366	378	397		1	400	407	419	440		1	577	586	604	635
	0	428	435	448	471		0	475	483	498	523		0	685	696	718	754
	5	174	176	182	191		5	225	228	235	247		5	225	228	235	247
	3	263	267	275	289	08	3	341	346	357	375		3	341	346	357	375
03	2	324	329	339	356	09	2	419	426	439	461	13	2	419	426	439	461
	1	379	385	397	417		1	491	498	514	540		1	491	498	514	540
	0	450	457	471	495		0	583	592	610	641		0	583	592	610	641

		200	300	500	1000
	5	180	183	189	198
18	3	273	277	286	300
19	2	336	341	352	369
	1	393	399	412	432
	0	467	474	489	514

Figure 10.1

CLASS 01
(a) Pleasure
(b) Principal operator, whether applicant or not, is
    (i) unmarried male 30 years of age or over,
    (ii) married male 25 years of age or over residing with his spouse,
    (iii) female 25 years of age or over.
(c) No male driver under 25 years of age
(d) No unmarried female driver under 25 years of age
(e) Not more than two drivers per automobile in the household, each driver having held a valid operator's licence for the past three years

Figure 10.2

(f) Automobile not used for driving to and from work or for vocational purposes

(g) Average and anticipated number of kilometres not exceeding 16 000 per year

CLASS 02

(a) Pleasure

(b) Principal operator, whether applicant or not, is

    (i)   unmarried male 30 years of age or over,

    (ii) married male 25 years of age or over residing with his spouse,

    (iii) female 25 years of age or over.

(c) No male driver under 25 years of age

(d) No unmarried female driver under 25 years of age

(e) Not more than two drivers per automobile in the household

(f) Automobile not used for driving to or from work more than 16 kilometres one way.

CLASS 03

(a) Pleasure

(b) Principal operator, whether applicant or not, is

    (i)   unmarried male 30 years of age or over,

    (ii) married male 25 years of age or over residing with his spouse,

    (iii) female 25 years of age or over

(c) No male driver under 25 years of age

Rating Note: Third Party Liability. All Perils and Collisions

CLASS 06

Occasional male driver under 25 years of age where the principal operator is rated as 01, 02, 03, 04, or 07.

Note   The policy will be rated under Class 01, 02, 03, 04, or 07 as though there is no occasional male driver or drivers under 25 years of age. Cover for such driver or drivers will be charged for as Class 06 under "Endorsements" on the policy face and the "Occasional Driver Certificate".

CLASS 07

(a) Business or business and pleasure

(b) Principal operator, whether applicant or not, is

    (i)   unmarried male 30 years of age or over,

    (ii) married male 25 years of age or over,

    (iii) female 25 years of age or over

(c) No male driver under 25 years of age

CLASS 08

Principal operator, whether applicant or not, married male under 21 years of age, residing with his spouse

CLASS 09

Principal operator, whether applicant or not, married male under 25 years of age, but not under 21 years of age, residing with his spouse

CLASS 10

Unmarried male principal operator, whether applicant or not, 16, 17, or 18 years of age

CLASS 11

Unmarried male principal operator, whether applicant or not, 19 or 20 years of age

CLASS 12

Unmarried male principal operator, whether applicant or not, 21 or 22 years of age

CLASS 13

Unmarried male principal operator, whether applicant or not, 23 or 24 years of age

CLASS 18

Principal operator, whether applicant or not, female under 21 years of age

CLASS 19

Principal operator, whether applicant or not, female under 25 years of age, but not under 21 years of age

Figure 10.2

Figure 10.2 explains the classification of the driver(s) by the numbers 01 to 19 under the heading CLASS in Figure 10.1.

Figure 10.3 explains how the driver's driving record is described by the numbers 5, 3, 2, 1, and 0 in Figure 10.1.

DRIVING RECORD	STAT. CODE
Clear Record for the five years immediately prior to the effective date of the policy or any renewal thereof.	5
Clear Record for the three years immediately prior to the effective date of the policy or any renewal thereof.	3
Clear Record for the two years immediately prior to the effective date of the policy or any renewal thereof.	2
Clear Record for the one year immediately prior to the effective date of the policy or any renewal thereof.	1
Risk not qualifying for 5, 3, 2, or 1.	0

Figure 10.3

Example
Trevor Jones, a driver classified as Class 10 and Driving Record 1, wishes to purchase $200 000 Third Party Liability insurance. Find the cost of such insurance. A portion of Figure 10.1 is shown.

THIRD PARTY LIABILITY (amounts given in 000's)

CLASS		200	300	500	1 000
	5	403	410	422	444
10	3	611	621	640	672
11	2	752	764	787	827
	1	880	894	921	968
	0	1 045	1 062	1 094	1 150

Solution
Trevor's Third Party Liability insurance premium would be $880 per annum.

EXERCISE 10.3
Look up the following premiums of Third Party Liability insurance in Figure 10.1.

	Class	*Driving Record*	*Amount of Insurance*
(a)	19	3	$200 000
(b)	07	2	200 000
(c)	02	5	300 000
(d)	12	0	300 000
(e)	06	3	500 000
(f)	13	2	200 000
(g)	09	1	200 000
(h)	11	5	300 000
(i)	03	2	200 000
(j)	18	0	200 000

10.4   SURCHARGES

It is important to note that a driver with Driving Record 0 does not have a clear record. In other words, he or she must have had either an accident or a conviction, or both, within the last year. If the driver does not have a clear record, then an *additional premium* to that shown in Figure 10.1 must be paid. The additional premium, or surcharge, might be calculated as follows.

Surcharges to be Added to Premiums in Figures 10.1

Add 25%.
Then add 15%
of the result.

Accidents: Two accidents within the last 3 years – add 25%.
Each additional accident – add 15% for each.

Convictions: 100% For any conviction under the Criminal Code of Canada including
  (1) Criminal negligence
  (2) Manslaughter
  (3) Failing to stop at scene
  (4) Intoxicated driving
  (5) Impaired driving
  (6) Driving while licence suspended
  (7) Dangerous driving
 50% For any conviction under any act governing highway traffic including
  (1) Careless driving
  (2) Failing to report an accident
  (3) Improper passing of school buses
  (4) Driving without due care and attention
  (5) Racing
 25% Improper passing of schools or playgrounds

Example 1
If the regular premium is $470, what is the surcharge for three accidents within the last three years?

Solution

Regular premium	$470.00
Surcharge for two accidents ($470 × 0.25)	117.50
	$587.50
Surcharge for third accident ($587.50 × 0.15)	88.13
Total premium	$675.63

Example 2
Michael William, a driver classified as Class 10, was convicted for racing his car within one year of applying for a new policy for Third Party Liability of $200 000. Find the cost of his insurance. A portion of Figure 10.1 is shown. What would a female driver, Class 19, with the same conviction pay for similar coverage? Why?

THIRD PARTY LIABILITY (amounts given in 000's)

CLASS		200	300	500	1 000
	5	403	410	422	444
10	3	611	621	640	672
11	2	752	764	787	827
	1	880	894	921	968
	0	1 045	1 062	1 094	1 150

Solution
Michael's basic premium for Third Party Liability would be $1 045, but because of his driving conviction, he must pay a 50% surcharge.

Basic premium	$1 045.00	$467.00	Female
Add surcharge (50%)	522.50	233.50	Driver
Total premium	$1 567.50	$700.50	

EXERCISE 10.4
Calculate the Third Party Liability premiums using Figure 10.1 and adding surcharges in the following situations.

	Class	Driving Record	Amount of Insurance	Accident or Conviction
(a)	13	0	$1 000 000	2 accidents within last 3 a
(b)	18	0	200 000	Failing to stop at scene
(c)	07	0	200 000	Driving without due care and attention
(d)	12	0	500 000	Careless driving
(e)	01	0	300 000	Improper passing of school bus
(f)	03	0	500 000	Impaired driving
(g)	08	0	1 000 000	3 accidents within last 3 a
(h)	11	0	200 000	Improper passing of schools
(i)	06	0	500 000	Criminal negligence
(j)	02	0	300 000	Failing to report an accident

10.5 YOUR OWN CAR

All of the previous questions concerned Third Party Liability, that is, insurance to pay for damage to another person and/or property. To insure against damage to *your own car* caused by collision with another object, either moving or stationary, or by upset, you must buy *collision insurance*.

A lower premium can be obtained if the insured helps to pay for damages. The insured obtains lower premiums for collision by buying either $100 or $250 *deductible*. This means that if a collision occurs, the insured pays the amount deductible shown in the policy, and the insurance company pays the balance. The higher the amount deductible, the lower the premium for collision insurance.

FACILITY ASSOCIATION

PRIVATE PASSENGER

SCHEDULE OF RATES – ONTARIO – TERRITORY 4

COLLISION

CLASS	DR. REC.	RATING GROUP 1 DED. 100	1 DED. 250	2 DED. 100	2 DED. 250	3 DED. 100	3 DED. 250	4 DED. 100	4 DED. 250	5 DED. 100	5 DED. 250	6 DED. 100	6 DED. 250	7 DED. 100	7 DED. 250	8 DED. 100	8 DED. 250
01	5	50	42	59	50	70	59	83	70	98	82	115	97	136	114	161	135
	3	73	62	87	73	103	86	122	103	144	121	170	143	200	168	237	199
	2	87	73	103	87	122	103	145	122	172	144	202	170	238	200	282	237
	1	103	86	121	102	144	121	171	144	202	170	238	200	281	236	332	279
	0	119	100	141	119	167	141	199	167	235	197	277	233	327	274	386	325
02	5	57	48	67	56	79	67	94	79	111	94	131	110	155	130	183	154
	3	83	70	99	83	117	98	139	117	164	138	193	162	228	191	269	226
	2	99	83	117	99	139	117	165	139	195	164	230	193	271	228	321	269
	1	117	98	138	116	163	137	194	163	229	193	270	227	319	268	377	317
	0	136	114	161	135	190	160	226	190	267	224	315	264	371	312	439	369
03	5	63	53	74	63	88	74	105	88	124	104	146	122	172	144	203	171
	3	92	78	109	92	129	109	154	129	182	153	214	180	253	212	299	251
	2	110	92	130	109	154	129	183	154	216	182	255	214	301	253	356	299
	1	129	109	153	129	181	152	216	181	255	214	300	252	354	297	419	352
	0	151	127	178	150	211	177	251	211	296	249	349	293	412	346	487	409
06	5	33	28	40	33	47	39	56	47	66	55	77	65	91	77	108	91
	3	49	41	58	49	69	58	82	69	97	81	114	96	134	113	159	133
	2	58	49	69	58	82	69	97	82	115	97	135	114	160	134	189	159
	1	69	58	81	68	96	81	115	96	135	114	159	134	188	158	222	187
	0	80	67	95	80	112	94	134	112	158	132	186	156	219	184	259	218
07	5	70	59	83	70	98	83	117	98	138	116	163	137	192	161	227	191
	3	103	87	122	103	145	121	172	145	203	171	239	201	282	237	334	281
	2	123	103	145	122	172	145	205	172	242	203	285	239	336	282	397	334
	1	145	121	171	144	202	170	241	202	284	239	335	281	395	332	468	393
	0	168	141	199	167	236	198	281	236	331	278	390	328	460	387	544	457
08 09	5	81	68	96	81	113	95	135	113	159	134	188	158	221	186	262	220
	3	119	100	141	118	167	140	199	167	234	197	276	232	326	274	385	324
	2	142	119	168	141	198	167	236	198	279	234	328	276	387	325	458	385
	1	167	140	197	166	233	196	278	233	328	276	386	325	456	383	539	453
	0	194	163	230	193	272	228	324	272	382	321	450	378	531	446	628	527
18 19	5	78	66	93	78	109	92	130	109	154	129	181	152	214	179	253	212
	3	115	97	136	114	161	135	192	161	226	190	266	224	314	264	372	312
	2	137	115	162	136	192	161	228	192	269	226	317	266	374	314	442	372
	1	161	135	190	160	225	189	268	225	317	266	373	313	440	370	520	437
	0	187	157	222	186	262	220	312	262	369	310	434	365	512	430	606	509
10 11	5	173	146	205	172	243	204	289	243	341	286	402	337	474	398	560	471
	3	255	214	302	253	357	300	425	357	501	421	591	496	697	585	824	692
	2	303	255	359	302	425	357	506	425	597	501	765	590	829	696	981	824
	1	357	300	422	355	500	420	595	500	702	590	827	694	975	819	1154	969
	0	416	349	492	413	582	489	693	582	817	686	963	809	1136	954	1343	1129
12	5	123	104	146	123	173	145	206	173	243	204	286	240	338	284	399	335
	3	182	153	215	181	254	214	303	254	357	300	421	353	496	417	587	493
	2	216	182	256	215	303	254	360	303	425	357	501	421	591	496	699	587
	1	254	214	301	253	356	299	424	356	500	420	589	495	695	584	822	691
	0	296	249	350	294	414	348	493	414	582	489	686	576	809	680	957	804
13	5	97	82	115	97	136	115	162	136	192	161	226	190	266	221	315	265
	3	143	120	170	142	201	169	239	201	282	237	332	279	392	329	463	389
	2	171	143	202	169	239	201	284	239	335	282	395	332	446	391	551	463
	1	201	169	237	199	281	236	334	281	395	331	465	390	548	461	649	545
	0	234	196	276	232	327	275	389	327	459	386	541	454	638	536	755	634

Figure 10.4

In Figure 10.4 note that there is a *rating group* heading with the numbers 1 to 8. These numbers refer to the make, model, number of cylinders, and year of the car. For example, a 1981 Dodge Omni is rated as number 5 whereas a 1981 Lincoln Continental is rated as number 8. Why do you think different cars have different rates for collision insurance?

Example
Keith Strojek applied for $250 deductible collision insurance. Keith, the driver, was classified as 08, Driving Record 3. Keith's car was rated as 4. Using Figure 10.4, look up Keith's premium for $250 deductible collision insurance. A portion of figure 10.4 is shown.

FACILITY ASSOCIATION
PRIVATE PASSENGER   PAGE 35

SCHEDULE OF RATES – ONTARIO – TERRITORY 4

COLLISION

CLASS		RATING GROUP														
		1		2		3		4		5		6		7		8
	DR.	DED.		DED.		DED.		DED.		DED.		DED.		DED.		DED.
	REC.	100	250	100	250	100	250	100	250	100	250	100	250	100	250	100	250
	5	81	68	96	81	113	95	135	113	159	134	188	158	221	186	262	220
08	3	119	100	141	118	167	140	199	167	234	197	276	232	326	274	385	324
09	2	142	119	168	141	198	167	236	198	279	234	328	276	387	325	458	385
	1	167	140	197	166	233	196	278	233	328	276	386	325	456	383	539	453
	0	194	163	230	193	272	228	324	272	382	321	450	378	531	446	628	527

Solution
Keith's premium for collision insurance would be $167 per annum.

EXERCISE 10.5

1. Using Figure 10.4 calculate the premium for the following collision insurance situations.

	Driver Class	Driver Record	Car Make and Model Rating	Amount Deductible
(a)	19	3	2	$100
(b)	03	5	1	250
(c)	11	2	6	100
(d)	08	1	8	100
(e)	13	5	4	250
(f)	12	0	3	250
(g)	13	2	7	100
(h)	01	3	6	250
(i)	07	1	5	100
(j)	03	2	7	100

2. As with Third Party Liability insurance, for a driver with certain convictions under the Criminal Code of Canada and/or with two or more accidents within the last three years, a surcharge is added to the basic premium for collision insurance. Calculate the following collision premiums using Figure 10.4 and adding surcharges in the following situations.

	Driver Class	Record	Car Make and Model Rating	Amount Deductible	Accident or Conviction(s)
(a)	13	0	8	$100	Driving without due care and attention
(b)	12	0	6	100	Impaired driving
(c)	19	0	4	250	Careless driving
(d)	08	0	3	250	Manslaughter
(e)	11	0	7	250	2 accidents within last 3 a
(f)	07	0	5	100	Improper passing of schools
(g)	13	0	2	100	Racing
(h)	03	0	1	250	Failing to report an accident
(i)	01	0	6	250	3 accidents within last 3 a
(j)	06	0	2	100	Failing to stop at scene

3. Ed Bennett wanted $300 000 Third Party Liability insurance and $100 deductible collision insurance. Ed was classified as Class 09 with a driving record of 0 as he had been convicted of impaired driving a short time before. If Ed's car was rated as 7, how much total insurance premium would Ed pay per annum?

4. Adrienne Morrow had been in two accidents in the past three years. She wanted $200 000 Third Party Liability and $250 deductible collision. Adrienne was classified as Class 07, and her car was rated as 4. How much total insurance premium would she pay per annum if her driving record was rated as 0?

5. Dieter Furlong took a driver education course at high school and was told by his insurance company that he would be eligible for Third Party Liability and collision. What would Dieter's total premium per annum be if he was classified as Class 12, his car rated as 4, and he wanted $200 000 Third Party Liability and $100 deductible collision? Dieter's driving record was rated as 1.

REVIEW EXERCISE 10.6

1. Debbie wishes to purchase a car worth $7 525. She wishes to take out a conditional sales contract for 24 months with interest at $14\frac{3}{4}\%$. How much interest will she pay?

2. Kris has decided to buy a car worth $13 365. If she takes out a promissory demand note for 75 d at 16%, how much interest would she have to pay?

3. Bryan wants to buy a car worth $10 565. If he takes out a promissory demand note for 125 d at $17\frac{1}{4}$%, how much interest would he have to pay?

4. If Nancy borrows $2 500 to buy a car and plans to repay it in 18 months, what is the effective annual interest rate? (Schedule 1, page 151)

5. If Jason borrows $3 500 to buy a car and plans to repay it in 24 months, what is the effective annual interest rate? (Schedule 1, page 151)

6. Cindy drove her medium-size Mustang 25 km on Monday, 15 km on Tuesday, 30 km on Wednesday, 20 km on Thursday, and 50 km on Friday. How much did it cost Cindy to drive her car that week?

7. Jaime drives his full-size station wagon back and forth to school every day. He lives about 5 km from the school. How much does it cost to drive back and forth for a week?

8. Isabelle drives 65 km to work every day. If she owns a medium-size car, how much does it cost for a week?

9. Miguel lives in a small town and drives 68 km to the city to work every day. If he drives a compact Honda and works five days a week, how much does it cost for Miguel to drive back and forth for a week?

10. Angela wanted $200 000 Third Party Liability insurance and $250 deductible collision insurance. She was classified as Class 02 with a driving record of 0 as she had been convicted of careless driving within the previous two years. If her car was rated as 5, how much total premium did she pay per annum?

11. Ed Hewitt had been in two accidents in the previous three years. He wanted $300 000 Third Party Liability and $100 deductible collision. Ed was classified as Class 08 and his car was rated as 6. How much total insurance premium would Ed pay per annum if his driving record was rated as 0?

CUMULATIVE REVIEW 8

1. Change the following percents to fractions.
   (a) 55%   (b) $16\frac{2}{3}$%   (c) 80%   (d) $62\frac{1}{2}$%   (e) 75%

2. $42.50 increased by $12\frac{1}{2}$% of itself equals what number?

3. Factor the following.
   (a) $8a + 32ab + 48c - 32ac$ (c) $bA + bZ$
   (b) $4ab + 8ac + 16a$

4. Calculate the following if the broker gets 55% and the agent gets 45% of the $ commission as per listing.

	House Sold For	% Comm. as per Listing	$ Comm. as per Listing	$ Comm. for Broker	$ Comm. for Agent
(a)	$52 900	6%	■	■	■
(b)	46 700	5%	■	■	■
(c)	65 500	$4\frac{1}{2}$%	■	■	■
(d)	38 900	$5\frac{1}{2}$%	■	■	■

5. Fill in the blanks.

	Cost of Goods	Retail	% Margin of Retail	% Markup on Cost
(a)	$ 8.60	$19.95	■	■
(b)	42.50	■	■	55%
(c)	■	79.50	44%	■
(d)	■	23.95	58%	■
(e)	63.90	■	■	65%

6. Find the rate at which interest is earned for each of the following.

	Principal	Interest Earned	Time
(a)	$4 500	$765.00	2 a
(b)	2 000	77.50	6 months
(c)	3 600	54.00	73 d
(d)	5 200	120.25	3 months
(e)	1 500	472.50	3 a

7. Calculate the amount of interest paid and the effective rate of interest for the following loans. (Assume the principal does not decrease with monthly payments.)

	Princ.	Int. Paid	Rate of Int. Paid	Time	Interest Rebate	Annual Effective Rate of Interest
(a)	$3 500	■	$14\frac{1}{2}$%	1 year	$62	■
(b)	1 800	■	$15\frac{1}{4}$%	1 year	55	■
(c)	4 200	■	$14\frac{3}{4}$%	1 year	65	■
(d)	2 600	■	$13\frac{3}{4}$%	1 year	45	■

8. Erik worked a 44 h week. He received $6.75/h for the first 40 h and time-and-one-half for overtime. How much did he earn?

9. Debbie picked raspberries last week. On Monday she picked 40 boxes, Tuesday 62 boxes, Wednesday 68 boxes, Thursday 47 boxes, and Friday 75 boxes. If the farmer paid 55¢/box up to 50 boxes per day, and 70¢/box for all boxes picked over 50 per day, how much did she earn?

UNIT 11

Presentation of Data

11.1 AVERAGE

The word "average" has different meanings for different situations, just as other words in our language have come to have many meanings. The word "nice", for example, is used in "nice day" to describe the weather, or in "nice play" to describe a successful play in football or some other sport. We may have a general idea what people mean when they use the adjective "nice", but we cannot be certain of a specific meaning. Similarly, the word "average" has a general meaning.

A   Mean

The best known and most commonly used average is the *mean*. Examine the following results of a December examination for a class of 17 students in mathematics. The mean is calculated as follows.

Frequency	100	1 student
Distribution 1	96	1 student
	87	1 student
	78	1 student
	73	1 student
	72	1 student
	68	1 student
	68	1 student
	65	1 student
	64	1 student
	62	1 student
	59	1 student
	56	1 student
	55	1 student
	52	1 student
	46	1 student
	38	1 student
	1 139 Total Marks	17 Total

Note: **Frequency distributions have data arranged in values from highest to lowest**

$$\text{Mean} = \frac{\text{Total Marks}}{\text{Number of Students}} = \frac{1139}{17} = 67$$

The mean of a group of items then, is obtained by dividing the sum of the items in the group by the number of items.

The disadvantage of the mean is that the mean is affected by extreme values. Extreme values, such as illustrated in the example, should be pointed out if a mean is to have significance.

Example 1
One student had a mark of 55, another student had a mark of 53, and another student had a mark of 90. Find the mean.

Solution

$$\begin{array}{r} 90 \\ 55 \\ \underline{53} \\ 198 \end{array}$$

$$\text{Mean} = \frac{198}{3} = 66$$

Because of the extreme value of the mark by *one* student, the mean is quite a bit higher than the marks by the other *two* students.

This mean is considered to be unweighted, or a simple average, because, even though the students' marks were of unequal value, each student was considered to be of equal value ($\frac{1}{5}$). When there is only 1 of each item in the group, the mean is called a *simple average* because it is considered to be unweighted. When there are varied numbers of each item in the group, the mean is a *weighted average*. The different values are weighted according to the number of items at each value.

Example 2
On a recent test Amy scored 58, Guy got 50, Charlotte 58, Doug 72, and Juanita 72. Find the mean of their marks.

Solution

$$
\begin{array}{r}
2 \times 72 = 144 \\
2 \times 58 = 116 \\
1 \times 50 = \underline{50} \\
\overline{5} \qquad 310
\end{array}
\qquad \text{Mean} = \frac{310}{5} = 62
$$

This is a weighted average because the different marks are weighted according to the number of students having each mark.

B Median

Another average that can be determined from Frequency Distribution 1 is the *median*. There are 17 students involved in the frequency distribution. The median mark is the mark that has half the students with a higher mark, and half the students with a lower mark.

$$17 \div 2 = 8.5$$

Frequency
Distribution 2

100	1 student	⎫
96	1 student	⎪
87	1 student	⎪
78	1 student	⎬ 8 students
73	1 student	⎪
72	1 student	⎪
68	1 student	⎪
68	1 student	⎭
65	1 student	
64	1 student	⎫
62	1 student	⎪
59	1 student	⎪
56	1 student	⎬ 8 students
55	1 student	⎪
52	1 student	⎪
46	1 student	⎪
38	1 student	⎭

The median mark, therefore, is 65. Half the students had a mark higher than 65 and half the students had a mark lower than 65. Hence the median is an average of position.

Example 3

Students	Marks
1	90
1	70
1	60
1	50

Median $= \dfrac{70 + 60}{2} = 65$

> *Note:* **When there is an even number of items in a group, the median is the mean of the two middle numbers.**

C   Mode

A third average from Frequency Distribution 1 is the mark of 68. This average is called the *mode*, the mark which more students had. In the given mark, or frequency, distribution, more students had a mark of 68 than any other mark.

What would you think, however, if 5 students had a mark of 51? Could you take a report card home and say that the class average was 51? In that case, the word average would mean one thing to you and something else to parents or guardians. Saying that the mode was 51 would give meaningful information. That tells us that more students had a mark of 51 than any other mark.

Could a group contain more than one mode? Explain how.

Could a group not have a mode? Explain how.

If we think of average as meaning a central tendency, would the mode, or the median, best fit this definition? Why? Would the same answer be true for all situations?

EXERCISE 11.1

1. Joon Sik Kim bought one dozen cookies at 79¢, a dozen at 92¢, and a dozen at $1.10.
   (a) What was the mean price?
   (b) What was the median price?

2. On his first 9 weeks of weekly tests in mathematics Akil Khan's marks were 85, 72, 78, 91, 86, 79, 75, 81, and 89. Find Akil's mean mark and his median mark.

3. (a) From the following set of test results, calculate the mean, the median, and the mode.

    98 – 1 student; 96 – 1 student; 53 – 6 students; 44 – 4 students; 89 – 1 student; 75 – 2 students; 30 – 1 student; 40 – 1 student; 91 – 1 student; 50 – 3 students; 59 – 3 students; 92 – 1 student; 54 – 2 students; 87 – 1 student; 84 – 2 students.

   (b) Which average is the *least* suitable description? Why?

4. From the following series of incomes, calculate the mean, the median, and the mode.

   1 person earned $525 000, 1 person earned $55 000, 3 people earned $40 000, 5 people earned $30 000, 10 people earned $20 000, 25 people earned $15 000, 15 people earned $10 000, and 5 people earned $7 000.

   (a) Is any one average better used to describe this series of incomes?
   (b) Is the mean a weighted or a simple average?

5. (a) Using the income figures of Question 4 and assuming that only one person received each different income, which average is the most suitable description?
   (b) Why are the other averages unsuitable?

6. (a) A manager of a clothing store wants to advertise for a new salesperson and wants to tell the prospect the average income that the salespeople in the store are now earning. Arrange the following raw data into a frequency distribution, and determine the mean, median, and mode.

Salesperson	Sales for the Year	Rate of Commission
Bryce	$150 000	11%
Cheong	225 000	11%
Bruba	185 500	11%
Manji	122 000	11%
Wilhelm	195 500	11%
Macdonald	182 250	11%
Dufour	130 000	11%
Cody	142 350	11%

   Would the manager tell the prospect the mean, the median, or the mode? Why?
   (b) Is the mean a weighted or a simple average?

7. A local TV station held an auction and it was determined that bids were made on the following basis: 301 people made only one bid, 100 people made 2 bids, 45 people made 3 bids, 24 people made 4 bids, 28 people made 5 bids, 6 people made 6 bids, 7 people made 7 bids, 4 people made 8 bids, 2 people made 9 bids, 2 people made 10 bids, 3 people made 11 bids, 2 people made 12 bids, 3 people made 13 bids, 2 people made 14 bids, 1 person made 15 bids, 1 person made 16 bids, 1 person made 17 bids, 1 person made 18 bids, 1 person made 19 bids, 1 person made 20 bids, 1 person made 21 bids, 1 person made 27 bids, 1 person made 33 bids, and 1 person made 67 bids.

   (a) Arrange the raw data into a frequency distribution and determine the mode, median, and mean.
   (b) Which of the mode, median, or mean would be most meaningful to the organizers of the TV auction? Why?

8. The number of tow tickets sold at a local ski slope was as follows.

Monday	383
Tuesday	468
Wednesday	645
Thursday	122
Friday	289
Saturday	1 052
Sunday	1 541

   (a) What was the daily mean average of tow tickets sold during the week? What needs to be pointed out when mentioning this average?
   (b) If tow tickets were sold for $4.50 each on Monday through Friday inclusive, and $6.50 each on Saturday and Sunday, what was the daily mean average of income?

9. Consumer purchases for the year from a TV and Appliance store were as follows.

January	$ 4 058.25
February	5 241.98
March	4 892.59
April	5 389.65
May	6 482.75
June	5 967.58
July	4 076.48
August	6 785.25
September	5 055.85
October	5 298.25
November	8 468.95
December	10 595.60

   What was the monthly mean average?

10. Real estate purchases for one week in a medium-size city were as follows.

Monday:	2 homes sold for $65 000; 1 home @ $42 000
Tuesday:	1 home @ $85 000; 1 @ $59 500; 1 @ $72 400; 1 @ $78 900; 2 @ $61 500
Wednesday:	1 home @ $72 500
Thursday:	1 home @ $110 000; 2 @ $74 900; 1 @ $62 900; 1 @ $75 400; 1 @ $63 200; 1 @ $64 800
Friday:	1 home @ $71 900; 1 @ $76 700; 1 @ $78 500; 3 @ $61 000
Saturday:	1 home @ $55 900; 1 @ $43 700; 2 @ $62 500

   (a) What was the mean price for the week?
   (b) What was the median price for the week?
   (c) Was there a mode average price?
   (d) Which average would best describe the average real estate price of homes bought? Why?

11. A farmer who sold tomatoes on a "pick your own" basis, sold the following during August.

> 50 baskets @ $4.99
> 225 baskets @   3.25
> 75 baskets @   2.50
> 50 baskets @   1.89

(a) Calculate the simple mean average of the four prices.
(b) Calculate the weighted mean average of the four prices.

11.2   CUMULATIVE AND MOVING AVERAGES

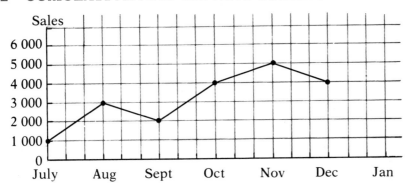

The line graph shows sales for each month from July through December. Sometimes businesspeople want to see the trend in sales rather than the specific figures. One way to show a gradual trend is to graph a *cumulative average*. The cumulative average is found by dividing the cumulative total by the number of months during which the total was accumulated. Using the material from the previous graph, we calculate the cumulative average as follows.

Month	Sales	Cumulative Sales Total	Cumulative Average
July	$1 000	$ 1 000	$1 000
August	3 000	4 000	$\dfrac{4\ 000}{2} = 2\ 000$
September	2 000	6 000	$\dfrac{6\ 000}{3} = 2\ 000$
October	4 000	10 000	$\dfrac{10\ 000}{4} = 2\ 500$
November	5 000	15 000	$\dfrac{15\ 000}{5} = 3\ 000$
December	4 000	19 000	$\dfrac{19\ 000}{6} = 3\ 166.67$

We graph the cumulative average on the previous graph using a dotted line or a colored line to distinguish it from the first graph.

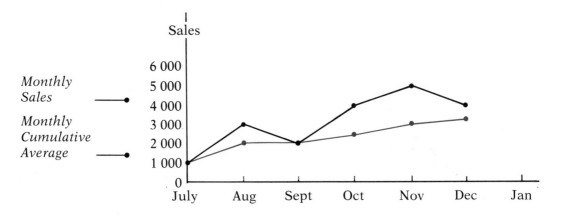

A *moving average* also can be used to show a general trend over a period of time. The following chart shows how to calculate a moving average.

Month	Sales	3 Month Moving Average	How Calculated
July	$1 000		
August	3 000		
September	2 000	$2 000	$\dfrac{1\,000 + 3\,000 + 2\,000}{3}$
October	4 000	3 000	$\dfrac{3\,000 + 2\,000 + 4\,000}{3}$
November	5 000	3 666.67	$\dfrac{2\,000 + 4\,000 + 5\,000}{3}$
December	4 000	4 333.33	$\dfrac{4\,000 + 5\,000 + 4\,000}{3}$

Note that the longer the period of time, the more significant cumulative and moving averages become.

EXERCISE 11.2

1. Sales for a sporting goods salesperson from Year 1 to Year 5 were as follows.

Year	Sales
1	$ 60 000
2	100 000
3	110 000
4	140 000
5	145 000

(a) What were the mean sales for the five year period?
(b) Compute the cumulative averages for the five year period.
(c) Construct a line graph and plot the sales for the five year period.

2. Commissions earned during a nine year period were as follows.

Year	$ Commissions Earned
1	$30 000
2	12 000
3	10 000
4	15 000
5	35 000
6	32 000
7	47 000
8	40 000
9	60 000

(a) What were the mean commissions earned for the nine year period?
(b) Compute the two year moving average.
(c) Construct a line graph and plot the sales and the two year moving average for the nine year period.

3. Record purchases over a nine year period were as follows.

Year	Purchases
1	$ 525 000
2	375 000
3	350 000
4	500 000
5	550 000
6	1 000 000
7	1 300 000
8	1 500 000
9	1 800 000

(a) What were the mean purchases for the nine year period?
(b) Compute the cumulative averages.
(c) Compute the two year moving average.
(d) Construct a line graph and plot the sales and the two year moving average for the nine year period.

11.3 INTERPRETING TABLES

Many times in your life you will want to find information that can be obtained from tables. It is a good idea to learn now how to read them. Below is part of a page from a book showing the monthly payments you would make if you were paying off a mortgage. This is called an *amortization table*. To *amortize* a mortgage is simply to pay back the money borrowed with regular payments over a period of time, usually several years.

13%

BLENDED MONTHLY PAYMENTS
AMORTIZATION IN YEARS

AMOUNT	1	2	3	4	5	6	7	8
$ 25	2.23	1.19	0.84	0.67	0.57	0.50	0.46	0.41
50	4.46	2.37	1.68	1.34	1.13	1.00	0.91	0.84
100	8.92	4.74	3.36	2.67	2.26	1.99	1.81	1.67
200	17.84	9.48	6.71	5.34	4.52	3.98	3.61	3.33
300	26.75	14.22	10.06	8.00	6.78	5.97	5.41	4.99
400	35.67	18.96	13.42	10.67	9.04	7.96	7.21	6.65
500	44.58	23.70	16.77	13.33	11.30	9.95	9.01	8.31
600	53.50	28.43	20.12	16.00	13.55	11.94	10.81	9.98
700	62.42	33.17	23.48	18.67	15.81	13.93	12.61	11.64
800	71.33	37.91	26.83	21.33	18.07	15.92	14.41	13.30
900	80.25	42.65	30.18	24.00	20.33	17.91	16.21	14.96
1 000	89.16	47.39	33.54	26.66	22.59	19.90	18.01	16.62
1 500	133.74	71.08	50.30	39.99	33.88	29.85	27.02	24.93
2 000	178.32	94.77	67.07	53.32	45.17	39.80	36.02	33.24
2 500	221.90	118.46	83.83	66.65	56.46	49.74	45.03	41.55
3 000	267.48	142.15	100.60	79.98	67.75	59.69	54.03	49.86
3 500	318.06	165.85	117.36	93.31	79.04	69.64	63.03	58.17
4 000	356.64	189.54	134.13	106.64	90.33	79.59	72.04	66.48
4 500	401.22	213.23	150.89	119.97	101.62	89.54	81.04	74.79
5 000	445.80	236.92	167.66	133.30	112.91	99.48	90.05	83.10
5 500	490.38	260.61	184.43	146.63	124.20	109.43	99.05	91.41
6 000	534.96	284.30	201.19	159.96	135.49	119.38	108.05	99.72
6 500	579.53	307.99	217.96	173.29	146.78	129.33	117.06	108.02
7 000	624.11	331.69	234.72	186.62	158.07	139.28	126.06	116.33
7 500	668.69	355.38	251.49	199.95	169.36	149.22	135.07	124.64
8 000	713.27	379.07	268.25	213.28	180.65	159.17	144.07	132.95
8 500	757.85	402.76	285.02	.226.61	191.94	169.12	153.08	141.26
9 000	802.43	426.45	301.78	239.94	203.23	179.07	162.08	149.57
9 500	847.01	450.14	318.55	253.27	214.52	189.01	171.08	157.88
10 000	891.59	473.83	335.32	266.60	225.81	198.96	180.09	166.19

Source:
Monthly
Payments
for Mortgages
Computofacts

Figure 11.1

This page shows the monthly payment required to pay off a mortgage when the interest rate is 13%. Other pages show the payments for different interest rates.

The column of figures on the left side shows the amount of money borrowed. The numbers across the top show the number of years over which the mortgage is amortized or paid off. Can you locate the monthly payments for a mortgage of $7 000 to be repaid over a period of six years? Look down the left hand column to find 7 000, then look across to the column headed 6. You should find the number 139.28, which represents a monthly payment of $139.28.

Sometimes you want to find a value not shown on a table. This is done by *interpolating*.

Example
Find the monthly payment required to amortize a mortgage of $7 200 over a period of five years.

Solution
From the table

$7 000 for 5 a is $158.07
　　200 for 5 a is 　　4.52
$7 200 for 5 a is $162.59

EXERCISE 11.3

1. Using the table in Figure 11.1, find the monthly payment required to amortize the following mortgages.

	Amount of Mortgage	Amortization Time (years)
(a)	$3 000	3
(b)	3 500	6
(c)	900	8
(d)	8 000	4
(e)	6 500	5
(f)	5 400	3
(g)	7 300	4
(h)	1 800	2

2. Anyone between 18 and 70 who is employed in Canada and earns over a minimum amount that varies from year to year is required to contribute to the Canada Pension Plan.

Canada Pension Plan Contributions – Weekly Pay Period

Remuneration Rémunération		C.P.P. R.P.C.	Remuneration Rémunération		C.P.P. R.P.C.
From-*de*	To-*à*		From-*de*	To-*à*	
198.19 –	198.73	2.88	238.19 –	238.73	3.60
198.74 –	199.29	2.89	238.74 –	239.29	3.61
199.30 –	199.84	2.90	239.30 –	239.84	3.62
199.85 –	200.40	2.91	239.85 –	240.40	3.63
200.41 –	200.95	2.92	240.41 –	240.95	3.64
200.96 –	201.51	2.93	240.96 –	241.51	3.65
201.52 –	202.07	2.94	241.52 –	242.07	3.66
202.08 –	202.62	2.95	242.08 –	242.62	3.67
202.63 –	203.18	2.96	242.63 –	243.18	3.68
203.19 –	203.73	2.97	243.19 –	243.73	3.69
203.74 –	204.29	2.98	243.74 –	244.29	3.70
204.30 –	204.84	2.99	244.30 –	244.84	3.71
204.85 –	205.40	3.00	244.85 –	245.40	3.72
205.41 –	205.95	3.01	245.41 –	245.95	3.73
205.96 –	206.51	3.02	245.96 –	246.51	3.74
206.52 –	207.07	3.03	246.52 –	247.07	3.75
207.08 –	207.62	3.04	247.08 –	247.62	3.76
207.63 –	208.18	3.05	247.63 –	248.18	3.77

To find how much you have to contribute, look under Remuneration to find your weekly earnings, and then look across to the C.P.P. column. Find the contributions for the following earnings.

(a) $200.00
(b) $239.67
(c) $242.69
(d) $244.23
(e) $205.84
(f) $198.74
(g) $246.75
(h) $204.62
(i) $238.18
(j) $248.19

3. When you start working full time, you find that unemployment insurance premiums are deducted from your pay.

Unemployment Insurance
Premiums
– Weekly Pay Period

198.05 – 198.47	4.56	237.18 – 237.60	5.46
198.48 – 198.91	4.57	237.61 – 238.04	5.47
198.92 – 199.34	4.58	238.05 – 238.47	5.48
199.35 – 199.78	4.59	238.48 – 238.91	5.49
199.79 – 200.21	4.60	238.92 – 239.34	5.50
200.22 – 200.64	4.61	239.35 – 239.78	5.51
200.65 – 201.08	4.62	239.79 – 240.21	5.52
201.09 – 201.51	4.63	240.22 – 240.64	5.53
201.52 – 201.95	4.64	240.65 – 241.08	5.54
201.96 – 202.38	4.65	241.09 – 241.51	5.55
202.39 – 202.82	4.66	241.52 – 241.95	5.56
202.83 – 203.25	4.67	241.96 – 242.38	5.57
203.26 – 203.69	4.68	242.39 – 242.82	5.58
203.70 – 204.12	4.69	242.83 – 243.25	5.59
204.13 – 204.56	4.70	243.26 – 243.69	5.60
204.57 – 204.99	4.71	243.70 – 244.12	5.61
205.00 – 205.43	4.72	244.13 – 244.56	5.62
205.44 – 205.86	4.73	244.57 – 244.99	5.63

Find the weekly unemployment insurance premium for the following earnings.

(a) $199.25
(b) $238.65
(c) $242.79
(d) $203.16
(e) $205.75

(f) $239.68
(g) $243.02
(h) $201.69
(i) $205.87
(j) $237.17

4. When you mail a parcel, the amount of postage you have to buy depends on the mass of the parcel and its destination. This information is found in a table of postal rates. Using the information on page 241, find the cost of sending the following parcels.

(a) A Christmas present having a mass of 45 g to a friend in Winnipeg

(b) A package of cookies having a mass of 950 g to a brother in university at Ottawa

(c) A birthday present weighing 2.73 kg to a sister-in-law in Vancouver

(d) A parcel of clothes, weighing 3.46 kg, that your friend from Halifax left at your place on her last visit

(e) A book weighing 650 g to a friend in Fredericton

5. What is the maximum size for a first class parcel mailing?

Canada

USE THE POSTAL CODE on all mail. The Postal Code should appear as the last line of the address. Always show the Postal Code in the return address.

FIRST CLASS PARCELS (over 500 g) Maximum 30 kg

First Class parcels receive priority air service.

Note: First class parcels exceeding the prescribed limits of size are subject to a surcharge of $2. These will receive priority surface service.

From ONT. "L & M" Over 500 g Up to and including

Destination	Postal Code	Zone	2 lb / 4 oz / 1 kg	3 / 5 / 1.5	4 / 7 / 2	5 / 9 / 2.5	6 / 10 / 3	7 / 12 / 3.5	8 / 14 / 4	13 / 4 / 6	17 / 11 / 8	22 / 1 / 10	26 / 8 / 12	30 / 14 / 14	35 / 5 / 16	39 / 11 / 18	44 / 2 / 20	48 / 9 / 22	52 / 15 / 24	57 / 6 / 26	61 / 12 / 28	65 lb / 3 oz / 30 kg
Short Haul* Ont.	L,M		$1.85	2.05	2.25	2.45	2.65	2.85	3.05	3.35	3.65	3.95	4.25	4.55	4.85	5.10	5.40	5.70	6.00	6.30	6.60	6.90
Ont.	N		2.15	2.35	2.55	2.75	2.95	3.15	3.35	3.70	4.05	4.40	4.80	5.15	5.50	5.85	6.20	6.55	6.95	7.30	7.65	8.00
Ont. Que.	K,P G,H,J		2.30	2.55	2.80	3.00	3.25	3.50	3.75	4.30	4.85	5.35	5.90	6.45	7.00	7.50	8.05	8.60	9.15	9.65	10.20	10.75
Man. NS, NB, PEI	R B,E,C		2.65	3.05	3.40	3.80	4.20	4.55	4.95	6.00	7.05	8.10	9.10	10.15	11.20	12.25	13.30	14.35	15.35	16.40	17.45	18.50
Sask.	S		2.80	3.30	3.75	4.25	4.70	5.20	5.65	7.05	8.50	9.90	11.30	12.75	14.15	15.55	16.95	18.40	19.80	21.20	22.65	24.05
Nfld. Alta.	A T		3.10	3.70	4.30	4.85	5.45	6.05	6.65	8.50	10.35	12.20	14.05	15.90	17.75	19.55	21.40	23.25	25.10	26.95	28.80	30.65
BC	V		3.35	4.10	4.80	5.55	6.25	7.00	7.70	9.80	11.90	14.00	16.10	18.20	20.30	22.40	24.50	26.60	28.70	30.80	32.90	35.00
Yukon	Y		3.60	4.50	5.40	6.30	7.20	8.10	9.00	11.75	14.55	17.30	20.10	22.85	25.60	28.40	31.15	33.90	36.70	39.45	42.25	45.00
NWT	X		2.95	4.35	5.75	7.15	8.60	10.00	11.40	14.75	18.05	21.40	24.75	28.05	31.40	34.75	38.10	41.40	44.75	48.10	51.40	54.75

*Call your Marketing representative or postmaster for a list of Short Haul destinations.

	Maximum size	
	Length, width or depth – 1 metre	
	Length plus girth – 2 metres	
With $2 surcharge		
	Length width or depth – 2 metres	
	Length plus girth – 3 metres	

THIRD CLASS SMALL PARCELS – MAXIMUM 500 g

Addressed loose items in "FLAT" or "OVERSIZE" letter configuration are subject to First Class mail rates and receive First Class service.
Addressed loose items in "BULKY" or "SMALL PARCEL" form are subject to the following rates.

Up to and including	50 g	100 g	150 g	200 g	250 g	300 g	350 g	400 g	450 g	500 g
	$0.37	0.48	0.64	0.80	0.95	1.11	1.27	1.43	1.59	1.75

NOTE: Items of Third Class mail in bulky or small parcel or small parcel form weighing up to 500 g may, at the option of the mailer be paid as a Fourth Class zoned parcel weighing up to 1 kg where this results in a lower rate.

6. In most provinces in Canada you have to pay provincial sales tax on almost everything you buy except food.

Province of Ontario
Sales Tax Schedule at 7%

AMOUNT	TAX	AMOUNT	TAX
15.79 to 15.92	$1.11	23.65 to 23.78	$ 1.66
15.93 to 16.07	1.12	23.79 to 23.92	1.67
16.08 to 16.21	1.13	23.93 to 24.07	1.68
16.22 to 16.35	1.14	24.08 to 24.21	1.69
16.36 to 16.49	1.15	24.22 to 24.35	1.70
16.50 to 16.64	1.16	24.36 to 24.49	1.71
16.65 to 16.78	1.17	24.50 to 24.64	1.72
16.79 to 16.92	1.18	24.65 to 24.78	1.73
16.93 to 17.07	1.19	24.79 to 24.92	1.74
17.08 to 17.21	1.20	24.93 to 25.07	1.75
17.22 to 17.35	1.21	25.08 to 25.21	1.76
17.36 to 17.49	1.22	25.22 to 25.35	1.77
17.50 to 17.64	1.23	25.36 to 25.49	1.78
17.65 to 17.78	1.24	25.50 to 25.64	1.79
17.79 to 17.92	1.25	25.65 to 25.78	1.80
20.79 to 20.92	1.46	28.65 to 28.78	2.01
20.93 to 21.07	1.47	28.79 to 28.92	2.02
21.08 to 21.21	1.48	28.93 to 29.07	2.03
21.22 to 21.35	1.49	29.08 to 29.21	2.04
21.36 to 21.49	1.50	29.22 to 29.35	2.05
21.50 to 21.64	1.51	29.36 to 29.49	2.06
21.65 to 21.78	1.52	29.50 to 29.64	2.07
21.79 to 21.92	1.53	29.65 to 29.78	2.08
21.93 to 22.07	1.54	29.79 to 29.92	2.09
22.08 to 22.21	1.55	29.93 to 30.07	2.10
22.22 to 22.35	1.56	40.00	2.80
22.36 to 22.49	1.57	50.00	3.50
22.50 to 22.64	1.58	60.00	4.20
22.65 to 22.78	1.59	70.00	4.90
22.79 to 22.92	1.60	80.00	5.60
22.93 to 23.07	1.61	90.00	6.30
23.08 to 23.21	1.62	100.00	7.00
23.22 to 23.35	1.63	300.00	21.00
23.36 to 23.49	1.64	400.00	28.00
23.50 to 23.64	1.65	1 000.00	70.00

Find the amount of sales tax for the following purchases.
(a) A pair of jeans priced at $28.95
(b) A hand-held calculator priced at $15.95
(c) Three records at $9.95 each
(d) A portable radio cassette player priced at $240
(e) A personalized jean jacket for $29.50

11.4   INTERPRETING CHARTS AND GRAPHS

How often have you heard the phrase "A picture is worth a thousand words"? A great deal of data is published in numerical form. How much more effective it might be in picture or graph form! In this and the following sections you will learn to read and interpret graphs, to use good graphic techniques, and to construct different types of graphs.

Graphs are used frequently by government and business to show the relationship among quantities of data for different subjects and to illustrate trends. Awareness of these trends helps government and business-people make the decisions that eventually affect the consumer.

Much has been said about Canada's energy crisis. Since 1960, the average energy consumed by each of us has almost doubled. Available resources are shrinking. Here is a chart showing the forecast relationship between Canadian supply and demand.

•••• Total Canadian demand
— Demand west of Ottawa valley
--- Canadian supply

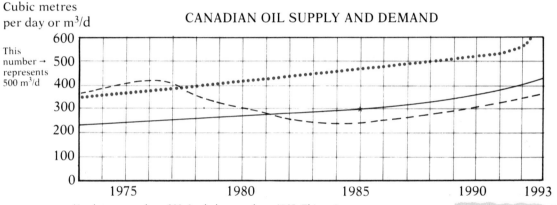

CANADIAN OIL SUPPLY AND DEMAND

Cubic metres per day or m³/d

This number → represents 500 m³/d

*Look across and see 300. Look down and see 1985. This point represents 300 m³/d demand west of the Ottawa valley in the year 1985.

The scale shows the time in 5 year periods

There are many kinds of graphs or charts but the following are the ones most frequently seen in newspapers, magazines, and pamphlets.

Line graphs: single line
                   multiple line
                   component line

Bar graphs: vertical bar
                   horizontal bar
                   component bar

Circle graph: also called a pie chart

Rectangle graph: also called a 100% chart

Pictogram: also called a picture chart

All of these will be discussed in this unit. Selecting the one that illustrates data best depends upon the relationships to be emphasized.

General Techniques for Good Graphic Presentation

(1) Graphs are drawn on graph paper, which is ruled horizontally and vertically. These lines are equidistant and called *grid lines*. Sometimes every tenth grid line is more heavily printed.

(2) The left hand vertical grid line and the bottom horizontal grid line are called *scale lines* or *axes*.

Should numbers below 0 be needed, they may be used.

(3) The *vertical axis* should show the scale unit at the top and should be divided to indicate the value of the horizontal grid lines. The lowest number is often 0.

(4) The *horizontal axis* should be divided to indicate the value of units and the basis of calculation of the vertical grid lines.

(5) If time elements are used they should always appear on the horizontal scale.

(6) Every graph should have a short descriptive title, preferably at the top.

(7) Graphs should be neat and attractive.

(8) Lettering and digits should be plain and clear.

EXERCISE 11.4

1. When did the Canadian supply of oil cease to meet the national demand?

2. When did the supply cease to meet the demand west of the Ottawa Valley?

3. Approximately what is the forecast production for 1990?

4. If demand increases at its current rate, how much will it be in 1990?

5. What was the total forecast Canadian demand for oil in 1980?

6. What was the forecast Canadian supply of oil for 1980?

7. What was the total forecast Canadian demand for oil in 1985?

8. What was the forecast Canadian supply of oil in 1985?

9. Assuming that the lines continue their present trend, determine the values for 1995.

11.5 GRAPHING A SET OF ORDERED PAIRS

(6, 8)

An ordered pair consists of two numbers written in brackets and separated by a comma. The order is important. The first number in the bracket represents the value of one item and the second number represents the value of the other or second item.

The graph of a set of ordered pairs is really a simple line graph.

Example
If chocolate bars sell for 25¢ each, construct a graph to show the cost of any number of bars up to ten.

Solution
You are required to graph the set of ordered pairs (0,0), (1,25), (2,50), (3,75), (4,100), (5,125), (6,150), (7,175), (8,200), (9,225), (10,250)

 Plot the points for each ordered pair and then join the points with a smooth line.

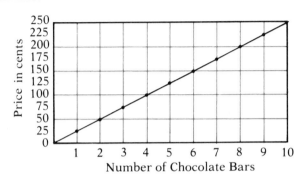

COST OF CHOCOLATE BARS

EXERCISE 11.5
Draw a line graph to illustrate the following.

1. The total height of a building from one to six storeys high, if each storey represents an additional 3 m.

2. The temperature increase of 2°/h over a period of eight hours.

3. The total distance travelled by a train from ten minutes to one hour, if the train is travelling at 120 km/h.

4. The total cost of four to ten ballpoint pens, if each pen costs $0.69.

11.6 LINE GRAPHS

A line graph illustrates the relationship between 2 sets of data, one of which is usually time. The values for one set of data are marked on the vertical axis and the values for the other on the horizontal axis. The graph is constructed by plotting each point of the given data and joining these points with a straight line or sometimes a curved line. Figure 11.2 illustrates a *single line graph*.

Point A represents $140 in 1980.
Point B represents $150 in 1983.
Point C represents $120 in 1986.
What does point D represent?
What do points E, F, and G represent?

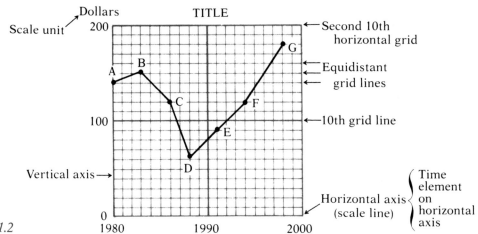

Figure 11.2

Multiple Line Graphs

These graphs are used to compare lines drawn from 2 or more sets of similar data. The lines can be distinguished by using various types of lines. For example, broken lines (-------), dotted lines (.......), combinations of lines and dots (---------), or colors. The lines must be labelled or a key provided.

Example 1

The local school board wants a line graph to visually illustrate the changes in enrolment in Year I Keyboarding classes in its secondary schools. The statistics are as follows.

September Enrolment in Year I Keyboarding Classes
Percent of Year I Enrolment

School	1980	1981	1982	1983	1984	1985	1986	1987
Greenspan	70	44	32	70	69	72	73	72
Blackely	52	36	44	65	70	74	75	76
Redstar	67	46	54	77	75	82	77	73

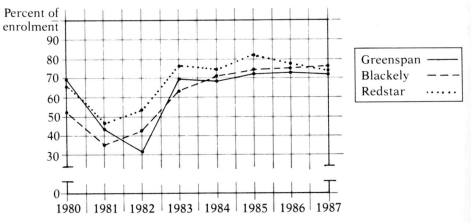

Figure 11.3

Figure 11.3 shows the completed graph. Since the graph represents a time series, the horizontal scale is used for the years and the vertical scale for the percent of enrolment. The large dots show the enrolment for each year. The dots are connected by straight lines for Greenspan, dotted lines for Redstar, and broken lines for Blackely. A key is provided to identify each line.

Since the percents ranged from 32 to 82, it was decided to *break* the vertical scale. Vertical scales may be broken in 2 ways.

Break in vertical scale only   OR   *Break across whole graph*

Component Line Graphs
These graphs can be used to show the total and the component parts that make up the total. Shading, hatching, or cross-hatching can be used to distinguish between the various components.

Hatching

Example 2
Draw a component line graph to compare Canada's import trade with the United States and the United Kingdom using the following statistics prepared by Statistics Canada.

Cross-Hatching

Year	United States $000 000	United Kingdom $000 000
1	6 045	619
2	8 016	673
3	10 313	719
4	10 951	837
5	16 484	1 005
6	23 616	1 222
7	29 630	1 281
8	45 203	1 926

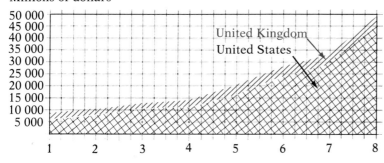

CANADA'S IMPORT TRADE
WITH
THE UNITED STATES
AND
THE UNITED KINGDOM

EXERCISE 11.6

1. The following figures represent the average monthly rainfall in the Ottawa area as published in a Canada Year Book.

January	67.8 mm	July	89.7 mm
February	55.9 mm	August	75.2 mm
March	71.4 mm	September	79.2 mm
April	66.5 mm	October	68.6 mm
May	72.1 mm	November	75.2 mm
June	87.1 mm	December	77.0 mm

Construct a single line graph to compare the average monthly precipitations.

2. A Grade 11 typing teacher averaged the typing speeds of the students in her class for monthly intervals. Prepare a line graph using her information. Let each square on the horizontal axis represent 1 month and each square on the vertical axis represent 2 words per minute.

Month	Words per Minute	Month	Words per Minute
September	35	February	43
October	37	March	40
November	35	April	45
December	36	May	46
January	40	June	57

3. In searching for a suitable location for a new branch store, the Elton Company took a population survey of several neighborhoods. The survey of the Orville neighborhoods showed the percent of population in each of the following age groups.

Under 12	8%	24 to 35	10%
12 to 15	5%	35 to 45	18%
15 to 19	13%	45 to 55	27%
19 to 24	7%	over 55	12%

Construct a single line graph to illustrate the above facts.

4. Construct a single line graph to illustrate what a typical family of four spends on food during a year. Use the following figures.

January	$357	July	$290
February	306	August	316
March	290	September	367
April	316	October	537
May	331	November	562
June	290	December	493

5. Three salespeople wanted to compare their selling records for the past year. Prepare a component line graph to compare each person's sales with the total sales. Use 1 square on the vertical axis to represent $1 000 and 1 square on the horizontal axis to represent 1 month.

	Sales		
Month	Joanne	Ivor	Marc
January	$2 456	$2 260	$3 450
February	2 560	2 725	2 892
March	2 675	2 650	2 300
April	3 892	3 984	2 138
May	2 450	1 985	4 000
June	5 125	5 010	3 600
July	5 680	5 975	4 000
August	3 100	2 800	4 500
September	4 410	4 135	4 580
October	3 250	4 150	4 800
November	6 100	6 255	5 215
December	7 500	8 125	7 230

6. Prepare a component line graph to compare the production of cars and trucks over a recent six week period.

Week	*Cars*	*Trucks*
1	22 932	12 706
2	23 438	11 783
3	23 296	13 463
4	20 109	11 276
5	16 612	10 541
6	23 061	12 680

7. Construct a multiple line graph to compare the sources of CBC revenues for seven selected years.

CBC Revenues, Years Ended March 31 (in millions of dollars)

Source	Year 1	Year 2	Year 3	Year 4	Year 5	Year 6	Year 7
Public Funds	181	207	233	299	560	522	577
Advertising	37	28	43	50	108	119	127

8. Draw a multiple line chart to illustrate the changes in temperature of a patient in hospital. Use one line for the morning temperature and one for the evening temperature.

Day		Degrees Celsius
Monday	morning	38.2
	evening	38.3
Tuesday	morning	38.8
	evening	38.1
Wednesday	morning	37.9
	evening	38.7
Thursday	morning	38.6
	evening	38.1
Friday	morning	37.7
	evening	37.9
Saturday	morning	36.9
	evening	37.1
Sunday	morning	36.4
	evening	36.8

9. The figures below show the total number of shares traded on different stock exchanges during a recent five week period.

Source: Financial Post

	First Week	Second Week	Third Week	Fourth Week	Fifth Week
Alberta	73 000	31 000	39 000	63 000	71 000
Montreal	461 000	397 000	419 000	501 000	469 000
Toronto	1 443 000	1 834 000	1 388 000	1 391 000	1 858 000
Vancouver	1 324 000	2 207 000	2 357 000	2 051 000	1 588 000

Construct a multiple line graph to compare the sales of the different stock exchanges.

10. Canadian tourists spend a great deal of money in other countries. Using the following figures, construct a component line graph to compare the amounts spent overseas with the amounts spent in the United States in six selected years.

	Year 1	Year 2	Year 3	Year 4	Year 5	Year 6
			(in millions of dollars)			
United States	$930	$930	$903	$1 558	$2 553	$2 451
Overseas	524	567	553	953	1 531	1 512

11.7   BAR GRAPHS

A bar graph can also be used to compare sets of data in picture form. Instead of connecting dots, you draw a bar from the axis to the dot. The bars should all be the same width but the widths do not affect the values. Select the width that makes the graph the most attractive. If the graph depicts a time series, the time periods should be on the horizontal axis. When time is not part of the comparison, the bars may run in either a horizontal or a vertical direction.

Example 1

Construct a horizontal bar graph to compare the points won by teams in the Eastern and Western Conferences at a point part way through a recent football season.

Team	Points
Montreal	8
Saskatchewan	10
Winnipeg	18
Ottawa	5
Edmonton	14
Toronto	16
Calgary	17
Hamilton	7
B.C.	13

POINTS GAINED
IN
EASTERN AND
WESTERN
CONFERENCES

Example 2

Construct a vertical single bar graph to illustrate the changes in the whole-sale price of eggs over a recent six month period. Use the following statistics taken from the local newspaper.

October	$0.83
November	0.857
December	0.891
January	0.866
February	0.852 5
March	0.932

EGG PRICES

Multiple Bar Graphs

Bar graphs can show two or more bars for each category or date. This is an excellent method for comparisons.

Example 3

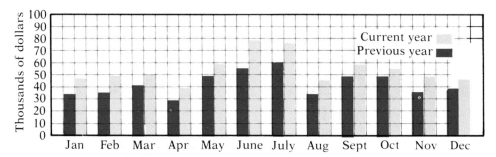

Component Bar Graphs

A component bar graph is a useful way to present several sets of data for a series of time periods.

Example 4

Lesslie Electronics produces desk electronic calculators and hand electronic calculators. Over a period of one year monthly production is as follows.

	Desk Models	Hand Models
January	1 896	5 420
February	2 010	3 678
March	3 000	4 250
April	3 280	6 780
May	2 960	2 430
June	3 480	5 680
July	2 460	6 000
August	1 900	5 870
September	2 180	4 910
October	2 460	6 700
November	2 500	6 200
December	2 300	4 980

Construct a component bar chart to illustrate the above data.

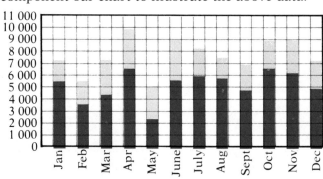

LESSLIE ELECTRONICS
MONTHLY
PRODUCTION
OF
CALCULATORS

EXERCISE 11.7

1. Canada has 7 870 km of Trans-Canada highway. Prepare a horizontal
   bar graph to compare the kilometres of highway in each province.

Newfoundland	891	Manitoba	497
Prince Edward Island	114	Saskatchewan	653
Nova Scotia	512	Alberta	454
New Brunswick	628	British Columbia	914
Quebec	644	National Parks	225
Ontario	2 338		

2. Construct a horizontal bar graph to compare the heights of principal
   Canadian mountain peaks using the following data.

Alberta Rockies, Columbia	19 781
British Columbia Rockies, Robson	20 872
Manitoba, Porcupine Hills	4 344
New Brunswick, Carleton	4 328
Newfoundland, Lewis Hills	4 227
Nova Scotia, Franey	2 261
Ontario, Ogidaki	3 512
Quebec Appalachians, Jacques Cartier	6 693
Vancouver Island, Albert Edward	11 051

   Source:
   Quick Canadian Facts

3. A Guidance teacher decided to make a horizontal bar graph showing
   the salaries paid in various occupations. The occupations were listed
   on the left axis and each square on the horizontal axis represented
   $1 000. Using the following information, construct a similar graph.

Superintendent	9 900
Bookkeeper	12 100
Interior Decorator	11 500
Butcher	12 600
Retail Salesperson	10 500
Upholsterer	10 900
Travel Consultant	12 600
Dental Hygienist	14 700
Stenographer	13 600
Word processing operator	14 500

4. Bell Canada recently calculated the average price increases in selected
   items (using data compiled from Statistics Canada) since 1971.

Poultry, Meat, and Fish	169.5%
Gasoline	140.1%
Electricity	124.1%
Telephone Service	59.5%

   Construct a vertical bar graph to illustrate the above statistics.

5. After a Business Mathematics examination, the following statistics were compiled.

Topic	Correct Answers
Compound Interest	39%
Foreign Exchange	63%
Home Ownership	72%
Income Tax	58%
Payroll	85%
Property Taxes	74%
Stocks and Bonds	69%

(a) Construct a vertical bar graph to illustrate the above facts.
(b) What was the overall average mark?

6. Construct a multiple vertical bar graph to illustrate the following information.

Area by Tenure, by Economic Region,
in Canada in Square Kilometres

	Private Lands	Provincial Lands	Federal Lands	
Atlantic	103 292	431 368	5 764	
Quebec	112 616	1 424 795	2 610	
Ontario	116 903	941 692	9 530	*Source:*
Prairies	444 124	1 207 529	76 666	*Quick Canadian*
British Columbia	53 789	885 596	8 960	*Facts*

7. Construct a multiple horizontal bar graph to compare the mean temperatures for the following selected meteorological stations.

Mean Temperatures in Degrees Celsius

	January	July	
Vancouver	3.3	17.8	
Whitehorse	− 15.0	16.1	
Edmonton	− 13.3	17.2	
Regina	− 16.7	19.4	
Winnipeg	− 17.2	18.9	
Toronto	− 3.9	21.7	
Ottawa	− 11.1	20.6	
Quebec	− 11.1	18.9	
Halifax	− 4.4	18.3	
Charlottetown	− 7.2	19.4	
St. John's	− 4.4	15.6	*Source:*
Saint John	− 6.7	16.7	*Quick Canadian Facts*

8. The booklet *How Your Tax Dollar is Spent* published by the Treasury Board shows the following distribution of federal public servants excluding those in the capital region.

	Proportion of Federal Public Servants	Proportion of Total Population
Alberta	8.4%	7.8%
British Columbia	14.0%	10.6%
Manitoba	6.3%	4.7%
New Brunswick	4.3%	3.0%
Newfoundland	2.7%	2.5%
Nova Scotia	8.2%	3.8%
Ontario (Ottawa excluded)	27.5%	34.7%
Quebec (Hull excluded)	21.8%	27.8%
Prince Edward Island	0.7%	0.5%
Saskatchewan	4.6%	4.3%
Yukon & Northwest Territories	1.5%	0.3%

Construct a multiple horizontal bar graph to illustrate these statistics in chart form.

9. Construct a component bar graph to compare a local school board's expenditures for elementary and secondary schools.

	Expenditures in Thousands of Dollars	
	Elementary	Secondary
Business administration	309	314
Instruction	14 553	14 622
Plant operation and maintenance	2 530	2 150
Transportation	1 491	1 276
Capital expenditures	876	180
Debt charges	788	468
Other	313	2 131

10. A census showed that the percent of the population classified as urban, non-farm rural, and farm rural by province was as follows.

	Urban	Rural Non-Farm	Rural Farm	
Newfoundland	57.2	41.9	0.9	
Prince Edward Island	38.3	42.7	18.9	
Nova Scotia	56.7	40.0	3.3	
New Brunswick	56.9	39.1	4.0	
Quebec	80.6	14.3	5.1	
Ontario	82.4	12.9	4.7	
Manitoba	69.5	17.3	13.2	
Saskatchewan	53.0	21.8	25.2	
Alberta	73.5	12.0	14.5	
British Columbia	75.7	20.9	3.4	
Yukon Territory	61.0	38.7	0.3	
Northwest Territories	48.4	51.6	0.1	*Source:*
Canada	76.1	17.3	6.6	*Canada Year Book*

Prepare a multiple horizontal bar graph to compare percents of the three population classifications.

11.8   CIRCLE GRAPHS

Circle graphs or *pie charts* as they are often called are an attractive and meaningful way to present data that is given in percents. The whole circle is 100% and each "slice of pie" represents the percent that each part is of the whole.

Since a circle has 360°, each part must be expressed as a percent of 360°. For example, if a part is 40% of the whole, it will be represented by 40% of 360° or 144°.

Example

Construct a pie chart to show the relationship between the types of errors in a shorthand test given to a Grade 11 class.

Type of Error	Number of Errors	Errors as %	Number of Degrees
Punctuation	38	34	122.4
Word form	30	27	97.2
Erasing	12	11	39.6
Spelling	19	17	61.2
Paragraphing	8	7	25.2
Capitalization	5	4	14.4
		100	360.0

The first and largest segment usually begins at 12 o'clock and the rest of the segments are constructed in a clockwise direction. Place the centre of the protractor on the centre of the circle with the edge of the protractor along the diameter of the circle. Place a mark at the required point (122.4°). Using a ruler, join the circle centre and this mark. Draw a line from the centre to the circumference of the circle. This is your first segment.

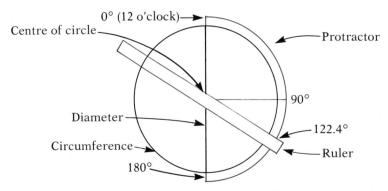

The rest of the segments can be drawn by shifting the edge of the protractor to the edge of the previous segment and marking the number of degrees required for the next segment. An alternative method is to leave the protractor in its original position and calculate where the next point would be by adding the degrees for the next segment to those already plotted until you reach 180°. Replace the protractor on the other side of the circle with its straight edge along the diameter. Continue marking the number of degrees required for each segment until all have been plotted.

When the segments are completed, they may be colored or marked in different ways to make them more visually effective.

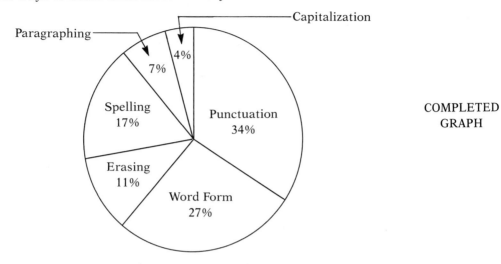

COMPLETED
GRAPH

EXERCISE 11.8

1. The town of Greenspan spends the money it receives in taxes as follows: education, 28.4%; health and welfare, 15.2%; police and fire protection, 10.5%; public works, 11.6%; debt charges, 18.5%; all other items, 15.8%. Draw a pie graph to illustrate to the taxpayers how their tax money is spent.

2. A spice dispenser on the market contains the following spices in separate compartments.

Paprika	8g	Pepper	8g
Nutmeg	7g	Curry	7.5g
Salt	33g	Cayenne Pepper	4.5g

Construct a circle graph to compare the proportions of each spice in the dispenser.

3. The town of Caseyville spends the money it receives in taxes as follows.

General Government	$145 000
Protective Services	171 000
Transportation Services	246 000
Environmental Services	19 000
Family and Social Services	13 000
Recreation Services	385 000
Community Planning and Development	43 000
Financial Expense	60 000

Construct a circle graph to illustrate how the taxpayers' money is spent.

4. According to a census, the population of Canada is divided among the provinces and territories as follows.

Alberta	7.55%	
British Columbia	10.13%	
Manitoba	4.58%	
New Brunswick	2.94%	
Newfoundland	2.42%	
Nova Scotia	3.66%	
Ontario	35.71%	
Prince Edward Island	0.52%	
Quebec	27.95%	
Saskatchewan	4.29%	*Source:*
Yukon Territory	0.09%	*Canadian*
Northwest Territories	0.16%	*Almanac and*
Canada	100%	*Directory*

Construct a circle graph to show the proportion of the population in each province and territory.

11.9 RECTANGLE GRAPHS AND PICTOGRAMS

A *rectangle graph* or 100% chart is similar to a component bar graph where each bar is 100%. Each section of the rectangle represents a percent of the whole. By using percents we can compare the relative values of component parts of two or more whole units. The whole units may have different values but each will be 100%.

Example 1
Compare the proportion of a class receiving A, B, C, and failing grades in September with the grades earned in June.

	September	June
A	20%	12%
B	37%	28%
C	28%	42%
Failure	15%	18%

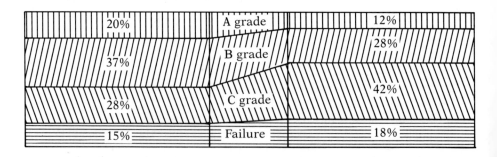

Pictograms are constructed in a manner similar to bar graphs. However, instead of a bar, the data is presented symbolically. For example, the local apple harvest might be shown by 👝👝👝. Numbers are increased by adding more symbols, not by increasing the size of the symbol. For example, if 👝 represents 100 kL of apples, then 👝 would represent 50 kL of apples.

Some Common Symbols Used for Pictograms

Example 2

The London Free Press delivers papers to households in Southwestern Ontario as follows.

Kent County	26% of households
Elgin County	35% of households
Oxford County	44% of households
Middlesex County	79% of households
Lambton County	31% of households
Perth County	29% of households
Huron County	52% of households

Construct a pictogram to illustrate this information.

DELIVERY OF LONDON FREE PRESS TO HOUSEHOLDS IN SOUTHWESTERN ONTARIO

(pictogram showing county delivery percentages, x-axis: Percent of households, 0 to 70)

EXERCISE 11.9

1. The following figures were calculated from data published by *Quick Canadian Facts.*

Expenditure of Municipal and Provincial Governments
(Fiscal Year Ended 19-- 12 31)

	Municipal Government	Provincial Government
General Government and Other	25.2	16.1
Protection of Persons and Property	8.2	3.8
Health, Social Welfare	16.2	7.7
Education	43.3	63.5
Transfers to Other Levels of Government	1.5	2.6
Debt Charges	5.6	6.3

Draw a rectangle or 100% chart to illustrate the distribution of a dollar spent by the municipal government and by the provincial government.

2. In two selected years the net advertising revenues by media were as follows.

	Year 1	Year 2	
Radio	110	135	
Television	138	153	
Newspapers	363	445	
Magazines	66	175	*Source:*
Other	358	420	*Quick Canadian Facts*

(a) Express these figures as percents of the yearly revenues for each of the two years and compare the distribution by means of a 100% graph.
(b) Which source of revenue showed the most significant change?
(c) Which source of revenue showed the least change?

3. The following figures show what the Canadian oil refinery industry made from crude oil in two different years.

	Year 1	Year 2	
Gasoline	35%	45%	
Aviation fuel	3%	—	
Light oil and diesel oil	28%	17%	
Stove oil and kerosene	5%	5%	
Heavy fuel oil	19%	22%	
Lube oil and other	7%	7%	*Source:*
Asphalt	3%	4%	*Financial Post*

Construct a 100% chart to compare the products produced by the refineries from crude oil in the two years.

4. Construct a pictogram to illustrate the monthly food expenditures of a family of four. See Question 4, Exercise 11.6, for the monthly figures.

5. Construct a pictogram to compare the number of boys and the number of girls in Grade 11 in your school.

6. Construct a pictogram to compare the number of boys and the number of girls in the following business education areas: Accounting, Computer Concepts, General Business, Marketing, and Secretarial.

7. (a) Construct a pictogram using the information given in the example in Section 11.8.
(b) In your opinion, which graph is more effective?

SUMMARY

The mean of a group of items is obtained by dividing the sum of the items in the group by the number of items.

The *median* of a group of items is the middle item.

The *mode* of a group of items is the item that occurs most frequently.

A *graph* is an illustration of the relationships between quantities of data for different subjects.

The *line graph* is constructed by plotting points from the given data and joining these points with a straight or curved line.

The *bar graph* is constructed by plotting points from the given data and drawing a bar from the axis to each point.

The *component graph* shows the total and the component parts that make up that total.

The *circle* or *pie graph* shows data as a percent of the whole circle.

The *pictogram* presents data in symbolic form.

REVIEW EXERCISE 11.10

1. Miras Miketich's used car lot sold the following during the month of April: MGB $4 895; TR6 $4 995; Datsun $3 395; XJ6 $4 995; TRS $4 195; Marina $2 595; Spitfire $3 195; Toyota $2 495; Jag $6 875; Buick Royal $3 495. Calculate the mode, median, and mean prices for the month of April.

2. At an auction sale, the following items were sold: settee $250; organ $600; freezer $225; dining room suite $1 995; TV $219; pool table $250; desk $25; bedroom suite $495; kitchen set $200.
   (a) What was the mode sale price?
   (b) What was the median sale price?
   (c) What was the mean sale price?
   (d) Which average best represents the situation? Why?

3. During the first two weeks of May, the school cafeteria reported the following sales.

Day	Sales	Number of Students Served
Monday	$485.20	960
Tuesday	542.65	1 008
Wednesday	368.90	726
Thursday	476.50	897
Friday	522.35	1 011
Monday	492.40	985
Tuesday	551.60	996
Wednesday	522.90	941
Thursday	485.10	862
Friday	389.40	743

(a) What is the mean daily sales figure?

(b) What is the median daily sales?

(c) What is the mean amount each student spent daily in the cafeteria?

(d) Compute the cumulative sales averages for the ten day period.

(e) Compute the two day moving average for the ten day period.

4. Construct a line graph to illustrate the absences recorded at the H. Thomson Secondary School during two typical weeks.

Day	A Week in September	A Week in December
Monday	25	33
Tuesday	19	40
Wednesday	20	42
Thursday	28	63
Friday	42	70

5. Construct a bar graph to show the marital status of the employees of H. B. Hutton Ltd. using the following information.

Marital Status	Number of Employees
Single	25
Married	45
Widow or Widower	10
Separated	15
Divorced	20

6. Construct a circle graph to illustrate the cost of owning and operating an automobile using the following information.

Depreciation	$1 800
Maintenance and repairs	600
Gasoline and oil	1 400
Insurance	540
Licence	45

7. Construct a pictogram to illustrate the range of earnings of the employees at Woodburn's manufacturing plant.

Weekly Earnings	Number of Employees
$ 200 - $ 500	63
500 - 800	114
800 - 1 100	196
1 100 - 1 400	245
1 400 - 1 700	86
1 700 - 2 000	12
2 000 - 2 300	25
2 300 - 2 600	5

8. Have a class project to interview a random selection of 25 students from each grade in your school about a current student issue and present your findings in graph form.

CUMULATIVE REVIEW 9

1. What percent is 8 of 64?

2. Find $\frac{1}{8}$ of $1 292.

3. What number increased by 40% of itself equals 462?

4. What number increased by 25% of itself, and the result decreased by 10% of itself, equals 393.75?

5. Solve for *a*.
   (a) $4(a + 3) = 3a - 12$
   (b) $6(6 - 3a) - 4(9 - 3a) = 0$
   (c) $11a + 2 = 26 + 7a$

6. Find the cost price for each of the following.

	List Price	Trade Discount	Quantity Discount
(a)	$ 75.50	55%	10%
(b)	98.60	45%	5%
(c)	187.90	35%	5%

7. An article was sold at $16 after discounts of 25% and 10% had been allowed. Find the list price.

8. Find the single equivalent discount if the trade discount is 40%, the quantity discount, 10%.

9. Geoff Byrne sold goods for G. E. Sales Ltd. at a commission rate of $10\frac{1}{2}$% on net sales over $4 500, plus a monthly salary of $285. During the month of August he had net sales of $15 500. How much did he earn for the month?

10. A real estate broker and an agent had an agreement whereby the broker would get 60% and the agent would get 40% of the $ commission if the broker listed the property but the agent sold it. The broker listed a hardware store for $185 000 at 5% commission. The agent sold the store for the listed price. How much would the agent's $ commission be? How much would the broker get?

11. If a retailer purchases goods for $940 and operates a store on a 53% markup on cost, how much will the goods sell for?

12. The retail price of an article is $66 and the % margin of retail is $33\frac{1}{3}$%. How much does the article cost?

13. If an article costs $1.50 and the % margin of retail is 50%, how much will the article sell for?

14. Find the simple interest.

	Principal	Rate	Time
(a)	$4 400	$11\frac{3}{4}\%$	73 d
(b)	3 500	$15\frac{1}{2}\%$	65 d
(c)	2 500	$16\frac{3}{4}\%$	36 d
(d)	3 850	$14\frac{1}{2}\%$	86 d

15. Compute the schedule of payments for the first six months for a loan of $2 200, where the monthly payment is $200.44 and the interest is $18\frac{1}{4}\%$ per annum.

16. Gerry Hagen borrowed $2 000 from his credit union. At the end of the year he had paid $240 interest but then received an 11% rebate of interest paid. What was the effective rate of interest for the year if the loan was repaid in the year by regular monthly payments?

17. Bond interest amounted to $120 when a coupon was cashed one year after the bond was issued. If the bond bore interest at 19%, what was the principal amount of the bond?

18. Sally Braun had a Net Federal Tax Payable of $2 675 and a Net Ontario Tax Payable of $1 380. Her T4 slip showed that $3 684.75 had been deducted at source. Find her total refund or balance due.

19. Heindrik had $862.73 in receipts for medical expenses. If his net income was $26 500, how much was the allowable portion of his medical expenses?

UNIT 12

Measurement

12.1   THE RECTANGLE

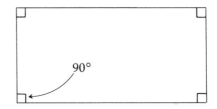

The Rectangle: Opposite sides are equal and parallel.
 All angles are right angles.

The width of a rectangle is the shorter distance between sides and is represented by w.

The length of a rectangle is the longer distance between sides and is represented by l.

A   Perimeter of a Rectangle

The perimeter, the measure of the boundary, is represented by P. The formula for the perimeter of a rectangle may be found as follows.

$$P = w + w + l + l$$
$$= 2w + 2l$$

Thus

$$P = 2(w + l)$$

Also

$$l = \frac{P - 2w}{2} \quad \text{and} \quad w = \frac{P - 2l}{2}$$

Example
Find the perimeter of a rug whose width is 3 m and whose length is 4 m.

Solution

$$P = 2(w + l)$$
$$= 2(3 + 4)$$
$$= 14$$

Perimeter of rug is 14 m.

B   Area of a Rectangle

The area, the measurement of the surface, is represented by A. The formula for the area of a rectangle is

The answer will be in square units

$$A = lw$$

Also

$$l = \frac{A}{w} \quad \text{and} \quad w = \frac{A}{l}$$

Example
If the length of a rectangle is 10 cm and the width is 5 cm, what is the area?

Solution

$$A = lw$$
$$= 10 \times 5$$
$$= 50$$

Area of rectangle is 50 cm².

EXERCISE 12.1

1. Find the missing dimensions of the following rectangles.

	Length	*Width*	*Perimeter*	*Area*
(a)	4 m	3 m	▮▮▮	▮▮▮
(b)	16 m	8 m	▮▮▮	▮▮▮
(c)	15 dm	14 dm	▮▮▮	▮▮▮
(d)	18 cm	15 cm	▮▮▮	▮▮▮
(e)	64 mm	▮▮▮	▮▮▮	1 600 mm²
(f)	45 m	23 m	▮▮▮	▮▮▮
(g)	18.5 cm	16 cm	▮▮▮	▮▮▮
(h)	▮▮▮	20 cm	▮▮▮	450 cm²
(i)	22.5 m	18.8 m	▮▮▮	▮▮▮
(j)	▮▮▮	36 cm	▮▮▮	1 980 cm²

2. A living room, 7.8 m long and 5.5 m wide, is to be covered with carpet costing $18.95/m². What will the cost of carpeting the room be, assuming there will be no waste?

3. (a) It is planned that one end of a recreation room measuring 4.2 m × 3 m will be tiled. Each tile measures 900 cm² and the tile sells for $32.95 a box. Part boxes are not sold and there are 50 tiles per box. How many tiles will be needed to cover the end of the recreation room?
   (b) How many tiles will be left over?
   (c) What will the total cost of the tiles be?

4. Jack wishes to tile a coffee table top. The tiles are 1 cm² and the coffee table measures 1.4 m × 0.3 m.
   (a) How many tiles will Jack need?
   (b) If the tiles are sold in sheets of 144 tiles each, how many sheets will he have to buy?

12.2   THE SQUARE

The Square: All sides are equal.
          All angles are right angles.

Since the length and width of a square are equal, both dimensions can be represented by the same letter, *s*.

$s = \dfrac{P}{4}$

Perimeter of a Square: $P = 4s$

$s = \sqrt{A}$

Area of a Square: $A = s^2$

Example
If one side of a square is 4.5 m, find its perimeter and area.

Solution

$$P = 4s \qquad\qquad A = s^2$$
$$= 4 \times 4.5 \qquad\qquad = 4.5 \times 4.5$$
$$= 18 \qquad\qquad\qquad = 20.25$$

Perimeter is 18 m and area is 20.25 m².

EXERCISE 12.2

1. Find the missing dimensions of the following squares.

	Length of Side	Perimeter	Area
(a)	16.5 m		
(b)	22.25 m		
(c)		78.24 cm	
(d)		856.24 cm	
(e)	18.7 m		
(f)			4 624 m²
(g)			1 260.25 cm²
(h)	9.9 m		
(i)		56.4 m	
(j)			3 433.96 cm²

2. Dennis Cunningham and his wife Sharon decide to paint their living room. One wall measures 3.5 m × 3.5 m; another measures 3.5 m × 7.8 m. A third wall measures 3.5 m × 7.8 m but includes a doorway that measures 1.2 m × 2.8 m. The fourth wall measures 3.5 m × 3.5 m, but includes a window that measures 1.4 m × 2.5 m.
   (a) What is the area to be covered by paint?
   (b) If a litre of paint covers 22.4 m², how many litres will have to be purchased?

12.3   THE TRIANGLE

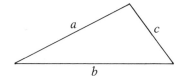

The perimeter of a triangle is the sum of the lengths of its three sides.

$$P = a + b + c$$

The common formula for the area of a triangle is

$$A = \tfrac{1}{2}bh$$

where b is the measure of the base and h is the height, that is, the measure of the perpendicular distance from that base to the opposite vertex.

Example 1
Find the area of a triangle whose base is 6 cm and whose height is 8 cm.

Solution

$$A = \tfrac{1}{2}bh$$
$$= \tfrac{1}{2} \times 6 \times 8$$
$$= 24$$

Area of triangle is 24 cm².

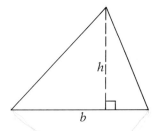

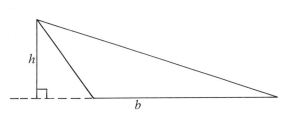

Since

$$A = \tfrac{1}{2}bh$$

it follows that

$$b = \frac{2A}{h}$$

and

$$h = \frac{2A}{b}$$

If you can measure the lengths of the three sides of any triangle, the area of the triangle can be calculated by using the formula

$$A = \sqrt{s(s - a)(s - b)(s - c)}$$

where a, b, and c are the lengths of the three sides of the triangle, and s is half the perimeter.

Example 2
Find the area of the given triangle.

Solution

$P = a + b + c$
$\quad = 7 + 5 + 4$
$\quad = 16$

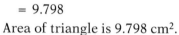

$s = \frac{1}{2}P$
$\quad = \frac{1}{2} \times 16$
$\quad = 8$

$A = \sqrt{s\,(s - a)(a - b)\,(s - c)}$
$\quad = \sqrt{8\,(8 - 7)\,(8 - 5)\,(8 - 4)}$
$\quad = \sqrt{8(1)(3)(4)}$
$\quad = \sqrt{96}$
$\quad = 9.798$

Area of triangle is 9.798 cm².

EXERCISE 12.3

1. Find the unknown dimension of each of the following triangles.

	Base	Height	Area
(a)	25.5 cm	32 cm	▮▮▮▮
(b)	5.8 m	8.5 m	▮▮▮▮
(c)	▮▮▮▮	6.2 m	13.95 m²
(d)	48.3 cm	▮▮▮▮	1 506.96 cm²
(e)	52.8 cm	65.4 cm	▮▮▮▮
(f)	▮▮▮▮	18.5 cm	138.75 cm²
(g)	13.5 m	▮▮▮▮	118.8 m²
(h)	48.5 cm	53.8 cm	▮▮▮▮
(i)	96.2 cm	1.5 cm	▮▮▮▮
(j)	1.85 m	98.3 cm	▮▮▮▮

2. Find the area of triangles whose sides are the following.

	Side a	Side b	Side c
(a)	7 m	24 m	25 m
(b)	6 m	8 m	10 m
(c)	15 cm	20 cm	25 cm
(d)	21 cm	72 cm	75 cm
(e)	30 cm	40 cm	50 cm
(f)	28 m	96 m	100 m
(g)	36 cm	48 cm	60 cm
(h)	45 cm	60 cm	75 cm
(i)	18 m	24 m	30 m
(j)	42 cm	56 cm	70 cm

3. Marilyn Rozinka wishes to seed an area of land that measures 5 m ×
   12 m × 13 m. How much seed will Marilyn need if 1 kg of seed covers
   10.5 m²?

4. When a dining area was carpeted, a piece measuring 14 cm × 48 cm ×
   50 cm was left over. If the carpeting cost $19.95/m², how much did the
   wasted carpet cost?

12.4   THE CIRCLE

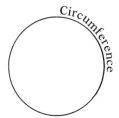  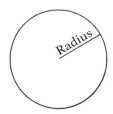

The *circumference* of a circle is the measure of its perimeter. The measure from the centre of a circle to any point on its circumference is the
radius. The *diameter* of a circle is the measure of a straight line drawn
through the centre, joining the circumference at either end. The diameter,
therefore, is twice the measure of the radius.

The formula for the circumference of a circle is

$$C = \pi d$$

π
Greek letter pi

where C represents the circumference, and d represents the diameter.

π is a constant factor and represents a number whose value we can only
approximate. In most cases we deal with, $3\frac{1}{7}$ or $\frac{22}{7}$ is a good approximation.
In other cases 3.141 59 (correct to 5 decimal places) may be used to be more
accurate.

$d = \dfrac{C}{\pi}$

Since $C = \pi d$

it follows that $C = 2\pi r,$ where r = radius.

$r = \dfrac{C}{2\pi}$

The formula for the area of a circle is

$$A = \pi r^2$$

$r = \sqrt{\dfrac{A}{\pi}}$

Example 1
Find the circumference of a circle whose diameter is 4 cm.

Solution
$$C = \pi d$$
$$= \tfrac{22}{7}(4)$$
$$= \tfrac{88}{7}$$
$$= 12.57$$

Circumference is 12.57 cm.

Example 2

Find the area of a circular swimming pool whose diameter is 6 m.

Solution

$$A = \pi r^2$$
$$= 3.142(\tfrac{6}{2})^2$$
$$= 3.142 \times 9$$
$$= 28.28$$

Area of pool is 28.28 m².

EXERCISE 12.4

1. Find the unknown dimensions of the following circles.

	Radius	Diameter	Circumference	Area
(a)		35 cm		
(b)	14 cm			
(c)			264 cm	
(d)			1 232 cm	
(e)		56 m		
(f)				154 m²
(g)	87.5 cm			
(h)		126 cm		
(i)				346.5 cm²
(j)				152 806.5 cm²

2. Liz Frampton is preparing to spray-paint bases for Christmas wreaths. She has 10 bases, each with a circumference of 1.12 m. Tins of fluorescent spray paint cost $2.89 each and each tin covers 10 000 cm². How many tins does she have to purchase?

3. A circular rug measures 160 cm across. If it costs $23.95/m², how much will you pay?

12.5   VOLUME – RECTANGULAR SOLIDS

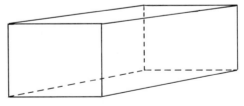

The Rectangular Solid: It has 6 sides.

All sides are rectangles.

The length of a rectangular solid is the longest distance between sides and is represented by *l*.

The width of a rectangular solid is the shorter distance between sides and is represented by *w*.

The height of a rectangular solid is represented by *h*.

The volume is represented by *V* and is expressed in cubic units.

The formula for the volume of a rectangular solid is

$$V = l \times w \times h$$

Example 1

Find the volume of a rectangular solid 6 m long, 4 m wide, and 2 m high.

Solution

$$V = 6\,\text{m} \times 4\,\text{m} \times 2\,\text{m}$$
$$= 48\,\text{m}^3$$

When each of the 6 sides is square, the solid is called a *cube*. Since all sides are equal, each side is represented by *s*.

$$V = s \times s \times s$$
$$= s^3$$

Example 2

Find the volume of a cube of ice if each side is 2 cm.

Solution

$$V = (2\,\text{cm})^3$$
$$= 8\,\text{cm}^3$$

EXERCISE 12.5

1. Find the volume of the following rectangular solids.

	Length	Width	Height
(a)	3 m	2 m	1 m
(b)	16 cm	10 cm	8 cm
(c)	10 m	8 m	3 m
(d)	15 mm	10 mm	4 mm
(e)	4 m	3 m	50 cm

2. Find the volume of the following.
    (a) a 6 mm cube
    (b) a 4 m cube
    (c) a 3 cm cube

3. How much water would be required to fill a swimming pool 10 m long, 6 m wide, and 3 m deep, if $1\,\text{m}^3 = 1\,\text{kL}$?

4. How many cubic metres of topsoil would you need to cover a lawn 30 m × 25 m with a 3 cm layer of soil?

5. What would be the cost of paving a driveway 20 m long by 8 m wide, if the cement was to be 10 cm deep and cost $19/m^3$?

12.6   VOLUME – CYLINDRICAL SOLIDS

The Cylindrical Solid: The ends are equal circles.

The sides meet the ends at right angles.

Following what you have learned about the rectangular solid, you can see that the volume of a cylindrical solid will be the area of its circular end times its height.

The area of the circular end is

$$A = \pi r^2$$

Therefore, the volume will be

$$V = \pi r^2 h$$

Example

Find the volume of a cylinder 12 cm high, having ends with a 4 cm radius.

Solution

$$V = \pi r^2 h$$
$$= \tfrac{22}{7} \times (4 \text{ cm})^2 \times 12 \text{ cm}$$
$$= 603.43 \text{ cm}^3$$

EXERCISE 12.6

1. Find the volume of the cylinders having the following measurements.

	Radius	*Diameter*	*Height*
(a)	3 cm	▮▮▮▮	8 cm
(b)	▮▮▮▮	6 mm	3 mm
(c)	4 cm	▮▮▮▮	10 cm
(d)	▮▮▮▮	9.2 cm	15 cm
(e)	▮▮▮▮	6 m	14 m
(f)	50 cm	▮▮▮▮	3 m

2. Find the volume of a can 6 cm across the top and 16 cm high.

3. A hot water tank has a diameter of 60 cm and stands 180 cm high. What is its volume in cubic metres?

4. Find the mass of a cylindrical piece of iron having a diameter of 2 cm and a height of 5 cm, if 1 cm³ has a mass of approximately 7.612 g.

5. A cylindrical water tank 6 m in diameter and 10 m high is full of water. How many kilolitres of water are in the tank? (1 m³ = 1 kL)

6. 1 000 cm³ of copper is rolled into wire with a 4 mm diameter. What is the length of the wire?

7. What is the diameter of a can whose volume is 100.57 cm³ and whose height is 8 cm?

SUMMARY

The Rectangle

$$P = 2(w + l) \qquad l = \frac{P - 2w}{2} \qquad w = \frac{P - 2l}{2}$$

$$A = lw \qquad l = \frac{A}{w} \qquad w = \frac{A}{l}$$

The Square

$$P = 4s \qquad s = \frac{P}{4}$$

$$A = s^2 \qquad s = \sqrt{A}$$

The Triangle

$$A = \sqrt{s\,(s - a)\,(s - b)\,(s - c)} \qquad \text{where} \qquad s = \frac{a + b + c}{2}$$

or

$$A = \frac{bh}{2}$$

The Circle

$$C = \pi d = 2\pi r \qquad d = \frac{C}{\pi} \qquad r = \frac{C}{2\pi}$$

$$A = \pi r^2 \qquad r = \sqrt{\frac{A}{\pi}}$$

The Rectangular Solid

$$V = lwh \qquad l = \frac{V}{wh} \qquad w = \frac{V}{lh} \qquad h = \frac{V}{lw}$$

The Cube

$$V = s^3$$

The Cylinder

$$V = \pi r^2 h$$

REVIEW EXERCISE 12.7

Diagrams will help you!

1. A 200 m roll of fencing is used to enclose a rectangular field 36 m wide. How long is the field?

2. Before a permit will be issued to install their inground swimming pool, Wayne and Suan have to build a fence surrounding the area where the pool will be placed. The length of the pool is 24 m and the width is 15 m. They want the fence to be 10 m from the edges of the pool.
   (a) How long must the fence be to surround the pool?
   (b) What would be the area of plastic needed to cover the pool for winter if there should be a 1 m overlap on each edge?

3. (a) A triangular lot measured 45 m × 60 m × 75 m. What would the area of the lot be?
   (b) If you could plant 12 trees/m², how many trees could be planted?

4. The area of a triangle is 144 cm² and the base is 12 cm. What is the height of the triangle?

5. The height of a triangle is 55 cm and the area is 605 cm². What is the base?

6. Find the radius, diameter, and area of a circle whose circumference is 1 100 m.

7. Find the radius, circumference, and area of a circle whose diameter is 21 cm.

8. Find the radius, diameter, and circumference of a circle whose area is 154 m².

9. Claudette's mother made her a butcher block measuring 75 cm long, 40 cm wide, and 5 cm deep. What is its volume?

10. (a) Find the volume of a pencil 15 cm long and having a diameter of 8 mm.
    (b) What is the volume of the lead in the pencil if it is 2 mm wide?

CUMULATIVE REVIEW 10

1. What is $\frac{7}{8}$% of 92?

2. $15.90 increased by $25\frac{1}{2}$% equals what amount?

3. $44.20 is what percent of $95.80?

4. What is the fractional equivalent of
   (a) 0.125?   (b) 0.833?

5. Factor $6b^2c + 12bc^3 + 24bc$.

6. Simplify $\dfrac{6m^2k}{2m}$.

7. Find the cost price of each of the following.
   (a) List price $298.90; discounts of 55%, 35%, and 2%
   (b) List price $3 045.80; discounts of 45%, 15%, and 1%

8. Mishka sells used cars. She earns $400 per month salary plus 15% commission on sales over $3 000. If her sales for the month of May were $10 300, how much did she earn for the month?

9. The cost price of a 10-speed bicycle is $125. What will the retail price of the bike be if the merchant needs a 38% markup on cost?

10. A pair of roller boots retailed for $69.95. If the merchant operated on a 45% markup on cost, what was the cost price of the roller boots?

11. Compute a schedule of payments for the first six months for a loan of $3 000 at $18\frac{1}{2}$% interest where the monthly payment is $129.58.

12. Compute the effective rate of interest per annum for each of the following.

	Amount Borrowed	Monthly Payment	Loan To Be Repaid in
(a)	$2 500	$ 88.19	36 months
(b)	1 500	138.13	12 months

13. Alec Pollington was applying for a credit card from a bank and was asked for his monthly salary. Alec could not give an answer because his commissions varied so much from month to month. In the previous 12 months Alec had earned the following:
   January $1 274; February $1 625; March $2 054; April $936; May $1 456; June $1 833; July $663; August $624; September $1 534; October $1 365; November $1 625; December $1 105.
   (a) What is Alec's mean salary?
   (b) What is Alec's mode salary?
   (c) What is Alec's median salary?
   (d) Which one should Alec use for his credit card application?

14. Bruce Black purchased a used car and applied for $250 deductible for collision and $200 000 Third Party Liability. His insurance agent told him that he would be classified as Class 10 with a driving record of 3. Bruce's car was rated as 6.
   (a) What would Bruce have to pay for insurance for one year?
   (b) If Bruce estimated that he would spend $300 per year for maintenance of the car and $800 per year for gasoline, how much would it cost him to operate his car per month, including insurance?
   Note: Refer to schedules in Unit 10.

15. Gail Carazza received $404.25 for a 46 h week. If she earned a regular wage for the first 40 h worked, and time-and–one-half for overtime, what was her regular hourly rate?

16. Bill Blake had a Net Federal Tax Payable of $842.68 and a Net Ontario Tax Payable of $500.49. His T4 slip showed that $1 306.93 had been deducted at source. Find Bill's total refund or balance due.

17. Malik had $695.82 in receipts for medical expenses. If his net income was $23 450, how much was the allowable portion of his medical expenses?

UNIT 13

Review

Reference:
Unit 1

EXERCISE 13.1

1. Add.

(a)	67	(b)	381	(c)	510
	71		472		728
	35		520		396
	72		679		205
	92		275		963
	49		928		478

(d)	35 698	(e)	546.8	(f)	580.46
	42 763		529.2		366.09
	78 620		672.9		578.11
	63 801		734.2		401.22
	10 276		825.6		739.46
	54 738		536.2		511.52

(g)	544	(h)	582	(i)	887
	877		872		790
	651		336		503
	755		267		126
	647		804		793
	551		507		353
	219		723		703
	848		894		521
	255		192		578
	975		521		954
	644		823		398
	998		952		885

(j)	65 982	(k)	91 506	(l)	800.73
	56 588		15 112		173.08
	12 599		76 432		520.45
	45 655		80 613		727.35
	32 859		95 648		483.80
	15 392		51 892		251.92
	65 489		52 305		442.30
	40 623		42 295		501.39
	14 539		67 895		628.54
	98 722		95 411		973.16
	69 723		41 589		850.14
	91 425		63 440		442.51

(m)   34 526.3
          8.236
         72.09
     72 849.1
        573.604 334
          0.572 396
      ―――――――――

(n)   483.456
       29.563 78
        0.902 41
   1 530.001 04
      386.72
       91.27
     ―――――――

(o) 982 673.528 1
        704.56
          0.790 8
         38.297
     73 592
      3 666.01
     ――――――――

(p)   0.2
        34.59
       367.296
     2 445.973
     3 006.073 76
       789.253 4
     ――――――――

(q) $56.24
       69.42
       31.72
       47.42
       22.65
       75.60
     ―――――

(r) $43.67
       48.09
       46.75
       85.44
       77.52
       24.11
     ―――――

(s) $29.98
       83.10
       67.83
       57.52
       32.57
       61.07
     ―――――

(t) $80.55
       75.10
       45.70
       80.20
       40.81
       24.31
     ―――――

2. Add horizontally.

(a) 74.89 + 213.80 + 5.17 + 85.623 + 532.43 + 17.3 + 19

(b) 153.67 + 47.71 + 15.02 + 4.822 53 + 0.830 + 946.192

(c) 48.2 + 48.23 + 85.24 + 74.239 + 0.37 + 1.387 + 16.2

(d) 28.705 + 633.54 + 2.86 + 1.09 + 0.15 + 35.368 + 376 245

(e) 36.75 + 11.061 + 22.122 45 + 74.483 + 71.071 34 + 193

3. Add using subtotals.

(a)	(b)	(c)	(d)	(e)
372.65	873.56	375.22	593.88	935.23
153.37	164.58	382.46	587.22	229.56
563.73	387.65	247.73	398.43	325.39
849.71	290.37	912.57	166.84	411.77
▮S	▮S	▮S	▮S	▮S
165.57	172.45	436.40	351.56	188.76
191.29	243.84	165.47	770.90	253.91
502.65	365.10	301.20	150.06	182.23
▮S	▮S	▮S	▮S	▮S
678.24	975.19	995.06	491.67	672.82
825.62	786.47	343.75	168.24	509.18
991.95	109.49	682.57	165.92	360.37
▮T	▮T	▮T	▮T	▮T

4. Calculate the total sales for each month, the total sales for each sales-person, and the total half-yearly sales.

	A	B	C	
Jan.	$12 689.11	$10 998.00	$24 382.49	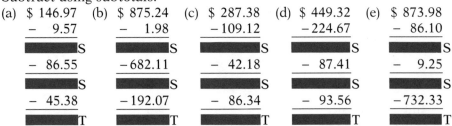
Feb.	9 375.55	10 392.49	13 862.46	
March	11 439.49	15 385.29	11 386.55	
April	12 385.22	14 887.39	12 387.42	
May	11 986.39	12 664.92	9 427.33	
June	12 754.38	13 500.00	18 226.75	

5. Subtract.

(a) 48 266
  − 7 378

(b) 76 833
  − 4 255

(c) 83 296
  − 4 793

(d) 38 764
  − 6 739

(e) 86 542
  − 2 914

6. Subtract using subtotals.

(a) $ 146.97
  − 9.57
  S
  − 86.55
  S
  − 45.38
  T

(b) $ 875.24
  − 1.98
  S
  −682.11
  S
  −192.07
  T

(c) $ 287.38
  −109.12
  S
  − 42.18
  S
  − 86.34
  T

(d) $ 449.32
  −224.67
  S
  − 87.41
  S
  − 93.56
  T

(e) $ 873.98
  − 86.10
  S
  − 9.25
  S
  −732.33
  T

7. Add or subtract as indicated and indicate credit balances where they occur.

(a) 74.89
  − 153.67
  48.2
  − 0.369
  − 15.2
  114.646

(b) 213.80
  47.71
  − 48.23
  −138.28
  71.23
  8.753

(c) 5.17
  15.02
  −74.239 2
  −98.4
  6.552
  0.102 3

(d) 532.43
  − 94.822
  45.229
  −487.3
  −135.86
  62.97

(e) 17.3
  0.345
  108.034 46
  − 67.2
  − 99.351 56
  1.230 42

8. Multiply.

(a) 37 × 69
(b) 42 × 89
(c) 72 × 41
(d) 89 × 33
(e) 48 × 56

(f) 356.44 × 59
(g) 3.5 × 7.89
(h) 18.43 × 0.001
(i) 367.23 × 54.332
(j) 1.874 × 34.6

9. Multiply and add the products using the memory key.

(a) 34.6 × 66.1 =
  23.8 × 8.32 =
  92.5 × 0.234 =
  Total =

(c) 78.4 × 6.13 =
  65.7 × 1.011 =
  4.9 × 1.82 =
  Total =

(b) $46.2 \times 56.99 = $ ▆▆▆▆▆▆

$37.4 \times 1.63 \ = $ ▆▆▆▆▆▆

$83.3 \times 5.27 \ = $ ▆▆▆▆▆▆

Total $= $ ▆▆▆▆▆

(d) $32.33 \times 4.5 \ \ = $ ▆▆▆▆▆

$0.192 \times 4.7 \ = $ ▆▆▆▆▆

$7.3 \times 88.3 \ \ \ = $ ▆▆▆▆▆

Total $= $ ▆▆▆▆▆

10. Multiply without using a calculator.
    (a) 384×99
    (b) 45×98
    (c) 386×25
    (d) 142×125
    (e) 467×2.5
    (f) $2.3 \times 1\ 000$
    (g) 0.008×536
    (h) $439 \times 10\ 000$
    (i) $1\ 000 \times 0.01$
    (j) $0.037\ 5 \times 0.2$
    (k) $9.463\ 487\ 2 \times 1\ 000$
    (l) 42×1.25

11. Multiply. Show your answer correct to 3 decimal places.
    (a) $35.6 \times 33.7 \times 84.1$
    (b) $87.3 \times 46.3 \times 335$
    (c) $0.356 \times 35.9 \times 1.72$
    (d) $4.35 \times 6.72 \times 4.88$
    (e) $8.44 \times 67.2 \times 39.7$

12. Divide.
    (a) $630 \div 14$
    (b) $384 \div 16$
    (e) $34\ 980 \div 165$
    (d) $3\ 208\ 329 \div 163$
    (e) $525 \div 35$

13. Divide correct to 2 decimal places.
    (a) $5.05 \div 15$
    (b) $16.78 \div 2.43$
    (c) $2\ 456 \div 4.6$
    (d) $88.6 \div 0.203$
    (e) $35.97 \div 0.012$

14. Multiply and divide the product by the given number using the memory key (correct to 2 decimal places).
    (a) $36.4 \times 48.9 \div 6.1$
    (b) $72.3 \times 59.3 \div 55.2$
    (c) $77 \times 1.378 \div 152$
    (d) $85.6 \times 49.36 \div 0.442$
    (e) $73.4 \times 4.52 \div 1.25$

15. Divide mentally.
    (a) $395 \div 25$
    (b) $65.37 \div 25$
    (c) $382 \div 2.5$
    (d) $793 \div 125$
    (e) $11\ 364 \div 1.25$
    (f) $876\ 492 \div 8$
    (g) $763\ 995 \div 7$
    (h) $876 \div 0.01$
    (i) $45 \div 0.25$
    (j) $0.668\ 34 \div 0.001$

EXERCISE 13.2

Reference: Unit 2

1. Add or subtract as indicated.
    (a) $6\frac{1}{4} + 3\frac{2}{3} - 4 - 1\frac{1}{2}$

    (b) $\frac{3}{4} - 1\frac{2}{3} + 16\frac{7}{8} + 9\frac{4}{5} - \frac{5}{6}$

2. Express each of the following fractions as a decimal and as a percent.
   - (a) $\frac{1}{2}$
   - (b) $\frac{3}{8}$
   - (c) $\frac{5}{6}$
   - (d) $\frac{5}{16}$
   - (e) $\frac{5}{12}$
   - (f) $\frac{1}{4}$
   - (g) $\frac{1}{12}$
   - (h) $\frac{2}{3}$
   - (i) $\frac{7}{10}$
   - (j) $\frac{7}{8}$
   - (k) $\frac{5}{8}$
   - (l) $\frac{2}{7}$
   - (m) $\frac{4}{5}$
   - (n) $\frac{3}{16}$
   - (o) $\frac{7}{12}$

3. Write in numerals.
   - (a) Thirteen thousandths
   - (b) One hundred forty-four thousand six hundred seventy-one and eight hundredths
   - (c) Twenty-eight million seven hundred fifty-six thousand four hundred nineteen and six hundred thirty-one thousand four hundred twenty-eight ten-millionths
   - (d) Five and four thousandths
   - (e) One hundred forty-five and six hundredths

4. Write in words.
   - (a) 62.48
   - (b) 741.389
   - (c) 42 691.005
   - (d) 38 729.036 482
   - (e) 18 672 486.02
   - (f) 0.001 43

5. What percent is 1 cm of 1 m?

6. What percent is $\frac{2}{3}$ of 12?

7. What percent is 19 of 95?

8. What is $9\frac{1}{2}\%$ of $760?

9. How much is 350% of 600?

10. Find $\frac{1}{8}\%$ of 84.

11. How much is $1\frac{1}{4}\%$ of $50?

12. If 250% of a number is 45, what is the number?

13. What number increased by 20% of itself equals 480?

14. What number decreased by 35% of itself equals 234?

15. What number increased by 25% of itself and the result decreased by 20% equals 375?

16. What value increased by 20% of itself and the result decreased by 40% equals $327.86?

17. Last year a firm sold $125 000 worth of goods. This year they increased their sales by 25%. How much did they sell this year?

18. Rajan withdrew 40% of the money he had on deposit at his bank. He spent 75% of the money he withdrew for a new car, which cost $8 100. How much did he have in the bank before he made the withdrawal?

19. Calculate the total cost without using your machine.

<table>
<tr><td>(a)</td><td>*Units*</td><td>*Unit Price*</td><td>*Amount*</td><td>(b)</td><td>*Units*</td><td>*Unit Price*</td><td>*Amount*</td></tr>
<tr><td></td><td>38</td><td>$12\frac{1}{2}$¢</td><td>■■■■</td><td></td><td>42</td><td>$87\frac{1}{2}$¢</td><td>■■■■</td></tr>
<tr><td></td><td>98</td><td>$37\frac{1}{2}$¢</td><td>■■■■</td><td></td><td>125</td><td>75¢</td><td>■■■■</td></tr>
<tr><td></td><td>64</td><td>70¢</td><td>■■■■</td><td></td><td>72</td><td>$62\frac{1}{2}$¢</td><td>■■■■</td></tr>
<tr><td></td><td>108</td><td>50¢</td><td>■■■■</td><td></td><td>680</td><td>80¢</td><td>■■■■</td></tr>
<tr><td></td><td>72</td><td>$6\frac{1}{4}$¢</td><td>■■■■</td><td></td><td>101</td><td>$16\frac{2}{3}$¢</td><td>■■■■</td></tr>
<tr><td></td><td>125</td><td>$66\frac{2}{3}$¢</td><td>■■■■</td><td></td><td>483</td><td>$33\frac{1}{3}$¢</td><td>■■■■</td></tr>
</table>

20. Find the number of items that may be purchased for the given amount at the given price, without using a machine.

	Amount	Unit Price
(a)	$460	$12\frac{1}{2}$¢
(b)	87.50	$37\frac{1}{2}$¢
(c)	678	$87\frac{1}{2}$¢
(d)	840	30¢
(e)	94	$6\frac{1}{4}$¢

EXERCISE 13.3

Reference:
Unit 3

1. Find the square of each of the following.
   (a) 15   (c) $5\frac{1}{2}$ (e) 32.5
   (b) 25   (d) 0.16   (f) 0.008

2. Find the cube of each of the following.
   (a) 3   (c) 5   (e) 1
   (b) 25   (d) 1.5   (f) 0.12

3. Add or subtract as indicated.
   (a) $4a + 6b - 2a - 4b$
   (b) $a^2 + 2a^2$
   (c) $3b^2 - b^2 + a^2$
   (d) $6a + 7b + c - 3a + b - 3c + 4a - 5b + 2c$
   (e) $3a^2b + ab - 3ab + 6a^2b + 4ab$

4. Expand.
   (a) $x(x^2 - 3x + 4)$
   (b) $3ab(2a + 3b)$
   (c) $\frac{1}{2}a(3a^2 + 6a - 2)$
   (d) $4(a - 2b + c)$
   (e) $(-2a)(6a + 2b - c)$

5. Simplify.

(a) $\dfrac{4a^3 - 8a^2 - 12a}{4a} + \dfrac{15a^4 + 10a^3 - 15a}{5a}$

(b) $\dfrac{2a(6a^3 + 4a^2 - 3a)}{3a^2} + \dfrac{13a^2 + 2a^3 - a}{2a}$

6. Factor.
   (a) $ab + a$
   (b) $a^2b + ab + a$
   (c) $2ab + 6a^2b + 8ab^2$

7. Solve the following equations.
   (a) $2a + 8 = 16$
   (b) $a^2 + 32 = 48$
   (c) $20\% \times 10a = 40$
   (d) $37\frac{1}{2}\%$ of Cost $= \$28.41$
   (e) $\frac{12}{a} \div 9 = 4$

Reference:
Unit 4

EXERCISE 13.4

1. Marsh Wells sold a house for $68 600. If the rate of real estate commission was 5%, how much commission was paid?

2. Joe Pasini collected 60% of a debt of $900. If he deducted 25% of the amount collected for his commission, how much did he make?

3. A homeowner wants to receive a net price of $42 000 for a home after the real estate commission is paid. If the rate of commission is $5\frac{1}{2}\%$, what will the selling price of the house have to be?

4. A salesperson received 20% commission on all sales over $2 000. For the person to earn a weekly income of $325, how much will have to be sold?

5. Another salesperson receives 20% commission on the first $2 000 of sales, 25% on sales between $2 000 and $5 000, and 40% on all sales over $5 000. If the total monthly sales are $6 530, how much does the salesperson earn?

6. Using the following information prepare
   (a) a payroll register showing the net pay of the three employees for the week ending 19-- 05 27. (Refer to Figures 4.1, 4.2, 4.3, and 4.4 for deductions for Canada Pension Plan, unemployment insurance, and income tax).
   (b) a payroll currency memorandum and a currency requisition.

Employee	Gross Pay	Income Tax Exemption	Group Ins.	Bond Payment	Hosp.
J. Baker SIN 998 202 340	$364.65	$4 670	$2.00	$3.00	$14.88
B. Dinsmore SIN 983 992 007	359.75	8 140	2.50	2.50	14.88
D. Prentiss SIN 883 772 396	362.98	3 960	2.25	2.50	7.44

7. Find the gross earnings for the following employees. (All time over 40 h/week is classed as overtime.)

(a) Employee: Albert Wong

	In	Out	In	Out	In	Out
M	7:56	12:01	12:58	16:55	17:10	19:15
T	7:59	12:02	13:03	17:06		
W	8:01	12:10	12:59	17:03	18:00	20:15
T	7:45	11:30	12:55	17:04	18:10	19:15
F	7:58	12:10	12:58	17:02		

Rate is $6.98/h; time-and-a-half for overtime.

(b) Employee: Andrea Gerrior

	In	Out	In	Out	In	Out
M	7:50	12:01	12:59	17:00	18:10	21:15
T	8:05	12:03	12:56	17:03		
W	7:49	12:00	12:58	16:35		
T	7:58	11:48	12:57	17:06	18:05	21:15
F	8:10	12:01	12:58	17:00	18:05	21:02
S	7:56	11:30				

Rate is $5.12/h; time-and-a-half for overtime.

(c) Employee: Ozzie Mariot

	In	Out	In	Out	In	Out
M	7:49	12:01	12:57	17:00		
T	7:58	12:08	12:59	16:30	17:30	18:48
W	7:50	12:09	12:58	17:01		
T	7:59	11:49	12:55	17:01	19:10	21:15
F	8:10	11:56	12:59	16:10		
S	7:50	12:01				

Rate is $6.20/h; time-and-a-half for overtime.

8. Baxter Sales and Services, Ltd. pays its salespeople a straight salary of $400 per month and a 5% commission on all sales over $5 000 per month. Find the monthly earnings for their two salespeople.

	Monthly Sales
Stephanie Li	$27 550
Dave London	30 600

9. Vijay Singh Manufacturing Ltd. pays its employees on a piecework basis. Each employee receives $2.10 per piece for the first 100 pieces completed, $2.25 per piece for the next 25 pieces completed, and $2.50 each for any pieces completed over 125. Calculate the weekly gross earnings for each employee.

Employee A	118 pieces
Employee B	98 pieces
Employee C	132 pieces

Reference:
Unit 5

EXERCISE 13.5

1. What is the simple interest on $840 if it is invested at $9\frac{3}{4}$% for 90 d?

2. How much simple interest did Stella earn on her $350 investment at $11\frac{1}{2}$% if the time was six months?

3. In what time will $1 800 earn $64.80 at 18%?

4. At what rate would Julie have to invest $1 000 to earn $367.50 in three years?

5. Jay Briggs deposits $500 in a trust account at the end of each year for fifteen years. If the account pays 12% compounded annually, how much will Jay have at the end of fifteen years?

6. Kurt wishes to have $6 000 at the end of four years. How much will he have to deposit at the end of every three months if his account pays interest at 10% compounded quarterly?

7. How much would Lorna Luksa have to invest now to provide herself with $5 000 at the end of every six months for twenty years if money is worth 12% compounded semi-annually?

8. Find the effective rate for
   (a) 9% compounded semi-annually,
   (b) 10% compounded quarterly,
   (c) 12% compounded monthly.

9. Nasser has received a bequest of $25 000. He deposits this sum in a fund that will provide him with a regular monthly income for four years. If money is worth 12% compounded monthly, how much will Nasser receive at the end of each month?

10. Cameron opened a savings account on May 15 with a deposit of $800. The daily interest was computed at the rate of $6\frac{1}{2}$% compounded daily. How much was in Cameron's account at the close of business May 18?

11. Last month Diane Hoekstra wrote 14 cheques on her chequing savings account. If the bank charged 27¢ for each cheque, how much was Diane's service charge?

EXERCISE 13.6

Reference:
Unit 6

1. Find the interest on a loan of $350 at a rate of 16% per annum if the loan is to be repaid in six months.

2. Find the amount of a loan when the interest at 16% per annum was $72 for one month.

3. A sum of money was borrowed on September 1 at 11% per annum and paid back on November 13 together with interest of $38.40. How much was borrowed?

4. If you borrowed $1 000 from a finance company and paid it back in 36 equal monthly payments of $35.77, what would the effective rate of interest be?

5. What sum of money was borrowed at 18% for two years if the amount paid back was $849.61?

6. What amount would be required to repay a loan of $1 000 at 19% for six months?

7. Natalie bought a new car priced at $7 440. She received a trade-in allowance on her old Chevy of $1 500 and promised to pay the balance in 24 monthly instalments of $306.90. Find
   (a) the carrying charge,
   (b) the effective rate of interest.

8. Tim Froese borrows $10 000. He wishes to repay it in equal annual instalments over ten years. How much will he pay at the end of each year if money is worth 8% compounded annually?

9. Claudette forgot to pay her charge card bill of $334.67 until one day after the due date. If the rate of interest charged was 22% per annum, how much did she have to pay then?

10. Kim Elias has the option of paying cash on a debt now or repaying it with 18 monthly instalments of $100 at the end of each month at 18% per annum compounded monthly. What is the cash value of Kim's debt?

11. Ming and Chan have just bought a house with a $22 000 mortgage. Payments are to be made at the end of each half year for six years. If the mortage bears interest at the rate of 16% compounded semi-annually, what is the amount of each payment?

Reference:
Unit 8

EXERCISE 13.8

1. Find the amount of cash discount, where applicable, and the amount of the payment.

	Terms	Invoice Amount	Date Paid	Date of Invoice
(a)	n/30	$ 430.37	April 25	April 10
(b)	2/10, n/30	75.50	April 27	April 20
(c)	3/10, n/60	1 980.00	April 28	April 23

2. Find the amount of provincial sales tax of 7% for each invoice amount in Question 1.

3. Find the amount of trade discount on goods listed at $45 when the net selling price to the retailer was $30.

4. Find the selling price of goods listed at $84.50 if the trade discount was 40%.

5. Find the selling price of goods listed at $48 with trade discounts of 20%, 10%, and 5%.

6. Find the single equivalent discount of a series of discounts of 40%, 25%, and 15%.

7. What is the list price of a lamp selling at $38 after trade discounts of $33\frac{1}{3}$% and 20% have been allowed?

8. Goods listed at $16 would sell for $12.80 after a discount of 20% was deducted. What additional discount would be required to lower the selling price to $11.52?

9. What would be the best trade discount: 40% and 25%? 30% and 35%? or 50% and 15%?

10. Calculate the amount of the invoice for the following items.

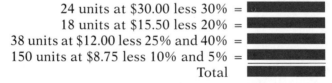

24 units at $30.00 less 30% =
18 units at $15.50 less 20% =
38 units at $12.00 less 25% and 40% =
150 units at $8.75 less 10% and 5% =
Total

11. The terms of sale of the invoice in Question 10 were 2/10, n/10. The invoice was dated May 2 and paid on May 8. If federal sales tax at 12% was added to the amount owing, how much was the cheque?

12. Goods listed at $84 were sold for $56. What was the rate of trade discount allowed?

13. On November 7, a firm mailed a cheque to pay for a $365 invoice dated October 29 with terms of 3/10, n/30. What was the amount of the cheque?

EXERCISE 13.9   *Reference:*
Unit 9

1. Find the retail price of each of the following items.

Item	Cost Price	*% of Markup or Margin*	*Selling Price Markup on Cost*	*Selling Price Margin of Retail*
Radio	$39.50	30%	▆▆▆▆	▆▆▆▆
Toaster	$12.00	25%	▆▆▆▆	▆▆▆▆

2. Find the retail price if the markup is based on cost.

	Cost	*Rate of Markup*	*Retail Price*
(a)	$ 0.75	25%	▆▆▆▆
(b)	3.00	40%	▆▆▆▆
(c)	189.40	125%	▆▆▆▆

3. Find the retail price if the margin is based on retail.

	Cost	*Rate of Margin*	*Retail Price*
(a)	$ 45.00	30%	▆▆▆▆
(b)	16.10	$37\frac{1}{2}\%$	▆▆▆▆
(c)	250.00	20%	▆▆▆▆

4. Find the rate of markup on cost correct to 2 decimal places.

	Cost	*Retail Price*	*Rate of Markup*
(a)	$156.00	$192.00	▆▆▆▆
(b)	1.40	1.96	▆▆▆▆
(c)	$0.03\frac{1}{2}$	0.04	▆▆▆▆

5. Find the rate of margin of retail correct to 2 decimal places for the items in Question 4.

6. What percent of markup on cost was used for an article costing $40 and selling for $50?

7. What percent of margin of selling price was used for an article costing $33.15 and selling for $44.20?

8. Find the cost price of a lighter selling for $1.80 when the markup on cost was 25%.

9. What was the cost price of a pen selling for $0.75 when the margin was 20% of the selling price?

10. Goods selling for $12.50 were originally marked up 20% of cost and later marked down 5% of the original selling price. Find the cost price.

11. A man bought a new stereo on which he paid a sales tax of $70. The rate of sales tax was 8%. How much did he pay for the stereo?

12. A retailer bought 100 suitcases and sold 40 at a profit of 20% on cost, 35 at a profit of 30% on cost, and the remainder at a loss of 10% of cost. The total selling price was $3 525.94. Find the cost price of each suitcase.

13. Joe Santelli's asking price for his house represented an increase of 50% over its cost. Later he reduced his price by 10% of the asking price. His profit on the sale was $22 400. What was the selling price?

14. Soiled goods marked to sell at $8.40 were marked down 28%.
    (a) What was the reduced price?
    (b) If the original price of $8.40 included a 25% markup on cost, what was the cost of the goods?

Reference:
Unit 10

EXERCISE 13.10

1. Bruce Barnes signed a $4 500 conditional sales contract for 24 months at $15\frac{1}{2}$%. What is the simple interest for this contract?

2. Donna bought a used car for $995. She signed a demand promissory note for that amount less her down payment of $200. If she paid the note in 90 d, how much did she pay if the note was $16\frac{3}{4}$%?

3. A car was insured under a $50 deductible collision policy. An accident resulted in damages of $835.45. How much should the policyholder recover from the insurance company?

4. John insured his car for one year. He paid $174.98 for public liability and property damage, $70 for $100 deductible collision, and $8 for $25 deductible comprehensive. Six months later he sold the car and cancelled the insurance. The short-term rate for a six month period was 68% of the annual premium. How much would John recover from the insurance company?

5. How much simple interest would Paul pay on a $2 300, 18% note given 30 months ago when he bought his Mustang?

6. Chantel made 36 payments of $137.69 for the balance of the purchase price of her car. She had paid $2 000 down on the $6 000 Plymouth. What was her effective rate of interest?

7. Using the chart of car driving costs in Unit 10, calculate the costs of the following.
   (a) a compact Rabbit driven for 193 km
   (b) a full-size Lincoln Continental driven for 13 500 km
   (c) a full-size Chevrolet driven for 675 km

8. Joan Wanski drives a class 3 car and is classified as class 02 with a driving record of 0. What would her annual premium be for $300 000 third party liability insurance and $250 deductible collision insurance?

9. Don Reven drives a class 6 car and he is classified as class 08 with a driving record of 0. Don was involved in two accidents in the past three years. What would he pay for $200 000 third party liability insurance and $100 deductible collision insurance?

EXERCISE 13.11

Reference:
Unit 11

1. A class in accounting had the following marks on a recent examination:
   24, 56, 55, 67, 66, 98, 95, 54, 53, 68, 70, 77, 73, 72, 76, 35, 42, 67, 51, 49, 69, 36, 53, 56, 59, 72, 63, 62, 68, 56.

   (a) Find the mean.
   (b) Find the median.
   (c) Find the mode.

2. A merchant mixed 36 kg of tea costing $10.00/kg, 20 kg costing $9.00/kg, 30 kg costing $8.00/kg, and 18 kg costing $12.00/kg. What is the average cost per kilogram of the resulting mixture of tea?

3. Karen worked as a salesperson in a retail store for a monthly salary plus commission. Her commissions for a six month period were as follows.

   $350 in May
   $325 in June
   $300 in July
   $288 in August
   $375 in September
   $382 in October

   (a) Find the total commissions for the six months.
   (b) Find the average monthly commission.
   (c) Find the three month moving average for July, August, September, and October.
   (d) Find the cumulative average.

4. Construct a single line graph to illustrate the commissions earned in Question 3.

5. The Crawley family had an annual income after payroll deductions of $18 000. They decided to budget $6 000 for housing, $5 000 for food, $4 000 for transportation, $2 000 for recreation, and the remainder for savings.

   (a) How much did they plan to save in one year?
   (b) Construct a circle graph to illustrate how the Crawleys plan to spend their money.

6. Construct a horizontal bar graph to compare the cost of operating the following appliances for one hour.

100 W light bulb	0.6¢
1 000 W toaster	6¢
1 600 W heater	10¢
2 200 W electric motor	13¢
375 W power saw	2¢
1 100 W vacuum cleaner	7¢

7. Construct a 100% rectangle graph to compare the cafeteria preferences of employees of H. B. Hirtz Ltd. and of Maitland Steel Inc. using the following information.

Menu Choice	H. B. Hirtz	Maitland Steel
Hot meal	1 220	960
Sandwich	380	820
Pizza	160	140
Others	240	80

Reference:
Unit 12

EXERCISE 13.12

1. Find the area of a rug measuring 3.4 m × 2.6 m.

2. How many metres of chain link fencing will you need to buy for a dog pen 30 m × 18 m if the gate to the pen is 1 m wide?

3. A circular fish pond measures 150 cm across. How much flexible molding will be required to edge the pond?

4. A circular area in a garden is to be filled with ornamental white gravel. The area measures 180 cm across and the gravel is to be 8 cm deep. How much gravel will be required?

5. How many knotty pine panels measuring 120 cm × 240 cm would be required to panel two sides and one end of a recreation room 5 m long, 4 m wide, and 240 cm high?

6. How much lace would you need to edge a tablecloth 135 cm square?

7. A garage floor 14 m × 8 m is being poured. How much cement would be used if the floor is to be 10 cm thick?

8. How many bricks would you need for a patio 350 cm × 200 cm if each brick measures 20 cm × 10 cm?

9. Jennifer Kim is pouring a foundation 1 200 cm × 750 cm. It will be 30 cm across and 90 cm high. Find the amount of cement Jennifer will need. Draw a diagram before you start calculating.

10. An oil drum 90 cm high and 40 cm across is to be filled with gravel to hold a flag pole 5 cm in diameter inserted in the drum. How much gravel will be needed?

SQUARES AND SQUARE ROOTS

n	n^2	$\sqrt{n}$	n	n^2	$\sqrt{n}$	n	n^2	$\sqrt{n}$	n	n^2	$\sqrt{n}$
1	1	1.000	51	2 601	7.141	101	10 201	10.050	151	22 801	12.288
2	4	1.414	52	2 704	7.211	102	10 404	10.100	152	23 104	12.329
3	9	1.732	53	2 809	7.280	103	10 609	10.149	153	23 409	12.369
4	16	2.000	54	2 916	7.348	104	10 816	10.198	154	23 716	12.410
5	25	2.236	55	3 025	7.416	105	11 025	10.247	155	24 025	12.450
6	36	2.449	56	3 136	7.483	106	11 236	10.296	156	24 336	12.490
7	49	2.646	57	3 249	7.550	107	11 449	10.344	157	24 649	12.530
8	64	2.828	58	3 364	7.616	108	11 664	10.392	158	24 964	12.570
9	81	3.000	59	3 481	7.681	109	11 881	10.440	159	25 281	12.610
10	100	3.162	60	3 600	7.746	110	12 100	10.488	160	25 600	12.649
11	121	3.317	61	3 721	7.810	111	12 321	10.536	161	25 921	12.689
12	144	3.464	62	3 844	7.874	112	12 544	10.583	162	26 244	12.728
13	169	3.606	63	3 969	7.937	113	12 769	10.630	163	26 569	12.767
14	196	3.742	64	4 096	8.000	114	12 996	10.677	164	26 896	12.806
15	225	3.873	65	4 225	8.062	115	13 225	10.724	165	27 225	12.845
16	256	4.000	66	4 356	8.124	116	13 456	10.770	166	27 556	12.884
17	289	4.123	67	4 489	8.185	117	13 689	10.817	167	27 889	12.923
18	324	4.243	68	4 624	8.246	118	13 924	10.863	168	28 224	12.961
19	361	4.359	69	4 761	8.307	119	14 161	10.909	169	28 561	13.000
20	400	4.472	70	4 900	8.367	120	14 400	10.954	170	28 900	13.038
21	441	4.583	71	5 041	8.426	121	14 641	11.000	171	29 241	13.077
22	484	4.690	72	5 184	8.485	122	14 884	11.045	172	29 584	13.115
23	529	4.796	73	5 329	8.544	123	15 129	11.091	173	29 929	13.153
24	576	4.899	74	5 476	8.602	124	15 376	11.136	174	30 276	13.191
25	625	5.000	75	5 625	8.660	125	15 625	11.180	175	30 625	13.229
26	676	5.099	76	5 776	8.718	126	15 876	11.225	176	30 976	13.267
27	729	5.196	77	5 929	8.775	127	16 129	11.269	177	31 329	13.304
28	784	5.292	78	6 084	8.832	128	16 384	11.314	178	31 684	13.342
29	841	5.385	79	6 241	8.888	129	16 641	11.358	179	32 041	13.379
30	900	5.477	80	6 400	8.944	130	16 900	11.402	180	32 400	13.416
31	961	5.568	81	6 561	9.000	131	17 161	11.446	181	32 761	13.454
32	1 024	5.657	82	6 724	9.055	132	17 424	11.489	182	33 124	13.491
33	1 089	5.745	83	6 889	9.110	133	17 689	11.533	183	33 489	13.528
34	1 156	5.831	84	7 056	9.165	134	17 956	11.576	184	33 856	13.565
35	1 225	5.916	85	7 225	9.220	135	18 225	11.619	185	34 225	13.601
36	1 296	6.000	86	7 396	9.274	136	18 496	11.662	186	34 596	13.638
37	1 369	6.083	87	7 569	9.327	137	18 769	11.705	187	34 969	13.675
38	1 444	6.164	88	7 744	9.381	138	19 044	11.747	188	35 344	13.711
39	1 521	6.245	89	7 921	9.434	139	19 321	11.790	189	35 721	13.748
40	1 600	6.325	90	8 100	9.487	140	19 600	11.832	190	36 100	13.784
41	1 681	6.403	91	8 281	9.539	141	19 881	11.874	191	36 481	13.820
42	1 764	6.481	92	8 464	9.592	142	20 164	11.916	192	36 864	13.856
43	1 849	6.557	93	8 649	9.644	143	20 449	11.958	193	37 249	13.892
44	1 936	6.633	94	8 836	9.695	144	20 736	12.000	194	37 636	13.928
45	2 025	6.708	95	9 025	9.747	145	21 025	12.042	195	38 025	13.964
46	2 116	6.782	96	9 216	9.798	146	21 316	12.083	196	38 416	14.000
47	2 209	6.856	97	9 409	9.849	147	21 609	12.124	197	38 809	14.036
48	2 304	6.928	98	9 604	9.899	148	21 904	12.166	198	39 204	14.071
49	2 401	7.000	99	9 801	9.950	149	22 201	12.207	199	39 601	14.107
50	2 500	7.071	100	10 000	10.000	150	22 500	12.247	200	40 000	14.142

TABLE 1

AMOUNT OF 1: $(1 + i)^n$

n	1%	1½%	2%	2½%	3%	3½%	4%	4½%	n
1	1.010 00	1.015 00	1.020 00	1.025 00	1.030 00	1.035 00	1.040 00	1.045 00	1
2	1.020 10	1.030 23	1.040 40	1.050 63	1.060 90	1.071 23	1.081 60	1.092 03	2
3	1.030 30	1.045 68	1.061 21	1.076 89	1.092 73	1.108 72	1.124 86	1.141 17	3
4	1.040 60	1.061 36	1.082 43	1.103 81	1.125 51	1.147 52	1.169 86	1.192 52	4
5	1.051 01	1.077 28	1.104 08	1.131 41	1.159 27	1.187 69	1.216 65	1.246 18	5
6	1.061 52	1.093 44	1.126 16	1.159 69	1.194 05	1.229 26	1.265 32	1.302 26	6
7	1.072 14	1.109 85	1.148 69	1.188 69	1.229 87	1.272 28	1.315 93	1.360 86	7
8	1.082 86	1.126 49	1.171 66	1.218 40	1.266 77	1.316 81	1.368 57	1.422 10	8
9	1.093 69	1.143 39	1.195 09	1.248 86	1.304 77	1.362 90	1.423 31	1.486 09	9
10	1.104 62	1.160 54	1.218 99	1.280 08	1.343 92	1.410 60	1.480 24	1.552 97	10
11	1.115 67	1.177 95	1.243 37	1.312 09	1.384 23	1.459 97	1.539 45	1.622 85	11
12	1.126 83	1.195 62	1.268 24	1.344 89	1.425 76	1.511 07	1.601 03	1.695 88	12
13	1.138 09	1.213 55	1.293 61	1.378 51	1.468 53	1.563 96	1.665 07	1.772 19	13
14	1.149 47	1.231 76	1.319 48	1.412 97	1.512 59	1.618 69	1.731 68	1.851 94	14
15	1.160 97	1.250 23	1.345 87	1.448 30	1.557 97	1.675 35	1.800 94	1.935 28	15
16	1.172 58	1.268 99	1.372 79	1.484 51	1.604 71	1.733 99	1.872 98	2.022 36	16
17	1.184 30	1.288 02	1.400 24	1.521 62	1.652 85	1.794 68	1.947 90	2.113 37	17
18	1.196 15	1.307 34	1.428 25	1.559 66	1.702 43	1.857 49	2.025 82	2.208 47	18
19	1.208 11	1.326 95	1.456 81	1.598 65	1.753 51	1.922 50	2.106 85	2.307 85	19
20	1.220 19	1.346 86	1.485 95	1.638 62	1.806 11	1.989 79	2.191 12	2.411 70	20
21	1.232 39	1.367 06	1.515 67	1.679 58	1.860 29	2.059 43	2.278 77	2.520 23	21
22	1.244 72	1.387 56	1.545 98	1.721 57	1.916 10	2.131 51	2.369 92	2.633 64	22
23	1.257 16	1.408 38	1.576 90	1.764 61	1.973 59	2.206 11	2.464 72	2.752 15	23
24	1.269 73	1.429 50	1.608 44	1.808 73	2.032 79	2.283 33	2.563 30	2.876 00	24
25	1.282 43	1.450 95	1.640 61	1.853 94	2.093 78	2.363 24	2.665 84	3.005 42	25
26	1.295 26	1.472 71	1.673 42	1.900 29	2.156 59	2.445 96	2.772 47	3.140 66	26
27	1.308 21	1.494 80	1.706 89	1.947 80	2.221 29	2.531 57	2.883 37	3.281 99	27
28	1.321 29	1.517 22	1.741 02	1.996 50	2.287 93	2.620 17	2.998 70	3.429 68	28
29	1.334 50	1.539 98	1.775 84	2.046 41	2.356 57	2.711 88	3.118 65	3.584 01	29
30	1.347 85	1.563 08	1.811 36	2.097 57	2.427 26	2.806 79	3.243 40	3.745 29	30
31	1.361 33	1.586 53	1.847 59	2.150 01	2.500 08	2.905 03	3.373 13	3.913 83	31
32	1.374 94	1.610 32	1.884 54	2.203 76	2.575 08	3.006 71	3.508 06	4.089 95	32
33	1.388 69	1.634 48	1.922 23	2.258 85	2.652 34	3.111 94	3.648 38	4.274 00	33
34	1.402 58	1.659 00	1.960 68	2.315 32	2.731 91	3.220 86	3.794 32	4.466 33	34
35	1.416 60	1.683 88	1.999 89	2.373 21	2.813 86	3.333 59	3.946 09	4.667 32	35
36	1.430 77	1.709 14	2.039 89	2.432 54	2.898 28	3.450 27	4.103 93	4.877 34	36
37	1.445 08	1.734 78	2.080 69	2.493 35	2.985 23	3.571 03	4.268 09	5.096 82	37
38	1.459 53	1.760 80	2.122 30	2.555 68	3.074 78	3.696 01	4.438 81	5.326 18	38
39	1.474 12	1.787 21	2.164 74	2.619 57	3.167 03	3.825 37	4.616 37	5.565 86	39
40	1.488 86	1.814 02	2.208 04	2.685 06	3.262 04	3.959 26	4.801 02	5.816 32	40
41	1.503 75	1.841 23	2.252 20	2.752 19	3.359 90	4.097 83	4.993 06	6.078 06	41
42	1.518 79	1.868 85	2.297 24	2.821 00	3.460 70	4.241 26	5.192 78	6.351 57	42
43	1.533 98	1.896 88	2.343 19	2.891 52	3.564 52	4.389 70	5.400 50	6.637 39	43
44	1.549 32	1.925 33	2.390 05	2.963 81	3.671 45	4.543 34	5.616 52	6.936 07	44
45	1.564 81	1.954 24	2.437 85	3.037 90	3.781 60	4.702 36	5.841 18	7.248 19	45
46	1.580 46	1.983 53	2.486 61	3.113 85	3.895 04	4.866 94	6.074 82	7.574 36	46
47	1.596 26	2.013 28	2.536 34	3.191 70	4.011 90	5.037 28	6.317 82	7.915 21	47
48	1.612 23	2.043 48	2.587 07	3.271 49	4.132 25	5.213 59	6.570 53	8.271 39	48
49	1.628 35	2.074 13	2.638 81	3.353 28	4.256 22	5.396 06	6.833 35	8.643 60	49
50	1.644 63	2.105 24	2.691 59	3.437 11	4.383 91	5.584 93	7.106 68	9.032 57	50
n	1%	1½%	2%	2½%	3%	3½%	4%	4½%	n

TABLE 1

AMOUNT OF 1: $(1 + i)^n$

n	6%	7%	8%	9%	10%	12%	16%	18%	n
1	1.060 00	1.070 00	1.080 00	1.090 00	1.100 00	1.120 00	1.160 00	1.180 00	1
2	1.123 60	1.144 90	1.166 40	1.188 10	1.210 00	1.254 40	1.345 60	1.392 40	2
3	1.191 02	1.225 04	1.259 71	1.295 03	1.331 00	1.404 93	1.560 90	1.643 03	3
4	1.262 48	1.310 80	1.360 49	1.411 58	1.464 10	1.573 52	1.810 64	1.938 78	4
5	1.338 23	1.402 55	1.469 33	1.538 62	1.610 51	1.762 34	2.100 34	2.287 76	5
6	1.418 52	1.500 73	1.586 87	1.677 10	1.771 56	1.973 82	2.436 40	2.699 55	6
7	1.503 63	1.605 78	1.713 82	1.828 04	1.948 72	2.210 68	2.826 22	3.185 47	7
8	1.593 85	1.718 19	1.850 93	1.992 56	2.143 59	2.475 96	3.278 41	3.758 86	8
9	1.689 48	1.838 46	1.999 00	2.171 89	2.357 95	2.773 08	3.802 96	4.435 45	9
10	1.790 85	1.967 15	2.158 92	2.367 36	2.593 74	3.105 84	4.411 43	5.233 83	10
11	1.898 30	2.104 85	2.331 64	2.580 43	2.853 12	3.478 55	5.117 26	6.175 92	11
12	2.012 20	2.252 19	2.518 17	2.812 66	3.138 43	3.895 97	5.936 02	7.287 58	12
13	2.132 93	2.409 85	2.719 62	3.065 80	3.452 27	4.363 49	6.885 78	8.599 35	13
14	2.260 90	2.578 53	2.937 19	3.341 73	3.797 50	4.887 10	7.987 51	10.147 23	14
15	2.396 56	2.759 03	3.172 17	3.642 48	4.177 25	5.473 56	9.265 51	11.973 73	15
16	2.540 35	2.952 16	3.425 94	3.970 31	4.594 97	6.130 38	10.747 99	14.129 00	16
17	2.692 77	3.158 82	3.700 02	4.327 63	5.054 47	6.866 03	12.467 67	16.672 22	17
18	2.854 34	3.379 93	3.996 02	4.717 12	5.559 92	7.689 95	14.462 49	19.673 22	18
19	3.025 60	3.616 53	4.315 70	5.141 66	6.115 91	8.612 74	16.776 49	23.214 40	19
20	3.207 14	3.869 68	4.660 96	5.604 41	6.727 50	9.646 27	19.460 73	27.392 99	20
21	3.399 56	4.140 56	5.033 83	6.108 81	7.400 25	10.803 83	22.574 45	32.323 73	21
22	3.603 54	4.430 40	5.436 54	6.658 60	8.140 27	12.100 28	26.186 36	38.142 00	22
23	3.819 75	4.740 53	5.871 46	7.257 87	8.954 30	13.552 32	30.376 17	45.007 56	23
24	4.048 93	5.072 37	6.341 18	7.911 08	9.849 73	15.178 60	35.236 36	53.108 92	24
25	4.291 87	5.427 43	6.848 48	8.623 08	10.834 71	17.000 03	40.874 18	62.668 52	25
26	4.549 38	5.807 35	7.396 35	9.399 16	11.918 18	19.040 03	47.414 04	73.948 85	26
27	4.822 35	6.213 87	7.988 06	10.245 08	13.109 99	21.324 83	55.000 29	87.259 65	27
28	5.111 69	6.648 84	8.627 11	11.167 14	14.420 99	23.883 81	63.800 34	102.966 38	28
29	5.418 39	7.114 26	9.317 27	12.172 18	15.863 09	26.749 87	74.008 39	121.500 33	29
30	5.743 49	7.612 26	10.062 66	13.267 68	17.449 40	29.959 85	85.849 73	143.370 39	30
31	6.088 10	8.145 11	10.867 67	14.461 77	19.194 34	33.555 04	99.585 69	169.177 06	31
32	6.453 39	8.715 27	11.737 08	15.763 33	21.113 78	37.581 64	115.519 40	199.628 93	32
33	6.840 59	9.325 34	12.676 05	17.182 03	23.225 15	42.091 44	134.002 50	235.562 14	33
34	7.251 03	9.978 11	13.690 13	18.728 41	25.547 67	47.142 41	155.442 90	277.963 32	34
35	7.686 09	10.676 58	14.785 34	20.413 97	28.102 44	52.799 50	180.313 77	327.996 72	35
36	8.147 25	11.423 94	15.968 17	22.251 23	30.912 68	59.135 43	209.163 97	387.036 13	36
37	8.636 09	12.223 62	17.245 63	24.253 84	34.003 95	66.231 69	242.630 20	456.702 63	37
38	9.154 25	13.079 27	18.625 28	26.436 68	37.404 34	74.179 49	281.451 03	538.909 10	38
39	9.703 51	13.994 82	20.115 30	28.815 98	41.144 78	83.081 03	326.483 20	635.912 74	39
40	10.285 72	14.974 46	21.724 52	31.409 42	45.259 26	93.050 75	378.720 51	750.377 03	40
41	10.902 86	16.022 67	23.462 48	34.236 27	49.785 18	104.216 84	439.315 79	885.444 90	41
42	11.557 03	17.144 26	25.339 48	37.317 53	54.763 70	116.722 86	509.606 32	1 044.824 98	42
43	12.250 45	18.344 35	27.366 64	40.676 11	60.240 07	130.729 60	591.143 33	1 232.893 47	43
44	12.985 48	19.628 46	29.555 97	44.336 96	66.264 08	146.417 15	685.726 26	1 454.814 30	44
45	13.764 61	21.002 45	31.920 45	48.327 29	72.890 48	163.987 21	795.442 46	1 716.680 87	45
46	14.590 49	22.472 62	34.474 09	52.676 74	80.179 53	183.665 68	922.713 25	2 025.683 43	46
47	15.465 92	24.045 71	37.232 01	57.417 65	88.197 49	205.705 56	1 070.347 37	2 390.306 45	47
48	16.393 87	25.728 91	40.210 57	62.585 24	97.017 23	230.390 22	1 241.602 95	2 820.561 61	48
49	17.377 50	27.529 93	43.427 42	68.217 91	106.718 96	258.037 05	1 440.259 42	3 328.262 69	49
50	18.420 15	29.457 03	46.901 61	74.357 52	117.390 85	289.001 49	1 670.700 93	3 927.349 98	50
n	6%	7%	8%	9%	10%	12%	16%	18%	n

TABLE 2

PRESENT VALUE OF 1: $\dfrac{1}{(1 + i)^n}$

n	1%	1½%	2%	2½%	3%	3½%	4%	4½%	n
1	0.990 10	0.985 22	0.980 39	0.975 61	0.970 87	0.966 18	0.961 54	0.956 94	1
2	0.980 30	0.970 66	0.961 17	0.951 81	0.942 60	0.933 51	0.924 56	0.915 73	2
3	0.970 59	0.956 32	0.942 32	0.928 60	0.915 14	0.901 94	0.889 00	0.876 29	3
4	0.960 98	0.942 18	0.923 85	0.905 95	0.888 49	0.871 44	0.854 80	0.838 56	4
5	0.951 47	0.928 26	0.905 73	0.883 85	0.862 61	0.841 97	0.821 93	0.802 45	5
6	0.942 05	0.914 54	0.887 97	0.862 30	0.837 48	0.813 50	0.790 31	0.767 90	6
7	0.932 72	0.901 03	0.870 56	0.841 27	0.813 09	0.785 99	0.759 92	0.734 83	7
8	0.923 48	0.887 71	0.853 49	0.820 75	0.789 41	0.759 41	0.730 69	0.703 19	8
9	0.914 34	0.874 59	0.836 76	0.800 73	0.766 42	0.733 73	0.702 59	0.672 91	9
10	0.905 29	0.861 67	0.820 35	0.781 20	0.744 09	0.708 92	0.675 56	0.643 93	10
11	0.896 32	0.848 93	0.804 26	0.762 14	0.722 42	0.684 95	0.649 58	0.616 20	11
12	0.887 45	0.836 39	0.788 49	0.743 56	0.701 38	0.661 78	0.624 60	0.589 66	12
13	0.878 66	0.824 03	0.773 03	0.725 42	0.680 95	0.639 40	0.600 57	0.564 27	13
14	0.869 96	0.811 85	0.757 88	0.707 73	0.661 12	0.617 78	0.577 48	0.539 97	14
15	0.861 35	0.799 85	0.743 01	0.690 47	0.641 86	0.596 89	0.555 26	0.516 72	15
16	0.852 82	0.788 03	0.728 45	0.673 62	0.623 17	0.576 71	0.533 91	0.494 47	16
17	0.844 38	0.776 39	0.714 16	0.657 20	0.605 02	0.557 20	0.513 37	0.473 18	17
18	0.836 02	0.764 91	0.700 16	0.641 17	0.587 39	0.538 36	0.493 63	0.452 80	18
19	0.827 74	0.753 61	0.686 43	0.625 53	0.570 29	0.520 16	0.474 64	0.433 30	19
20	0.819 54	0.742 47	0.672 97	0.610 27	0.553 68	0.502 57	0.456 39	0.414 65	20
21	0.811 43	0.731 50	0.659 78	0.595 39	0.537 55	0.485 57	0.438 83	0.396 79	21
22	0.803 40	0.720 69	0.646 84	0.580 86	0.521 89	0.469 15	0.421 96	0.379 70	22
23	0.795 44	0.710 04	0.634 16	0.566 70	0.506 69	0.453 29	0.405 73	0.363 35	23
24	0.787 57	0.699 54	0.621 72	0.552 88	0.491 93	0.437 96	0.390 12	0.347 71	24
25	0.779 77	0.689 21	0.609 53	0.539 39	0.477 61	0.423 15	0.375 12	0.332 73	25
26	0.772 05	0.679 02	0.597 58	0.526 23	0.463 69	0.408 84	0.360 69	0.318 40	26
27	0.764 40	0.668 99	0.585 86	0.513 40	0.450 19	0.395 01	0.346 82	0.304 69	27
28	0.756 84	0.659 10	0.574 37	0.500 88	0.437 08	0.381 65	0.333 48	0.291 57	28
29	0.749 34	0.649 36	0.563 11	0.488 66	0.424 35	0.368 75	0.320 65	0.279 02	29
30	0.741 92	0.639 76	0.552 07	0.476 74	0.411 99	0.356 28	0.308 32	0.267 00	30
31	0.734 58	0.630 31	0.541 25	0.465 11	0.399 99	0.344 23	0.296 46	0.255 21	31
32	0.727 30	0.620 99	0.530 63	0.453 77	0.388 34	0.332 59	0.285 06	0.244 50	32
33	0.720 10	0.611 82	0.520 23	0.442 70	0.377 03	0.321 34	0.274 09	0.233 97	33
34	0.712 97	0.602 77	0.510 03	0.431 91	0.366 04	0.310 48	0.263 55	0.223 90	34
35	0.705 91	0.593 87	0.500 03	0.421 37	0.355 38	0.299 98	0.253 42	0.214 26	35
36	0.698 93	0.585 09	0.490 22	0.411 09	0.345 03	0.289 83	0.243 67	0.205 03	36
37	0.692 00	0.576 44	0.480 61	0.401 07	0.334 98	0.280 03	0.234 30	0.196 20	37
38	0.685 15	0.567 92	0.471 19	0.391 28	0.325 23	0.270 56	0.225 29	0.187 75	38
39	0.678 37	0.559 53	0.461 95	0.381 74	0.315 75	0.261 41	0.216 62	0.179 67	39
40	0.671 65	0.551 26	0.452 89	0.372 43	0.306 56	0.252 57	0.208 29	0.171 93	40
41	0.665 00	0.543 12	0.444 01	0.363 35	0.297 63	0.244 03	0.200 28	0.164 53	41
42	0.658 42	0.535 09	0.435 30	0.354 48	0.288 96	0.235 78	0.192 57	0.157 44	42
43	0.651 90	0.527 18	0.426 77	0.345 84	0.280 54	0.227 81	0.185 17	0.150 66	43
44	0.645 45	0.519 39	0.418 40	0.337 40	0.272 37	0.220 10	0.178 05	0.144 17	44
45	0.639 05	0.511 71	0.410 20	0.329 17	0.264 44	0.212 66	0.171 20	0.137 97	45
46	0.632 73	0.504 15	0.402 15	0.321 15	0.256 74	0.205 47	0.164 61	0.132 02	46
47	0.626 46	0.496 70	0.394 27	0.313 31	0.249 26	0.198 52	0.158 28	0.126 34	47
48	0.620 26	0.489 36	0.386 54	0.305 67	0.242 00	0.191 81	0.152 19	0.120 90	48
49	0.614 12	0.482 13	0.378 96	0.298 22	0.234 95	0.185 32	0.146 34	0.115 69	49
50	0.608 04	0.475 00	0.371 53	0.290 94	0.228 11	0.179 05	0.140 71	0.110 71	50
n	1%	1½%	2%	2½%	3%	3½%	4%	4½%	n

TABLE 2 299

PRESENT VALUE OF 1: $\dfrac{1}{(1 + i)^n}$

n	6%	7%	8%	9%	10%	12%	16%	18%	n
1	0.943 40	0.934 58	0.925 93	0.917 43	0.909 09	0.892 86	0.862 07	0.847 46	1
2	0.890 00	0.873 44	0.857 34	0.841 68	0.826 45	0.797 19	0.743 16	0.718 18	2
3	0.839 62	0.816 30	0.793 83	0.772 18	0.751 31	0.711 78	0.640 66	0.608 63	3
4	0.792 09	0.762 90	0.735 03	0.708 43	0.683 01	0.635 52	0.552 29	0.515 79	4
5	0.747 26	0.712 99	0.680 58	0.649 93	0.620 92	0.567 43	0.476 11	0.437 11	5
6	0.704 96	0.666 34	0.630 17	0.596 27	0.564 47	0.506 63	0.410 44	0.370 43	6
7	0.665 06	0.622 75	0.583 49	0.547 03	0.513 16	0.452 35	0.353 83	0.313 93	7
8	0.627 41	0.582 01	0.540 27	0.501 87	0.466 51	0.403 88	0.305 03	0.266 04	8
9	0.591 90	0.543 93	0.500 25	0.460 43	0.424 10	0.360 61	0.262 95	0.225 46	9
10	0.558 39	0.508 35	0.463 19	0.422 41	0.385 54	0.321 97	0.226 68	0.191 07	10
11	0.526 79	0.475 09	0.428 88	0.387 53	0.350 49	0.287 48	0.195 42	0.161 92	11
12	0.496 97	0.444 01	0.397 11	0.355 53	0.318 63	0.256 68	0.168 46	0.137 22	12
13	0.468 84	0.414 96	0.367 70	0.326 18	0.289 66	0.229 17	0.145 23	0.116 29	13
14	0.442 30	0.387 82	0.340 46	0.299 25	0.263 33	0.204 62	0.125 20	0.098 55	14
15	0.417 27	0.362 45	0.315 24	0.274 54	0.239 39	0.182 70	0.107 93	0.083 52	15
16	0.393 65	0.338 73	0.291 89	0.251 87	0.217 63	0.163 12	0.093 04	0.070 78	16
17	0.371 36	0.316 57	0.270 27	0.231 07	0.197 84	0.145 65	0.080 21	0.059 98	17
18	0.350 34	0.295 86	0.250 25	0.211 99	0.179 86	0.130 04	0.069 14	0.050 83	18
19	0.330 51	0.276 51	0.231 71	0.194 49	0.163 51	0.116 11	0.059 61	0.043 08	19
20	0.311 80	0.258 42	0.214 55	0.178 43	0.148 64	0.103 67	0.051 39	0.036 51	20
21	0.294 16	0.241 51	0.198 66	0.163 70	0.135 13	0.092 56	0.044 30	0.030 94	21
22	0.277 51	0.225 71	0.183 94	0.150 18	0.122 85	0.082 64	0.038 19	0.026 22	22
23	0.261 80	0.210 95	0.170 32	0.137 78	0.111 68	0.073 79	0.032 92	0.022 22	23
24	0.246 98	0.197 15	0.157 70	0.126 40	0.101 53	0.065 88	0.028 38	0.018 83	24
25	0.233 00	0.184 25	0.146 02	0.115 97	0.092 30	0.058 82	0.024 47	0.015 96	25
26	0.219 81	0.172 20	0.135 20	0.106 39	0.083 90	0.052 52	0.021 09	0.013 52	26
27	0.207 37	0.160 93	0.125 19	0.097 61	0.076 28	0.046 89	0.018 18	0.011 46	27
28	0.195 63	0.150 40	0.115 91	0.089 55	0.069 34	0.041 87	0.015 67	0.009 71	28
29	0.184 56	0.140 56	0.107 33	0.082 15	0.063 04	0.037 38	0.013 51	0.008 23	29
30	0.174 11	0.131 37	0.099 38	0.075 37	0.057 31	0.033 38	0.011 65	0.006 98	30
31	0.164 26	0.122 77	0.092 02	0.069 15	0.052 10	0.029 80	0.010 04	0.005 91	31
32	0.154 96	0.114 74	0.085 20	0.063 44	0.047 36	0.026 61	0.008 66	0.005 01	32
33	0.146 19	0.107 23	0.078 89	0.058 20	0.043 06	0.023 76	0.007 46	0.004 25	33
34	0.137 91	0.100 22	0.073 05	0.053 39	0.039 14	0.021 21	0.006 43	0.003 60	34
35	0.130 11	0.093 66	0.067 63	0.048 99	0.035 58	0.018 94	0.005 55	0.003 05	35
36	0.122 74	0.087 54	0.062 62	0.044 94	0.032 35	0.016 91	0.004 78	0.002 58	36
37	0.115 79	0.081 81	0.057 99	0.041 23	0.029 41	0.015 10	0.004 72	0.002 19	37
38	0.109 24	0.076 46	0.053 69	0.037 83	0.026 73	0.013 48	0.003 55	0.001 86	38
39	0.103 06	0.071 46	0.049 71	0.034 70	0.024 30	0.012 04	0.003 06	0.001 57	39
40	0.097 22	0.066 78	0.046 03	0.031 84	0.022 09	0.010 75	0.002 64	0.001 33	40
41	0.091 72	0.062 41	0.042 62	0.029 21	0.020 09	0.009 60	0.002 28	0.001 13	41
42	0.086 53	0.058 33	0.039 46	0.026 80	0.018 26	0.008 57	0.001 96	0.000 96	42
43	0.081 63	0.054 51	0.036 54	0.024 58	0.016 60	0.007 65	0.001 69	0.000 81	43
44	0.077 01	0.050 95	0.033 83	0.022 55	0.015 09	0.006 83	0.001 46	0.000 69	44
45	0.072 65	0.047 61	0.031 33	0.020 69	0.013 72	0.006 10	0.001 26	0.000 58	45
46	0.068 54	0.044 50	0.029 01	0.018 98	0.012 47	0.005 45	0.001 08	0.000 49	46
47	0.064 66	0.041 59	0.026 86	0.017 42	0.011 34	0.004 86	0.000 93	0.000 42	47
48	0.061 00	0.038 87	0.024 87	0.015 98	0.010 31	0.004 34	0.000 81	0.000 36	48
49	0.057 55	0.036 32	0.023 02	0.014 66	0.009 37	0.003 88	0.000 69	0.000 30	49
50	0.054 29	0.033 94	0.021 32	0.013 45	0.008 52	0.003 46	0.000 60	0.000 26	50
n	6%	7%	8%	9%	10%	12%	16%	18%	n

TABLE 3

AMOUNT OF AN ANNUITY: $\quad s_{\overline{n}|\,i} = \dfrac{(1+i)^n - 1}{i}$

n	1%	1½%	2%	2½%	3%	3½%	4%	4½%	n
1	1.000 00	1.000 00	1.000 00	1.000 00	1.000 00	1.000 00	1.000 00	1.000 00	1
2	2.010 00	2.015 00	2.020 00	2.025 00	2.030 00	2.035 00	2.040 00	2.045 11	2
3	3.030 10	3.045 23	3.060 40	3.075 63	3.090 90	3.106 23	3.121 60	3.137 11	3
4	4.060 40	4.090 90	4.121 61	4.152 52	4.183 63	4.214 94	4.246 46	4.278 22	4
5	5.101 01	5.152 27	5.204 04	5.256 33	5.309 14	5.362 47	5.416 32	5.470 67	5
6	6.152 02	6.229 55	6.308 12	6.387 74	6.468 41	6.550 15	6.632 98	6.716 89	6
7	7.213 54	7.322 99	7.434 28	7.547 43	7.662 46	7.779 48	7.898 29	8.019 11	7
8	8.285 67	8.432 84	8.582 97	8.736 12	8.892 37	9.051 69	9.214 23	9.380 00	8
9	9.368 53	9.559 33	9.754 63	9.954 52	10.159 11	10.368 50	10.582 80	10.802 00	9
10	10.462 21	10.702 72	10.949 72	11.203 38	11.463 88	11.731 39	12.006 11	12.288 22	10
11	11.566 83	11.863 26	12.168 72	12.483 47	12.807 80	13.141 99	13.486 35	13.841 11	11
12	12.682 50	13.041 21	13.412 09	13.795 55	14.192 03	14.601 96	15.025 81	15.464 00	12
13	13.809 33	14.236 83	14.680 33	15.140 44	15.617 79	16.113 03	16.626 84	17.159 78	13
14	14.947 42	15.450 38	15.973 94	16.518 95	17.086 32	17.676 98	18.291 91	18.932 00	14
15	16.096 90	16.682 14	17.293 42	17.931 93	18.598 91	19.295 68	20.023 59	20.784 00	15
16	17.257 86	17.932 37	18.639 29	19.380 22	20.156 88	20.971 03	21.824 53	22.719 11	16
17	18.430 44	19.201 36	20.012 07	20.864 73	21.761 59	22.705 02	23.697 51	24.741 56	17
18	19.614 75	20.489 38	21.412 31	22.386 35	23.414 44	24.499 69	25.645 41	26.854 89	18
19	20.810 90	21.796 72	22.840 56	23.946 01	25.116 87	26.357 18	27.671 23	29.063 33	19
20	22.019 00	23.123 67	24.297 37	25.544 66	26.870 37	28.279 68	29.778 08	31.371 11	20
21	23.239 19	24.470 52	25.783 32	27.183 27	28.676 49	30.269 47	31.969 20	33.782 89	21
22	24.471 59	25.837 58	27.298 98	28.862 86	30.536 78	32.328 90	34.247 97	36.303 11	22
23	25.716 30	27.225 14	28.844 96	30.584 43	32.452 88	34.460 41	36.617 89	38.936 67	23
24	26.973 46	28.633 52	30.421 86	32.349 04	34.426 47	36.666 53	39.082 60	41.688 89	24
25	28.243 20	30.063 02	32.030 30	34.157 76	36.459 26	38.949 86	41.645 91	44.564 89	25
26	29.525 63	31.513 97	33.670 91	36.011 71	38.553 04	41.313 10	44.311 74	47.570 22	26
27	30.820 89	32.986 68	35.344 32	37.912 00	40.709 63	43.759 06	47.084 21	50.710 89	27
28	32.129 10	34.481 48	37.051 21	39.859 80	42.930 92	46.290 63	49.967 58	53 992 89	28
29	33.450 39	35.998 70	38.792 23	41.856 30	45.218 85	48.910 80	52.966 29	57.422 44	29
30	34.784 89	37.538 68	40.568 08	43.902 70	47.575 46	51.622 68	56.084 94	61.006 44	30
31	36.132 74	39.101 76	42.379 44	46.000 27	50.002 68	54.429 47	59.328 34	64.751 78	31
32	37.494 08	40.688 29	44.227 03	48.150 28	52.502 76	57.334 50	62.701 47	68.665 56	32
33	38.869 01	42.298 61	46.111 57	50.354 03	55.077 84	60.341 21	66.209 53	72.755 56	33
34	40.257 70	43.933 09	48.033 80	52.612 89	57.730 18	63.453 15	69.857 91	77.029 56	34
35	41.660 28	45.592 09	49.994 48	54.928 21	60.462 08	66.674 01	73.652 22	81.496 00	35
36	43.076 88	47.275 97	51.994 37	57.301 41	63.275 94	70.007 60	77.598 31	86.163 11	36
37	44.507 65	48.985 11	54.034 25	59.733 95	66.174 22	73.457 87	81.702 25	91.040 44	37
38	45.952 72	50.719 89	56.114 94	62.227 30	69.159 45	77.028 89	85.970 34	96.137 33	38
39	47.412 25	52.480 68	58.237 24	64.782 98	72.234 23	80.724 91	90.409 15	101.463 56	39
40	48.886 37	54.267 89	60.401 98	67.402 55	75.401 26	84.550 28	95.025 52	107.029 33	40
41	50.375 24	56.081 91	62.610 02	70.087 62	78 663 30	88.509 54	99.826 54	112.845 78	41
42	51.878 99	57.923 14	64.862 22	72.839 81	82.023 20	92.607 37	104.819 60	118.923 78	42
43	53.397 78	59.791 99	67.159 47	75.660 80	85.483 89	96.848 63	110.012 38	125.275 33	43
44	54.931 76	61.688 87	69.502 66	78.552 32	89.048 41	101.238 31	115.412 88	131.912 67	44
45	56.481 07	63.614 20	71.892 71	81.516 13	92.719 86	105.781 62	121.029 39	138.848 67	45
46	58.045 89	65.568 41	74.330 56	84.554 03	96.501 46	110.484 03	126.870 57	146.096 89	46
47	59.626 34	67.551 94	76.817 18	87.667 89	100.396 50	115.350 97	132.945 39	153.671 33	47
48	61.222 61	69.565 22	79.353 52	90.859 58	104.408 40	120.388 26	139.263 21	161.586 44	48
49	62.834 83	71.608 70	81.940 59	94.131 07	108.540 65	125.601 85	145.833 73	169.857 78	49
50	64.463 18	73.682 83	84.579 40	97.484 35	112.796 87	130.997 91	152.667 08	178.501 56	50
n	1%	1½%	2%	2½%	3%	3½%	4%	4½%	n

TABLE 3

301

AMOUNT OF AN ANNUITY: $\quad s_{\overline{n}|i} = \dfrac{(1 + i)^n - 1}{i}$

n	6%	7%	8%	9%	10%	12%	16%	18%	n
1	1.000 00	1.000 00	1.000 00	1.000 00	1.000 00	1.000 00	1.000 00	1.000 00	1
2	2.060 00	2.070 00	2.080 00	2.090 00	2.100 00	2.120 00	2.160 00	2.180 00	2
3	3.183 60	3.214 90	3.246 40	3.278 10	3.310 00	3.374 42	3.505 63	3.572 39	3
4	4.374 62	4.439 94	4.506 11	4.573 13	4.641 00	4.779 33	5.066 50	5.215 44	4
5	5.637 09	5.750 74	5.866 60	5.984 71	6.105 10	6.352 83	6.877 13	7.154 22	5
6	6.975 32	7.153 29	7.335 93	7.523 33	7.715 61	8.115 17	8.977 50	9.441 94	6
7	8.393 84	8.654 02	8.922 80	9.200 43	9.487 17	10.089 00	11.413 88	12.141 50	7
8	9.897 47	10.259 80	10.636 63	11.028 47	11.435 89	12.299 67	14.240 06	15.327 00	8
9	11.491 32	11.977 99	12.487 56	13.021 04	13.579 48	14.775 67	17.518 50	19.085 83	9
10	13.180 79	13.816 45	14.486 56	15.192 93	15.937 42	17.548 67	21.321 44	23.521 28	10
11	14.971 64	15.783 60	16.645 49	17.560 29	18.531 17	20.654 58	25.732 94	28.755 11	11
12	16.869 94	17.888 45	18.977 13	20.140 72	21.384 28	24.133 08	30.850 13	34.931 00	12
13	18.882 14	20.140 64	21.495 30	22.953 38	24.522 71	28.029 08	36.786 13	42.218 61	13
14	21.015 07	22.550 49	24.214 92	26.019 19	27.974 98	32.392 50	43.671 94	50.817 94	14
15	23.275 97	25.129 02	27.152 11	29.360 92	31.772 48	37.279 67	51.659 44	60.965 17	15
16	25.672 53	27.888 05	30.324 28	33.003 30	35.949 73	42.753 17	60.924 94	72.938 89	16
17	28.212 88	30.840 22	33.750 23	36.973 70	40.544 70	48.883 58	71.672 94	87.067 89	17
18	30.905 65	33.999 03	37.450 24	41.301 34	45.599 17	55.749 58	84.140 56	103.740 11	18
19	33.759 99	37.378 96	41.446 26	46.018 46	51.159 09	63.439 50	98.603 06	123.413 33	19
20	36.785 59	40.995 49	45.761 96	51.160 12	57.275 00	72.052 25	115.379 56	146.627 72	20
21	39.992 73	44.865 18	50.422 92	56.764 53	64.002 50	81.698 58	134.840 31	174.020 72	21
22	43.392 29	49.005 74	55.456 76	62.873 34	71.402 75	92.502 33	157.414 75	206.344 44	22
23	46.995 83	53.436 14	60.893 30	69.531 94	79.543 02	104.602 67	183.601 06	244.486 44	23
24	50.815 58	58.176 67	66.764 76	76.789 81	88.497 33	118.155 00	213.977 25	289.494 00	24
25	54.864 51	63.249 04	73.105 94	84.700 90	98.347 06	133.333 58	249.213 63	342.602 89	25
26	59.156 38	68.676 47	79.954 42	93.323 98	109.181 77	150.333 58	290.087 75	405.271 39	26
27	63.705 77	74.483 82	87.350 77	102.723 13	121.099 94	169.373 58	337.501 81	479.220 28	27
28	68.528 11	80.697 69	95.338 83	112.968 22	134.209 94	190.698 42	392.502 13	566.479 89	28
29	73.639 80	87.346 53	103.965 94	124.135 36	148.630 93	214.582 25	456.302 44	669.446 28	29
30	79.058 19	94.460 79	113.283 21	136.307 54	164.494 02	241.332 08	530.310 81	790.946 61	30
31	84.801 68	102.073 04	123.345 87	149.575 22	181.943 42	271.292 00	616.160 56	934.317 00	31
32	90.889 78	110.218 15	134.213 54	164.036 99	201.137 77	304.847 00	715.746 25	1 103.494 06	32
33	97.343 16	118.933 43	145.950 62	179.800 32	222.251 54	342.428 67	831.265 63	1 303.123 00	33
34	104.183 75	128.258 76	158.626 67	196.982 34	245.476 70	384.520 08	965.268 13	1 538.685 11	34
35	111.434 78	138.236 88	172.316 80	215.710 75	271.024 37	431.662 50	1 120.711 06	1 816.648 44	35
36	119.120 87	148.913 46	187.102 15	236.124 72	299.126 81	484.461 92	1 301.024 81	2 144.645 17	36
37	127.268 12	160.337 40	203.070 32	258.375 95	330.039 49	543.597 42	1 510.188 75	2 531.681 28	37
38	135.904 21	172.561 02	220.315 95	282.629 78	364.043 43	609.829 08	1 752.818 94	2 988.383 89	38
39	145.058 46	185.640 29	238.941 22	309.066 46	401.447 78	684.008 58	2 034.270 00	3 527.293 00	39
40	154.761 97	199.635 11	259.056 52	337.882 45	442.592 56	767.089 58	2 360.753 19	4 163.205 72	40
41	165.047 68	214.609 57	280.781 04	369.291 87	487.851 81	860.140 33	2 739.473 69	4 913.582 78	41
42	175.950 54	230.632 24	304.243 52	403.528 13	537.636 99	964.357 17	3 178.789 50	5 799.027 67	42
43	187.507 58	247.776 50	329.583 01	440.845 66	592.400 69	1 081.080 00	3 688.395 81	6 843.852 61	43
44	199.758 03	266.120 85	356.949 65	481.521 77	652.640 76	1 211.809 58	4 279.539 13	8 076.746 11	44
45	212.743 51	285.749 31	386.505 62	525.858 73	718.904 84	1 358.226 75	4 965.265 38	9 531.560 39	45
46	226.508 12	306.751 76	418.426 07	574.186 02	791.795 32	1 522.214 00	5 760.707 81	11 248.241 28	46
47	241.098 61	329.224 39	452.900 15	626.862 76	871.974 85	1 705.879 67	6 683.421 06	13 273.924 72	47
48	256.564 53	353.270 09	490.132 16	684.280 41	960.172 34	1 911.585 17	7 753.768 44	15 664.231 17	48
49	272.958 40	378.999 00	530.342 74	746.865 65	1 057.189 57	2 141.975 42	8 995.371 38	18 484.792 72	49
50	290.335 90	406.528 93	573.770 16	815.083 56	1 163.908 53	2 400.012 42	10 435.630 81	21 813.055 44	50
n	6%	7%	8%	9%	10%	12%	16%	18%	n

TABLE 4

THE ANNUITY THAT WILL AMOUNT TO 1: $\dfrac{1}{s_{\overline{n}|i}}$

n	1%	1½%	2%	2½%	3%	3½%	4%	4½%	n
1	1.000 00	1.000 00	1.000 00	1.000 00	1.000 00	1.000 00	1.000 00	1.000 00	1
2	0.497 51	0.496 28	0.495 05	0.493 83	0.492 61	0.491 40	0.490 20	0.488 97	2
3	0.330 02	0.328 38	0.326 75	0.325 14	0.323 53	0.321 93	0.320 35	0.318 77	3
4	0.246 28	0.244 44	0.242 62	0.240 82	0.239 03	0.237 25	0.235 49	0.233 74	4
5	0.196 04	0.194 09	0.192 16	0.190 25	0.188 35	0.186 48	0.184 63	0.182 79	5
6	0.162 55	0.160 53	0.158 53	0.156 55	0.154 60	0.152 67	0.150 76	0.148 88	6
7	0.138 63	0.136 56	0.134 51	0.132 50	0.130 51	0.128 54	0.126 61	0.124 70	7
8	0.120 69	0.118 58	0.116 51	0.114 47	0.112 46	0.110 48	0.108 53	0.106 61	8
9	0.106 74	0.104 61	0.102 52	0.100 46	0.098 43	0.096 45	0.094 49	0.092 58	9
10	0.095 58	0.093 43	0.091 33	0.089 26	0.087 23	0.085 24	0.083 29	0.081 38	10
11	0.086 45	0.084 29	0.082 18	0.080 11	0.078 08	0.076 09	0.074 15	0.072 25	11
12	0.078 85	0.076 68	0.074 56	0.072 49	0.070 46	0.068 48	0.066 55	0.064 67	12
13	0.072 41	0.070 24	0.068 12	0.066 05	0.064 03	0.062 06	0.060 14	0.058 28	13
14	0.066 90	0.064 72	0.062 60	0.060 54	0.058 53	0.056 57	0.054 67	0.052 82	14
15	0.062 12	0.059 94	0.057 83	0.055 77	0.053 77	0.051 83	0.049 94	0.048 11	15
16	0.057 94	0.055 77	0.053 65	0.051 60	0.049 61	0.047 68	0.045 82	0.044 02	16
17	0.054 26	0.052 08	0.049 97	0.047 93	0.045 95	0.044 04	0.042 20	0.040 42	17
18	0.050 98	0.048 81	0.046 70	0.044 67	0.042 71	0.040 82	0.038 99	0.037 24	18
19	0.048 05	0.045 88	0.043 78	0.041 76	0.039 81	0.037 94	0.036 14	0.034 41	19
20	0.045 42	0.043 25	0.041 16	0.039 15	0.037 22	0.035 36	0.033 58	0.031 88	20
21	0.043 03	0.040 87	0.038 78	0.036 79	0.034 87	0.033 04	0.031 28	0.029 60	21
22	0.040 86	0.038 70	0.036 63	0.034 65	0.032 75	0.030 93	0.029 20	0.027 55	22
23	0.038 89	0.036 73	0.034 67	0.032 70	0.030 81	0.029 02	0.027 31	0.025 68	23
24	0.037 07	0.034 92	0.032 87	0.030 91	0.029 05	0.027 27	0.025 59	0.023 99	24
25	0.035 41	0.033 26	0.031 22	0.029 28	0.027 43	0.025 67	0.024 01	0.022 44	25
26	0.033 87	0.031 73	0.029 70	0.027 77	0.025 94	0.024 21	0.022 57	0.021 02	26
27	0.032 45	0.030 32	0.028 29	0.026 38	0.024 56	0.022 85	0.021 24	0.019 72	27
28	0.031 11	0.029 00	0.026 99	0.025 09	0.023 29	0.021 60	0.020 01	0.018 52	28
29	0.029 90	0.027 78	0.025 78	0.023 89	0.022 11	0.020 45	0.018 88	0.017 42	29
30	0.028 75	0.026 64	0.024 65	0.022 78	0.021 02	0.019 37	0.017 83	0.016 39	30
31	0.027 68	0.025 57	0.023 60	0.021 74	0.020 00	0.018 37	0.016 86	0.015 44	31
32	0.026 66	0.024 58	0.022 61	0.020 77	0.019 05	0.017 44	0.015 95	0.014 69	32
33	0.025 73	0.023 64	0.021 69	0.019 86	0.018 16	0.016 57	0.015 10	0.013 75	33
34	0.024 84	0.022 76	0.020 82	0.019 01	0.017 32	0.015 76	0.014 31	0.012 98	34
35	0.024 00	0.021 93	0.020 00	0.018 21	0.016 54	0.015 00	0.013 58	0.012 27	35
36	0.023 21	0.021 15	0.019 23	0.017 45	0.015 80	0.014 28	0.012 89	0.011 61	36
37	0.022 47	0.020 41	0.018 51	0.016 74	0.015 11	0.013 61	0.012 24	0.010 98	37
38	0.021 76	0.019 72	0.017 82	0.016 07	0.014 46	0.012 98	0.011 63	0.010 40	38
39	0.021 09	0.019 05	0.017 17	0.015 44	0.013 84	0.012 39	0.011 06	0.009 86	39
40	0.020 46	0.018 43	0.016 56	0.014 84	0.013 26	0.011 83	0.010 52	0.009 34	40
41	0.019 85	0.017 83	0.015 97	0.014 27	0.012 71	0.011 30	0.010 02	0.008 86	41
42	0.019 28	0.017 26	0.015 42	0.013 73	0.012 19	0.010 80	0.009 54	0.008 41	42
43	0.018 73	0.016 72	0.014 89	0.013 22	0.011 70	0.010 33	0.009 09	0.007 98	43
44	0.018 20	0.016 21	0.014 39	0.012 73	0.011 23	0.009 88	0.008 66	0.007 58	44
45	0.017 71	0.015 72	0.013 91	0.012 27	0.010 79	0.009 45	0.008 26	0.007 20	45
46	0.017 23	0.015 25	0.013 45	0.011 83	0.010 36	0.009 05	0.007 88	0.006 85	46
47	0.016 77	0.014 80	0.013 02	0.011 41	0.009 96	0.008 67	0.007 52	0.006 51	47
48	0.016 33	0.014 38	0.012 60	0.011 01	0.009 58	0.008 31	0.007 18	0.006 19	48
49	0.015 91	0.013 96	0.012 20	0.010 62	0.009 21	0.007 96	0.006 86	0.005 89	49
50	0.015 51	0.013 57	0.011 82	0.010 26	0.008 87	0.007 63	0.006 55	0.005 60	50
n	1%	1½%	2%	2½%	3%	3½%	4%	4½%	n

n	6%	7%	8%	9%	10%	12%	16%	18%	n
1	1.000 00	1.000 00	1.000 00	1.000 00	1.000 00	1.000 00	1.000 00	1.000 00	1
2	0.485 44	0.483 09	0.480 77	0.478 47	0.476 19	0.471 70	0.462 96	0.458 72	2
3	0.314 11	0.311 05	0.308 03	0.305 05	0.302 11	0.296 35	0.285 26	0.279 03	3
4	0.228 59	0.225 23	0.221 92	0.218 67	0.215 47	0.209 23	0.197 37	0.191 74	4
5	0.177 40	0.173 89	0.170 46	0.167 09	0.163 80	0.157 41	0.145 41	0.139 78	5
6	0.143 86	0.139 80	0.136 32	0.132 92	0.129 61	0.123 23	0.111 39	0.105 91	6
7	0.119 14	0.115 55	0.112 07	0.108 69	0.105 41	0.099 12	0.087 61	0.082 36	7
8	0.101 04	0.097 47	0.094 01	0.090 67	0.087 44	0.081 30	0.070 22	0.065 24	8
9	0.087 02	0.083 49	0.080 08	0.076 80	0.073 64	0.067 68	0.057 08	0.052 40	9
10	0.075 87	0.072 38	0.069 03	0.065 82	0.062 75	0.056 98	0.046 90	0.042 51	10
11	0.066 79	0.063 36	0.060 08	0.056 95	0.053 96	0.048 42	0.038 86	0.034 78	11
12	0.059 28	0.055 90	0.052 70	0.049 65	0.046 76	0.041 44	0.032 42	0.028 63	12
13	0.052 96	0.049 65	0.046 52	0.043 57	0.040 78	0.035 68	0.027 18	0.023 69	13
14	0.047 58	0.044 34	0.041 30	0.038 43	0.035 75	0.030 87	0.022 90	0.019 68	14
15	0.042 96	0.039 79	0.036 83	0.034 06	0.031 47	0.026 82	0.019 36	0.016 40	15
16	0.038 95	0.035 86	0.032 98	0.030 30	0.027 82	0.023 39	0.016 41	0.013 71	16
17	0.035 44	0.032 43	0.029 63	0.027 05	0.024 66	0.020 46	0.013 95	0.011 49	17
18	0.032 36	0.029 41	0.026 70	0.024 21	0.021 93	0.017 94	0.011 89	0.009 64	18
19	0.029 62	0.026 75	0.024 13	0.021 73	0.019 55	0.015 76	0.010 14	0.008 10	19
20	0.027 18	0.024 39	0.021 85	0.019 55	0.017 46	0.013 88	0.008 67	0.006 82	20
21	0.025 00	0.022 29	0.019 83	0.017 62	0.015 62	0.012 24	0.007 42	0.005 75	21
22	0.023 05	0.020 41	0.018 03	0.015 91	0.014 01	0.010 81	0.006 35	0.004 85	22
23	0.021 28	0.018 71	0.016 42	0.014 38	0.012 57	0.009 56	0.005 45	0.004 09	23
24	0.019 68	0.017 19	0.014 98	0.013 02	0.011 30	0.008 46	0.004 67	0.003 45	24
25	0.018 23	0.015 81	0.013 68	0.011 81	0.010 17	0.007 50	0.004 01	0.002 92	25
26	0.016 90	0.014 56	0.012 51	0.010 72	0.009 16	0.006 65	0.003 45	0.002 47	26
27	0.015 70	0.013 43	0.011 45	0.009 73	0.008 26	0.005 90	0.002 96	0.002 09	27
28	0.014 59	0.012 39	0.010 49	0.008 85	0.007 45	0.005 24	0.002 55	0.001 77	28
29	0.013 58	0.011 45	0.009 62	0.008 06	0.006 73	0.004 66	0.002 19	0.001 49	29
30	0.012 65	0.010 59	0.008 83	0.007 34	0.006 08	0.004 14	0.001 89	0.001 26	30
31	0.011 79	0.009 80	0.008 11	0.006 69	0.005 50	0.003 69	0.001 62	0.001 07	31
32	0.011 00	0.009 07	0.007 45	0.006 10	0.004 97	0.003 28	0.001 40	0.000 91	32
33	0.010 27	0.008 41	0.006 85	0.005 56	0.004 50	0.002 92	0.001 20	0.000 77	33
34	0.009 60	0.007 80	0.006 30	0.005 08	0.004 07	0.002 60	0.001 04	0.000 65	34
35	0.008 97	0.007 23	0.005 80	0.004 64	0.003 69	0.002 32	0.000 89	0.000 55	35
36	0.008 39	0.006 72	0.005 34	0.004 24	0.003 34	0.002 06	0.000 77	0.000 47	36
37	0.007 86	0.006 24	0.004 92	0.003 87	0.003 03	0.001 84	0.000 66	0.000 40	37
38	0.007 36	0.005 80	0.004 54	0.003 54	0.002 75	0.001 64	0.000 57	0.000 34	38
39	0.006 89	0.005 39	0.004 19	0.003 24	0.002 49	0.001 46	0.000 49	0.000 28	39
40	0.006 46	0.005 01	0.003 86	0.002 96	0.002 26	0.001 30	0.000 42	0.000 24	40
41	0.006 06	0.004 66	0.003 56	0.002 71	0.002 05	0.001 16	0.000 37	0.000 20	41
42	0.005 68	0.004 34	0.003 29	0.002 48	0.001 86	0.001 04	0.000 32	0.000 17	42
43	0.005 33	0.004 04	0.003 03	0.002 27	0.001 69	0.000 93	0.000 27	0.000 15	43
44	0.005 01	0.003 76	0.002 80	0.002 08	0.001 53	0.000 83	0.000 24	0.000 12	44
45	0.004 70	0.003 50	0.002 59	0.001 90	0.001 39	0.000 74	0.000 20	0.000 11	45
46	0.004 41	0.003 26	0.002 39	0.001 74	0.001 26	0.000 66	0.000 17	0.000 09	46
47	0.004 15	0.003 04	0.002 21	0.001 60	0.001 15	0.000 59	0.000 15	0.000 08	47
48	0.003 90	0.002 83	0.002 04	0.001 46	0.001 04	0.000 52	0.000 13	0.000 06	48
49	0.003 66	0.002 64	0.001 89	0.001 34	0.000 95	0.000 47	0.000 11	0.000 05	49
50	0.003 44	0.002 46	0.001 74	0.001 23	0.000 86	0.000 42	0.000 10	0.000 05	50
n	6%	7%	8%	9%	10%	12%	16%	18%	n

TABLE 5

PRESENT VALUE OF AN ANNUITY: $a_{\overline{n}|\,i} = \dfrac{1-(1+i)^{-n}}{i}$

n	1%	1½%	2%	2½%	3%	3½%	4%	4½%	n
1	0.990 10	0.985 22	0.980 39	0.975 61	0.970 87	0.966 18	0.961 54	0.056 89	1
2	1.970 46	1.955 88	1.941 56	1.927 42	1.913 47	1.899 69	1.886 09	1.872 67	2
3	2.940 99	2.912 20	2.883 88	2.856 02	2.828 61	2.801 64	2.775 09	2.749 11	3
4	3.901 97	3.854 38	3.807 73	3.761 97	3.717 10	3.673 08	3.629 90	3.587 56	4
5	4.853 43	4.782 65	4.713 46	4.645 83	4.579 71	4.515 05	4.451 82	4.390 00	5
6	5.795 48	5.697 19	5.601 43	5.508 13	5.417 19	5.328 55	5.242 14	5.157 78	6
7	6.728 19	6.598 21	6.471 99	6.349 39	6.230 28	6.114 54	6.002 05	5.892 67	7
8	7.651 68	7.485 93	7.325 48	7.170 14	7.019 69	6.873 96	6.732 74	6.595 78	8
9	8.566 02	8.360 52	8.162 24	7.970 87	7.786 11	7.607 69	7.435 33	7.268 67	9
10	9.471 30	9.222 18	8.982 59	8.752 06	8.530 20	8.316 61	8.110 90	7.912 67	10
11	10.367 63	10.071 12	9.786 85	9.514 20	9.252 66	9.001 55	8.760 48	8.528 89	11
12	11.255 08	10.907 51	10.575 34	10.257 76	9.954 00	9.663 33	9.385 07	9.118 67	12
13	12.133 74	11.731 53	11.348 37	10.983 18	10.634 96	10.302 74	9.985 65	9.682 89	13
14	13.003 70	12.543 38	12.106 25	11.690 91	11.296 07	10.920 52	10.563 12	10.222 89	14
15	13.865 05	13.343 23	12.849 26	12.381 38	11.937 94	11.517 41	11.118 39	10.739 56	15
16	14.717 87	14.131 26	13.577 71	13.055 00	12.561 10	12.094 12	11.652 30	11.234 00	16
17	15.562 25	14.907 65	14.291 87	13.712 20	13.166 12	12.651 32	12.165 67	11.707 11	17
18	16.398 27	15.672 56	14.992 03	14.353 36	13.753 51	13.189 68	12.659 30	12.160 00	18
19	17.226 01	16.426 17	15.678 46	14.978 89	14.323 80	13.709 84	13.133 94	12.593 33	19
20	18.045 55	17.168 64	16.351 43	15.589 16	14.877 47	14.212 40	13.590 33	13.007 78	20
21	18.856 98	17.900 14	17.011 21	16.184 55	15.415 02	14.697 97	14.029 16	13.404 67	21
22	19.660 38	18.620 82	17.658 05	16.765 41	15.936 92	15.167 12	14.451 12	13.784 44	22
23	20.455 82	19.330 86	18.292 20	17.332 11	16.443 61	15.620 41	14.856 84	14.147 78	23
24	21.243 39	20.030 41	18.913 93	17.884 99	16.935 54	16.058 37	15.246 96	14.495 33	24
25	22.023 16	20.719 61	19.523 46	18.424 38	17.413 15	16.481 51	15.622 08	14.828 22	25
26	22.795 20	21.398 63	20.121 04	18.950 61	17.876 84	16.890 35	15.982 77	15.146 67	26
27	23.559 61	22.067 62	20.706 90	19.464 01	18.327 03	17.285 36	16.329 59	15.451 33	27
28	24.316 44	22.726 72	21.281 27	19.964 89	18.764 11	17.667 02	16.663 06	15.742 89	28
29	25.065 79	23.376 08	21.844 38	20.453 50	19.188 45	18.035 77	16.983 71	16.021 78	29
30	25.807 71	24.015 84	22.396 46	20.930 23	19.600 44	18.392 05	17.292 03	16.288 89	30
31	26.542 29	24.646 15	22.937 70	21.395 40	20.000 43	18.736 28	17.588 49	16.550 89	31
32	27.269 59	25.267 14	23.468 34	21.849 18	20.388 77	19.068 87	17.873 55	16.788 89	32
33	27.989 69	25.878 95	23.988 56	22.291 81	20.765 79	19.390 21	18.147 65	17.022 89	33
34	28.702 67	26.481 73	24.498 59	22.723 79	21.131 84	19.700 68	18.411 20	17.246 67	34
35	29.408 58	27.075 59	24.998 62	23.145 16	21.487 22	20.000 66	18.664 61	17.460 89	35
36	30.107 51	27.660 68	25.488 84	23.556 25	21.832 25	20.290 49	18.908 28	17.666 00	36
37	30.799 51	28.237 13	25.969 45	23.957 32	22.167 24	20.570 53	19.142 58	17.862 22	37
38	31.484 66	28.805 05	26.440 64	24.348 60	22.492 46	20.841 09	19.367 86	18.050 00	38
39	32.163 03	29.364 58	26.902 59	24.730 34	22.808 22	21.102 50	19.584 48	18.229 56	39
40	32.834 69	29.915 85	27.355 48	25.102 78	23.114 77	21.355 07	19.792 77	18.401 56	40
41	33.499 69	30.458 96	27.799 49	25.466 12	23.412 40	21.599 10	19.993 05	18.566 00	41
42	34.158 11	30.994 05	28.234 79	25.820 61	23.701 36	21.834 88	20.185 63	18.723 56	42
43	34.810 01	31.521 23	28.661 56	26.166 45	23.981 90	22.062 69	20.370 79	18.874 22	43
44	35.455 45	32.040 62	29.079 96	26.503 85	24.254 27	22.282 79	20.548 84	19.018 44	44
45	36.094 51	32.552 34	29.490 16	26.833 02	24.518 71	22.495 45	20.720 04	19.156 22	45
46	36.727 24	33.056 49	29.892 31	27.154 17	24.775 45	22.700 92	20.884 65	19.288 44	46
47	37.353 70	22.553 19	30.286 58	27.467 48	25.024 71	22.899 44	21.042 94	19.414 67	47
48	37.973 96	34.042 55	30.673 12	27.773 15	25.266 71	23.091 24	21.195 13	19.535 56	48
49	38.588 08	34.524 68	31.052 08	28.071 37	25.501 66	23.276 56	21.341 47	19.651 33	49
50	39.196 12	34.999 69	31.423 61	28.362 31	25.729 76	23.455 62	21.482 18	19.762 00	50
n	1%	1½%	2%	2½%	3%	3½%	4%	4½%	n

TABLE 5

305

PRESENT VALUE OF AN ANNUITY: $a_{\overline{n}|i} = \dfrac{1 - (1+i)^{-n}}{i}$

n	6%	7%	8%	9%	10%	12%	16%	18%	n
1	0.943 40	0.934 58	0.925 93	0.917 43	0.909 09	0.892 83	0.862 06	0.847 44	1
2	1.833 39	1.808 02	1.783 26	1.759 11	1.735 54	1.690 08	1.605 25	1.565 67	2
3	2.673 01	2.624 32	2.577 10	2.531 29	2.486 85	2.401 83	2.245 88	2.174 28	3
4	3.465 11	3.387 21	3.312 13	3.239 72	3.169 87	3.037 33	2.798 19	2.690 06	4
5	4.212 36	4.100 20	3.992 71	3.889 65	3.790 79	3.604 75	3.274 31	3.127 17	5
6	4.917 32	4.766 54	4.622 88	4.485 92	4.355 26	4.111 42	3.684 75	3.497 61	6
7	5.582 38	5.389 29	5.206 37	5.032 95	4.868 42	4.563 75	4.038 56	3.811 50	7
8	6.209 79	5.971 30	5.746 64	5.534 82	5.334 93	4.967 67	4.343 56	4.077 56	8
9	6.801 69	6.515 23	6.246 89	5.995 25	5.759 02	5.328 25	4.606 56	4.303 00	9
10	7.360 09	7.023 58	6.710 08	6.417 66	6.144 57	5.650 25	4.833 25	4.494 06	10
11	7.886 87	7.498 67	7.138 96	6.805 19	6.495 06	5.937 67	5.028 63	4.656 00	11
12	8.383 84	7.942 69	7.536 08	7.160 73	6.813 69	6.194 33	5.197 13	4.793 22	12
13	8.852 68	8.357 65	7.903 78	7.486 90	7.103 36	6.423 58	5.342 31	4.909 50	13
14	9.294 98	8.745 47	8.244 24	7.786 15	7.366 69	6.628 17	5.467 50	5.008 06	14
15	9.712 25	9.107 91	8.559 48	8.060 69	7.606 08	6.810 83	5.575 44	5.091 56	15
16	10.105 90	9.446 65	8.851 37	8.312 56	7.823 71	6.973 98	5.668 50	5.162 33	16
17	10.477 26	9.763 22	9.121 64	8.543 63	8.021 55	7.119 58	5.748 69	5.222 33	17
18	10.827 60	10.059 09	9.371 89	8.755 63	8.201 41	7.249 67	5.817 88	5.273 17	18
19	11.158 12	10.335 60	9.603 60	8.950 11	8.364 92	7.365 75	5.877 44	5.316 22	19
20	11.469 02	10.594 01	9.818 15	9.128 55	8.513 56	7.469 42	5.928 81	5.352 72	20
21	11.764 08	10.835 53	10.016 80	9.292 24	8.648 69	7.562 00	5.973 13	5.383 67	21
22	12.041 58	11.061 24	10.200 74	9.442 43	8.771 54	7.644 67	6.011 31	5.409 89	22
23	12.303 38	11.272 19	10.371 06	9.580 21	8.883 22	7.718 42	6.044 25	5.432 11	23
24	12.550 36	11.469 33	10.528 76	9.706 61	8.984 74	7.784 33	6.072 63	5.450 94	24
25	12.783 36	11.653 58	10.674 78	9.822 58	9.077 04	7.843 17	6.097 06	5.466 89	25
26	13.003 17	11.825 78	10.809 98	9.928 97	9.160 95	7.895 67	6.118 19	5.480 44	26
27	13.210 53	11.986 71	10.935 16	10.026 58	9.237 22	7.942 58	6.136 38	5.491 89	27
28	13.406 16	12.137 11	11.051 08	10.116 13	9.306 57	7.984 42	6.152 06	5.501 61	28
29	13.590 72	12.277 67	11.158 41	10.198 28	9.369 61	8.021 83	6.165 56	5.509 83	29
30	13.764 83	12.409 04	11.257 78	10.273 65	9.426 91	8.055 17	6.177 19	5.516 78	30
31	13.929 09	12.531 81	11.349 80	10.342 80	9.479 01	8.085 00	6.187 25	5.522 72	31
32	14.084 04	12.646 56	11.435 00	10.406 24	9.526 38	8.111 58	6.195 88	5.527 72	32
33	14.230 23	12.753 79	11.513 89	10.464 44	9.569 43	8.135 33	6.203 88	5.531 94	33
34	14.368 14	12.854 01	11.586 93	10.517 84	9.608 57	8.156 58	6.209 81	5.535 56	34
35	14.498 25	12.947 67	11.654 57	10.566 82	9.644 16	8.175 50	6.215 31	5.538 61	35
36	14.620 99	13.035 21	11.717 19	10.611 76	9.676 51	8.192 42	6.220 13	5.541 22	36
37	14.736 78	13.117 02	11.775 18	10.652 99	9.705 92	8.207 50	6.224 25	5.543 39	37
38	14.846 02	13.193 47	11.828 87	10.690 82	9.732 65	8.221 00	6.227 81	5.545 22	38
39	14.949 07	13.264 93	11.878 58	10.725 52	9.756 96	8.233 00	6.230 88	5.546 83	39
40	15.046 30	13.331 71	11.924 61	10.757 36	9.779 05	8.243 75	6.233 50	5.548 17	40
41	15.138 02	13.394 12	11.967 23	10.786 57	9.799 14	8.253 33	6.235 75	5.549 28	41
42	15.224 54	13.452 45	12.006 70	10.813 37	9.817 40	8.261 92	6.237 75	5.550 22	42
43	15.306 17	13.506 96	12.043 24	10.837 95	9.834 00	8.269 58	6.239 44	5.551 06	43
44	15.383 18	13.557 91	12.077 07	10.860 51	9.849 09	8.276 42	6.240 88	5.551 72	44
45	15.455 83	13.605 52	12.108 40	10.881 20	9.862 81	8.282 50	6.242 13	5.552 33	45
46	15.524 37	13.650 02	12.137 41	10.900 18	9.875 28	8.287 92	6.243 25	5.552 83	46
47	15.589 03	13.691 61	12.164 27	10.917 60	9.886 62	8.292 83	6.244 19	5.553 22	47
48	15.650 03	13.730 47	12.189 14	10.933 58	9.896 93	8.297 17	6.244 94	5.553 56	48
49	15.707 57	13.766 80	12.212 16	10.948 23	9.906 30	8.301 00	6.245 69	5.553 89	49
50	15.761 86	13.800 75	12.233 48	10.961 68	9.914 81	8.304 50	6.246 25	5.554 11	50
n	6%	7%	8%	9%	10%	12%	16%	18%	n

TABLE 6   THE ANNUITY THAT 1 WILL BUY: $\dfrac{1}{(a_{\overline{n}|i})} = (a_{\overline{n}|i})^{-1} = (s_{\overline{n}|i})^{-1} + i$

n	1%	1½%	2%	2½%	3%	3½%	4%	4½%	n
1	1.010 00	1.015 00	1.020 00	1.025 00	1.030 00	1.035 00	1.040 00	1.045 05	1
2	0.507 51	0.511 28	0.515 05	0.518 83	0.522 61	0.526 40	0.530 20	0.534 00	2
3	0.340 02	0.343 38	0.346 75	0.350 14	0.353 53	0.356 93	0.360 35	0.363 75	3
4	0.256 28	0.259 44	0.262 62	0.265 82	0.269 03	0.272 25	0.275 49	0.278 74	4
5	0.206 04	0.209 09	0.212 16	0.215 25	0.218 35	0.221 48	0.224 63	0.227 79	5
6	0.172 55	0.175 53	0.178 53	0.181 55	0.184 60	0.187 67	0.190 76	0.193 88	6
7	0.148 63	0.151 56	0.154 51	0.157 50	0.160 51	0.163 54	0.166 61	0.169 70	7
8	0.130 69	0.133 58	0.136 51	0.139 47	0.142 46	0.145 48	0.148 53	0.151 61	8
9	0.116 74	0.119 61	0.122 52	0.125 46	0.128 43	0.131 45	0.134 49	0.137 58	9
10	0.105 58	0.108 43	0.111 33	0.114 26	0.117 23	0.120 24	0.123 29	0.126 38	10
11	0.096 45	0.099 29	0.102 18	0.105 10	0.108 08	0.111 09	0.114 15	0.117 25	11
12	0.088 85	0.091 68	0.094 56	0.097 49	0.100 46	0.103 48	0.106 55	0.109 67	12
13	0.082 41	0.085 24	0.088 12	0.091 05	0.094 03	0.097 06	0.100 14	0.103 28	13
14	0.076 90	0.079 72	0.082 60	0.085 54	0.088 53	0.091 57	0.094 67	0.097 82	14
15	0.072 12	0.074 94	0.077 83	0.080 77	0.083 77	0.086 83	0.089 94	0.093 11	15
16	0.067 94	0.070 77	0.073 65	0.076 60	0.079 61	0.082 68	0.085 82	0.089 02	16
17	0.064 26	0.067 08	0.069 97	0.072 93	0.075 95	0.079 04	0.082 20	0.085 42	17
18	0.060 98	0.063 81	0.066 70	0.069 67	0.072 71	0.075 82	0.078 99	0.082 24	18
19	0.058 05	0.060 88	0.063 78	0.066 76	0.069 81	0.072 94	0.076 14	0.079 41	19
20	0.055 42	0.058 25	0.061 16	0.064 15	0.067 22	0.070 36	0.073 58	0.076 88	20
21	0.053 03	0.055 87	0.058 78	0.061 79	0.064 87	0.068 04	0.071 28	0.074 60	21
22	0.050 86	0.053 70	0.056 63	0.059 65	0.062 75	0.065 93	0.069 20	0.072 55	22
23	0.048 89	0.051 73	0.054 67	0.057 70	0.060 81	0.064 02	0.067 31	0.070 68	23
24	0.047 07	0.049 92	0.052 87	0.055 91	0.059 05	0.062 27	0.065 59	0.068 99	24
25	0.045 41	0.048 26	0.051 22	0.054 28	0.057 43	0.060 67	0.064 01	0.067 44	25
26	0.043 87	0.046 73	0.049 70	0.052 77	0.055 94	0.059 21	0.062 57	0.066 02	26
27	0.042 45	0.045 32	0.048 29	0.051 38	0.054 56	0.057 85	0.061 24	0.064 72	27
28	0.041 12	0.044 00	0.046 99	0.050 09	0.053 29	0.056 60	0.060 01	0.063 52	28
29	0.039 90	0.042 78	0.045 78	0.048 89	0.052 11	0.055 45	0.058 88	0.062 42	29
30	0.038 75	0.041 64	0.044 65	0.047 78	0.051 02	0.054 37	0.057 83	0.061 39	30
31	0.037 68	0.040 57	0.043 60	0.046 74	0.050 00	0.053 37	0.056 86	0.060 42	31
32	0.036 67	0.039 58	0.042 61	0.045 77	0.049 05	0.052 44	0.055 95	0.059 56	32
33	0.035 73	0.038 64	0.041 69	0.044 86	0.048 16	0.051 57	0.055 10	0.058 74	33
34	0.034 84	0.037 76	0.040 82	0.044 01	0.047 32	0.050 76	0.054 31	0.057 98	34
35	0.034 00	0.036 93	0.040 00	0.043 21	0.046 54	0.050 00	0.053 58	0.057 27	35
36	0.033 21	0.036 15	0.039 23	0.042 45	0.045 80	0.049 28	0.052 89	0.056 61	36
37	0.032 47	0.035 41	0.038 51	0.041 74	0.045 11	0.048 61	0.052 24	0.055 98	37
38	0.031 76	0.034 72	0.037 82	0.041 07	0.044 46	0.047 98	0.051 63	0.055 40	38
39	0.031 09	0.034 05	0.037 17	0.040 44	0.043 84	0.047 39	0.051 06	0.054 86	39
40	0.030 46	0.033 43	0.036 56	0.039 84	0.043 26	0.046 83	0.050 52	0.054 34	40
41	0.029 85	0.032 83	0.035 97	0.039 27	0.042 71	0.046 30	0.050 02	0.053 86	41
42	0.029 28	0.032 26	0.035 42	0.038 73	0.042 19	0.045 80	0.049 54	0.053 41	42
43	0.028 73	0.031 72	0.034 89	0.038 22	0.041 70	0.045 33	0.049 09	0.052 98	43
44	0.028 20	0.031 21	0.034 39	0.037 73	0.041 23	0.044 88	0.048 66	0.052 58	44
45	0.027 71	0.030 72	0.033 91	0.037 27	0.040 79	0.044 45	0.048 26	0.052 20	45
46	0.027 23	0.030 25	0.033 45	0.036 83	0.040 36	0.044 05	0.047 88	0.051 85	46
47	0.026 77	0.029 80	0.033 02	0.036 41	0.039 96	0.043 67	0.047 52	0.051 51	47
48	0.026 33	0.029 38	0.032 60	0.036 01	0.039 58	0.043 31	0.047 18	0.051 19	48
49	0.025 91	0.028 96	0.032 20	0.035 62	0.039 21	0.042 96	0.046 86	0.050 89	49
50	0.025 51	0.028 57	0.031 82	0.035 26	0.038 87	0.042 63	0.046 55	0.050 60	50
n	1%	1½%	2%	2½%	3%	3½%	4%	4½%	n

TABLE 6

THE ANNUITY THAT 1 WILL BUY: $\dfrac{1}{(a_{\overline{n}|i})} = (a_{\overline{n}|i})^{-1} = (s_{\overline{n}|i})^{-1} + i$

n	6%	7%	8%	9%	10%	12%	16%	18%	n
1	1.060 00	1.070 00	1.080 00	1.090 00	1.100 00	1.120 03	1.160 01	1.180 03	1
2	0.545 44	0.553 09	0.560 77	0.568 47	0.576 19	0.591 69	0.622 96	0.638 70	2
3	0.374 11	0.381 05	0.388 03	0.395 05	0.402 11	0.416 35	0.445 26	0.459 92	3
4	0.288 59	0.295 23	0.301 92	0.308 67	0.315 47	0.329 24	0.357 37	0.440 72	4
5	0.237 40	0.243 89	0.250 46	0.257 09	0.263 80	0.277 41	0.305 41	0.319 78	5
6	0.203 36	0.209 80	0.216 32	0.222 92	0.229 61	0.243 22	0.271 39	0.285 91	6
7	0.179 14	0.185 55	0.192 07	0.198 69	0.205 41	0.219 12	0.247 61	0.262 36	7
8	0.161 04	0.167 47	0.174 01	0.180 67	0.187 44	0.201 30	0.230 23	0.245 25	8
9	0.147 02	0.153 49	0.160 08	0.166 80	0.173 64	0.187 68	0.217 08	0.232 40	9
10	0.135 87	0.142 38	0.149 03	0.155 82	0.162 75	0.176 98	0.206 90	0.222 52	10
11	0.126 79	0.133 36	0.140 08	0.146 95	0.153 96	0.168 42	0.198 86	0.214 78	11
12	0.119 28	0.125 90	0.132 70	0.139 65	0.146 76	0.161 44	0.192 41	0.208 63	12
13	0.112 96	0.119 65	0.126 52	0.133 57	0.140 78	0.155 68	0.187 19	0.203 69	13
14	0.107 58	0.114 34	0.121 30	0.128 43	0.135 75	0.150 87	0.182 90	0.199 68	14
15	0.102 96	0.109 79	0.116 83	0.124 06	0.131 47	0.146 82	0.179 36	0.196 40	15
16	0.098 95	0.105 86	0.112 98	0.120 30	0.127 82	0.143 39	0.176 41	0.193 71	16
17	0.095 44	0.102 43	0.109 63	0.117 05	0.124 66	0.140 46	0.173 95	0.191 49	17
18	0.092 36	0.099 41	0.106 70	0.114 21	0.121 93	0.137 94	0.171 88	0.189 64	18
19	0.089 62	0.096 75	0.104 13	0.111 73	0.119 55	0.135 76	0.170 14	0.188 10	19
20	0.087 18	0.094 39	0.101 85	0.109 55	0.117 46	0.133 88	0.168 67	0.186 82	20
21	0.085 00	0.092 29	0.099 83	0.107 62	0.115 62	0.132 24	0.167 42	0.185 75	21
22	0.083 05	0.090 41	0.098 03	0.105 91	0.114 01	0.130 81	0.166 35	0.184 85	22
23	0.081 28	0.088 71	0.096 42	0.104 38	0.112 57	0.129 56	0.165 45	0.184 09	23
24	0.079 68	0.087 19	0.094 98	0.103 02	0.111 30	0.128 46	0.164 67	0.183 46	24
25	0.078 23	0.085 81	0.093 68	0.101 81	0.110 17	0.127 50	0.164 01	0.182 92	25
26	0.076 90	0.084 56	0.092 51	0.100 72	0.109 16	0.126 65	0.163 45	0.182 47	26
27	0.075 70	0.083 43	0.091 45	0.099 73	0.108 26	0.125 90	0.162 96	0.182 09	27
28	0.074 59	0.082 30	0.090 49	0.098 85	0.107 45	0.125 24	0.162 55	0.181 76	28
29	0.073 58	0.081 45	0.089 62	0.098 06	0.106 73	0.124 66	0.162 19	0.181 49	29
30	0.072 65	0.080 59	0.088 83	0.097 34	0.106 08	0.124 14	0.161 89	0.181 27	30
31	0.071 79	0.079 80	0.088 11	0.096 69	0.105 50	0.123 69	0.161 62	0.181 07	31
32	0.071 00	0.079 07	0.087 45	0.096 10	0.104 97	0.123 28	0.161 40	0.180 91	32
33	0.070 27	0.078 41	0.086 85	0.095 56	0.104 50	0.122 92	0.161 20	0.180 77	33
34	0.069 60	0.077 80	0.086 31	0.095 08	0.104 07	0.122 60	0.161 04	0.180 65	34
35	0.068 97	0.077 23	0.085 80	0.094 64	0.103 69	0.122 32	0.160 89	0.180 55	35
36	0.068 39	0.076 72	0.085 34	0.094 24	0.103 34	0.122 06	0.160 77	0.180 47	36
37	0.067 86	0.076 24	0.084 92	0.093 87	0.103 03	0.121 84	0.160 66	0.180 40	37
38	0.067 36	0.075 80	0.084 54	0.093 54	0.102 75	0.121 64	0.160 57	0.180 34	38
39	0.066 89	0.075 39	0.084 19	0.093 24	0.102 49	0.121 46	0.160 49	0.180 28	39
40	0.066 46	0.075 01	0.083 86	0.092 96	0.102 26	0.121 30	0.160 42	0.180 24	40
41	0.066 06	0.074 66	0.083 56	0.092 71	0.102 05	0.121 16	0.160 37	0.180 20	41
42	0.065 68	0.074 34	0.083 29	0.092 48	0.101 86	0.121 04	0.160 31	0.180 17	42
43	0.065 33	0.074 04	0.083 03	0.092 27	0.101 69	0.120 93	0.160 27	0.180 15	43
44	0.065 01	0.073 76	0.082 80	0.092 08	0.101 53	0.120 83	0.160 23	0.180 12	44
45	0.064 70	0.073 50	0.082 59	0.091 90	0.101 39	0.120 74	0.160 20	0.180 11	45
46	0.064 41	0.073 26	0.082 39	0.091 74	0.101 26	0.120 66	0.160 17	0.180 09	46
47	0.064 15	0.073 04	0.082 21	0.091 60	0.101 15	0.120 59	0.160 15	0.180 08	47
48	0.063 90	0.072 83	0.082 04	0.091 46	0.101 04	0.120 52	0.160 13	0.180 07	48
49	0.063 66	0.072 64	0.081 89	0.091 34	0.100 95	0.120 47	0.160 11	0.180 05	49
50	0.063 44	0.072 46	0.081 74	0.091 23	0.100 86	0.120 42	0.160 10	0.180 05	50
n	6%	7%	8%	9%	10%	12%	16%	18%	n

ANSWERS

EXERCISE 1.1, page 5

1. (a) 211   (b) 341   (c) 88

2. (a) 2 319   (b) 3 462   (c) 798

3. (a) 2 239   (b) 1 199   (c) 2 174

4. (a) 6 442   (b) 7 247   (c) 5 448

5. (a) 1 405   (b) 734   (c) 1 222

6. (a) 994 003 735
     (b) 1 851 738 101

7. (a) 1 924   (b) 1 880   (c) 2 064

8. (a) 1 300 060 494
     (b) 128 312 564
     (c) 1 794 610 938

EXERCISE 1.2, page 9

1. (a) 248   (b) 155   (c) 202

2. (a) 3 651   (b) 996   (c) 2 220

3. (a) 2 668   (b) 2 168   (c) 1 686

4. (a) 5 667   (b) 6 389   (c) 7 024

5. (a) 728   (b) 1 255   (c) 1 261

6. (a) 24 314 058
     (b) 1 188 693 562

7. (a) 2 891   (b) 1 938   (c) 2 922

8. (a) 921 706 353
     (b) 679 579 040
     (c) 522 719 178

EXERCISE 1.3, page 12

1. (a) 317.06   **2.** (a) 33 721.02
     (b) 314.70   (b) 33 058.29
     (c) 456.22   (c) 361 479.72
     (d) 460.79
     (e) 240.65
     (f) 209.73

3. (a) 1 489.97
     (b) 868.49
     (c) 14 710.37
     (d) 2 797.07
     (e) 16 521.76

EXERCISE 1.4, page 14

1. 261, 455, 788

2. 2 569, 4 004, 6 091

3. 3 596.30, 5 966.51, 7 591.07

4. 693.27, 1 246.16, 2 836.60

5. 1 899.86, 3 290.61, 4 348.21

6. 73 364.43, 100 075.39,
     143 495.98, 203 005.89

EXERCISE 1.5, page 15

1. (a) 554.197 99
     (b) 163.292 11
     (c) 180.489
     (d) 370.395 3
     (e) 69.533 82

2. (a) 214.711 1
     (b) 3 392.533 1
     (c) 1 625.793 1
     (d) 24 930.531 9
     (e) 2 280.704

EXERCISE 1.6, page 16

April : $ 44 785
May   :   42 637
June :   47 330

Ranu :   43 851
Camil :   29 974
Callas: 28 617
Grey :   32 310

Total : $134 752

EXERCISE 1.7, page 18

1. (a) 6 007
     (b) 7 651
     (c)   447
     (d) 8 328
     (e) 7 513

2. (a) 434.88
     (b) 982.73
     (c) 892.43
     (d) 808.02
     (e) 124.98

3. (a) 430.011 4
     (b) 19.878
     (c) 7.732
     (d) 2.778
     (e) 0.005

4. (a) 262.76, 153.52, 149.92, 57.50
     (b) 769.31, 765.86, 703.08, 424.62
     (c) 607.06, 507.06, 487.34, 196.84
     (d) 896.97, 877.62, 532.62, 503.20
     (e) 792.05, 446.38, 429.15, 340.13
     (f) 459, 337, 81, 67
     (g) 370, 336, 317, 204
     (h) 444, 336, 274, 73

5. (a) 224
     (b) 547.87 cr
     (c) 35.033
     (d) 41.251 cr
     (e) 500.359

6. 2 074.16   1 264.36
     2 169.64   1 274.36
     2 177.35   1 167.36
     2 082.29   1 131.60
     2 532.29   1 114.45
     1 661.31   1 090.89
     1 342.21   966.89
     1 279.78   964.71
     1 278.03

7. (a) 182   1 327   (b)   96   1 196
         264   − 1 044   188   − 1 110
         152   182   196   96
         193   465   249   182
         271   119
         360   221
         215   126
         358   42
         335   97
         322   178
         410   46
         371   179
         437   86
         465   182

EXERCISE 1.8, page 26

1. (a) 66 528   **3.** (a) 736 890
     (b) 10 900   (b) 455 672
     (c) 65 125   (c) 79 827
     (d) 84 476   (d) 250 536
     (e) 69 768   (e) 266 496
     (f) 84 700   (f) 36 386
     (g) 66 375   (g) 429 357
     (h) 91 278   (h) 63 360
     (i) 18 150   (i) 363 216
     (j) 11 760   (j) 469 044
     (k) 41 650   (k) 435 554
     (l) 3 232   (l) 53 669
     (m) 36 200
     (n) 32 742   **4.** (a) 22 271 067
     (o) 86 700   (b) 2 520 825
                         (c) 57 565 710
2. (a) 3 015   (d) 2 920 898
     (b) 4 648   (e) 155 740
     (c) 3 096   (f) 6 508 928
     (d) 2 890   (g) 1 530 100 638
     (e) 2 442   (h) 24 560 756
     (f) 3 312   (i) 62 112 128
     (g) 3 002
     (h) 3 770   **5.** (a) 2 194.89
     (i) 5 824   (b) 4 578.90
     (j) 2 736   (c) 6 232.44
     (k) 1 554   (d) 2 715.34
     (l) 3 402   (e) 879.63
                         (f) 808.45

6. (a) 3.792
(b) 8.880
(c) 14.438
(d) 108.480
(e) 1.245
(f) 206.050

7. (a) 0.004
(b) 3 763.669
(c) 37.966
(d) 0.001
(e) 18.405
(f) 211.906

8. (a)   142.67
  1 303.02
      7.03
  1 452.72

(b) 78 437.88
      0.94
   217.38
78 656.20

(c)   501.77
  363.20
  696.72
1 561.69

(d) 744.08
  46.03
  54.00
844.11

(e) 3 744.89
  110.02
    0.85
3 855.76

(f)   53.38
3 639.38
4 602.44
8 295.20

(g) 1 816.74
    6.96
  198.39
2 022.09

(h)   98.90
 146.69
   1.61
 247.20

9. (a) 6.60 (b) 6.86
  3.48   1.70
  1.77   1.58
  6.65   2.64
  0.94   31.43
  4.43   4.89
23.87   5.04
            3.52
         57.66

10. (a) 1 410 728
(b) 117 936
(c) 92 736
(d) 1 469.66
(e) 11 406.76
(f) 30 037.68
(g) 19 127.30
(h) 15 032.56
(i) 267.85
(j) 11.43

EXERCISE 1.9, page 30

1. (a) 115.75
(b) 14 941.33
(c) 125 267.49
(d) 620.00
(e) 3 646.63
(f) 25.00
(g) 3 100.00
(h) 3 120.00
(i) 80 000.00
(j) 3.50

2. (a) 13   (f) 130
(b) 48   (g) 14
(c) 32   (h) 98
(d) 22   (i) 36
(e) 189   (j) 76

3. (a) 26.27   (j) 5.61
(b) 2.75   (k) 882.61
(c) 18.20   (l) 262.35
(d) 566.07 (m) 32.37
(e) 3.74   (n) 0.95
(f) 13.44   (o) 0.72
(g) 597.41 (p) 2.21
(h) 171 000.00 (q) 6.80
(i) 1.78   (r) 238.32

REVIEW EXERCISE 1.10, page 30

1. 1 101.921

2. 414.914

3. (a) 4 143.32, 5 011.05, 6 951.98
(b) 1 784.80, 2 792.06, 5 566.63
(c) 2 486.64, 4 081.78, 5 365.73

4. 0.30
0.98
0.65
0.30
1.52
0.30
2.16
1.76
0.69
8.66

5. (a) 390.94, 311.59, 185.42, 92.94
(b) 529.94, 521,22, 189.27, 103.81
(c) 8 874.03, 7 917.77, 2 192.59, 1 340.20

6. (a) 784.022 2
(b) 174.741 11 cr
(c) 422.551 cr

7. (a) 368   (b)   984
    387   1 008
    439   916
    563   347
    521   498
    407   337
    691   321
    739   229
    683   253
    784   215
    408   86
    290   306
    271   311

8. (a) 9 200
(b) 223 000
(c) 7.78
(d) 14.8

9. (a) 1 515.49
(b) 302.32
(c) 341 905.83
(d) 27.00
(e) 36 815.26
(f) 0.10
(g) 1 422.56
(h) 8 373.46
(i) 53 724.99

10. (a) 1 748 (b) 6 840 (c) 9 085
      1 872   3 776   13 356
      5 355   1 656   16 576
      8 975   12 272   39 017

EXERCISE 2.1, page 36

1. (a) $\frac{1}{9}$ **2.** (a) $\frac{1}{2}$

(b) $\frac{3}{4}$ (b) $\frac{3}{4}$

(c) $\frac{7}{8}$ (c) $\frac{7}{8}$

(d) $\frac{2}{3}$ (d) $\frac{4}{5}$

(e) $\frac{3}{4}$ (e) $\frac{29}{30}$

(f) $\frac{15}{19}$ (f) $\frac{9}{11}$

(g) $\frac{4}{5}$ (g) $\frac{9}{35}$

(h) $\frac{6}{11}$ (h) $\frac{28}{30}$

                      (i) $\frac{8}{9}$

3. (a) $\frac{9}{6}, \frac{4}{6}, \frac{5}{6}, \frac{3}{6}$

(b) $\frac{25}{40}, \frac{36}{40}, \frac{30}{40}, \frac{24}{40}$

(c) $\frac{135}{150}, \frac{132}{150}, \frac{90}{150}, \frac{80}{150}$

EXERCISE 2.2, page 38

1. $1\frac{5}{28}$ 3. $\frac{5}{9}$ 5. $\frac{29}{40}$ 7. $8\frac{2}{3}$ 9. $4\frac{15}{28}$

2. $1\frac{11}{24}$ 4. $\frac{3}{8}$ 6. $\frac{23}{24}$ 8. $7\frac{41}{42}$ 10. $11\frac{6}{7}$

EXERCISE 2.3, page 38

1. $\frac{2}{15}$ 5. $\frac{2}{3}$ 9. $\frac{27}{80}$ 13. $29\frac{3}{4}$ 17. $4\frac{55}{56}$

2. $\frac{8}{13}$ 6. $\frac{63}{88}$ 10. $\frac{1}{2}$ 14. $\frac{111}{224}$ 18. $\frac{1}{144}$

3. $\frac{35}{128}$ 7. $\frac{21}{64}$ 11. $\frac{5}{8}$ 15. $19\frac{1}{2}$ 19. $351\frac{1}{9}$

4. $\frac{14}{25}$ 8. $\frac{5}{18}$ 12. $25\frac{1}{2}$ 16. 235   20. $143\frac{1}{3}$

EXERCISE 2.4, page 39

1. 9   4. $5\frac{7}{10}$ 7. 15   10. $1\frac{6}{7}$ 13. $7\frac{7}{8}$

2. 2   5. $\frac{35}{48}$ 8. $1\frac{43}{45}$ 11. $13\frac{1}{2}$ 14. $7\frac{5}{6}$

3. $\frac{2}{5}$ 6. $\frac{21}{40}$ 9. $\frac{19}{30}$ 12. $1\frac{4}{5}$ 15. 12

EXERCISE 2.5, page 40

1. $1\frac{1}{48}$ 2. $12\frac{73}{216}$ 3. -6

EXERCISE 2.6, page 41

1. (a) 0.500   (e) 0.875   (i) 0.125   (m) 0.682   (q) 4.167
   (b) 0.333   (f) 0.286   (j) 0.063   (n) 0.320   (r) 7.900
   (c) 0.667   (g) 0.778   (k) 0.083   (o) 0.188   (s) 36.667
   (d) 0.375   (h) 0.833   (l) 0.786   (p) 0.129   (t) 41.400

2. (a) $\frac{2}{5}$ (c) $\frac{3}{8}$ (e) $\frac{1}{8}$ (g) $\frac{1}{2}$ (i) $\frac{221}{50}$ (k) $\frac{18}{5}$

   (b) $\frac{23}{25}$ (d) $\frac{7}{8}$ (f) $\frac{5}{8}$ (h) $\frac{21}{4}$ (j) $\frac{65}{8}$ (l) $\frac{31}{5}$

EXERCISE 2.7, page 42

1. $\frac{1}{6}$ 4. $\frac{5}{6}$ 7. $4\frac{1}{3}$

2. $\frac{1}{12}$ 5. $\frac{7}{12}$ 8. $5\frac{2}{3}$

3. $\frac{2}{3}$ 6. $2\frac{1}{6}$ 9. $\frac{5}{12}$

EXERCISE 2.8, page 44

1. (a) $\frac{1}{2}$ (d) $\frac{1}{6}$ (g) $\frac{1}{4}$ (j) $\frac{1}{10}$ (m) $\frac{3}{4}$ (p) $\frac{1}{3}$

   (b) $\frac{5}{6}$ (e) $\frac{7}{8}$ (h) $\frac{11}{12}$ (k) $\frac{1}{16}$ (n) $\frac{7}{12}$ (q) $\frac{5}{8}$

   (c) $\frac{3}{8}$ (f) $\frac{1}{12}$ (i) $\frac{3}{10}$ (l) $\frac{2}{5}$ (o) $\frac{3}{8}$ (r) $\frac{4}{5}$

2. (a) $ 60.00   (c) $ 3.00   (e) $151.25
        33.00   100.00   288.75
       108.80   15.00   21.00
        38.40   8.00   1.75
        19.20   49.00   13.50
      ―――――   ―――――   ―――――
      $259.40 $175.00 $476.25

   (b) $ 45.34   (d) $ 12.00   (f) $ 46.00
        27.00   60.00   42.00
       130.00   41.25   13.00
        37.34   90.00   140.00
        42.00   44.00   14.00
      ―――――   ―――――   ―――――
      $281.68 $247.25 $255.00

EXERCISE 2.9, page 45

1. 250   5. 170   8. 1 536
2. 185   6. 100   9. 56
3. 101   7. 64   10. 84
4. 126

EXERCISE 2.10, page 45

1. $\frac{2}{5}$ 6. $\frac{2}{1}$ 11. $\frac{3}{4}$

2. $\frac{3}{5}$ 7. $\frac{9}{4}$ 12. $\frac{9}{10}$

3. $\frac{1}{2}$ 8. $\frac{1}{400}$ 13. $\frac{3}{8}$

4. $\frac{1}{3}$ 9. $\frac{1}{800}$ 14. $\frac{5}{8}$

5. $\frac{1}{6}$ 10. $\frac{11}{800}$ 15. $\frac{1}{16}$

EXERCISE 2.11, page 46

1. 50%   5. $37\frac{1}{2}$%   9. $28\frac{4}{7}$%

2. $66\frac{2}{3}$%   6. $41\frac{2}{3}$%   10. $152\frac{16}{17}$%

3. 75%   4. $387\frac{1}{2}$%   11. 216%

4. 60%   8. $31\frac{1}{4}$%   12. $192\frac{2}{19}$%

EXERCISE 2.12, page 46

1. 0.1   5. $0.00\overline{6}$ 9. 0.375

2. 0.875   6. 11   10. $0.08\overline{3}$

3. 8.15   7. 0.045   11. 0.062 5

4. 0.005   8. 0.002 5   12. 0.008 75

EXERCISE 2.13, page 47

1. (a) 4%   (e) $\frac{1}{8}$%   (i) 166%
   (b) $12\frac{1}{2}$%   (f) 213%   (j) 375%
   (c) $83\frac{1}{3}$%   (g) 12 525%   (k) $80\frac{1}{8}$%
   (d) 2.65%   (h) 108%   (l) $\frac{1}{4}$%

2. $\frac{1}{5}$ 4. 60%

3. 40%   5. Brown

EXERCISE 2.14, page 49

1. (a) 163.00   (d) 361.76
   (b) 20.16   (e) 15.81
   (c) 5.17   (f) 1 617.63

2. (a) 450.00   (d) 1 170.00
   (b) 128.43   (e) 8 231.35
   (c) 2.35   (f) 1 222.80

EXERCISE 2.15, page 51

1. 18%   5. 33%, 10%

2. $22\frac{1}{2}$%   6. (a) 10%   (b) 5%

3. 11.8%   7. (a) 25%   (b) 20%

4. 50%

EXERCISE 2.16, page 53

1. 752.00
2. 12.00
3. 968.75
4. 33.75
5. 16.83
6. 46.66
7. 10.50
8. 215.25
9. 0.27
10. 324.00
11. 142.50
12. 360.36

EXERCISE 2.17, page 53

1. 0.15
2. 7.2
3. 45.44
4. 1.26
5. 0.2
6. $8.75
7. 7.2
8. 5.6
9. 0.525
10. 0.735
11. $36
12. $34.38

EXERCISE 2.18, page 54

1. 200.00
2. 173.33
3. 700.00
4. 6.63 m
5. $16.80
6. $109.00
7. 16 dozen
8. $70.00
9. 6.67
10. 4.76
11. 225.00
12. 1 125.00
13. 14.81
14. 0.33
15. 3 125.00
16. $250.00
17. $310.50
18. $54.00
19. 182
20. $72 500.00

EXERCISE 2.19, page 55

1. (a) 18.75%
   (b) 300%
   (c) 20%
   (d) 6.25%
   (e) $16\frac{2}{3}$%
   (f) 12.5%
   (g) 200%
   (h) 1 200%
   (i) 37.5%
   (j) $33\frac{1}{3}$%
2. 6%
3. 4.44%
4. 9.98%
5. $83\frac{1}{3}$%
6. 6.23%
7. 28.57%
8. 20%
9. 2 000%
10. 5.27%
11. 50%

EXERCISE 2.20, page 57

1. 111
2. 200
3. $329.70
4. 25%
5. 250%
6. 8.64
7. 279%
8. 0.035
9. 14
10. (a) 61% (b) 39%
11. Food: $6 790
    Rent: 4 850
    Clothing: 2 328
    Education: 2 716
    Savings: 1 164
    Other: 1 552
12. 18%
13. (a) 5.03% (b) $16\frac{2}{3}$%
14. $1 333.33

EXERCISE 2.21, page 59

1. $33\frac{1}{3}$%
2. $33\frac{1}{3}$%
3. 50%
4. 20%
5. 16.33%
6. 55.38%
7. 25%
8. 18%
9. $12\frac{1}{2}$%
10. 200%
11. 1 100%
12. 99.4%
13. 150%, 40%

EXERCISE 2.22, page 61

1. 16.4
2. 36
3. 14
4. 20.5
5. 32.8
6. $8.80
7. $3.23
8. 72
9. 356
10. $\frac{1}{3}$
11. 96
12. (a) $25.45 (b) Increase, $0.77
13. 11%

EXERCISE 2.23, page 63

1. 48.57
2. 60
3. 21
4. 12
5. 100
6. 300
7. $74.88
8. $\frac{7}{9}$
9. $222.05
10. $9.20

EXERCISE 2.24, page 64

1. (a) $\frac{3}{5}$
   (b) $\frac{8}{13}$
   (c) $\frac{2}{3}$
   (d) $\frac{1}{3}$
   (e) $\frac{1}{2}$
   (f) $\frac{1}{4}$
   (g) $\frac{1}{3}$
   (h) $\frac{1}{2}$
   (i) $\frac{20}{1}$
   (j) $\frac{3}{1}$
2. (a) 16, 24 (b) 40, 48

EXERCISE 2.25, page 65

1. 12
2. 6
3. 39
4. 100
5. 18
6. 16
7. 63
8. 2
9. 50
10. 1.5

REVIEW EXERCISE 2.26, page 66

1. (a) 0.5 = 50%
   (b) $0.\overline{3} = 33\frac{1}{3}$%
   (c) 0.25 = 25%
   (d) $0.375 = 37\frac{1}{2}$%
   (e) $0.875 = 87\frac{1}{2}$%
   (f) $0.08\overline{3} = 83\frac{1}{3}$%
   (g) 0.8 = 80%
   (h) $0.125 = 12\frac{1}{2}$%
   (i) $0.062\ 5 = 6\frac{1}{4}$%
   (j) 0.75 = 75%

2. (a) $\frac{253}{320}$ (b) $2\frac{38}{135}$

3. (a) $2\% = \frac{1}{50}$
   (b) $12.5\% = \frac{1}{8}$
   (c) $75\% = \frac{3}{4}$
   (d) $40\% = \frac{2}{5}$
   (e) $83.\overline{3}\% = \frac{5}{6}$
   (f) $16\frac{2}{3}\% = \frac{1}{6}$
   (g) $37.5\% = \frac{3}{8}$
   (h) $162.5\% = 1\frac{5}{8}$
   (i) $32\ 020\% = 320\frac{1}{5}$
   (j) $60\% = \frac{3}{5}$
   (k) $287.5\% = 2\frac{7}{8}$
   (l) $366.\overline{6}\% = 3\frac{2}{3}$

4. 3 900%
5. 1.2%
6. $0.3\overline{3}$%
7. 36
8. 85
9. 7.41%
10. $16\frac{2}{3}$%
11. 78.08%
12. 20%
13. $540
14. 50
15. $33\frac{1}{3}$%
16. $\frac{3}{80}$, $8\frac{3}{4}$, $\frac{3}{4}$
17. 0.875
18. $0.3\overline{3}$, $0.1\overline{6}$, $0.41\overline{6}$
19. $0.93
20. 14 m
21. (a) 525, 234, 466, 175
    (b) 0.125
22. (a) 0.362 5
    (b) $26 000
    (c) $5 200, $3 250,
        $6 500
23. (a) 240 ha
    (b) 140 ha
24. (a) 0.375
    (b) Germaine:
        $20 737.50
        Claude: 8 887.50
        Klaus: 17 775.00

25. (a) $\frac{5}{6}$ (g) $\frac{1}{6}$
   (b) $\frac{1}{16}$ (h) $\frac{1}{3}$
   (c) $\frac{7}{8}$ (i) $\frac{5}{16}$
   (d) $\frac{5}{8}$ (j) $\frac{1}{8}$
   (e) $\frac{3}{8}$ (k) $\frac{3}{4}$
   (f) $\frac{4}{5}$ (l) $\frac{2}{3}$

26. (a) $20   (f) $1.50
   (b) $24.50   (g) $11.67
   (c) $151.25   (h) $45
   (d) $44.80   (i) $20.67
   (e) $36   (j) $132

27. (a) 560   (f) 123
   (b) 87   (g) 384
   (c) 640   (h) 192
   (d) 266   (i) 192
   (e) 220   (j) 3 300

28. (a) $21   (b) 0.625

29. 12, 18

30. 1 : 10

31. (a) 24   (b) 115

EXERCISE 3.1, page 71

1. (a) 125   (d) 243
   (b) 16   (e) 256
   (c) 8   (f) 3 125

2. (a) $4a^7b^4$ (d) $\frac{4ab^6}{3}$
   (b) $72a^6b^5$
   (c) $36a^4b^2$ (e) $\frac{18a^6c^9}{b}$

EXERCISE 3.2, page 72

1. 2.24   **6.** 3.87
2. 8.66   **7.** 5.48
3. 7.87   **8.** 6.71
4. 2.83   **9.** 9.90
5. 3.46   **10.** 0.94

EXERCISE 3.3, page 72

(a) 0.86   (e) 0.69
(b) 0.3   (f) 0.58
(c) $1.\overline{3}$ (g) 0.71
(d) 0.91   (h) 0.5

EXERCISE 3.4, page 73

1. $4x + 5y + 4z$
2. $3ab + 9ac + 3ad$
3. $3a^3 + 6a^2 + 4a^2b + b^2 + 7b^3$

EXERCISE 3.5, page 74

1. $10x$ **6.** $12a^2b$
2. $28a - 6b$ **7.** $2 + 60x^2$
3. $-7xy^2$ **8.** $\dfrac{5ab - 6a^2b^2}{5}$
4. $7r + 12$ **9.** $27r - 3$
5. $20a^2$ **10.** $-3x^2y^2$

EXERCISE 3.6, page 75

1. $7a + 3b + ab$
2. $17a - 18b - 6ab$
3. $2a^2 + 2ab - 2b^2 + 8ac$

EXERCISE 3.7, page 75

1. $a + b$
2. $3 + 4y$
3. $6a^2 - 3a + 1$
4. $4x^2 + 6x - 2$
5. $a + 5b - 6ab$

EXERCISE 3.8, page 76

1. $2(a + 2b)$ **4.** $2(a + 4ab + 6c - 4ac)$
2. $r(V + A)$ **5.** $C(1 + \frac{P}{4})$
3. $2a(b + 2c + 4)$ **6.** $6ab(5a^2 + 7ab + 2b^2)$

EXERCISE 3.9, page 76

1. 12   **4.** -1
2. 16   **5.** $\frac{5}{9}$
3. 22   **6.** 12

EXERCISE 3.10, page 78

1. 8   **6.** $\frac{7}{13}$
2. -12 **7.** ± 4
3. $\frac{3}{2}$ **8.** $200
4. 6   **9.** $40
5. 4   **10.** $288

EXERCISE 3.11, page 80

1. 2 086.538   **4.** 804.249
2. 1 037.443   **5.** 80.479
3. 6 464.646

EXERCISE 3.12, page 80

1. (a) (i) $60   (ii) $410.71
   (b) (i) 16%   (ii) 17%
   (c) (i) 2 a   (ii) 60 d

2. (a) (i) $30 000   (ii) $2 777 777.78
   (b) (i) 40 mills   (ii) 72 mills

3. (a) (i) $28 000   (ii) $9.54
   (b) (i) $4.40   (ii) $3.15

4. (a) (i) $1 320 (ii) $1 077
   (b) 18%
   (c) 3 months

5. (a) $17 800
   (b) $949 200

6. (a) $4.80
   (b) $6.56
   (c) $3.75

7. (a) $4 500
   (b) 20%
   (c) $5 850

8. (a) $911.18
   (b) 17%

EXERCISE 3.13, page 83

1. 1 363.2   **5.** $2 886
2. $12   **6.** $3.50
3. 10%   **7.** $8/h
4. $240

REVIEW EXERCISE 3.14, page 85

1. (a) $\dfrac{8a^3c^5}{b^3}$
   (b) $\frac{299}{480}$
   (c) $6a^2 + 11ax + 10ab$
2. (a) $3ab(a + 2b^2 + 4)$
   (b) $4m(r^2 + 3m^2r + \frac{2}{3}m)$
3. (a) -12 (b) $\frac{1}{4}$ (c) $\frac{15}{4}$
4. $1 280
5. $13 076.92

CUMULATIVE REVIEW 1, page 85

1. 37.5%   **8.** 45
2. 87.5%   **9.** 138
3. 0.625   **10.** 50%
4. $\frac{5}{6}$ **11.** 0.8%
5. $\frac{51}{400}$ **12.** 600
6. 25%   **13.** 312
7. 25%
14. (a) 540.345
   (b) 1 357.434
15. (a) 1 437, 2 702, 4 380
   (b) 1 512.72, 2 531.34, 3 427.48
16. (a) 900
   (b) 16 000
17. (a) 195
   (b) 134

EXERCISE 4.1, page 88

1. (a) $14.09 (d) $442.35
   (b) $38.20 (e) $553.91
   (c) $189.30

2. $525

3. $159.96

4. $103.28

5. Less, $175

6. (a) $21.90 (d) $25.50
   (b) $17.50 (e) $10.28
   (c) $33.03

EXERCISE 4.2, page 90

1. $752.25

2. $1 210

3. (a) $8 457.50
   (b) $12 338

4. (a) $12 495
   (b) $20 206.20, $32 701.20
   (c) $431 375

EXERCISE 4.3, page 92

1.

	Listing	Broker	Agent
(a)	$2 975	$1 785	$1 190
(b)	2 435	1 461	974
(c)	3 495	2 097	1 398
(d)	3 775	2 265	1 510
(e)	2 335	1 401	934

2.

	Listing	Broker	Agent
(a)	$2 245.00	$ 673.50	$1 571.50
(b)	2 635.00	790.50	1 844.50
(c)	3 242.50	972.75	2 269.75
(d)	3 745.00	1 123.50	2 621.50
(e)	4 435.00	1 330.50	3 104.50

3. Agent $1 600.50
   Broker   1 309.50

4. Broker $4 350.00
   Agent   2 900.00

EXERCISE 4.4, page 93

1. Pauluk: $295.10
   Smith: $208.32
   Reytag: $189.55
   Collins: $263.90
   Storey: $314.24

2. $254.60

3. $243.78

4. $143

5. $35, 40, $39.24

EXERCISE 4.5, page 95

1. (a) $6\frac{1}{2}$ (b) $7\frac{1}{4}$ (c) $6\frac{1}{2}$

2. (a) $8.28   (c) $13.185
   (b) $9.225   (d) $11.925

3. (a) $234.38 (e) $333.25
   (b) $249.60 (f) $256.70
   (c) $499.39 (g) $453.65
   (d) $315.06 (h) $403.75

EXERCISE 4.6, page 98

1. $4.54   6. $5.70
2. $4.57   7. $4.60
3. $4.52   8. $5.54
4. $4.60   9. $6.56
5. $4.90   10. $6.74

EXERCISE 4.7, page 101

1. $8.35   6. $9.75
2. $9.56   7. $9.78
3. $6.89   8. $8.08
4. $8.89   9. $8.79
5. $7.35   10. $9.25

EXERCISE 4.8, page 102

1. $46.70
2. $20.70
3. $40.30
4. $64.35
5. $45.90

EXERCISE 4.9, page 105 ▶

1.

	EMPLOYEE DATA				EARNINGS			DEDUCTIONS								NET PAY
NO	NAME	SIN	TAX EXEMP	HOURS	REG	O/T	TOTAL	CPP	UIC	INC TAX	GROUP INS	HOSP	UNION DUES	CREDIT UNION	TOTAL	
110	BRUNET	354 567 754	$3 960	45	$ 346.00	$ 64.88	$ 410.88	$ 6.74	$ 9.45	$ 76.30	$3.00	$ 29.75	$12.98	$ 2.00	$140.22	$270.66
111	O'HARA	777 654 652	4 460	42½	$ 356.00	33.38	389.38	6.32	8.96	68.15	3.00	59.50	13.35	20.00	179.28	210.10
112	RAMJI	846 399 288	4 280	46	304.00	68.40	372.40	6.01	8.57	63.65	—	59.50	11.40	17.50	166.63	205.77
					$1 006.00	$166.66	$1 172.66	$19.07	$26.98	$208.10	$6.00	$148.75	$37.73	$39.50	$486.13	$686.53

2.

NO	SIN	NAME	TAX EXEMP	HOURS	REG	O/T	TOTAL	CPP	UIC	INC TAX	GROUP INS	HOSP	BONDS	UNITED APPEAL	TOTAL	NET PAY
			EMPLOYEE DATA		EARNINGS			DEDUCTIONS								NET PAY
1	782 111 325	BAIE	$8 790	45½	$ 270.00	$ 55.69	$ 325.69	$ 5.17	$ 7.49	$ 27.50	$1.50	$14.88	$2.00	$0.25	$58.79	$ 266.90
2	338 287 852	HAMID	3 960	43	276.00	31.05	307.05	4.83	7.06	48.15	1.50	7.44	2.00	0.25	71.23	235.82
3	334 765 762	CHU	5 320	38	289.56	—	289.56	4.52	6.66	36.80	0.75	14.88	3.00	0.25	66.86	222.70
4	782 000 625	RIVERS	8 850	44	294.00	44.10	338.10	5.39	7.78	30.25	2.00	14.88	2.50	0.25	63.05	275.05
					$1 129.56	$130.84	$1 260.40	$19.91	$28.99	$142.70	$5.75	$52.08	$9.50	$1.00	$259.93	$1 000.47

3.

NO	SIN	TAX EXEMP	PIECES	REG	O/T	TOTAL	CPP	UIC	INC TAX	HOSP	TOTAL	NET PAY
		EMPLOYEE DATA		EARNINGS			DEDUCTIONS					NET PAY
1	378 982 000	$3 960	118	$ 260.00	$ 48.60	$ 308.60	$ 4.86	$ 7.10	$ 48.15	$ 7.44	$ 67.55	$ 241.05
2	090 287 339	3 960	115	260.00	40.50	300.50	4.72	6.91	45.30	7.44	64.37	236.13
3	937 883 265	3 960	124	260.00	64.80	324.80	5.15	7.47	52.40	7.44	72.46	252.34
4	352 039 376	8 790	132	260.00	86.40	346.40	5.54	7.97	33.15	14.88	61.54	284.86
				$1 040.00	$240.30	$1 280.30	$20.27	$29.45	$179.00	$37.20	$265.92	$1 014.38

EXERCISE 4.10, page 106

1. $270.96   **3.** $230.11

2. $234.32   **4.** $267.42

EXERCISE 4.11, page 108

1. 46 × $20   **2.** 48 × $20
    2 × 10   2 × 10
    3 × 5   3 × 5
    5 × 2   5 × 2
    2 × 1   1 × 1
    8 × 0.25   6 × 0.25
    4 × 0.10   3 × 0.10
    1 × 0.05   3 × 0.05
    12 × 0.12   12 × 0.12

EXERCISE 4.12, page 109

1.

NAME BRUNET, GISELLE
ADDRESS 38 WILLO CRES
TELEPHONE 345 6782
DATE OF BIRTH 1960 01 01

EMPLOYEE NO. 110
SOCIAL INSURANCE NO. 354 567 754
MARITAL STATUS S
TAX EXEMPTIONS $3 960
POSITION RECEIVING CLERK
DATE EMPLOYED 1984 05 04

PAY PERIOD ENDING	RATE PER HOUR	HOURS	REG	O/T	TOTAL	CPP	UIC	INC TAX	GROUP INS.	HOSP	UNION DUES	CREDIT UNION	TOTAL	NET PAY
			EARNINGS			DEDUCTIONS								NET PAY
MAR. 29	$8.65	45	$346.00	$64.88	$410.88	$6.74	$9.45	$76.30	$3.00	$29.75	$12.98	$2.00	$140.22	$270.66

2. (a)

PAY PERIOD ENDING	EARN-INGS TOTAL	CPP	UIC	INC TAX	GROUP INS	HOSP	UNION DUES	BONDS	TOTAL	NET PAY	ACC EARN

NAME BLAKE, ALLEN

EMPLOYEE NO. 1
SOCIAL INSURANCE NO. 456 764 009
MARITAL STATUS S
TAX EXEMPTIONS $3 960

PAY PERIOD ENDING	EARNINGS TOTAL	CPP	UIC	INC TAX	GROUP INS	HOSP	UNION DUES	BONDS	TOTAL	NET PAY	ACC EARN
JAN. 31											$1 160.92
FEB. 7	$309.00	$4.87	$7.11	$48.15	—	$7.44	—	—	$67.57	$241.43	$1 469.92
FEB. 14	309.00	4.87	7.11	48.15	—	7.44	—	$10	77.57	231.43	1 778.92
FEB. 21	312.50	4.93	7.19	49.55	—	7.44	$13.45	—	82.56	229.94	2 091.42
FEB. 28	309.00	4.87	7.11	48.15	$6	7.44	—	—	73.57	235.43	2 400.42

REVIEW EXERCISE 4.13, page 110

1. (a) No, too low by $126
   (b) 1.84%
   (c) 2.14%

2. (a) $11.78 (c) $19.30
   (b) $22.74 (d) $1 076.40

3. $2 954

4. A: $190.02
   B: $245.48
   C: $230.78

6. (a) $328.34
   (b) $338.10
   (c) $347.09

5. (a)

NO	SIN NO	NAME	TAX EXEMP	EARN-INGS TOTAL	CPP	UIC	INC TAX	GROUP INS	HOSP	BOND	TOTAL	NET PAY
1	573 555 908	ADAM	$7 430	$ 365.78	$ 5.89	$ 8.41	$ 42.90	$1.50	$59.50	$2.00	$120.20	$ 245.58
2	477 834 867	ALALOUF	5 320	373.56	6.03	8.59	59.80	2.40	59.50	2.00	138.32	235.24
3	548 574 879	COLICO	3 960	368.97	5.95	8.49	64.25	2.50	29.75	2.50	113.44	255.53
4	439 203 208	PRADO	9 500	362.67	5.84	8.34	33.05	1.50	29.75	—	78.48	284.19
				$1 470.98	$23.71	$33.83	$200.00	$7.90	$178.50	$6.50	$450.44	$1 020.54

(b)

		$20	$10	$5	$2	$1	0.25	0.10	0.05	0.01
ADAM	$ 245.58	12		1		2			1	3
ALALOUF	235.24	11	1	1			2			4
COLICO	255.53	12	1	1		2				3
PRADO	284.19	14			2			1	1	4
TOTAL	$1 020.54	49	2	3	2	—	4	3	2	14

Currency Requisition

49 × $20	=	$	980.00
2 × 10	=		20.00
3 × 5	=		15.00
2 × 2	=		4.00
4 × 0.25	=		1.00
3 × 0.10	=		0.30
2 × 0.05	=		0.10
14 × 0.01	=		0.14
			$1 020.54

7.

NO	PERS EXEMP	HOURS	REG	O/T	TOTAL	VAC PAY	GROSS PAY	CCP	UIC	INC TAX	VAC PAY	TOTAL	NET PAY
1	$8 790	42½	$318.00	$29.81	$ 347.81	$13.91	$ 361.72	$ 5.82	$ 8.32	$ 37.40	$13.91	$ 65.45	$ 296.27
2	3 960	36¾	316.05	—	316.05	12.64	328.69	5.22	7.56	53.85	12.64	79.27	249.42
3	7 430	44¼	284.00	45.26	329.26	13.17	342.43	5.47	7.88	35.75	13.17	62.27	280.16
4	8 140	41	322.00	12.08	334.08	13.36	347.44	5.56	7.99	33.15	13.36	60.06	287.38
			$1 240.05	$87.15	$1 327.20	$53.08	$1 380.28	$22.07	$31.75	$160.15	$53.08	$267.05	$1 113.23

CUMULATIVE REVIEW 2, page 113

1. $288
2. $582
3. 25%
4. 12% increase
5. $325.20
6. 18.18% increase
7. $0.38
8. 12.5%
9. $266\frac{2}{3}$%
10. (a) $4ab(a + 2b^2 + 4)$
    (b) $5m(r^2 + 3m^2r + \frac{2}{3}m)$
11. 0.375
12. 6.25%
13. $41\frac{2}{3}$%
14. (a) -9 (b) $\frac{1}{4}$ (c) $7\frac{1}{2}$
15. (a) $897.60 (b) $26 153.85
16. 123
17. (a) 10 250 (b) 31 284
18. (a) 153 (b) 114
19. 1.8 20. 480

EXERCISE 5.1, page 118

1. (a) $810 (f) $91.78
   (b) $85 (g) $2 371.88
   (c) $14.15 (h) $381.51
   (d) $115.28 (i) $668.80
   (e) $44.38 (j) $326.46
2. $3.75 4. $9.50
3. $327.82 5. $5.38

EXERCISE 5.2, page 119

1. (a) 13.5% (f) 14.55%
   (b) 10.5% (g) 9%
   (c) 16% (h) 7.56%
   (d) 3.5% (i) 10.8%
   (e) 15.17% (j) 17.25%
2. 6.5%
3. 10.5%
4. (a) $10.20 (b) 12%
5. 9.5%

EXERCISE 5.3, page 120

1. (a) 182 d (f) 1 a 236 d
   (b) 91 d (g) 108 d
   (c) 3 a 130 d (h) 227 d
   (d) 110 d (i) 165 d
   (e) 3 a 300 d (j) 1 a 274 d
2. 1 a 4. 91 d
3. 329 d 5. 93 d

EXERCISE 5.4, page 121

1. (a) $1 242 (f) $11 487
   (b) $867 (g) $917
   (c) $865 (h) $3 532
   (d) $5 308 (i) $5 719
   (e) $650 (j) $904
2. $504
3. $950
4. $1 764
5. $5 000

EXERCISE 5.5, page 122

1. (a) $8 348.31
   (b) $5 105.41
   (c) $1 436.76
   (d) $501.12
   (e) $909.36
2. 9.47%
3. $49.15
4. $1 000
5. 1 a 175 d
6. $41 880.80

EXERCISE 5.6, page 124

1. 6, 10%
2. 10, 6%
3. 7, $5\frac{1}{2}$%
4. 44, $3\frac{1}{2}$%
5. 17, $2\frac{1}{2}$%

EXERCISE 5.7, page 125

(a) 12.36% (e) 16.64%
(b) 12.55% (f) 16.99%
(c) 12.68% (g) 8.16%
(d) 10.38% (h) 9.20%

EXERCISE 5.8, page 126

1. (a) $13 113.64 (e) $20 661.25
   (b) $11 111.64 (f) $57 251.35
   (c) $5 370.12 (g) $12 527.80
   (d) $30 020.25
2. $1 143.60
3. $3 678.49
4. $983 451

EXERCISE 5.9, page 128

1. (a) $4 371.10 (d) $1 860.78
   (b) $298.14 (e) $7 286.89
   (c) $734.61
2. $4 857.99 5. $2 506.70
3. $442.30 6. $39.71
4. $847.66

EXERCISE 5.10, page 130

1. (a) $733.59 (d) $5 116.01
   (b) $20 704.73 (e) $14 567.96
   (c) $1 542.51
2. $93 625.60
3. $31 981.77
4. $16 334.19
5. $8 616.31
6. $10 748.15

EXERCISE 5.11, page 131

1. (a) $11.83 (d) $69.78
   (b) $85.96 (e) $5.14
   (c) $476.25
2. $1 021.80
3. $344.36
4. $35.22
5. $389.50
6. $38.29

EXERCISE 5.12, page 133

1. (a) $536.81 (d) $48 176.91
   (b) $1 052.88 (e) $7 951.16
   (c) $1 014.52
2. $30 583.70
3. $4 256.78
4. A
5. $22 575.79
6. $922.22

EXERCISE 5.13, page 134

1. (a) $7 039 (d) $888.30
   (b) $163.02 (e) $17.30
   (c) $117.08
2. $814.93
3. $146.40
4. $2 972.34
5. $170
6. $661.30

EXERCISE 5.14, page 139

1. Oct. 1 Balance $2 809.82
2. $1 007.22 6. $6.72
3. $1 043.63 7. $836.01
4. $1 045 8. 28¢
5. $4.80 9. $4.48
10. (a) $1.29 (b) $0.90

EXERCISE 5.15, page 141

(a) $86.30 (d) $49.62
(b) $405 (e) $469.24
(c) $650 (f) $4 080

EXERCISE 5.16, page 144

1. (a) $67.50
   (b) $945
   (c) $1 000

2. (a) $4 450
   (b) $5 000
   (c) discount

3. $300

4. $4 350

5. (a) (i) $498.35 (ii) $465.75 (iii) $453
   (b) (i) $12.90 (ii) $45.50 (iii) $47
   (c) (i) 2.6% (ii) 9.8% (iii) 10.4%

6. (a) $6 505
   (b) 9.3%

REVIEW EXERCISE 5.17, page 146

1. (a) $43.97
   (b) $44.63
   (c) $73.52
   (d) $143.24
   (e) $151.32

4. (a) $11 069
   (b) $1 153
   (c) $2 355
   (d) $8 020
   (e) $8 853

2. (a) 10.45%
   (b) 10.3%
   (c) 12.5%
   (d) 16.5%
   (e) 4%

5. 2 a 22 d

6. $2 000

7. $3 061.13

3. (a) 219 d
   (b) 90 d
   (c) 3.5 a
   (d) 60 d
   (e) 173 d

8. $2 525.26

9. $113 283.21

10. $4 110.90

11. $117.50

12. $325

CUMULATIVE REVIEW 3, page 147

1. (a) 50% (d) 80% (g) $66\frac{2}{3}$%
   (b) $37\frac{1}{2}$% (e) 10% (h) $87\frac{1}{2}$%
   (c) 75% (f) $8.\overline{3}$% (i) $33\frac{1}{3}$%

2. 7%

3. 20%

4. 9.91

5. 0.585

6. 3

7. (a) 3 (b) 1

8. 25%

9. $40\frac{1}{2}$

10. $387.13

11. $1 580

12. 17.2%

13. 67.2

14. 960

15. (a) 10 800 (b) 85 000

16. (a) 67 (b) 29

17. (a) 817.85 (b) 286 860.2

18. (a) $104 (b) $158 (c) $309

EXERCISE 6.1, page 152

1. Up to $3 000: Bank – $13\frac{1}{2}$%
   Trust Company – 15%
   Over $3 000: Bank – $13\frac{1}{2}$%
   Trust Company – $14\frac{1}{2}$%

2. (a) $1 074.60 (b) $83.12, $1 083.12

3. (a) $2 866.56, $2 909.52 (b) Smaller loan payments

EXERCISE 6.2, page 153

(a) End of	1st	$121.23	$31.25	$89.98	$2 410.02
	2nd	121.23	30.13	91.10	2 318.92
	3rd	121.23	28.99	92.24	2 226.68
	4th	121.23	27.83	93.40	2 133.28
	5th	121.23	26.67	94.56	2 038.72
	6th	121.23	25.48	95.75	1 942.97
(b) End of	1st	98.64	28.13	70.51	2 429.49
	2nd	98.64	27.33	71.31	2 358.18
	3rd	98.64	26.53	72.11	2 286.07
	4th	98.64	25.72	72.92	2 213.15
	5th	98.64	24.90	73.74	2 139.41
	6th	98.64	24.07	74.57	2 064.84

EXERCISE 6.3, page 154

1. (a) 14.22%
   (b) 14.06%
   (c) 14.37%

2. (a) 15.73%
   (b) 15.52%
   (c) 15.86%

EXERCISE 6.4, page 156

1. $157.19

2. $196.95

3. (a) $89.92
   (b) $171.14
   (c) $261.06

4.
January 27			$3 500.00
February 27	100.00	60.94	3 460.94
March 27	100.00	54.43	3 415.37
April 27	100.00	59.46	3 374.83

EXERCISE 6.5, page 157

1. (a) $652.50, 19.92%
   (b) $518.75, 19.15%
   (c) $956.25, 19.25%
   (d) $726.25, 18.46%
   (e) $333.75, 19.92%

2. 19.23%

3. (a) 12 months, $4.59 (b) 13.9%

4. (a) 6 months, $29.62 (b) 15.7%

EXERCISE 6.6, page 158

1. 21.12%

2. (a) 15.28%
   (b) 12.67%
   (c) 13.99%
   (d) 24.16%

EXERCISE 6.7, page 161

1. (a)

Date	Interest	Off Principal	Balance
			$65.00
End of 1st	$1.30	$5.70	59.30
2nd	1.19	5.81	53.49
3rd	1.07	5.93	47.56
4th	0.95	6.05	41.51
5th	0.83	6.17	35.34
6th	0.71	6.29	29.05
7th	0.58	6.42	22.63
8th	0.45	6.55	16.08
9th	0.32	6.68	9.40
10th	0.19	6.81	2.59
11th	0.05	2.59	0

(b) 23.51%

2. (a)

Date	Interest	Off Principal	Balance
			$625.50
End of 1st	$10.95	$58.55	566.95
2nd	9.92	59.58	507.37
3rd	8.88	60.62	446.75
4th	7.82	61.68	385.07
5th	6.74	62.76	322.31
6th	5.64	63.86	258.45
7th	4.52	64.98	193.47
8th	3.39	66.11	127.36
9th	2.23	67.27	60.09
10th	1.05	60.09	0

(b) 21.33%

3. 18.55%

4. The interest is calculated more than once during the year. Therefore, Sharon is incorrect. *Nominal* interest rate would be 1 × 12 = 12%.

5. 11.69%

REVIEW EXERCISE 6.8, page 162

1. (a) $101.02
(b) $114.75
(c) $148.83
(d) $184.17
(e) $226.97

2. (a) 10.45%
(b) 10.31%
(c) 13.54%
(d) 19.82%
(e) 6.0%

3. (a) 87 d
(b) 186 d
(c) 326 d
(d) 131 d
(e) 369 d

4. (a) $8 713
(b) $451
(c) $1 455
(d) $4 150
(e) $4 368

5. 1 a 258 d

6. $1 797.47

7.

			$2 500.00
$200.44	$44.79	$155.65	2 344.35
200.44	42.00	158.44	2 185.91
200.44	39.16	161.28	2 024.63
200.44	36.27	164.17	1 860.46
200.44	33.33	167.11	1 693.35
200.44	30.34	170.10	1 523.25

8. (a) 14.38%
(b) 15.73%
(c) 16.20%
(d) 15.86%
(e) 15.35%

9. $32

10.

Date	Interest	Off Principal	Balance
			$1 500.00
End of 1st	$16.88	$ 98.12	$1 401.88
2nd	15.77	99.23	1 302.65
3rd	14.65	100.35	1 202.30
4th	13.53	101.47	1 100.83
5th	12.38	102.62	998.21
6th	11.23	103.77	894.44
7th	10.06	104.94	789.50
8th	8.88	106.12	683.38
9th	7.69	107.31	576.07
10th	6.48	108.52	467.55
11th	5.26	109.74	357.81
12th	4.03	110.97	246.84

11. 18.83%

12. (a)

Date	Interest	Off Principal	Balance
			$314.95
End of 1st	$4.72	$31.28	$283.67
2nd	4.26	31.74	251.93
3rd	3.78	32.22	219.71
4th	3.30	32.70	187.01
5th	2.81	33.19	153.82
6th	2.31	33.69	120.13
7th	1.80	34.20	85.93
8th	1.29	34.71	51.22
9th	0.77	35.23	15.99
10th	0.24	15.99	0

(b) $25.28   (c) 17.51%

CUMULATIVE REVIEW 4, page 163

1. $\frac{31}{120}$

2. 12.07%

3. $\frac{3}{20}, \frac{3}{5}, \frac{11}{20}$

4. 200

5. (a) $\frac{1}{6}$ (d) $\frac{3}{4}$

(b) $\frac{1}{32}$ (e) $\frac{1}{8}$

(c) $\frac{5}{8}$

6. 39

7. 896.55

8. 2.58 m

9. $4x^2y(3y + x^2 + z)$

10. (a) −0.9
(b) 12
(c) 2

11. $545.90

12. $720

13. $490.88

14. $9.80

15. $5 000

16. $583.20

17. $3.64

EXERCISE 7.1, page 180

1.
Earnings before deductions		$4 525.00
Less: employment expense deduction		500.00
Net employment earnings		$4 025.00
Interest income		226.02
Total income		$4 251.02
Canada Pension Plan contribution	$ 49.05	
Unemployment Insurance premiums	104.08	
Safety Deposit box	14.00	167.13
Net income		$4 083.89
Basic personal exemption		3 770.00
		$ 313.89
Standard deduction for medical expenses		100.00
		$ 213.89
Interest, dividend and capital gains deductions		226.02
Taxable Income		0

Refund claimed, $127.50

2.
Earnings before deductions		$7 475.00
Less: employment expense deduction		500.00
Net employment earnings		$6 975.00
Interest income		163.98
Total income		$7 138.98
Canada Pension Plan contribution	$102.15	
Unemployment Insurance premiums	171.93	
Tuition	550.00	824.08
Net income		$6 314.90
Basic personal exemption		3 770.00
		$2 544.90
Charitable donations	$120.00	
Interest, dividend and capital gains deduction	163.98	283.98
Taxable Income		$2 260.92

Federal tax		$ 45.00
Provincial tax		117.60
Total tax		$162.60
Ontario Tax Credit	$215.68	
Income Tax deducted	307.10	522.78
Refund claimed		$360.18

3.
Earnings before deductions		$16 400.00
Less: employment expense deduction		500.00
Net employment earnings		$15 900.00
Interest income		361.93
Total income		$16 261.93
Canada Pension Plan contribution	$ 262.80	
Unemployment Insurance premiums	377.20	
Registered Retirement Savings Plan	1000.00	1 640.00
Net income		$14 621.93
Basic personal exemption		3 770.00
		$10 851.93

Medical expenses	$538.00	
Less: 3% Net income	438.66	
	99.34	
Charitable donations	110.00	$ 209.34
Interest, dividend and capital gains deduction		361.93	571.27
Taxable Income		$10 280.66
Federal tax	$1 495.00	
Provincial tax	831.20	
Total tax	$2 326.20	
Ontario Tax Credit	$ 74.47	
Income Tax deducted	2 200.20	2 274.67
Balance owing	$ 51.53	

CUMULATIVE REVIEW 5, page 181

1. (a) 900   (b) 12 000
2. (a) 2.28   (b) 5.28
3. $x = 1$
4. 148.8
5. 64
6. (a) 15   (b) 13
7. (a) 6   (b) 41
8. 24.32
9. 20%
10. 425.88
11. 8%
12. 500
13. $12 800
14. $38.22
15. 1 a
16. (a) 48, 0.025   (b) 36, 0.045
17. $478.40
18. $4.67
19. $11\frac{1}{4}$%
20. $49

EXERCISE 8.1, page 186

1. (a) $6
   (b) 28.8%
   (c) $2.77
2. $0.40
3. 18.6%
4. (a) $5.68
   (b) $11.64
5. (a) 0.8%
   (b) 4%
   (c) decrease

EXERCISE 8.2, page 187

1. $ 35.80
       34.50
     313.76
   $384.06
2. $24.50
     9.00
   53.00
   $86.50
3. $ 59.04
     97.90
     19.00
     97.65
   $273.59
4. $562.50
     94.25
      1.23
     14.63
      7.61
   $680.22

EXERCISE 8.3, page 189

(a) August 2 $ 8.47 $ 838.03
(b) January 19   9.63   953.12
(c) September 7   124.07   6 079.34
(d) April 4   170.52   8 355.58
(e) July 10   4.95   490.31
(f) September 21   104.81   5 135.84
(g) April 18   4.68   463.12
(h) October 25   72.52   3 553.40
(i) November 22   24.70   2 444.88
(j) July 8   119.30   3 857.53

EXERCISE 8.4, page 191

1. (a) $218.25
   (b) $312.93
   (c) $58.76
   (d) $23.74
   (e) $23.35
2. (a) $26.98
   (b) $37.83
   (c) $282.15
   (d) $163.60
   (e) $59.10
3. B is 83¢ less.
4. B
5. regular

EXERCISE 8.5, page 193

1. (a) 50.5%
   (b) 61.75%
   (c) 55%
   (d) 57.25%
   (e) 59.5%
2. (a) $123.48
   (b) $42.51
   (c) $47.02
   (d) $74.81
   (e) $23.73
3. (a) $29.68
   (b) $32.53
   (c) $121.30
   (d) $131.22
   (e) $191.25
   (f) $41.77
   (g) $206.98
4. (a) $40.45, $25.05
   (b) $113.99, $184.01
   (c) $208.04, $281.46
   (d) $171.25, $174.70
   (e) $39.69, $58.31

REVIEW EXERCISE 8.6, page 194

1. $ 5.94
    56.98
     5.19
    41.85
    52.64
   119.92
   $282.52

2. Sept. 7, $1 063.65
3. $136.81, $68.40
4. $4 334.68
5. $2 285.47, 63.662 5%
6. June 21, $3 592.87, $3 485.09
7. 20%

CUMULATIVE REVIEW 6, page 195

1. (a) 0.08, 8%
   (b) $0.6\overline{6}$, $66\frac{2}{3}$%
   (c) 0.375, $37\frac{1}{2}$%
   (d) 0.625, $62\frac{1}{2}$%
   (e) 0.60, 60%
2. (a) $\frac{1}{20}$, 5%
   (b) $4\frac{163}{250}$, 465.2%
   (c) $3\frac{3}{4}$, 375%
   (d) $\frac{1}{200}$, 0.5%
   (e) $\frac{7}{8}$, 87.5%
3. 78.4
4. (a) $8a^2c^8$
   (b) $-\frac{31}{21}$
   (c) $7ab + 6a^2 - 6ax - 6b^2$
5. (a) $2ab(6 + 3a^2 + 4b)$
   (b) $ab(33ab^2 + 8b + 7a^2)$
6. (a) 8.6
   (b) -19
   (c) 13
7. 23.45
8. $132
9. 90 d
10. $2 399.93
11. $498.41
12. (a) $6.19, $8.80
    (b) $4.71, $6.90
    (c) $4.93, $7.19
    (d) $6.65, $9.35
13. (a) $8
    (b) $146
    (c) $21
    (d) $30
14. $612.52
15. $11.25
16. April 30
17. student

EXERCISE 9.1, page 199

1. (a) $0.35
   (b) $0.72
   (c) $12.34
   (d) $47.91
   (e) $59.80
   (f) $70.20
   (g) $244.30
   (h) $171.40
   (i) $244.81
   (j) $1 262.81

2. (a) 23.69%
   (b) 47.92%
   (c) 46.97%
   (d) 34.25%
   (e) 40.13%
   (f) 32.42%
   (g) 54.44%
   (h) 36.57%
   (i) 49.50%
   (j) 49.48%

3. $7.98

4. $40

5. $0.58

6. $55.25

7. 35%

EXERCISE 9.2, page 202

	$ Margin	% Margin of Retail
1. (a)	0.50	50%
(b)	1.79	35.87%
(c)	18.15	25.95%
(d)	17.21	11.51%
(e)	60.33	24.14%
(f)	8.68	34.79%
(g)	73.08	27.58%
(h)	15.83	45.88%
(i)	36.55	28.13%
(j)	115.45	32.07%

2.   Cost

   (a) $ 53.97
   (b) $ 83.33
   (c) $335.21
   (d) $ 41.51
   (e) $ 56.64
   (f) $496.23
   (g) $266.80

3. Total retail $574.08
         cost $355.93

4. (a) $72 500
   (b) Jan $ 1 450
       Feb   2 175
       Mar   2 900
       Apr   5 075
       May   7 975
       June   8 700
       July   5 800
       Aug   4 350
       Sept   2 900
       Oct   13 050
       Nov   14 500
       Dec   3 625

5. (a) Meat   33.92%
       Produce   21.5%
       Grocery   13.22%
       Dairy   12.86%
   (b) Whole store 18.28%
       Dairy; meat
   (c) Answers will vary.

EXERCISE 9.3, page 205

1.			
(a)		32.55%	48.25%
(b)	8.96		33.37%
(c)		13.22	35.48%
(d)			39.93% 66.48%
(e)	2.75		66.91%
(f)		6.35	37.48%
(g)			33.23% 49.77%
(h)	3.59		61.28%
(i)		10.31	42.87%
(j)			25.15% 33.60%

2. $2.00   4. $22.50

3. $11.82   5. $3.10

EXERCISE 9.4, page 206

1.	Cost of Goods	Retail
(a)	$4 294.50	$6 227.03
(b)	2 615.37	3 923.06
(c)	1 000.99	1 551.53
(d)	1 493.79	2 121.18
(e)	23.21	38.30
(f)	3 668.23	5 062.16
(g)	5 692.22	8 196.80
(h)	3 112.64	4 824.59
(i)	24.75	33.17
(j)	191.30	309.91

2. (a) On Cost = 29.63%
   (b) Of Retail = 22.86%

3. $13.62

4. $2.62

EXERCISE 9.5, page 209

1. (a)

Bette's Boutique
Income Statement
For the Year Ended 19-- 12 31

Revenue from Sales		$ 4 100
Expenses: Rent	$ 900	
Salaries	1 200	
Advertising	240	
Utilities	320	
Total Operating Expenses		2 660
Net Income		$ 1 440

(b)

Koski's Bicycle Repair Service
Income Statement
For the Year Ended 19-- 12 31

Revenue from Repair Services		$21 900
Expenses: Rent	$1 200	
Salaries	9 800	
Utilities	1 100	
Advertising	350	
Telephone	90	
Miscellaneous	500	
Total Operating Expenses		13 040
Net Income		$ 8 860

(c)

April Sales Company
Income Statement
For the Year Ended 19-- 12 31

Revenue from Sales		$124 000
Cost of Goods Sold		
Inventory January 1	$50 000	
Add: Purchases	45 000	
Cost Goods Available for Sale	95 000	
Less: Inventory December 31	52 000	
	43 000	
Gross Trading Margin		$81 000
Expenses: Advertising	320	
Miscellaneous	820	
Office Expense	1 000	
Insurance	400	
Supplies Expense	600	
Utilities	320	
Salaries	21 000	
Total Operating Expenses		24 460
Net Income		$56 540

2. (a) $3 000, $400
   (b) $35 000, $18 000
   (c) $100 000, $22 000
   (d) $2 000, $1 500 loss
   (e) $11 155, $2 900

REVIEW EXERCISE 9.6, page 210

1. (a) 163.64%
   (b) 62.07%

2. (a) $24 750
   (b) $24 165

3. $21 916.67

4. (a) $31 612.90
   (b) $16 612.90

5. $21.14

6. Yes. $6.52 + $0.55 = $7.07. This cost will yield a 69.02% markup on cost if the article sells for $11.95.

7. $131.97

8.

Syd's Cycle Shop
Statement of Cost of Goods Sold
For the Month Ending 19-- 12 31

Inventory January 1	$1 800
Add: Purchases	3 900
	$5 700
Less: Inventory January 31	2 100
Cost of Goods Sold	$3 600

9.

The Bay City Brothers
Income Statement
For Month Ended 19--- 02 28

Sales Revenue		$18 500
Cost of Goods Sold		
Inventory February 1	$ 2 200	
Add Purchases	14 000	
	$16 200	
Inventory February 28	3 000	
Cost of Goods Sold		13 200
Gross Margin of Profit		$ 5 300
Operating Expenses		
Advertising	$ 200	
Salaries	1 200	
Taxes	150	
Utilities	65	
Miscellaneous	350	
Total Expenses		1 965
Net Income		$ 3 335

CUMULATIVE REVIEW 7, page 211

1. 60

2. 16.13%

3. 42.86%

4. 15.56%

5. (a) 12.5   (d) 60.25
   (b) 91.67   (e) 8.4
   (c) 37.5

6. 7.06%

7. 39%

8. (a) $4pq + 11pr$
   (b) $36a + 3b$
   (c) $13xp - 3xr$
   (d) $19xy$
   (e) x^9
   (f) $11x^2 + 11y^2$

9. (a) $3x + 18$
   (b) $7x + 6$
   (c) $2 - 8x$
   (d) $9 - 2p$
   (e) $x + 3$

10. (a) 14 m   (b) $41.72

11. $4.35

12. $1 447.60

13. $53.55

14. (a) 11.65%   (d) 43.57%
    (b) 61.525%   (e) 39.49%
    (c) 66.34%

15. $121.91

16. $50.27

17. $242.60

18. $3 890

19. (a) $193.64   (b) $197.59

20. CPP, UIC, Union dues, bonds, health insurance, . . .

EXERCISE 10.1, page 215

1. (a) $101.02   (d) $184.17
   (b) $114.75   (e) $226.97
   (c) $148.83

2. 13.93%

3. $1 441.13

4. $190.03

5. 13.78%

6. $1 237.50

7. $11.91

8. 14.38%

9. (a) $375   (b) 13.78%

10. $48.19

EXERCISE 10.2, page 216

1. (a) $31.50
   (b) $765.81
   (c) $132.36
2. $27.30
3. (a) $7.62   (b) $30.48
4. (a) $65.27   (b) $261.08
5. (a) $142.80
   (b) $690.88
   (c) Public transit
6. (a) $34.35   (b) $137.40
7. (a) $63
   (b) $8.50
   (c) Bus
8. (a) $147.00
   (b) $48
   (c) Public transit, car
9. (a) Lui: $111.30, Niki: $111.30,
       Cheryl: $134.62,
       Donna: $121.37
   (b) Cheryl, Lui and Niki, yes
10. Plymouth to work, station
    wagon on weekend.

EXERCISE 10.3, page 221

(a) $373   (f) $419
(b) $342   (g) $491
(c) $168   (h) $410
(d) $696   (i) $324
(e) $142   (j) $467

EXERCISE 10.4, page 223

(a) $801.25   (f) $942
(b) $934   (g) $921.44
(c) $712.50   (h) $1 295.80
(d) $1 077   (i) $484
(e) $535.50   (j) $652.50

EXERCISE 10.5, page 225

1. (a) $136   2. (a) $1 132.50
   (b) $53   (b) $1 372
   (c) $765   (c) $393
   (d) $539   (d) $456
   (e) $136   (e) $1 192.50
   (f) $348   (f) $410.44
   (g) $446   (g) $414
   (h) $143   (h) $190.50
   (i) $284   (i) $334.94
   (j) $301   (j) $190
3. $2 246
4. $888.75
5. $1 001

REVIEW EXERCISE 10.6, page 226

1. $2 219.88
2. $439.40
3. $624.13
4. 13.93%
5. 14.07%
6. $32.06
7. $12.70
8. $148.85
9. $142.80
10. $978
11. $1 135.25

CUMULATIVE REVIEW 8, page 227

1. (a) $\frac{11}{20}$ (b) $\frac{1}{6}$ (c) $\frac{4}{5}$ (d) $\frac{5}{8}$ (e) $\frac{3}{4}$
2. 47.81
3. (a) $8(a + 4ab + 6c - 4ac)$
   (b) $4a(b + 2c + 4)$
   (c) $b(A + Z)$
4.

	Listing	Broker	Agent
(a)	$3 174.00	$1 745.70	$1 428.30
(b)	2 335.00	1 284.25	1 050.75
(c)	2 947.50	1 621.13	1 326.37
(d)	2 139.50	1 176.73	962.77

5. (a) 56.89%, 131.98%   6. (a) 8.5%
   (b) $65.88, 35.49%   (b) 7.75%
   (c) $44.52, 78.57%   (c) 7.5%
   (d) $10.06, 138.07%   (d) 9.62%
   (e) $105.44, 39.40%   (e) 10.5%
7.

	Interest	Annual Effective Rate
(a)	$507.50	12.73%
(b)	274.50	12.19%
(c)	619.50	13.20%
(d)	357.50	12.02%

8. $310.50
9. $168.85

EXERCISE 11.1, page 232

1. (a) 94¢ (b) 92¢
2. mean: 81.78; median: 81
3. (a) mean: 62.3; median: 53.5; mode: 53
   (b) The mean would not indicate the
       extreme values.
4. mean: $24 769.23; median: $15 000;
   mode: $15 000
   (a) median and mode
   (b) weighted
5. (a) median: $25 000
   (b) There is no mode. The mean
       includes extreme values.

6. (a) mean: $166 575;
       median: $166 125;
       no mode
   (b) simple
7. (a) mean: 2.6;
       median: 1;
       mode: 1
   (b) The mode because
       of the very high
       number of people
       it involves.
8. (a) 642.86
       Extreme values on
       Saturday and
       Sunday
   (b) $3 633.71
9. $6 026.10
10. (a) $67 559.26
    (b) $64 800
    (c) $61 000
    (d) median
11. (a) $3.16
    (b) $3.16

EXERCISE 11.2, page 236

1. (a) $111 000
   (b) $60 000
       80 000
       90 000
       102 500
       111 000
2. (a) $31 222.22
   (b) $21 000
       11 000
       12 500
       25 000
       33 500
       39 500
       43 500
       50 000
3. (a) $877 777.78
   (b) $525 000
       450 000
       416 666.67
       437 500
       460 000
       550 000
       657 142.86
       762 500
       877 777.78
   (c) $ 450 000
          362 500
          425 000
          525 000
          775 000
        1 150 000
        1 400 000
        1 650 000

324

EXERCISE 11.3, page 239

1. (a) $100.60 (e) $146.78
   (b) $69.64   (f) $181.08
   (c) $14.96   (g) $194.62
   (d) $213.28 (h) $85.30

2. (a) $2.91   (f) $2.89
   (b) $3.62   (g) $3.75
   (c) $3.68   (h) $2.99
   (d) $3.70   (i) $3.59
   (e) $3.01   (j) $3.78

3. (a) $4.58   (f) $5.51
   (b) $5.49   (g) $5.59
   (c) $5.58   (h) $4.64
   (d) $4.67   (i) $4.74
   (e) $4.73   (j) $5.45

4. (a) $0.37   (d) $4.55
   (b) $2.30   (e) $2.65
   (c) $6.25

5. 30 kg: length, width or depth – 1 m
           length plus girth – 2 m

6. (a) $2.03   (d) $16.80
   (b) $1.12   (e) $2.07
   (c) $2.09

EXERCISE 11.4, page 244

1. 1977

2. 1982

3. 300 m³/d

4. 540 m³/d

5. 420 m³/d

6. 310 m³/d

7. 475 m³/d

8. 250 m³/d

9. 700 m³/d; 460 m³/d; 390 m³/d

EXERCISE 11.5, page 245

1.

HEIGHT OF BUILDING

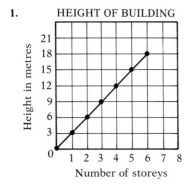

2.

TEMPERATURE INCREASE

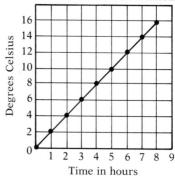

3.

DISTANCE TRAVELLED AT 120 km/h

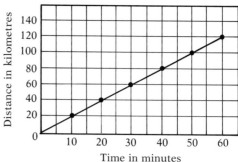

4.

COST OF PENS

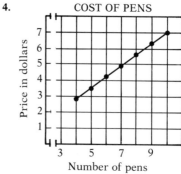

EXERCISE 11.6, page 248

1. THE AVERAGE MONTHLY RAINFALL IN THE OTTAWA AREA

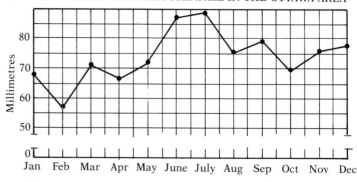

2.

GRADE 11 AVERAGE TYPING SPEEDS

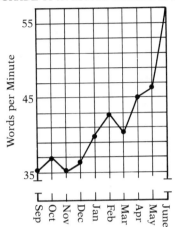

3.

PERCENT OF POPULATION PER AGE GROUP IN ORVILLE

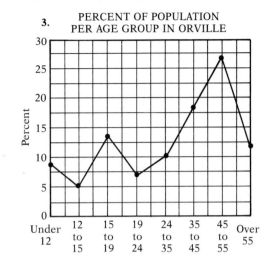

4.

FOOD EXPENDITURES – FAMILY OF FOUR

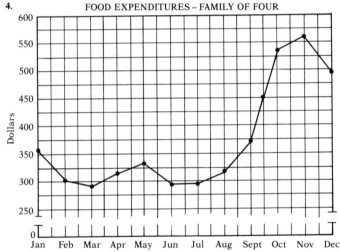

5.

SALES

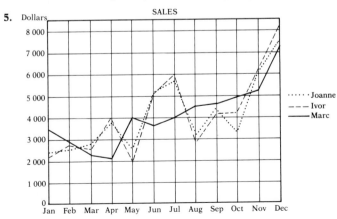

6.

CAR AND TRUCK PRODUCTION

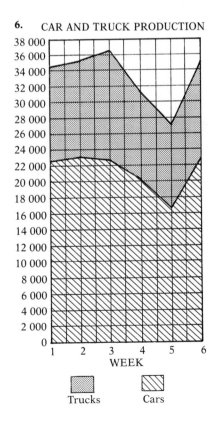

7.

CBC REVENUES, YEARS ENDED MARCH 31

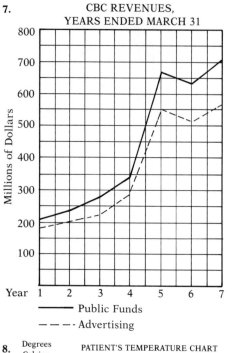

Millions of Dollars

——— Public Funds

– – – Advertising

8.

PATIENT'S TEMPERATURE CHART

Degrees Celsius

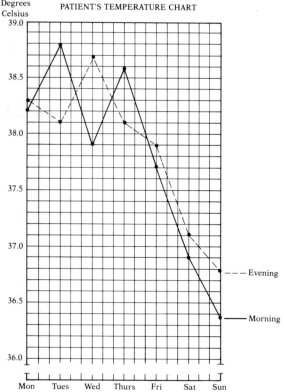

– – – Evening

——— Morning

9.

TRADING ACTIVITY ON STOCK EXCHANGES

Thousands of Shares

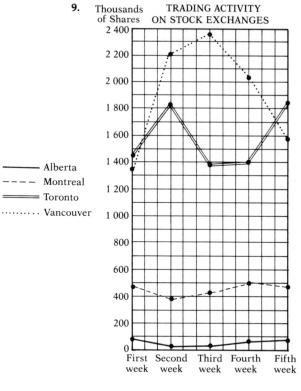

——— Alberta
– – – Montreal
═══ Toronto
·········· Vancouver

10.

CANADIAN TOURIST EXPENDITURES

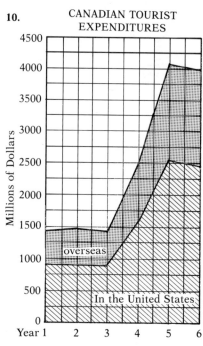

Millions of Dollars

overseas

In the United States

EXERCISE 11.7, page 253

1.

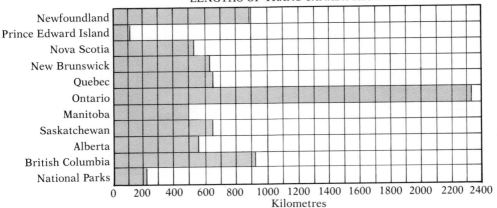

LENGTHS OF TRANS-CANADA HIGHWAY

2.

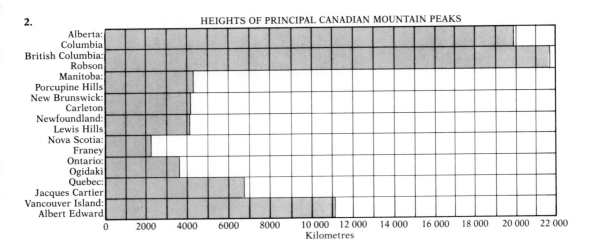

HEIGHTS OF PRINCIPAL CANADIAN MOUNTAIN PEAKS

3.

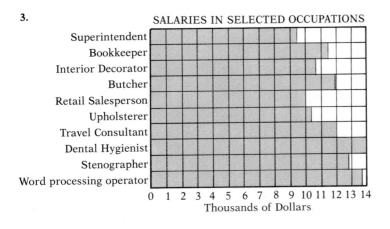

SALARIES IN SELECTED OCCUPATIONS

4.

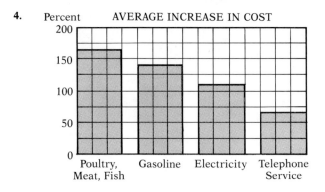

Percent — AVERAGE INCREASE IN COST

5. (a)

RESULTS OF BUSINESS MATHEMATICS EXAMINATION

(b) 65.7%

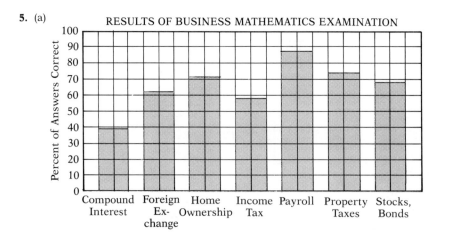

6.

AREA BY TENURE, BY ECONOMIC REGION

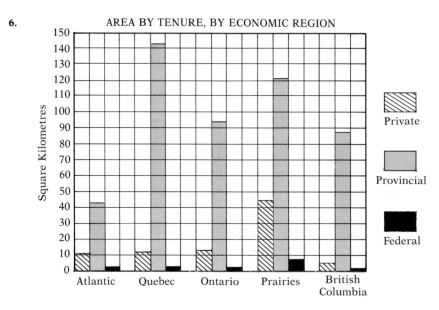

7.

MEAN TEMPERATURES

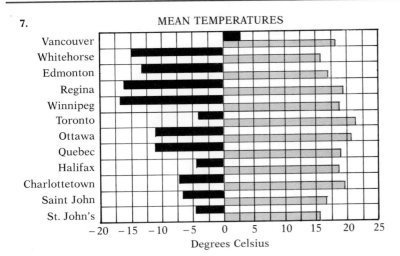

8.

DISTRIBUTION OF FEDERAL PUBLIC SERVANTS
(excluding those in capital region)

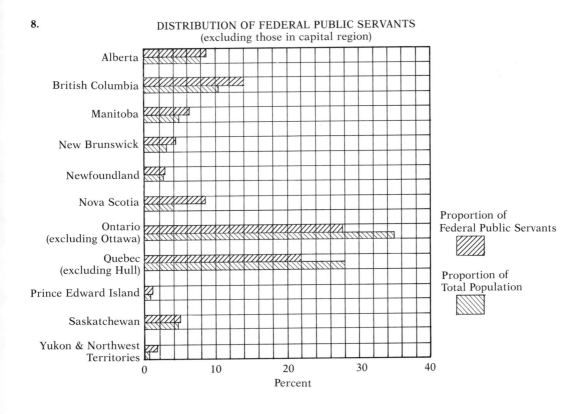

9.

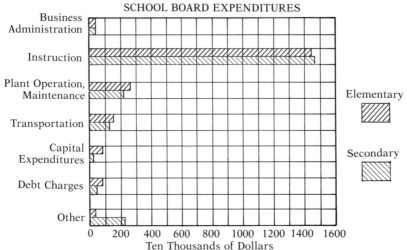

SCHOOL BOARD EXPENDITURES

Business Administration

Instruction

Plant Operation, Maintenance

Transportation

Capital Expenditures

Debt Charges

Other

0   200   400   600   800   1000 1200 1400 1600
Ten Thousands of Dollars

Elementary

Secondary

10.

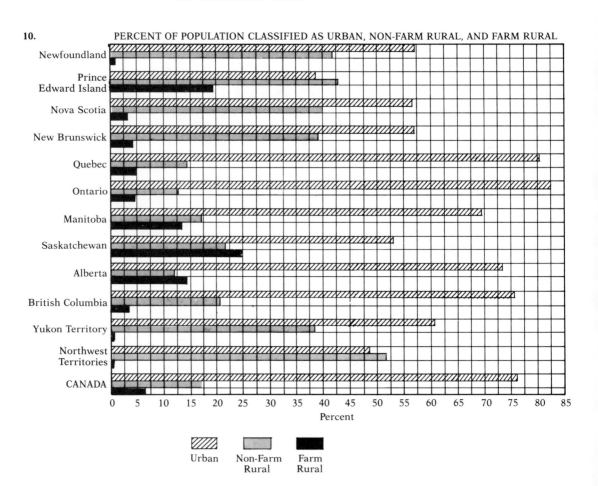

PERCENT OF POPULATION CLASSIFIED AS URBAN, NON-FARM RURAL, AND FARM RURAL

Newfoundland
Prince Edward Island
Nova Scotia
New Brunswick
Quebec
Ontario
Manitoba
Saskatchewan
Alberta
British Columbia
Yukon Territory
Northwest Territories
CANADA

0   5   10   15   20   25   30   35   40   45   50   55   60   65   70   75   80   85
Percent

Urban   Non-Farm   Farm
            Rural   Rural

EXERCISE 11.8, page 257

1. HOW GREENSPAN SPENDS ITS MONEY

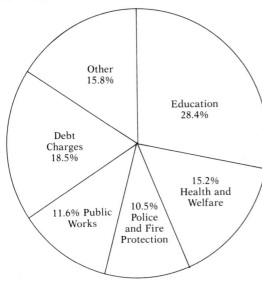

Other 15.8%

Education 28.4%

Debt Charges 18.5%

11.6% Public Works

10.5% Police and Fire Protection

15.2% Health and Welfare

2. SPICES IN SPICE DISPENSER

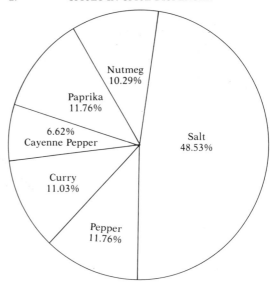

Nutmeg 10.29%

Paprika 11.76%

6.62% Cayenne Pepper

Curry 11.03%

Salt 48.53%

Pepper 11.76%

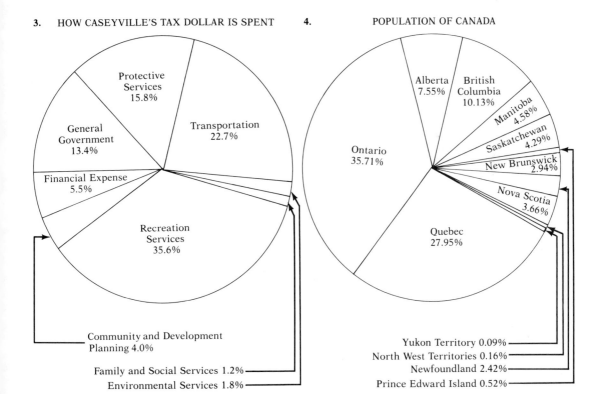

3. HOW CASEYVILLE'S TAX DOLLAR IS SPENT

Protective Services 15.8%

General Government 13.4%

Transportation 22.7%

Financial Expense 5.5%

Recreation Services 35.6%

Community and Development Planning 4.0%

Family and Social Services 1.2%

Environmental Services 1.8%

4. POPULATION OF CANADA

Alberta 7.55%

British Columbia 10.13%

Manitoba 4.58%

Saskatchewan 4.29%

New Brunswick 2.94%

Nova Scotia 3.66%

Ontario 35.71%

Quebec 27.95%

Yukon Territory 0.09%

North West Territories 0.16%

Newfoundland 2.42%

Prince Edward Island 0.52%

EXERCISE 11.9, page 259

1.   GOVERNMENT EXPENDITURES

Municipal   Provincial

General Government 25.2%	6.1%
	3.8%
Protection	7.7%
8.2% Health and Welfare	
16.2%	
Education 43.3%	63.5%
Transfers 1.5%	2.6%
Debt Charges 5.6%	6.3%

2. (a)   (b) Magazine
                                                          (c) Radio
    NET ADVERTISING REVENUES BY MEDIA
    Year 1   Year 2

Radio 10.6%	10.2%
Television 13.3%	11.5%
Newspapers 35.1%	33.5%
Magazines 6.4%	13.2%
Other 34.6%	31.6%

3. CANADIAN PRODUCTION FROM CRUDE OIL

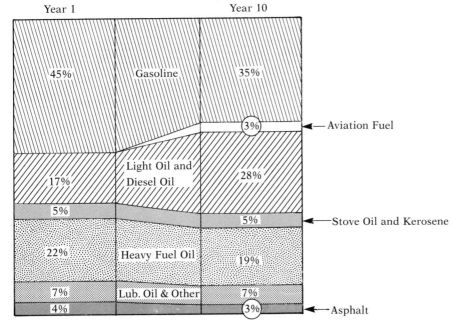

Year 1   Year 10

45%	Gasoline	35%
		◄── (3%) ──── Aviation Fuel
17%	Light Oil and Diesel Oil	28%
5%		5% ◄───── Stove Oil and Kerosene
22%	Heavy Fuel Oil	19%
7%	Lub. Oil & Other	7%
4%		(3%) ◄──── Asphalt

4.   MONTHLY FOOD EXPENDITURE

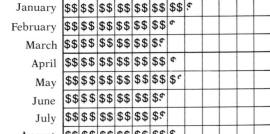

	0	100	200	300	400	500	600
January	$$ $$ $$ $$ $$ $$ $$ ¢						
February	$$ $$ $$ $$ $$ $$ ¢						
March	$$ $$ $$ $$ $$ $¢						
April	$$ $$ $$ $$ $$ $$ ¢						
May	$$ $$ $$ $$ $$ $$ $¢						
June	$$ $$ $$ $$ $$ $¢						
July	$$ $$ $$ $$ $$ $¢						
August	$$ $$ $$ $$ $$ $$ ¢						
September	$$ $$ $$ $$ $$ $$ $$ $						
October	$$ $$ $$ $$ $$ $$ $$ $$ $$ $$ $¢					
November	$$ $$ $$ $$ $$ $$ $$ $$ $$ $$ $$ $¢				
December	$$ $$ $$ $$ $$ $$ $$ $$ $$ $¢					

Dollars

5. Answers will vary.

6. Answers will vary.

7. (a)   ERRORS IN GRADE 11 SHORTHAND TEST

	0	5	10	15	20	25	30	35	40	45
Punctuation	xxxxx	xxxxx	xxxxx	xxxxx	xxxxx	xxxxx	xxxxx	xxx		
Word Form	xxxxx	xxxxx	xxxxx	xxxxx	xxxxx	xxxxx				
Erasing	xxxxx	xxxxx	xx							
Spelling	xxxxx	xxxxx	xxxxx	xxxx						
Paragraphing	xxxxx	xxx								
Capitalization	xxxxx									

Number of Errors

REVIEW EXERCISE 11.10, page 261

1. Mode = $4 995
   Median = $3 845
   Mean = $4 113

2. (a) $250
   (b) $250
   (c) $473.22
   (d) Median and mode

3. (a) $483.70
   (b) $488.80
   (c) $0.53
   (d) $485.20   (e) $485.20
       513.93   513.93
       465.58   455.78
       468.31   422.70
       479.12   499.43
       481.33   507.38
       491.37   522.00
       495.31   537.25
       494.18   504.00
       483.70   437.25

6. COST OF OWNING AND OPERATING A CAR

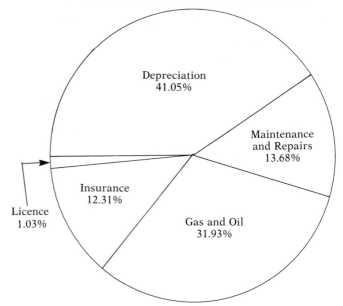

4.

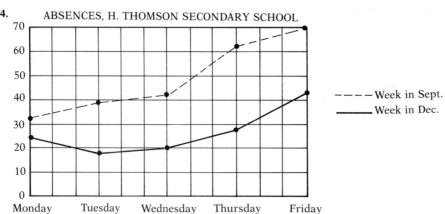

ABSENCES, H. THOMSON SECONDARY SCHOOL

5.   MARITAL STATUS, EMPLOYEES OF H. B. HUTTON LTD.

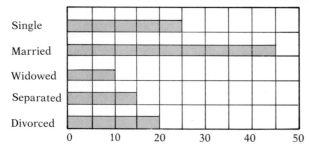

7. Weekly
Earnings
in $

EARNINGS AT WOODBURN'S

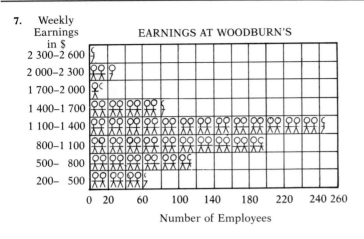

Number of Employees

8. Answers will vary.

CUMULATIVE REVIEW 9, page 263

1. 12.5%
2. $161.50
3. 330
4. 350
5. (a) −24
   (b) 0
   (c) 6
6. (a) $30.58
   (b) $51.52
   (c) $116.03
7. $23.70
8. 46%
9. $1 440
10. $3 700, $5 550
11. $1 438.20
12. $44
13. $3
14. (a) $103.40
    (b) $96.61
    (c) $41.30
    (d) $131.53

15.

			$2 200.00
200.44	33.46	166.98	2 033.02
200.44	30.92	169.52	1 863.50
200.44	28.34	172.10	1 691.40
200.44	25.72	174.72	1 516.68
200.44	23.07	177.37	1 339.31
200.44	20.37	180.07	1 159.24

16. 19.72%
17. $631.58
18. $370.25
19. $167.73

EXERCISE 12.1, page 267

1. (a) 14 m, 12 m²
   (b) 48 m, 128 m²
   (c) 58 dm, 210 dm²
   (d) 66 cm, 270 cm²
   (e) 25 mm, 178 mm
   (f) 136 m, 1 035 m²
   (g) 69 cm, 296 cm²
   (h) 22.5 cm, 85 cm
   (i) 82.6 m, 423 m²
   (j) 55 cm, 182 cm

2. $812.96

3. (a) 140
   (b) 10
   (c) $98.85

4. (a) 4 200
   (b) 30

EXERCISE 12.2, page 268

1. (a) 66 m, 272.25 m²
   (b) 89 m, 495.062 5 m²
   (c) 19.56 cm, 382.593 6 cm²
   (d) 214.06 cm, 45 821.683 6 cm²
   (e) 74.8 m, 349.69 m²
   (f) 68 m, 272 m
   (g) 35.5 cm, 142 cm
   (h) 39.6 m, 98.01 m²
   (i) 14.1 m, 198.81 m²
   (j) 58.6 cm, 234.4 cm

2. (a) 72.24 m²
   (b) 4 L

EXERCISE 12.3, page 270

1. (a) 408 cm²
   (b) 24.65 m²
   (c) 4.5 m
   (d) 62.4 cm
   (e) 1 726.56 cm²
   (f) 15 cm
   (g) 17.6 m
   (h) 1 304.65 cm²
   (i) 7 215 cm²
   (j) 9 092.75 cm²

2. (a) 84 m²
   (b) 24 m²
   (c) 150 cm²
   (d) 756 cm²
   (e) 600 cm²
   (f) 1 344 m²
   (g) 864 cm²
   (h) 1 350 cm²
   (i) 216 m²
   (j) 1 176 cm²

3. 3 kg

4. $0.67

EXERCISE 12.4, page 272

1. (a) 17.5 cm, 110 cm, 962.5 cm²
   (b) 28 cm, 88 cm, 616 cm²
   (c) 42 cm, 84 cm, 5 544 cm²
   (d) 196 cm, 392 cm, 120 736 cm²
   (e) 28 m, 176 m, 2 464 m²
   (f) 7 m, 14 m, 44 m
   (g) 175 cm, 550 cm, 24 062.5 cm²
   (h) 63 cm, 396 cm, 12 474 cm²
   (i) 10.5 cm, 21 cm, 66 cm
   (j) 220.5 cm, 441 cm, 1 386 cm

2. 1

3. $48.17

EXERCISE 12.5, page 273

1. (a) 6 m^3
   (b) 1 280 cm^3
   (c) 240 m^3
   (d) 600 mm^3
   (e) 6 m^3

2. (a) 216 mm^3
   (b) 64 m^3
   (c) 27 cm^3

3. 180 kL

4. 22.5 m^3

5. $304

EXERCISE 12.6, page 275

1. (a) 226.29 cm^3
   (b) 84.86 mm^3
   (c) 502.86 cm^3
   (d) 997.54 cm^3
   (e) 396 m^3
   (f) 2.36 m^3

2. 452.57 cm^3

3. 0.51 m^3

4. 119.62 g

5. 282.86 kL

6. 7 954.5 cm

7. 4 cm

REVIEW EXERCISE 12.7, page 276

1. 64 m

2. (a) 160 m   (b) 459 m^2

3. (a) 1 350 m^2 (b) 16 200

4. 24 cm

5. 22 cm

6. 175 m, 350 m, 96 250 m^2

7. 10.5 cm, 66 cm, 346.5 cm^2

8. 7 m, 14 m, 44 m

9. 15 000 cm^3

10. (a) 7.54 cm^3 (b) 471.43 mm^3

CUMULATIVE REVIEW 10, page 276

1. 0.805

2. $19.95

3. 46.14%

4. (a) $\frac{1}{8}$ (b) $\frac{5}{6}$

5. $6bc(b + 2c^2 + 4)$

6. $3mk$

7. (a) $85.68   (b) $1 409.67

8. $1 495

9. $172.50

10. $48.24

11.
			$3 000.00
129.58	46.25	83.33	2 916.67
129.58	44.97	84.61	2 832.06
129.58	43.66	85.92	2 746.14
129.58	42.34	87.24	2 658.90
129.58	40.99	88.59	2 570.31
129.58	39.63	89.95	2 480.36

12. (a) 17.51%   (b) 19.39%

13. (a) $1 341.17
    (b) $1 625
    (c) $1 410.50
    (d) Mean

14. (a) $1 107   (b) $183.92

15. $8.25

16. $36.24 balance due   17. None

EXERCISE 13.1, page 280

1. (a) 386
   (b) 3 255
   (c) 3 280
   (d) 285 896
   (e) 3 844.9
   (f) 3 176.86
   (g) 7 964
   (h) 7 473
   (i) 7 491
   (j) 609 596
   (k) 774 138
   (l) 6 795.37
   (m) 108 029.902 730
   (n) 2 521.913 23
   (o) 1 060 675.185 9
   (p) 6 643.386 16
   (q) $303.05
   (r) $325.58
   (s) $332.07
   (t) $346.67

2. (a) 948.213
   (b) 1 168.244 53
   (c) 273.866
   (d) 376 946.713
   (e) 408.487 79

3. (a) 1 939.46 S
       2 798.97 S
       5 294.78 T
   (b) 1 716.16 S
       2 497.55 S
       4 368.70 T
   (c) 1 917.98 S
       2 821.05 S
       4 842.43 T
   (d) 1 746.37 S
       3 018.89 S
       3 844.72 T
   (e) 1 901.95 S
       2 526.85 S
       4 069.22 T

4. A $70 630.14
   B $77 828.09
   C $89 673.00

   Jan $48 069.60
   Feb $33 630.50
   Mar $38 211.33
   Apr $39 660.03
   May $34 078.64
   June $44 481.13

   Total $238 131.23

5. (a) 40 888
   (b) 72 578
   (c) 78 503
   (d) 32 025
   (e) 83 628

6. (a) 137.40
       50.85
        5.47

   (b) 873.26
       191.15
       −0.92

   (c) 178.26
       136.08
       49.74

   (d) 224.65
       137.24
       43.68

   (e) 787.88
       778.63
       46.30

7. (a) 68 497
   (b) 154 983
   (c) 145.794 9 cr
   (d) 77.253 cr
   (e) 39.641 68 cr

8. (a) 2 553
(b) 3 738
(c) 2 952
(d) 2 937
(e) 2 688
(f) 21 029.96
(g) 27 615
(h) 0.018 43
(i) 19 952.340 36
(j) 64.480 4

9. (a) 2 506.721
(b) 3 132.891
(c) 555.932 7
(d) 790.977 4

10. (a) 38 016
(b) 4 410
(c) 9 650
(d) 17 750
(e) 1 167.5
(f) 2 300
(g) 4.288
(h) 4 390 000
(i) 10
(j) 0.007 5
(k) 9 463.487 2
(l) 52.5

11. (a) 100 896.452
(b) 1 354 066.650
(c) 21.982
(d) 142.652
(e) 22 516.570

12. (a) 45
(b) 24
(c) 212
(d) 19 683
(e) 15

13. (a) 0.34
(b) 6.91
(c) 533.91
(d) 436.45
(e) 2 997.50

14. (a) 291.80
(b) 77.67
(c) 0.70
(d) 9 559.31
(e) 265.41

15. (a) 15.8
(b) 2.614 8
(c) 152.8
(d) 6.344
(e) 9 091.2
(f) 109 561.5
(g) 109 142.14
(h) 87 600
(i) 180
(j) 668.34

EXERCISE 13.2, page 283

1. (a) $4\frac{5}{12}$ (b) $24\frac{37}{40}$

2. (a) 0.5, 50%
(b) 0.375, 37.5%
(c) $0.83\overline{3}$, 83.33%
(d) 0.312 5, 31.25%
(e) $0.41\overline{6}$, 41.67%
(f) 0.25, 25%
(g) $0.08\overline{3}$, 8.33%
(h) $0.66\overline{6}$, 66.67%
(i) 0.7, 70%
(j) 0.875, 87.5%
(k) 0.625, 62.5%
(l) 0.285 7, 28.57%
(m) 0.8, 80%
(n) 0.187 5, 18.75%
(o) $0.58\overline{3}$, 58.33%

3. (a) 0.013
(b) 144 671.08
(c) 28 756 419.063 142 8
(d) 5.004
(e) 145.06

4. (a) Sixty-two and forty-eight hundredths
(b) Seven hundred forty-one and three hundred eighty-nine thousandths
(c) Forty-two thousand six hundred ninety-one and five thousandths
(d) Thirty-eight thousand seven hundred twenty-nine and thirty-six thousand four hundred eighty-two millionths
(e) Eighteen million six hundred seventy-two thousand four hundred eighty-six and two hundredths
(f) One hundred forty-three hundred-thousandths

5. 1%

6. 5.56%

7. 20%

8. $72.20

9. 2 100

10. 0.105

11. $0.625

12. 18

13. 400

14. 360

15. $375

16. $455.36

17. $156 250

18. $27 000

19. (a) $228.13   (b) $897.33

20. (a) 3 680
(b) 233
(c) 774
(d) 2 800
(e) 1 504

EXERCISE 13.3, page 285

1. (a) 225
(b) 625
(c) 30.25
(d) 0.025 6
(e) 1 056.25
(f) 0.000 064

2. (a) 27
(b) 15 625
(c) 125
(d) 3.375
(e) 1
(f) 0.001 728

3. (a) $2a + 2b$
(b) $3a^2$
(c) $2b^2 + a^2$
(d) $7a + 3b$
(e) $9a^2b + 2ab$

4. (a) $x^3 - 3x^2 + 4x$
(b) $6a^2b + 9ab^2$
(c) $1\frac{1}{2}a^3 + 3a^2 - a$
(d) $4a - 8b + 4c$
(e) $-12a^2 - 4ab + 2ac$

5. (a) $3a^3 + 3a^2 - 2a - 6$
(b) $5a^2 + \frac{55}{6}a - \frac{5}{2}$

6. (a) $a(b + 1)$
(b) $a(ab + b + 1)$
(c) $2ab(1 + 3a + 4b)$

7. (a) $a = 4$
(b) $a = \pm 4$
(c) $a = 20$
(d) $75.76
(e) $a = \frac{1}{3}$

EXERCISE 13.4, page 286

1. $3 430

2. $135

3. $44 444.44

4. $3 625

5. $1 762

6. Baker: $272.21
Dinsmore: $288.42
Prentiss: $273.85

7. (a) $321.08
(b) $289.28
(c) $294.50

8. Li: $1 527.50
London: $1 680

9. A: $250.50
B: $205.80
C: $283.75

EXERCISE 13.5, page 288

1. $20.19
2. $20.13
3. 73 d
4. 12.25%
5. $18 639.84
6. $309.60
7. $75 231.50
8. (a) 9.203%
   (b) 10.381%
   (c) 12.683%
9. $658.25
10. $800.43
11. $3.78

EXERCISE 13.6, page 289

1. $28
2. $5 400
3. $1 745.45
4. 18.66%
5. $624.71
6. $1 095
7. (a) $1 425.60   (b) 23.04%
8. $1 490.30
9. $340.81
10. $1 567.26
11. $2 919.40

EXERCISE 13.8, page 290

1. (a) 0, $430.37
   (b) $1.51, $73.99
   (c) $59.40, $1 920.60
2. $30.13, $5.29, $138.60
3. $33\frac{1}{3}$%
4. $50.70
5. $32.83
6. 61.75%
7. $71.25
8. 10%
9. 50% and 15%
10. $ 504.00
            223.20
            205.20
          1 122.19
       _____
         $2 054.59
11. $2 255.12
12. $33\frac{1}{3}$%
13. $354.05

EXERCISE 13.9, page 291

1.	Markup on Cost	Margin on Retail
Radio	$51.35	$56.43
Toaster	15.00	16.00

2. (a) $0.94
   (b) $4.20
   (c) $426.15
3. (a) $64.29
   (b) $25.76
   (c) $312.50
4. (a) 23.08%
   (b) 40%
   (c) 14.29%
5. 18.75%, 28.57%, 12.5%
6. 25%
7. 25%
8. $1.44
9. $0.60
10. $10.96
11. $875   13. $86 400
12. $30.40   14. (a) $6.05   (b) $6.72

EXERCISE 13.10, page 292

1. $1 395
2. $827.83
3. $785.45
4. $80.95
5. $1 035
6. 15.52%
7. (a) $40.53
   (b) $3 429.00
   (c) $154.58
8. $595
9. $1 291.25

EXERCISE 13.11, page 293

1. (a) 61.4
   (b) 62.5
   (c) 56
2. $9.58/kg
3. (a) $2 020
   (b) $336.67
   (c) July $325
       Aug   304.33
       Sept   321
       Oct   348.33
   (d) June $337.50
       July   325.00
       Aug   315.75
       Sept   327.60
       Oct   336.67

4.

COMMISSIONS EARNED

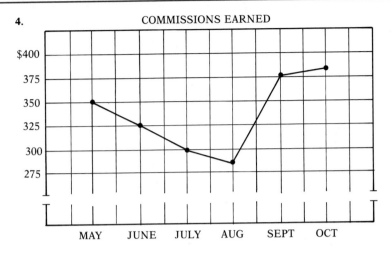

5. (a) $1000

(b)

CRAWLEY FAMILY BUDGET

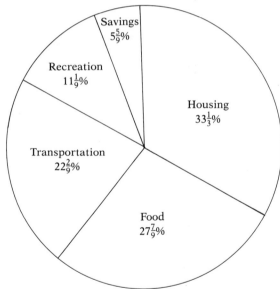

Savings $5\frac{5}{9}\%$

Recreation $11\frac{1}{9}\%$

Housing $33\frac{1}{3}\%$

Transportation $22\frac{2}{9}\%$

Food $27\frac{7}{9}\%$

6.

COST OF
OPERATING APPLIANCES

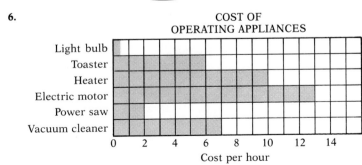

Cost per hour

7.

CAFETERIA PREFERENCES

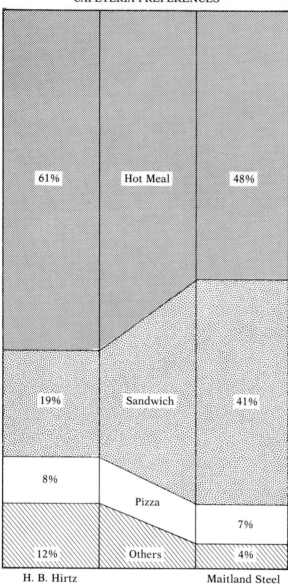

61%	Hot Meal	48%
19%	Sandwich	41%
8%		
	Pizza	7%
12%	Others	4%

H. B. Hirtz   Maitland Steel

EXERCISE 13.12, page 294

1. 8.84 m^2
2. 95 m
3. 471 cm
4. $203\ 472 \text{ cm}^3$
5. 12
6. 540 cm
7. 11.2 m^3
8. 350
9. 10.854 m^3
10. $111\ 375 \text{ cm}^3$

INDEX